Islas Baleares

ROYAL CRUISING CLUB
PILOTAGE FOUNDATION

Robin Brandon
Revised by Anne Hammick

Imray Laurie Norie & Wilson Ltd

St Ives Cambridgeshire England

Published by
Imray Laurie Norie & Wilson Ltd
Wych House St Ives Huntingdon
Cambridgeshire PE17 4BT, England
☎ +44 (0)1480 462114,
Fax +44 (0)1480 496109
E-mail ilnw@imray.com

© Royal Cruising Club Pilotage Foundation 1997
© Plans. Imray Laurie Norie & Wilson Ltd 1997
1st Edition 1977 (as *East Spain Pilot – Chapter VII, Islas Baleares*)
2nd Edition 1980
3rd Edition 1984
4th Edition 1989 (including *East Spain Pilot Chapter I*, Introduction and General Information)
5th Edition 1991, updated 1995
6th Edition 1997

ISBN 0 85288 389 7

British Library Cataloguing in Publication Data.
A catalogue record for this book is available from the British Library.

This work, based on surveys over a period of many years, has been corrected to June 1997 from land-based visits to the ports and harbours of the coast, from contributions by visiting yachtsmen and from official notices. All photographs were taken during 1996.

CAUTION

Every effort has been made to ensure the accuracy of this book. It contains selected information and thus is not definitive and does not include all known information on the subject in hand; this is particularly relevant to the plans, which should not be used for navigation. The RCC Pilotage Foundation believes that this selection represents a useful aid to prudent navigation, but the safety of a vessel depends ultimately on the judgement of the navigator, who should assess all information, published or unpublished.

CORRECTIONS

The RCC Pilotage Foundation would be glad to receive any corrections, information or suggestions which readers may consider would improve the book. Letters should be addressed to the Editor, Islas Baleares, care of the publishers.

CORRECTIONAL SUPPLEMENTS

This pilot book is amended at intervals by the issue of correctional supplements prepared by the RCC Pilotage Foundation. Supplements are supplied free of charge with the books when they are purchased. Additional supplements are also available free from the publishers on receipt of a stamped, addressed A4 envelope and a note of the name of the book for which the supplement is required.

PLANS

The plans in this guide are not to be used for navigation. They are designed to support the text and should always be used with navigational charts.

Where lights on the plans are identified by a number in red (the international index number, as in the Admiralty *List of Lights*) the reader should refer to the relevant list of lights in the text for details. All bearings are from seaward and refer to true north. Symbols are based on those used by the British Admiralty – users are referred to *Symbols and Abbreviations (NP 5011)*.

Note on using the plans

Every effort has been made to locate harbour and anchorage plans on the same page as the relevant text. Plainly this is impossible in the case of coastal plans, which are normally placed adjacent to the first harbour or anchorage covered on the plan, in a CLOCKWISE direction. If sailing 'anti-clockwise' the coastal plan is likely to be found a number of pages earlier in the text.

Key to symbols

	English	Spanish
⚓	harbourmaster/ port office	*Capitán de Puerto*
	fuel	*gasoil, gasolina*
A	yacht chandler	*efectos navales*
	crane	*grua*
	travel-lift	*grua giratoria*
	yacht club	*Club Náutico*
	showers	*ducha*
i	information	*información*
✉	post office	*correos*
	slipway	*grada*
⚓	anchorage	*fondeadero*
	anchoring prohibited	*fondeadero prohibido*
	yachts	*yates*

See Appendix III, page 229, for further Spanish terms commonly used in a marine context.

Printed in Great Britain by Butler and Tanner Ltd, Frome, Somerset.

Contents

Dedicated to the memory of
Orianne Tucker
who rests forever on a
mountaintop within sight
of the sea.

Foreword

The Royal Cruising Club Pilotage Foundation was created by members of the RCC to enable them and others to bring their experience of sailing and cruising to a wider public and to encourage the aspiring sailor to cruise further afield with confidence.

The Pilotage Foundation, a registered charity whose object is 'to advance the education of the public in the science and practice of navigation', was established with a generous grant by an American member of the RCC, Dr Fred Ellis, and fulfills its remit by producing and maintaining Pilot Books and Cruising Guides. Present volumes range from the Baltic to the West Indies and from Greenland to the Río Grande.

The Foundation is extremely grateful and privileged to have been given the copyrights to pilots written by a number of distinguished authors and yachtsmen, charged with the willingly accepted task of keeping the original books up to date. Amongst such authors was the late Robin Brandon, and this volume is the first of his to be updated by means of a new edition so ably edited on behalf of the Pilotage Foundation by Anne Hammick.

W H Batten
Chairman and Director
RCC Pilotage Foundation
June 1997

Acknowledgements

Hundreds of yachtsmen and women have, over the years, supplied information which has been incorporated into the *Islas Baleares*. Much of their input continues to be of value for edition after edition.

Incomparably the greatest assistance on this occasion has come from Claire James, who with her husband Jimmy explored the islands in 1993 and again in 1996 aboard their Voyager 38 *Phoenician*. During both these cruises Claire amassed and recorded a great deal of factual data, and on a brief visit to England agreed to read and comment on the draft text, resulting in many practical suggestions regarding the content and layout of the book.

Other valuable information was supplied by the crews of *Shaheen*, *Timolisa* and *Tobago Clipper* and members of the Royal Cruising Club over a number of years. Christopher and Joana Maidment and Roger Shallcross helped greatly with my researches in Menorca, as did Brian and Jill White (Whites International Yachts) and Terry Purkiss in Mallorca. Prue Farrington contributed useful contacts and cheerful company to my early researches in the field. Oz Robinson, currently undertaking major revisions of the companion volumes in the *East Spain Pilot* series – *Costas del Azahar, Dorada and Brava* and *Costas del Sol and Blanca* – collaborated on the introductory sections and appendices. Marine Instruments of Falmouth allowed me unrestricted access to research materials.

That I was able to take an almost complete set of aerial photographs of the islands during a single week in May 1996 was entirely thanks to Alastair Sutherland of Sloane Helicopters. His claim that a helicopter was much better suited to the task than a fixed-wing aeroplane proved well founded, complemented by his own skill in positioning it for each shot. The Balearics are beautiful islands and seeing them at close range from the air was quite unforgettable. For interest, the cameras used were a Canon Epoca 135, Practica Spotmatic F and ANSCO Pix Panorama. Film was mainly Kodak EKTAR 100 with some EKTAR 25. Unless otherwise credited, all photographs, including the cover, were taken by the author.

As always my thanks go to the skill and patience of the team at Imray Laurie Norie and Wilson Ltd, in particular to Willie Wilson and Nell Stuart, and with a special mention for Debbie Lee and Jill Eaton in the drawing office who between them redrew and updated all the plans in the *Islas Baleares*. Debbie was also responsible for the clear and user-friendly layout, while my two volunteer proofreaders, Cdr Mike Grubb and Brian L Builder, provided an essential safety net to my efforts.

Anne Hammick
June 1997

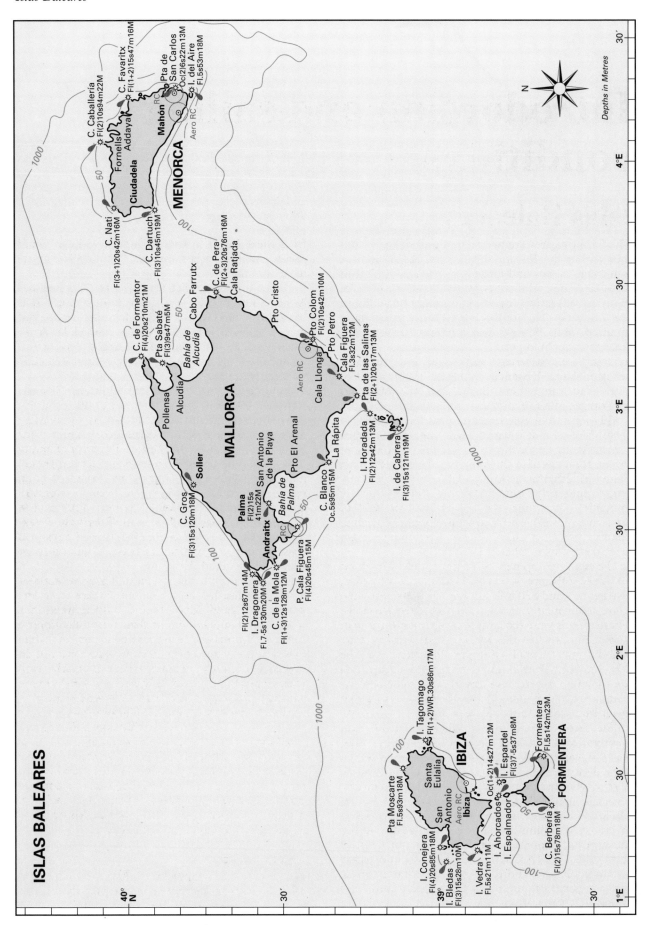

ISLAS BALEARES

Introduction and sailing conditions

Islas Baleares

The Islas Baleares are an integral part of Spain and thus within the European Union. They consist of four main islands and a number of smaller islets in three separate and distinct groups, and form one of the most attractive and varied cruising grounds in the western Mediterranean. There are many hundreds of harbours and anchorages, varying from large cosmopolitan ports such as Palma de Mallorca to completely deserted anchorages in exquisitely beautiful bays. Distances between islands are not great and those between ports, harbours and anchorages often very small.

Although Mallorca in particular has become a byword for all that is worst in holiday development, in practice this applies only to a small percentage of the coastline, notably the beaches running west from Palma. In other areas it is possible to sail for hours past apparently untouched – and frequently dramatic – coastline. The same may be said of western and northern Ibiza, while Menorca, though possibly less spectacular, has managed to preserve a great deal of its rural charm.

The island group nearest to the mainland – about 50 miles offshore – includes Ibiza, Espalmador, Formentera and half a dozen smaller islets separated from the mainland and Mallorca by deep channels. These islands were recognised as a separate group in Roman times when they were called *Pityusae* (Pine Islands) and are still sometimes referred to as the *Islas Pitiusas*. They offer many secluded bays and *calas* (coves) where it is possible to anchor. The islands are higher and more rocky to the north with lower sandy bays to the south.

The second group, which consists of Mallorca, Cabrera, Menorca and some small inshore islands, was known by the Romans as *Insulae Baleares*, possibly from the Phoenician '*baal laaron*' meaning 'a man who throws stones' (seemingly the islanders' favourite method of resisting attack). The names Mallorca and Menorca are derived from the Latin 'Major' and 'Minor'. Mallorca, the largest island of the group, is approximately 45 miles northeast of Ibiza and roughly square in shape with sides some 45 miles long. The northern part is mountainous. It has a major port, several harbours and many bays and *calas* where it is possible to anchor. There is one large off-lying island, Cabrera, which has a well protected bay, several *calas* and a number of off-lying islets, but it is a national park with restricted access. Anchoring is forbidden but mooring buoys have been laid.

Menorca lies 25 miles northeast of Mallorca and is much lower and flatter than its neighbour. It is some 30 miles long, with few harbours but numerous *calas* where anchoring is possible. As in Mallorca the northern part is higher and more rugged than further south, but even there sea cliffs predominate.

The Islas Baleares are attractive, particularly away from 'developed' areas, and form an excellent cruising ground. However they have suffered badly from the rapid growth in tourism in the same way as has the coast of mainland Spain. The days of empty anchorages and uncrowded harbours are long gone, particularly July and August, and there is good reason for the cruising yachtsman to venture elsewhere during the holiday season – if any less teeming alternative can be found. Otherwise cheek-by-jowl existence, disturbance from speed boats and jet-skis, and the occasional noisy disco must be accepted as part of the cruise.

For those accustomed to more northern latitudes a winter cruise has its attractions – there are many days with a good sailing breeze and the weather is warmer and much sunnier than a normal English summer. Storms and heavy rain do occur, and when they do they are worse than in summer, but in general the climate is mild and, particularly from January to March, reasonably pleasant. Offshore the Mediterranean in winter can be horrid, but it is feasible to dodge bad weather and slip from harbour to harbour as they are seldom far apart. Sailing out of season not only has the great advantage that there are no crowds, but the shops and services are freer to serve the winter visitor. Local people can be met, places of interest enjoyed and the empty beaches and coves used in privacy. Many *Clubs Náutico*, which in summer have to turn away cruising sailors, welcome visitors during the off-season.

Local economy

Tourism is now a significant contributor to the local economy, but agriculture and light industry manage to co-exist with it in the islands. These latter industries form a reserve, incidentally, from which an established boat building industry draws skilled labour for the increased demands of marinas.

Language

Each island has two official languages, Castilian and Catalan, the latter transformed into local dialects referred to as *Mallorquín*, *Menorquín* and *Ibicenco*. Catalan alternatives for Castilian Spanish phrases include: *bondia* – good morning (rather than *buenos días*), *bona tarde* – good afternoon (*buenos tardes*), *s'es plau* – please (*por favor*).

Many local people speak English or German, often learnt from tourists, and French is taught as a second language at school.

Place names appear in the Spanish (ie. Castilian) form where possible – the spelling normally used on British Admiralty charts – with local alternatives in brackets. Where there is no Castilian form the local name is used.

Currency

The unit of currency is the *peseta* (pta/ptas). Major credit cards are widely accepted, as are Eurocheques. Bank hours are normally 0830 to 1400, Monday to Friday, with a few also open 0830 to 1300 on Saturday. Most banks have credit card machines.

Regional weather – the Western Mediterranean

General

The weather pattern in the basin of the western Mediterranean is affected by many different systems. It is largely unpredictable, quick to change and often very different at places only a short distance apart. See Appendix III, page 229, for Spanish meteorological terms.

Winds

Winds most frequently blow from the west, northwest, north and east but are considerably altered by the effects of local topography. The Mediterranean is an area of calms and gales and the old saying that in summer there are nine days of light winds followed by a gale is very close to reality. Close to the coast normal sea and land breezes are experienced on calm days.

The winds in the Mediterranean have been given special names dependent on their direction and characteristics. Those that affect this area are detailed below.

Northwest – tramontana
This wind, also known as the *maestral* near Río Ebro and the *mistral* in France, is a strong, dry wind, cold in winter, which can be dangerous. It is caused by a secondary depression forming in the Golfo de León or the Golfo de Génova on the cold front of a major depression crossing France. The northwesterly airflow generated is compressed between the Alps and the Pyrenees and flows into the Mediterranean basin. In Spain it chiefly affects the coast to the north of Barcelona, the Islas Baleares, and is strongest at the northern end of the Costa Brava.

The *tramontana* can be dangerous in that it can arrive and reach gale force in as little as fifteen minutes, on a calm sunny day with virtually no warning. Signs to watch for are brilliant visibility, clear sky – sometimes with cigar-shaped clouds – very dry air and a steady or slightly rising barometer. On rare occasions the sky may be cloudy when the wind first arrives although it clears later. Sometimes

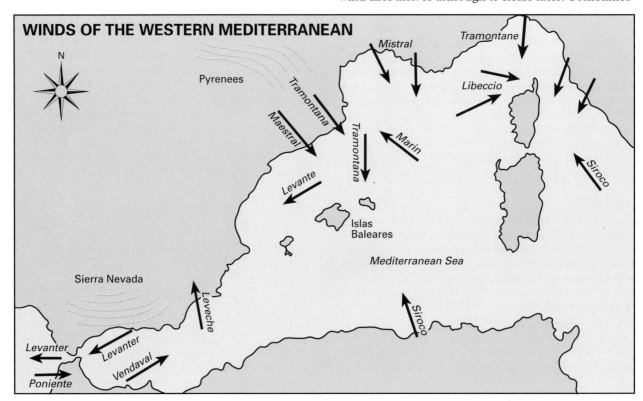

WINDS OF THE WESTERN MEDITERRANEAN

N

Pyrenees

Mistral

Tramontane

Tramontana

Maestral

Tramontana

Libeccio

Marin

Levante

Siroco

Islas Baleares

Mediterranean Sea

Sierra Nevada

Leveche

Siroco

Levanter

Levanter

Vendaval

Poniente

the barometer will plunge in normal fashion, rising quickly after the gale has passed. If at sea and some way from land, a line of white on the horizon and a developing swell give a few minutes' warning. The only effective warning that can be obtained is by radio – Marseille (in French) and Monaco (in French and English) are probably the best bet. See pages 16 and 17 for transmission details.

The *tramontana* normally blows for at least three days and, on occasions, may last for a week or longer. It is very frequent in the winter months, blowing for a third of the time, and on occasions can reach force 10 (50 knots) or above. In summer it is neither as strong nor as frequent.

West – vendaval

A depression crossing Spain or southern France creates a strong southwest to west wind, the *vendaval* or *poniente*, which funnels through the Strait of Gibraltar and along the south coast of Spain. Though normally confined to the south and southeast coasts, it occasionally blows in the northeast of the area. It is usually short-lived and at its strongest from late autumn to early spring.

East – levante

Encountered from Gibraltar to Valencia and beyond, the *levante*, sometimes called the *llevantade* when it blows at gale force, is caused by a depression located between the Islas Baleares and the North African coast. It is preceded by a heavy swell (*las tascas*), cold damp air, poor visibility and low cloud which forms first around the higher hills. Heavy and prolonged rainfall is more likely in spring and autumn than summer. A *levante* may last for three or four days.

South – siroco

The hot wind from the south is created by a depression moving east along or just south of the North African coast. By the time this dry wind reaches Spain or the Islas Baleares it can be very humid, with haze and cloud. If strong it carries dust, and should it rain when the cold front comes through the water may be red or brown and the dust will set like cement. This wind is sometimes called the *leveche* in southeast Spain. It occurs most frequently in summer, seldom lasting more than one or two days.

Clouds

Cloud cover of between 4/8ths and 5/8ths in the winter months is about double the summer average of 2/8ths. The cloud is normally cumulus and high level. In strong winds with a southerly component complete cloud cover can be expected.

Precipitation

Annual rainfall is moderate, between 450mm and 500mm, and tends to be higher in the east of the area. It is heaviest in the last quarter of the year and lightest in the third quarter – July averages 4–5mm.

Thunderstorms

Thunderstorms are most frequent in the autumn at up to four or five each month, and can be accompanied by hail.

Visibility

Fog is very rare in summer but may occur about three times a month in winter. On occasions dust carried by the southerly *siroco* can reduce visibility.

Temperature

Winter temperatures average 10°C–15°C, rising steadily after March to average 20°C–29°C in July and August. Afternoon (maximum) temperatures may reach 30°–33°C in these months.

Humidity

The relative humidity is moderate at around 60% to 80%. With winds from west, northwest or north low humidity can be expected; with winds off the sea, high humidity is normal. The relative humidity increases throughout the night and falls by day.

Local weather – the Islas Baleares

The two main weather areas in the Islas Baleares lie either side of a line roughly bisecting Mallorca from north-northwest to south-southeast.

The southwestern area is influenced by the weather over mainland Spain – winds are variable but, in general, those from the southeast semicircle prevail in summer and those from the northwest in winter. Gales are rare in summer but may blow for 5–10% of the time in winter, generally the result of a *tramontana* though they may blow from anywhere between west through north to northeast. Winds from the southeast semicircle can bring clouds, rain and poor visibility, though these are are more frequent in the winter months.

In the northeastern area, northwest, north and northeast winds are most common, especially in winter, though winds from other directions frequently occur. This area is influenced by the weather in the Golfo de León and is in the direct path of the northwesterly *tramontana*, making it particularly important to listen to regular weather forecasts. Gales or increased winds forecast for the Golfo de León almost invariably mean stronger winds in the northeastern Baleares. Gales may be experienced for 10% of the time during the winter, dropping to 2% in July and August, sometimes arriving with little warning and rapidly building to gale force. Although there is more rain than in the southwestern part of the archipelago visibility is generally better. Menorca is sometimes described as 'The Windy Isle', though this may be undeserved.

Local names for the principal winds, with Catalan names in brackets, are:

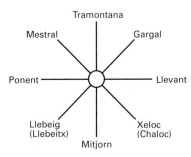

Local winds (Blowing towards the centre of the rose)

Throughout the area, in calm weather a sea breeze (*brisa de mar*) will be experienced near the coast, blowing more strongly where it is channelled into a large bay such as the Bahías de Palma, Pollensa or Alcudia. It usually gets up about 1100, is at its maximum between 1500 and 1600 and drops towards dusk. It can reach force 5 (20 knots) or more at times. In spite of its name it seldom blows directly onshore – more often at 45° to the coast or even along it.

A land breeze is sometimes present during the latter half of the night and lasts until the sun has had time to warm the land. This breeze can be quite strong where there are valleys leading inland.

Precipitation, visibility and temperature

Annual rainfall at Palma is 460mm, the wettest period being October to December. Fog may occur for up to 4% of the time in winter but is almost unknown in summer. Mean air temperatures range from 14°C in January up to 24°C in July and August, with afternoon (maximum) temperatures occasionally reaching 30°–33°C during these months.

Radio equipment and weather forecasts – *see pages 8 and 16–17*

The sea

Currents

The current past the islands normally sets southeast, south or southwest at a rate of 0·5 to 1 knot, though stronger in the channels between the islands and off promontories. Its direction and strength can also be modified by the effects of strong or prolonged winds, those from the south tending to reduce or reverse the current and those from the north increasing the rate of flow.

Tides

Even at springs tidal range is less than 0·3m, so can be disregarded. Sea level is more affected by the strength, direction and duration of winds and by variations in barometric pressure. In general, winds from the north combined with high pressure cause a fall in sea level and those from the south plus low pressure a rise in the level. In addition, the levels in harbours or *calas* facing an onshore wind will be higher than in those experiencing offshore winds.

Even with these factors the range of sea level is unlikely to exceed 1m, other than during a phenomenon known as *resaca* or *seiche* which occurs rarely, usually when a depression and spring tide coincide. The sea level rises and falls by as much as 1·5m every ten or fifteen minutes, an oscillation which may last for several days. *Resaca* most often affects Puerto de Ciudadela, Menorca and the deeply indented harbours and *calas* on the southeast coast of Mallorca, but has also been experienced as far west as Puerto de Arenal in the Bahía de Palma.

Swell

Swell from any direction can affect the Islas Baleares, and particularly the *cala* anchorages, though it never reaches the size of an ocean swell. A gale in the Golfo de León is likely to send a northerly swell of up to 2m down into the islands, possibly before the wind itself arrives.

Scouring and silting

In passages and anchorages where the bottom is of loose sand, depths may change due to the effects of rainfall and wind.

Sea temperature

Sea temperature ranges from around 14°C in February to 20°C or more in August. Winds from the south and east tend to raise the temperature and those from the west and north to lower them.

Water spouts

Water spouts may occasionally be encountered in spring and autumn, usually near promontories and often associated with thunderstorms.

Practicalities and preparation

OFFICIAL ADDRESSES
Spanish embassies and consulates
London – 20 Draycott Place, London SW3 2RZ
☎/fax 0171-235 5555, ☎ 0171-589 8989
Manchester – Suite 1a, Brook House, Manchester
M22 2BQ ☎ 0161-236 1233
Edinburgh – 63 North Castle Street, Edinburgh
EH2 3LJ ☎ 0131-220 1843, *Fax* 0131-226
4568
Washington DC – 2700 15th Street NW,
Washington DC 20009 ☎ 202 265-0190
New York – 150 E 58th Street, New York, NY
10155 ☎ 212 355-4090
Plus many others.

Spanish national tourist offices
London – 57-58 St James's Street, London SW1A
1LD ☎ 0171-499 0901, *Fax* 0171-629 4257
New York – 665 Fifth Avenue, New York, NY
10022 ☎ 212 759-8822

British representation in Islas Baleares
Mallorca – British Consulate, Plaza Mayor 3D,
07002 Palma de Mallorca, ☎ (71) 712445,
716048, *Fax* (71) 717520
Ibiza – British Vice-Consulate, Avenida Isidoro
Macabich 45-1, Apartado 307, 07800 Ibiza
☎ (71) 301818, 303816, *Fax* (71) 301972
Menorca – British Vice-Consulate, Torret 28, San
Luis, Menorca ☎ (71) 366439

American representation in Islas Baleares
Mallorca – Vice-Consulate, Avenida Rey Jaime III,
26, Entresuelo 2, 07012 Palma de Mallorca,
☎ (71) 722660, *Fax* (71) 718755

British and American embassies in Madrid
British Embassy – Calle Fernando el Santo 16,
28010 Madrid ☎ (91) 319 0200, *Fax* (91) 319
0423
American Embassy – Calle Serrano 75, 28006
Madrid ☎ (91) 577 4000, *Fax* (91) 577 5737
If using the telephone, see the note on page 11.

Formalities

Documentation
Spain is a member of the European Union. Other
EU nationals may visit the country for up to 90 days
with a passport but no visa, as may US citizens. EU
citizens wishing to remain in Spain may apply for a
permiso de residencia once in the country; non-EU
nationals can apply for a single 90-day extension, or
otherwise obtain a long-term visa from a Spanish
embassy or consulate before leaving home.

In practice the requirement to apply for a *permiso
de residencia* does not appear to be enforced in the
case of cruising yachtsmen, living aboard rather than
ashore and frequently on the move. Many
yachtsmen have cruised Spanish waters for extended
periods with no documentation beyond that
normally carried in the UK. If in doubt, check with
the authorities before departure.

Under EU regulations, EU registered boats are
not required to fly the Q flag on first arrival unless
they have non-EU nationals or dutiable goods
aboard. Nevertheless, clearance should be sought
either through a visit to or from officials or through
the offices of the larger marinas or yacht clubs.
Passports and the ship's registration papers will be
required. A Certificate of Competence (or
equivalent) and evidence of VAT status may also be
requested – see Appendices IV and V, page 231.
Other documents sometimes requested are a crew
list with passport details, the radio licence and
evidence of insurance. Subsequently, at other ports,
clearance need not be sought but the *Guarda Civil*
may wish to see papers, particularly passports.
Marina officials often ask to see yacht registration
documents and the skipper's passport, and
sometimes evidence of insurance.

Temporary import and laying up
A VAT paid or exempt yacht should apply for a
permiso aduanero on arrival in Spanish waters. This
is valid for twelve months and renewable annually,
allowing for an almost indefinite stay. As well as
establishing the status of a foreign-owned vessel,
possession of a *permiso aduanero* should enable the
owner to import equipment and spares from other
EU countries free of duty.

A boat registered outside the EU fiscal area on
which VAT has not been paid may be temporarily
imported into the EU for a period not exceeding six
months in any twelve before VAT is payable. This
period may sometimes be extended by prior
agreement with the local customs authorities (for
instance, some do not count time laid up as part of
the six months). While in EU waters the vessel may
only be used by its owner, and may not be chartered
or even lent to another person, on pain of paying
VAT (but see Appendix VI, page 231). If kept in the
EU longer than six months the vessel normally
becomes liable for VAT. There are marked
differences in the way the rules are applied from one
harbour to the next, let alone in different countries
– check the local situation on arrival.

See Appendix V, page 231, for information on
documentation and the EU fiscal area. The purely
practical side of laying up is covered on page 9.

Chartering
Chartering is a well-regulated business in the Islas
Baleares with somewhat different regulations to
those applied in mainland Spain, notably that there
is no blanket restriction on foreign-owned and/or
skippered vessels applying for charter authorisation.
However the necessary paperwork is time-
consuming and involved – see Appendix VI for
details.

Light dues

A charge known as Tarifa T-0 is now levied on all vessels. Locally based pleasure craft (the status of a charter yacht is not clear) pay at the rate of pesetas 800 per sq metre per year, area being calculated as LOA x beam. Visiting pleasure craft pay one tenth of that sum and are not charged again for ten days. Boats of less than 7m LOA and with engines of less than 25hp make a single payment of 5000 pesetas per year (whether actual or calendar is not known).

Insurance

Many marinas require evidence of insurance cover, though third party only may be sufficient. Many UK companies are willing to extend home waters cover for the Mediterranean, excluding certain areas.

Flag etiquette

A yacht in commission in foreign waters is legally required to fly her national maritime flag, normally the Red Ensign for a British yacht. If a special club ensign is worn it *must* be accompanied by the correct burgee. The courtesy flag of the country visited should be flown from the starboard signal halliard – note that in Spain, like the UK, the maritime ensign and national flags are not the same. The Islas Baleares have their own regional flags which may be flown below the national courtesy flag if desired.

General regulations

Harbour Restrictions

All harbours have speed limits, usually 3 knots or less. There is a blanket 5 knot speed limit along the whole coast extending 100m offshore, increasing to 250m off bathing beaches.

In most harbours anchoring is forbidden except in emergency or for a short period while sorting out a berth.

Garbage

It is an international offence to dump garbage at sea and, while the arrangements of local authorities may not be perfect, garbage on land should be dumped in the proper containers. Marinas require the use of their onshore facilities or holding tanks.

Scuba diving

Inshore scuba diving is strictly controlled and a licence is required from the *Comandancia Militar de Marina*. This involves a certificate of competence, a medical certificate, two passport photographs, the passport itself (for inspection), knowledge of the relevant laws and a declaration that they will be obeyed. The simplest approach is to enquire through marina staff. Any attempt to remove archaeological material from the seabed will result in serious trouble.

Snorkelling

Spearfishing while using a snorkel is controlled and, in some places, prohibited.

Water-skiing

There has been an explosive increase in the use of high powered outboards for water-skiing over the past decade, accompanied by a significant increase in accidents. In most of the main ports and at some beaches it is now controlled and enquiries should be made before skiing. It is essential to have third party insurance and, if possible, a bail bond. If bathing and water skiing areas are buoyed, yachts are excluded.

Harbours, marinas and anchorages

In spite of the growth in both the number and size of marinas and yacht harbours there is still a general shortage of berths in the islands, particularly in mid-summer. Thus it it always preferable to radio (VHF Ch 9) or telephone before arrival to check whether a berth is likely to be available.

Harbour charges

All harbours and marinas charge, at a scale which varies from season to season and year to year. July and August are normally considered to be 'high season', with some harbours citing May, June and September as 'mid season' while others go directly to 'low season' rates. High season charges in 1996 varied from 2192 to 12,722 ptas per day for a 15m yacht, and 1137 to 7633 ptas per day for 10m.

A banding system based on 1996 prices has been used in the text:

High season

	Band A ptas	Band B ptas	Band C ptas	Band D ptas
15m LOA	Over 8000	8000–6000	6000–4000	Under 4000
10m LOA	Over 5000	5000–3500	3500–2000	Under 2000

Low season

	Band A ptas	Band B ptas	Band C ptas	Band D ptas
15m LOA	Over 5000	5000–3500	3500–2500	Under 2500
10m LOA	Over 3000	3000–2000	2000–1500	Under 1500

All the above include IVA (VAT) at 16%, though some harbours quote charges ex-IVA in their brochures. Nearly all harbours accept payment by major credit cards (American Express, VISA, Mastercard etc.) and also by Eurocheque – where this is known not to be the case it is noted in the text. It must be remembered that these figures can only reflect rates charged in 1996, and that although average increases are likely to be broadly similar the occasional harbour may raise prices further, perhaps following an improvement in facilities. Multihulls are frequently charged up to 50% more than monohulls, while in a few harbours exceptionally beamy monohulls pay a surcharge.

A few harbours have public buoys or pontoons administered by the port authority which are often charged at a very much lower rate. Anchoring, where permitted within developed harbours, is generally (but not always) free.

Large yachts

Many harbours in the Islas Baleares are too small, or too shallow, for a large yacht, which must anchor outside whilst its crew visit the harbour by tender. It is essential that the skipper of such a yacht wishing to enter a small harbour telephones or radios the harbour authorities well in advance to reserve a berth (if available) and receive necessary instructions.

Berthing

Due to the vast numbers of yachts and limited space available, berthing stern-to the quays and pontoons is normal (and allows easiest shore access). For greater privacy berth bows-to, which has the added advantages of keeping the rudder away from possible underwater obstructions near the quay and making the approach a much easier manoeuvre. An anchor may occasionally be needed, but more often a bow (or stern) line will be provided, usually via a lazyline to the pontoon though sometimes buoyed. This line may be both heavy and dirty and gloves will be found useful. Either way, have plenty of fenders out and lines ready.

Most cruising skippers will have acquired some expertise at this manoeuvre before reaching the Islas Baleares, but if taking over a chartered or otherwise unfamiliar yacht it would be wise both to check handling characteristics and talk the manoeuvre through with the crew before attempting to enter a narrow berth. Detailed instructions regarding Mediterranean mooring techniques will be found in Imrays *Mediterranean Almanac*.

Mooring lines – surge in harbours is not uncommon and mooring lines must be both long and strong. It is sometimes useful to have a loop of chain made up at the shore end to slip over bollards, though in other places rings are in use. Carry plenty of mooring lines, especially if the boat is to be left unattended for any length of time.

Gangplanks – if a gangplank is not already part of the boat's equipment, a builder's scaffolding plank, with a couple of holes drilled at either end to take lines, serves well. As it is cheap and easily replaced it can also be used outside fenders to deal with an awkward lie or ward off an oily quay. A short ladder may also have its uses, particularly if berthing bows-to.

Moorings

Virtually all moorings are privately owned and if one is used it will have to be vacated should the owner return. There are often no markings to give any indication as to the weight and strength of moorings so they should be used with caution.

Anchorages

One of the main charms of the islands is the large number of attractive *cala* anchorages, although many are now somewhat spoilt by building work and the beaches are often crowded. However they must be used with care and good seamanship is essential – if possible set a lookout equipped with Polaroid sunglasses on the bow. A down-sun approach is to be preferred. Note that most of the anchorage plans (as against those of marinas and commercial harbours) are derived from limited observation and incomplete official data. Depths, shapes, distances etc. are approximate.

Many yachtsmen collect picture postcards (particularly aerial views) to augment the photographs in a book such as this. Though a potentially useful aid it is ABSOLUTELY ESSENTIAL to check against other photographs or a sketch plan that they really are of the place stated. During the 1996 research for *Islas Baleares* at least a dozen postcards proved to be incorrectly titled – in one case not merely the wrong *cala* but the wrong island! Also a number of *calas* have more than one name, whilst popular names – such as Cala Figuera – crop up several times. Be certain that a photograph really is of the assumed place before adding it to the navigational stockpile.

The weather in the Islas Baleares can be unexpectedly changeable and can deteriorate very quickly. During the day the sea breeze can be strong, especially if there is a valley at the head of an anchorage. Similarly a strong land breeze can flow down a valley in the early hours of the morning. If anchored near the head of a *cala* backed by a river valley, should there be a thunderstorm or heavy downpour in the hills above take precautions against the flood of water and debris which will descend into the *cala*.

Many *cala* anchorages suffer from swell even when not open to its apparent direction. This is because swell tends to run along the coast, curling around all but the most prominent headlands into the *cala* behind. Wash from boats entering and leaving, as well as from larger vessels passing outside, adds to the discomfort. If considering a second anchor or a line ashore in order to hold the yacht into the swell, first calculate the swinging room required by yachts on single anchors should the wind change.

In a high sided *cala* winds are often fluky and a sudden blow, even from the land, may make departure difficult. Plans for a swift and orderly exit – possibly in darkness – should be considered. This type of anchorage should only be used in settled weather and left in good time if swell or wind rise. It is unwise to leave an anchored yacht unattended for any length of time.

Choice of anchor – many popular anchorages are thoroughly ploughed up each year by the hundreds of anchors dropped and weighed by visiting yachts.

Others are of weed-covered compacted sand, and not without reason is the four-pronged grab the favourite anchor of local fishermen, though difficult to stow. A fisherman-type anchor is easier to stow and a useful ally. If using a patent anchor – Danforth, CQR, Bruce, Fortress etc. – an anchor weight (or Chum) is a worthwhile investment and will encourage the pull to remain horizontal.

Anchoring – once in a suitable depth of water, if clarity permits look for a weed-free patch to drop the anchor. In rocky or otherwise suspect areas – including those likely to contain wrecks, old chains etc. – use a sinking trip line with a float (an inviting buoy may be picked up by another yacht). Chain scope should be at least four times the maximum depth of water, nylon scope double this. It is always worth setting the anchor by reversing slowly until it holds, but on a hard or compacted bottom this must be done very gently in order to give the anchor a chance to bite – over enthusiasm with the throttle will cause it to skip without digging in.

Preparation – the yacht

A yacht properly equipped for cruising in northern waters should need little extra gear, but the following items are worth considering if not already on board.

Radio equipment – in order to receive weather forecasts and navigational warnings from Coast Radio Stations, a radio capable of receiving short and medium wave Single Sideband (SSB) transmissions will be needed. Do not make the mistake of buying a radio capable only of receiving the AM transmissions broadcast by national radio stations, or assume that SSB is only applicable to transmitting radios (transceivers).

Most SSB receivers are capable of receiving either Upper Side Band (USB) or Lower Side Band (LSB) at the flick of a switch. The UK Maritime Mobile Net covering the Eastern Atlantic and Mediterranean uses USB, and again it is not necessary to have either a transceiver or a transmitting licence to listen in. All Coast Radio Stations broadcast on SSB – whether on USB or LSB should be easy to determine by trial and error.

Digital tuning is very desirable, and the radio should be capable of tuning to a minimum of 1kHz and preferably to 0·1kHz. Several companies (including Sony, Grundig and Roberts) market suitable SSB receivers in the UK via high street retailers and marine outlets.

Ventilation – modern yachts are, as a rule, better ventilated than their older sisters though seldom better insulated. Consider adding an opening hatch in the main cabin, if not already fitted, and ideally another over the galley. A wind scoop for the forehatch helps increase the draft, particularly if the open hatch is not forward facing.

Awnings – an awning covering at least the cockpit provides much relief for the crew, while an even better combination is a bimini which can be kept rigged whilst sailing, plus a larger 'harbour' awning, preferably at boom height or above and extending forward to the mast.

Cockpit tables – it is pleasant to eat civilized meals in the cockpit, particularly while at anchor. If nothing else can be arranged, a small folding table might do.

Refrigerator/ice-box – if a refrigerator is not fitted it may be possible to build in an ice-box (a plastic picnic coolbox is a poor substitute), but this will be useless without adequate insulation. An ice-box designed for northern climes will almost certainly benefit from extra insulation, if this can be fitted – 100mm (4in) is a desirable minimum, 150mm (6in) even better. A drain is also essential.

If a refrigerator is fitted but electricity precious, placing ice inside will help minimise battery drain.

Hose – at least 25 metres. Standpipes tend to have bayonet couplings of a type unavailable in the UK – purchase them on arrival. Plenty of 5 or 10 litre plastic carriers will also be found useful.

Deck shower – if no shower is fitted below, a black-backed plastic bag plus rose heats very quickly when hung in the rigging. (At least one proprietary model is available in the UK).

Mosquito nets – some advocate fitting screens to all openings leading below. Others find this inconvenient, relying instead on mosquito coils and other insecticides and repellents. For some reason mosquitoes generally seem to bother new arrivals more than old hands, while anchoring well out will often decrease the problem.

Preparation – the crew

Clothing

Summer sunburn is an even more serious hazard at sea, where light is reflected, than on land. Lightweight, patterned cotton clothing is handy in this context – it washes and dries easily and the pattern camouflages the creases! Non-absorbent, heat retaining synthetic materials are best avoided. Until a good tan has been built up it may be wise to wear a T-shirt when swimming, while shoes give necessary protection against sea-urchin spines.

Some kind of headgear, preferably with a wide brim, is essential. A genuine Montecristi hat can be rolled up, shoved in a pocket and doesn't mind getting wet (they come from Ecuador, not Panama, which has usurped the name). A retaining string, tied either to clothing or around the neck, is a wise precaution whilst on the water.

Footwear at sea is a contentious subject. Many experienced cruisers habitually sail barefoot, but while this may be acceptable on a familiar vessel it would be courting injury on a less intimately known deck. In either case proper sailing shoes should always be worn for harbour work or anchor handling. Decks may become unexpectedly hot and very painful to unprotected feet, and if wearing sandals ashore the upper part of the foot is a prime area for sunburn.

Winters can be wet and cold, and foul weather gear as well as warm sweaters etc. will be needed.

Shoregoing clothes should be on a par with what one might wear at home – beachwear is not usually acceptable in restaurants and certainly not on more formal occasions in yacht clubs.

Medical

No inoculations are required. Minor ailments may best be treated by consulting a *farmacia* (often able to dispense drugs which in most other countries would be on prescription), or by contact with an English-speaking doctor (recommended by the *farmacia*, marina staff, a tourist office, the police or possibly a hotel). Specifically prescribed or branded drugs should be bought in Britain in sufficient quantity to cover the duration of the cruise. Medicines are expensive in Spain and often have different brand names from those used in Britain.

Apart from precautions against the well recognized hazards of sunburn and stomach upsets, heat exhaustion (or heat stroke) is most likely to affect newly joined crew not yet acclimatised to Mediterranean temperatures. Carry something such as Dioralyte to counteract dehydration. Insect deterrents, including mosquito coils, can be obtained locally.

UK citizens should complete a form E111 (see the Department of Health's leaflet *T4 Health Advice for Travellers*, to be found in most travel agents), which provides for free medical treatment under a reciprocal agreement with the National Health Service. Private medical treatment is likely to be expensive and it may be worth taking out medical insurance (which should also provide for an attended flight home should the need arise).

General information

Repairs and chandlery

There are many marinas equipped to handle all aspects of yacht maintenance from laying up to changing a washer. Nearly all have travel-hoists and the larger have specialist facilities – GRP work, electronics, sailmaking, stainless welding and so forth. Charges may differ widely so, if practicable, shop around.

The best equipped chandleries will be found near the larger marinas, where they may equal anything to be found in the UK (though generally with higher prices). Smaller harbours or marinas are often without a chandlery, though something may be found in the associated town. Basic items can sometimes be found in *ferreterias* (ironmongers).

Laying up

Laying up either afloat or ashore is possible at most marinas, though a few have no hard standing. Facilities and services provided vary considerably, as does the cost, and it is worth seeking local advice as to the quality of the services provided and the security of the berth or hard standing concerned.

The northwesterly *tramontana* (*mestral*) can be frequent and severe in winter and early spring, and this should be borne in mind when selecting the area and site to lay up. Yachts with wooden decks and varnished brightwork will need protection from the winter sun, and ideally arrangements should be made for the former to be hosed down each evening. It may well prove cheaper to return to mainland Spain rather than to lay up in the Islas Baleares.

The paperwork associated with temporary import and laying up is detailed on page 5.

Yacht clubs

Most harbours of any size support at least one *Club Náutico*. However the grander ones in particular are basically social clubs – often with tennis courts, swimming pools and other facilities – and may not welcome the crews of visiting yachts. There is usually both a marina and a club, and unless there are special circumstances the first option for a visitor is the marina. That said, many *Club Náuticos* have pleasant bars and excellent restaurants which appear to be open to all, while a few are notably helpful and friendly to visitors. The standard of dress and behaviour often appears to be somewhat more formal than that expected in a similar club in Britain.

Electricity

The standard is 220 volt, 50 cycle, generally via a two-pin socket for which an adapter will be needed, though some marinas provide 380 volt supplies to berths for yachts over 20–25m. If using 110 volt 60 cycle equipment seek advice – cycles may be a greater problem than volts. Even if the yacht is not wired for mains, a 25m length of cable and a trickle charger may be useful.

Bottled gas

Camping Gaz is widely available from marinas, supermarkets or *ferreterias* (ironmongers), the 1·9kg bottles identical to those in the UK. Its availability is therefore not listed in the text under individual harbour facilities.

Getting 4·5kg Calor Gas bottles refilled is much more difficult and can normally only be carried out at REPSOL/CAMPSOL depots. Where one is located near a harbour this is normally mentioned under harbour facilities, otherwise enquire of the staff. A test certificate may be required if the cylinder is more than five years old. A simpler option is to carry the appropriate fitting and regulator to permit the switch from Calor Gas to Camping Gaz – both are butane, the only real differences being the connector and regulator.

Yachts fitted for propane systems should certainly follow this course. If in doubt, consult the Calor Gas Boating Industry Liaison Officer (☎ 01753 540000, *Fax* 01753 586037).

Fuel

Diesel (*gasoleo*, *gasoil* or simply diesel) is sold in two forms throughout Spain, *Gasoleo B* which attracts a lower tax and is only available to fishing craft, and *Gasoleo A* which is available to yachts. Nearly all marinas and yacht harbours in the Islas Baleares sell *Gasoleo A* – Puerto de Bonaire on the Bahía de Pollensa is a notable exception – but this is not true on the Spanish mainland, particularly of smaller fishing harbours. A more limited number also have a pump for petrol (*gasolina*). *Petróleo* is paraffin (kerosene). Credit cards are widely, but not universally, accepted – if in doubt, check first.

Fresh water

In many places drinking water (*agua potable*) is scarce. Expect to pay for it, particularly if supplied by hose, and do not wash sails and decks before checking that it is acceptable to do so. In those harbours where a piped supply is not available for yachts a public tap can often be found – a good supply of 5 or 10 litre plastic cans will be useful.

Water quality in Mallorca and Menorca is generally good, less so in Ibiza, particularly at San Antonio. However water quality throughout all the islands appears to vary from year to year. Always check verbally and taste for salinity or over-chlorination before topping up tanks – the ideal is to have a tank specifically reserved for drinking water, with other tanks for general use. Failing this earmark some cans for the purpose, but stow them in a dark locker to discourage algae. Consider fitting an in-line filter.

Bottled water is readily available in bars and supermarkets.

Ice

Block ice for an ice-box is widely obtainable – use the largest blocks that will fit – while chemical ice is sometimes available in blocks measuring 100 x 20 x 20cms. The latter must not be used in drinks, the former only after close inspection. Cube or 'small' ice is widely obtainable and generally of drinks quality, particularly if bought in a sealed bag. An increasing number of marinas and yacht clubs now have ice machines.

Food and drink

There are many well stocked stores, supermarkets and hypermarkets in the larger towns and cities and it may be worth doing the occasional major stock-up by taxi. Conversely, some isolated anchorages have quite literally nothing. As a rule, availability and choice varies directly with the size of the town. Even the smallest has something and most older settlements (though not all tourist resorts) have a traditional style market offering excellent local produce at very reasonable prices. Alcohol is cheap by UK standards with, not surprisingly, Spanish wines particularly good value. Shop prices generally are noticeably lower away from tourist resorts.

Most shops, other than the largest supermarkets, close for *siesta* between 1400 and 1700 and remain closed on Sunday, though some smaller food shops do open on Sunday mornings. In larger towns the produce market may operate from 0800 to 1400, Monday to Saturday; in smaller towns it is more often a weekly affair.

Local gastronomic specialities include *ensaimadas*, flat spirals of flaky pastry ranging from one-person size to family size, nearly two feet across! Everyone is familiar with *mahonésa* (mayonnaise), but possibly not with its cousin *alioli*, a more powerful version made with garlic. An excellent way to sample unfamiliar delicacies in small portions is in the form of bar snacks or *tapas*, once served gratis but now almost invariably charged for – sometimes heavily.

Mallorca produces some local wines, including Binisalem and Felanitx, but most wine is imported from the mainland. Each island has its own apéritifs and liqueurs. Ibiza produces *Hierbas*, *Rumaniseta* and *La Frigola*, all made from herbs. Mallorca makes *Palo* from carob nuts, and Menorca specialises in gin – Bertram and Lord Nelson are the best known brands and are 70° proof.

Security

Crime afloat is not a major problem in most areas, and regrettably much of the theft which does occur can be laid at the door of other yachtsmen. It is sensible to take much the same precautions as at home – lock up before leaving the yacht, padlock the outboard to the dinghy, and secure the dinghy (particularly if an inflatable) with chain or wire rather than line. Folding bicycles are particularly vulnerable to theft, and should be chained up unless actually in use – even when on deck.

Ashore, the situation in the big towns is certainly no worse than in the UK, and providing common sense is applied to such matters as how handbags are carried, where not to go after the bars close etc., there should be no problems.

The officials most likely to be seen are the *Guardia Civil*, who wear grey uniforms and deal with immigration as well as more ordinary police work, the *Aduana* (customs) in navy blue uniforms, and the *Policía*, also in blue uniforms, who deal with traffic rather than criminal matters.

Time

Spain keeps Standard European Time (UT +1), advanced one hour in summer to UT +2 hours. Changeover dates are now standardised with the rest of the EU as the last weekends in March and October respectively.

Unless stated otherwise, times quoted are UT.

Telephones and fax

Telephone kiosks are common, both local and *teléfono internacional*, and most carry instructions in English. Both coins and phonecards, available from tobacconists (*estancos*), are used. If no kiosk is available marina offices have telephones and many have faxes. Most bars and hotels have metered telephones and the latter usually have faxes, though these are seldom metered.

To make an international call, dial 07 for the international exchange, wait for the next dialling tone and then dial the country code (44 for the UK), the area code (dropping the first zero, eg. 171 or 181 for London rather than 0171 or 0181) and the number. Dial 008 for the European International Operator.

If dialling the Islas Baleares from abroad, dial the international access code (00 in the UK), 34 (for Spain) followed by the area code (71) and the number.

When calling a number within Spain note the following points. If within the same area dial the number alone. If outside, or if in doubt, dial 9 followed by the area code and then the number, which normally has six digits. Some changes are being made to this system in mainland Spain, principally replacing six figure with seven figure numbers.

An area code of 908 or 909 denotes a mobile phone and must be dialled in full, as in the UK.

Mail

Letters may be sent *poste restante* to any post office (*oficina de corréos*). They should be addressed with the surname of the recipient followed by *Lista de Corréos* and the town, island and Islas Baleares. Collection is a fairly cumbersome procedure and a passport is likely to be needed on collection. Alternatively, most marinas and some *Club Náuticos* will hold mail for yachts, but it is always wise to check in advance if possible. Uncollected letters are seldom returned.

Mail to and from the UK should be marked 'air mail' (*por avión*) but even so may take up to ten days, so if speed is important it may be better to arrange fax contact. Post boxes are yellow, and stamps available from tobacconists (*estancos*) as well as post offices. Almost every town has a post office, so these are not listed under individual harbour facilities in the text.

Tourist offices

There is at least one tourist office in every major town or resort. They are graded as Provincial Tourist Office – one only in the Islas Baleares, at Plaça de la Reina 2, 07012 Palma de Mallorca (☎ 712216, *Fax* 710251); Insular Tourist Office – generally at the airport, and well stocked with literature, maps etc; and Municipal Tourist Office, to be found in most towns.

Of the many free handouts available, the A4-sized *I'd like to see you!* series published by IBATUR (The Balearic Institute for the Promotion of Tourism) is worth seeking out. Four beautifully illustrated booklets cover the main islands, giving a smattering of history, places to visit, *fiestas*, local folklore, island statistics and useful telephone numbers. Excellent value!

Transport and travel

Almost every community has some form of public transport, if only one *autobús* a day. Surprisingly, Mallorca boasts two railway lines – one is a narrow gauge affair dating back to Victorian times which links Palma to the town of Sóller in the north, the final connection to Puerto de Sóller being completed by vintage tram. The other line runs from Palma to Inca, about halfway to Alcúdia. Both are recommended for the experience and as a means of seeing some of Mallorca's unspoilt interior.

Taxis are easily found in the tourist resorts though less common outside them, but can always be ordered by telephone. Car hire is simple, but either a full national or international driving licence must be shown.

The three larger islands each have an international airport, Mallorca's being one of the busiest in Europe during the holiday season. There are still some real bargains to be found amongst charter flights from the UK.

Ferries run to mainland Spain, France and Italy and there are frequent inter-island ferry and hydrofoil services. The largest ferry company is Trasmediterránea with offices at Palma, Ibiza and Mahón.

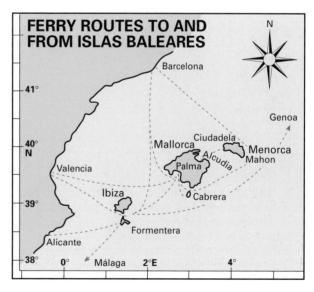

In addition to travel associated with crew changes and the like it is well worth exploring inland whenever possible, particularly in Mallorca where long stretches of the coast are fringed with new developments. Once away from the sea the countryside soon takes over, and it is possible to slip back several decades, if not centuries, in as many miles. All the islands are littered with historic remains and a good general guidebook will be useful - see Appendix II, page 228.

National holidays and *fiestas*

There are numerous official and local holidays, the latter often celebrating the local saint's day or some historical event. A useful *Fiestas Guide* is published annually by the Balearic Tourist Institute. They usually comprise a religious procession, sometimes by boat, followed by a *fiesta* in the evening. The *Fiesta del Virgen de la Carmen* is celebrated in many harbours during mid-July. Where feasible, dates of other local *fiestas* are included in the harbour information. Official holidays include:

1 January	*Año Nuevo* (New Year's Day)
6 January	*Reyes Magos* (Epiphany)
19 March	*San José* (St Joseph's Day)
	Viernes Santo (Good Friday)
	Easter Monday
1 May	*Día del Trabajo* (Labour Day)
(early/mid-June)	*Corpus Christi*
24 June	*Día de San Juan* (St John's Day, the King's name-day)
29 June	*San Pedro y San Pablo* (SS Peter and Paul)
25 July	*Día de Santiago* (St James' Day)
15 August	*Día del Asunción* (Feast of the Assumption)
11 September	Catalan National Day
12 October	*Día de la Hispanidad* (Day of the Spanish Nation)
1 November	*Todos los Santos* (All Saints)
6 December	*Día de la Constitución* (Constitution Day)
8 December	*Inmaculada Concepción* (Immaculate Conception)
25 December	*Navidad* (Christmas Day)

When a national holiday falls on a Sunday it may be celebrated the following day.

Wildlife

The Audouins Gull (rare elsewhere) can often be seen, particularly at San Antonio (Ibiza), Puerto de Andraitx, Puerto de Pollensa and Porto Colom (Mallorca), around Cabrera, and at Mahon (Menorca). They are somewhat smaller than herring gulls, and have a large red beak with black tip, and dark legs. Viewed from below in flight the wingtips appear considerably blacker than those of a herring gull. The cry is a nasal 'gee-ow'. Herring gulls are common (though with yellow legs rather than the pink of their northern relatives), together with shearwaters and many land birds.

Birds of prey such as osprey and both peregrine and the very rare Eleanora's falcon favour the more wild and rocky stretches, including parts of Mallorca's north coast and that of the Cabrera group. The Albufera Nature Reserve southwest of Alcudia is home to many rare waders and other water birds.

Essential Mallorca, Ibiza and Menorca (see Appendix II, page 228) includes a particularly interesting section entitled 'Countryside and Wildlife on the Balearic Islands', detailing bird migration as well as the flora and fauna of the various habitats.

Technical information

Approaches to the Islas Baleares

General

With the exception of a few inshore rocks and islands, and shallow water at the heads of some bays, there is generally deep water up to the coast with few offshore dangers. The islands, by virtue of their height and the usual good visibility, can often be seen from many miles and are well lit at night. The channels between the islands are free from obstructions, but in strong winds that between Mallorca and Menorca can be rough due to a shallow and uneven bottom. The passage from the mainland to the islands presents no particular problems with the one exception of the north or northwesterly *tramontana* or *mestral* which can be dangerous in winter and unpleasant in summer.

From the Spanish coast

From west and southwest – the shortest passage is from Puerto de Jávea or Puerto de Denia to Puerto de San Antonio, Ibiza, at about 55 miles. Should a *tramontana* arise during the crossing it will be on the beam or the quarter and San Antonio can, if necessary, be entered under gale conditions. For a flatter approach and better protection once in harbour it would be wise to continue around the island to Puerto de Santa Eulalia or Puerto de Ibiza.

From northwest and north – from the Spanish coasts between Valencia and Barcelona a choice of islands is offered at distances of 80 miles plus. The usual route is to leave the Spanish coast near Barcelona and to sail for Puerto de Andraitx (110 miles). If the *tramontana* or *mestral* blows it will be on the stern or quarter. Puerto de Andraitx can be entered in almost any conditions. In good and settled conditions Puerto de Sóller is nearer but, because the coast on either side is very dangerous, accurate navigation is vital. Note also the *Caution* on page 13.

From the French coast

Menorca is the nearest island to the French coast, being 170 miles from Port Vendres, 210 miles from Sète and Toulon and 270 miles from Nice. Probably the safest route is from the area of Cap Béar to Mahón, which can safely be entered in gale conditions. Should a *tramontana* blow it will be on the stern or quarter, and should this occur in the early part of the voyage the Spanish coast can be closed for shelter. Again note the *Caution* on page 13.

From the eastern Mediterranean

For yachts on passage from Sardinia, Tunisia, Malta or further east, Mahón is the obvious choice. Distances are approximately 200 miles from the west coast of Sardinia, 360 miles from Tunis and 550 from Valletta, Malta. Should a *tramontana* affect the last part of the passage it will of course be directly on the nose but the landfall will be relatively sheltered. Conversely a southerly *siroco* will be on or aft of the beam but may give rise to poor visibility.

Caution

The two lights marking the north end of the channel between Mallorca and Menorca have similar characteristics and are easy to confuse. Cabo Formentor (Mallorca) shows Fl(4)20s while Cabo Nati (Menorca) is Fl(3+1)20s. When running towards the islands in a northwesterly *tramontana*, mistaken identification could lead to a dangerous situation.

Harbours of refuge

In a sound yacht with a reliable engine the following harbours and anchorages can safely be entered in severe weather, albeit with some difficulty:

Isla de Ibiza

Puerto de Ibiza
Puerto de San Antonio

Isla de Mallorca

Puerto de Palma
Puerto Portals
Puerto de Andraitx
Puerto de Sóller
Anchorage northwest of Punta de la Avanzada, Bahía de Pollensa
Puerto de Alcudia
Porto Colom
Cala Llonga

Isla de Cabrera

Puerto de Cabrera (other than in a northwesterly gale)

Isla de Menorca

Puerto de Mahón
Puerto de Fornells

Many other harbours and anchorages can safely be entered in strong offshore winds and even gales, and even more provide excellent shelter from all directions once inside.

Rescue and emergency services

In addition to VHF Ch 16 (MAYDAY or PAN PAN as appropriate) the marine emergency services can be contacted by telephone at all times on **900 202 202**.

The National Centre for Sea Rescue is based in Madrid but has a string of communications towers, including one at Palma, Mallorca. On the spot responsibility for co-ordinating rescues lies with the *Capitanías Marítimas* with support from the Spanish Navy, Customs, *Guardia Civil* etc. Lifeboats are stationed at some of the larger harbours but the majority do not appear to be all-weather boats.

The other emergency services can be contacted by dialling **003** for the operator and asking for *policía* (police), *bomberos* (fire service) or *Cruz Roja* (Red Cross). Alternatively the police can be contacted direct on **091**.

Hazards

Restricted areas

Anchoring or fishing is banned in the following areas due to submarine cables: Cala de Puerto Roig, Punta Grosa and north of Islote Vedra in Ibiza, south of Cabo de Pera on the east coast of Mallorca and off Cabo Dartuch in southwest Menorca. Spanish naval vessels and submarines exercise around Isla de Cabrera and in the Bahía de Pollensa.

Night approaches

Approaches in darkness are often made more difficult by the plethora of background lights – fixed, flashing, occulting, interrupted – of all colours. Though there may be exceptions, this applies to nearly all harbours backed by a town of any size. Powerful shore lights make weaker navigation lights difficult to identify and mask unlit features such as exposed rocks or the line of a jetty. If at all possible, avoid closing an unknown harbour in darkness.

Skylines

Individual buildings on these developing islands – particularly prominent hotel blocks – are built and demolished, duplicated on a good site and change colour and shape, all with amazing rapidity. They are not nearly as reliable landmarks as might be thought. If a particular building on a chart or in a photograph can be positively identified on the ground, well and good. If not, you may be in the wrong place; but on the other hand it may have been demolished, or be obscured.

Tunny nets

During summer and autumn these nets, anchored to the sea bed and up to 6 miles long, are normally laid inshore in depths of 15-40m but may be placed as far as 10 miles offshore. The outer end should be marked by a float or a boat carrying a white flag with an 'A' (in black) by day, and two red or red and white lights by night. There should also be markers along the line of the net.

These nets are capable of stopping a small freighter but should you by accident, and successfully, sail over one, look out for a second within a few hundred metres. If seen, the best action may be to sail parallel to the nets until one end is reached.

Commercial fishing boats

Commercial fishing boats should be given a wide berth. They may be:

- Trawling singly or in pairs with a net between the boats.
- Laying a long net, the top of which is supported by floats.
- Picking up or laying pots either singly or in groups or lines.
- Trolling with one or more lines out astern.
- Drifting, trailing nets to windward.

Do not assume they know, or will observe, the law of the sea – keep well clear on principle.

Small fishing boats

Small fishing boats, including the traditional double-ended *llauds*, either use nets or troll with lines astern and should be avoided as far as possible. At night many *lámparas* put to sea and, using powerful electric or gas lights, attract fish to the surface. When seen from a distance these lights appear to flash as the boat moves up and down in the waves and can give the appearance of a lighthouse.

Speed boats etc.

Para-gliding, water ski-ing, speed boats and jet-skis are all popular, and are sometimes operated by unskilled and thoughtless drivers with small regard to collision risks. In theory they are not allowed to exceed 5 knots within 100m of the coast or within 250m of bathing beaches. Water-skiing is restricted to buoyed areas.

Scuba divers and swimmers

A good watch should be kept for scuba divers and swimmers, with or without snorkel equipment, particularly around harbour entrances. If accompanied by a boat, the presence of divers may be indicated either by International Code Flag A or by a square red flag with a single yellow diagonal, as commonly seen in north America and the Caribbean.

Navigation aids

Marine radiobeacons and aerobeacons

Two marine radiobeacons and three aerobeacons serve the Islas Baleares. Details will be found in both island and harbour details as appropriate.

Lights

The four-figure international numbering system has been used to identify lights in the text and on plans, the Mediterranean falling in Group E. As each light has its own number, correcting from *Notices to Mariners* or the annual *List of Lights and Fog Signals*, whether in Spanish or English, is straightforward.

Positions correspond to the largest scale British Admiralty chart of the area currently available. All bearings are given from seaward and refer to true north. Where a visibility sector is stated this is always expressed in a clockwise direction.

Harbour lights, which in the Islas Baleares adhere to the IALA A system, are normally listed in the order in which they become relevant upon approach and entry.

Buoyage

Buoys in the Balearics adhere to the IALA A system, based on the direction of the main flood tide. Yellow topped black or red rusty buoys some 500m offshore mark raw sewage outlets.

Yellow or white buoys in line mark the seaward side of areas reserved for swimming. Narrow lanes for water-skiing and sailboarding, also buoyed, may lead out from the shore.

Harbour traffic signals

Traffic signals are rare, and in any case are designed for commercial traffic and seldom apply to yachts.

Storm signals

The signal stations at major ports and harbours may show storm signals, but equally they may not. With minor exceptions they are similar to the International System of Visual Storm Warnings.

Charts

See Appendix I, page 225. Current British Admiralty information is largely obtained from Spanish sources. The Spanish Hydrographic Office re-issues and corrects its charts periodically, and issues weekly *Notices to Mariners*. Corrections are repeated by the British Admiralty, generally some months later. Spanish charts tend to be short on compass roses – carry a chart plotter or rule which incorporates a protractor.

Before departure – Spanish charts can be obtained through certain British agents, notably Imray Laurie Norie & Wilson Ltd, Wych House, The Broadway, St Ives, Huntingdon, Cambs PE17 4BT, (☎ (01480) 462114, *Fax* (01480) 496109), *e-mail* orders@imray.com; and Kelvin Hughes Ltd, Royal Crescent Road, Southampton S014 3NP, (☎ (01703) 634911, *Fax* (01703) 330014). However in both cases stocks held are very limited and it may take months to fill an order. It may be simpler to order direct from the Instituto Hidrográfico de la Marina, Tolosa Latour 1, DP 11007 Cádiz (☎ (956) 599412, *Fax* (956) 275358) and pay by Eurocheque.

In Spain and Islas Baleares – The only British Admiralty chart agent in the Islas Baleares is Rapid Transit Service SL, Network Yacht Team, Edificio Torremar, Paseo Maritimo, 44 – 07015, Palma de Mallorca (☎ 403703, 403903, *Fax* 400216). In Mallorca, Spanish charts are stocked by: Libreria

Fondevila, C/Costa de las Pols 18, Palma (☎ (71) 725616, *Fax* (71)713326); Casa del Mapa, Empresa Munic Informatica SA, Joan Maragall No 3, Palma ☎ (71) 466061, *Fax* (71) 771616); and Valnautica SL, Miquel Santadreu 10, Palma (☎ (71) 464990, *Fax* (71) 465422). In Ibiza, Spanish charts of the islands are held by Valnautica SL, Ibinave, Travesia del Mar, s/n, local 2, San Antonio. Spanish ☎/*Fax* (71) 345251. There is currently no approved Spanish chart stockist in Menorca.

In this book, listing of a chart under both *Approach* and *Harbour* headings normally implies that a large scale harbour plan appears as an insert on a smaller scale approach chart.

Pilot books

Details of principal harbours and some interesting background information appear in the British Admiralty Hydrographic Department's *Mediterranean Pilot Vol 1 (NP 45)*. Harbour descriptions are also to be found in *Guia del Navegante – La Costa de España y el Algarve* (PubliNáutic Rilnvest SL) written in colloquial English with a Spanish translation. Published annually, it carries many potentially useful advertisements for marine-related businesses.

For French speakers, *Votre Livre de Bord – Méditerranée* (Bloc Marine) and *Les Guides Nautiques-Baléares* (Edition Eskis) may be helpful. In German there are *Spanische Gewässer, Lissabon bis Golfe du Lion* (Delius Klasing), *Die Baleares* (Edition Maritim) and others, though possibly out of date in some aspects. See also Appendix II, page 227.

Horizontal Chart Datum: satellite derived positions

Positions given by GPS and other modern satellite navigation systems are normally expressed in terms of World Geodetic System 1984 (WGS 84) Datum unless the receiver is specifically adjusted otherwise. New editions of British Admiralty charts are either based on WGS 84 Datum or carry a note giving the correction necessary to comply with it, but charts published by other nations' hydrographic offices may use different datum references when covering the same area. Charts of various scales published by the same national authority may also use different datum references, particularly when the printing of one chart predates another. In practice, this means that care must be taken when plotting a position expressed in latitude and longitude, or when transferring such a position from one chart to another, particularly when no reference can be made to physical features.

Positions given in this volume can be plotted directly onto the largest scale British Admiralty chart of the area currently available, unless stated otherwise. At present all British Admiralty charts of the Islas Baleares are referred to European Datum 1950 – positions derived from systems working on WGS 84 Datum should be moved 0·07'N and 0·07'E in order to agree with these positions.

Waypoints

The Pilotage Foundation considers that waypoints should not be included in the text. The reasons are straightforward.

First, the estimation of latitude and longitude may vary by more than a mile between disciplines and there are three disciplines to be considered at any one moment: that used in this volume, that employed on the chart used by the navigator and that programmed into the aid in use. Each discipline may require its own correction and it is unlikely that all three will be the same. Only the first can be known to the author.

Second, waypoints should be chosen in relation to prevailing conditions. Given the inherent inaccuracies of all navigational aids, a waypoint which is safe and sensible when visibility is 10 miles may be dangerous and foolhardy when visibility is 100 metres. The detailed positioning of a ship in relation to the land depends upon interpretation of all information available, including that received by eye, and it does no harm to remind the navigator of this. When conditions are such that no information can be received by eye, encouragement of a false sense of security by adherence to a specified but possibly misleading waypoint is likely to create more problems than it solves.

Positions given in the text and on plans are intended purely as an aid to locating the place in question on the chart, and unless otherwise specified use the same datum as the largest scale Admiralty chart of the area currently available.

Magnetic variation

Magnetic variation throughout the Balearics is already slight and decreasing further. In 1997 the mean was:
Ibiza/Formentera – 1°45'W (decreasing 7'E annually)
Mallorca/Cabrera – 1°23'W (decreasing 6'E annually)
Menorca – 0°59'W (decreasing 6'E annually)

Radio and weather forecasts

Details of coast radio stations, weather forecasts, Weatherfax and Navtex follow. See individual harbours details for port and marina radio information. All times quoted are UT (universal time) unless otherwise specified. Only France Inter, Radio France International, BBC Radio 4 and one of the two Monaco stations observe local time (LT), thus altering the UT transmission times when the clocks change.

VHF

When calling a Spanish coast radio station on VHF use Ch 16 – the CRS will then specify which channel to switch to for further communication. When calling a marina or another vessel use Ch 9 unless stated otherwise in the text.

Coast radio stations

All coast radio stations in the Islas Baleares, as well as many on the Spanish Mediterranean coast, are remotely controlled from the Centro Regional de Comunicaciónes Radiomaritimas (CCR) at Valencia, Spain. Several CRS (including Punta da la Mola and Alcudia, both in Mallorca) were discontinued in late 1996, others on the mainland became VHF only and are therefore no longer listed.

In addition to the stations listed there is Pozuelo del Rey (Madrid) (EHY) which operates a comprehensive commercial service on the HF band. Full details will be found in the *Admiralty List of Radio Signals Vol 1 Part 1 (NP281/1)*.

Spanish coast radio stations no longer broadcast traffic lists on VHF. On receipt of traffic, vessels within VHF range will be called once on Ch 16, after that the vessel's call sign will be included in scheduled MF traffic lists.

See *Radio Equipment*, page 8, for information regarding radio receivers.

Ibiza 24 hrs (39°N 1°28'E)
VHF Ch **3**, 16
Navigational warnings: Ch 3 on receipt and at
    1033, 1633 UT (in Spanish only)

Palma, Mallorca (EAO) 24 hrs
(39°21'N 2°58'E)
Transmits: **1755**, 2182, 2799¹kHz SSB
Receives: 2099, 2182, 3283¹kHz SSB
Traffic lists: 1755kHz SSB at every odd H+33 UT,
    (0333–1933), 2333
Navigational warnings: 1755kHz SSB on receipt
    and at 0833, 2033 UT (urgent navigational
    warnings in English and Spanish)
VHF: Ch 7, **16**, **20**, 83¹
Navigational warnings: Ch 7, 20 on receipt and at
    0833, 1533 UT (in Spanish only)
Note VHF facilities are located at 39°44'N 2°43'E,
some 3½ miles inland from the north coast, at a
height of 1034.
1. Reserved for Autolink

Menorca 24 hrs (39°49'N 4°16'E)
VHF: Ch 16, **82**
Navigational warnings: Ch 82 on receipt and at
    0833, 1533 UT (in Spanish only)

Weather forecasts

Only Palma, Mallorca, both stations in Monaco, the UK Maritime Mobile Net and of course BBC Radio 4 transmit forecasts in English.

There are no scheduled VHF weather bulletins broadcast by Spanish coast radio stations. Storm warnings, weather messages and navigational warnings are announced on VHF Ch 16 before being broadcast on the scheduled frequency or channel.

Weather forecasts in Spanish
Palma, Mallorca (39°21'N 2°58'E)
On 1755kHz SSB at 0803, 1703 UT (gale or storm warnings, synopsis and 24 hr forecast, in Spanish, for areas 8–12: see diagram).

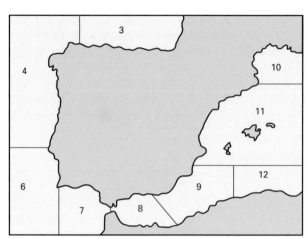

SPANISH WEATHER FORECAST AREAS

Madrid (EBA)
On 3790, 6930, 14641kHz SSB at 0830, 1700 UT (weather bulletin and synopsis in Spanish).

The Spanish word for 'gale' is '*temporal*' and the phrase for 'gale warning' is '*aviso temporal*'. More usually '*no hay temporal*', or 'no gale warning', will be heard. With a little Spanish the rest of the forecast may be deduced, especially if taped and replayed. See Appendix III, page 229, for other Spanish terms commonly heard in weather forecasts.

Weather forecasts in French and English
Monaco (43°43'N 7°43'E)
On 4363kHz SSB at 0903 LT (in French and English), 1403 LT (in French only), 1915 LT (in French and English), using the same forecast as Marseille but with an English translation, for areas 514(eastern part)–523, 531–534: see diagram page 17).

Monaco (43°43'N 7°43'E)
On 8728 and/or 8743kHz SSB at 0715, 1830¹ UT, in French and English, for the entire western Mediterranean, using the same forecast as Marseille but with an English translation.
1. In winter only broadcast if specifically requested

Note Transmissions from both stations in Monaco are reported to be irregular, particularly in winter.

Weather forecasts in French only
Marseille (FFM), France (43°19'N 5°21'E)
On 1906, 2649, 3792kHz SSB at 0703, 1303, 1803 UT (gale or storm warnings, synopsis and 24 hr forecast, in French, for areas 514(eastern part)–523, 531–534: see diagram). Repeated twice at dictation speed and read through a third time, followed by observations from ships at sea. (Recommended by yachtsmen as the most reliable local forecast).

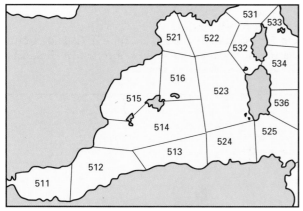

FRENCH WEATHER FORECAST AREAS

Mediterranean sea areas bear the following names in French forecasts and are usually given in this order: 511–Alboran, 512–Palos, 513–Alger, 514–West & East Cabrera, 515–Baleares, 516–Minorque, 521–Lion, 522–West & East Provence, 532–Corse, 523–Sardaigne, 531–Ligure, 533–Elbe, 534–Maddalena, 535–Circeo, 537–Lipari, 536–Carbonara, 525–Tunisie, 524–Annaba. (Areas in italics are included in forecasts for the northern part of the area, standard type in the southern part)

France Inter (Bulletin Inter-Service-Mer)

On 162kHz at 1005, 2005 LT (Mon–Fri), 0650, 2005 LT (Sat–Sun) LT (gale or storm warnings, synopsis and 24 hr forecast, in rapid French, for areas 1–25, 515, 516, 521–523, 531–534: see diagram). May be worth tape recording by the less fluent.

Radio France–Internationale

On 11845kHz SSB at 1145 UT (gale warnings, synopsis, development, 24 hr forecast, in French, for the West African coast and the western and central Mediterranean: see diagram).

Alger (7TA), Algeria (36°40'N 3°18'E)

On 1792kHz SSB at 0903, 1703 UT (12 hr forecast in French for area 3, followed by gale warnings, synopsis, 12 hr forecast and further 12 hr outlook, in French, for all areas: see diagram).

Note Transmissions (though not necessarily content) are reported to be unreliable.

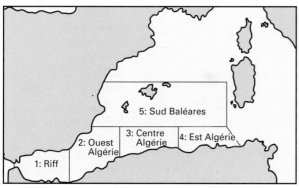

ALGERIAN WEATHER FORECAST AREAS

English language
UK Maritime Mobile Net

In addition to 'official' weather forecasts, that given by the UK Maritime Mobile Net covering the Eastern Atlantic and Mediterranean is reported to be useful. The Net can be heard on 14303kHz SSB on the Upper Side Band at 0800 and 1800 UT daily, the forecast following about 30 minutes later. On Saturday there is sometimes a preview of the coming week's weather prospects. It is not necessary to have either a transceiver or a transmitting licence to listen to the Net – see *Radio equipment*, page 8.

BBC Radio 4, UK

On 198kHz at 0048, 0555, 1355, 1750 LT. Occasionally the synopsis provides advance warning of the approach of an Atlantic depression which could lead to a northwesterly *tramontana*.

German language
Offenbach (Main) / Pinneberg (DDH)(DDK), Germany

On 147·3mHz at 0620, 0900, 1518, 1730 UT (5 day, 3 day, 5 day and 24 hr forecasts respectively, in German, for the Mediterranean and station reports for areas M1–M9: see diagram).

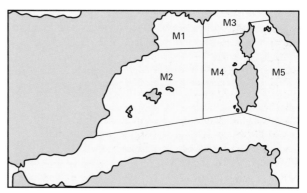

GERMAN WEATHER FORECAST AREAS

Non-radio weather forecasts

A forecast in Spanish can be obtained from the airport Met Office on each island (ask for *meteorologia*). Alternatively a pre-recorded marine forecast, again in Spanish, is available by telephoning (906) 365371. The 'High Seas' bulletin includes the Islas Baleares.

Spanish television shows a useful synoptic chart with its land weather forecast every evening after the news at approximately 2120 weekdays, 1520 Saturday and 2020 Sunday. Most national and local newspapers also carry some form of forecast.

Nearly all marinas and yacht harbours display a synoptic chart and forecast, generally updated daily (though often posted rather late to be of use).

Weatherfax

Rota (US Navy) (1030), Madrid (1005) and Rome (1265) broadcast weatherfax transmissions covering the Islas Baleares and suitable for reception via SSB and computer or dedicated weatherfax receiver. Refer to the *Admiralty List of Radio Signals Vol 3 Part 1 (NP 283/1)* for times and frequencies.

Navtex

Navtex is transmitted on the standard frequency of 518kHz. The Mediterranean and Black Sea fall within NAVAREA III.

Valencia (Cabo de la Nao), Spain

Identification letter X

Weather messages: 0750, 1950 (gale warnings, synopsis and 24 hr forecast, in English, for areas 8–12 (see diagram page 16).

Navigational warning:s: 0350, 0750, 1150, 1550, 1950, 2350 in English, for the Mediterranean coast of Spain and Islas Baleares.

La Garde (CROSS), France

Identification letter W

Storm warnings: On receipt and at 0340, 0740, 1140, 1540, 1940, 2340, in English, for areas 514(eastern part)–523, 531–534.

Weather messages: 1140, 2340 (gale or storm warnings, synopsis and 24 hr forecast, in English, for areas 514(eastern part)–523, 531–534: see diagram page 17).

Navigational warnings: in English, for the northwestern Mediterranean only.

Isla de Ibiza

General description

Ibiza, the most westerly of the Islas Baleares, lies 50 miles off Cabo de la Nao on the Spanish mainland. It is 26 miles long and 16 miles wide and covers an area of 22 square miles. The northern half and the southwestern extremity are mountainous, the highest point being Atalayasa at 475m. There are three true harbours and hundreds of small anchorages around the coast which, with the exception of some stretches of low sandy beaches on the south and southeast sides, is very rugged and broken. Rocky cliffs are interspersed with numerous *calas* (literally coves, but in practice often wide bays), many with small sandy beaches at their heads.

Inland, Ibiza is green and fertile with carpets of flowers in the spring and many pine forests which caused the Romans to name the group the '*Pityusae*' (Pine Islands). In common with the rest of the archipelago Ibiza suffers a massive invasion of holidaymakers each summer, and sadly many of the formerly deserted and exquisitely beautiful *calas* have been ruined by the construction of hotels and holiday apartments around their shores. The permanent population of Ibiza is around 72,000, more than a third of whom live in the capital city. Hotels, apartments and guest houses throughout the island are claimed to be able to accommodate a further 65,000 visitors.

History

Like many parts of the Mediterranean, Ibiza has experienced waves of invasion and settlement throughout its history.

Neolithic pottery discovered in a cave near Cala Vicente indicates that the inhabitants at the time of the Early Bronze Age were Iberian; this is borne out by drawings on the walls in a cave at the foot of Cabo Nono. But by 1200 BC the civilisations of the eastern Mediterranean were spreading westwards and there are many objects of Phoenician and Carthaginian origin, such as bronze axes and discs from San Juan, Salinas and Formentera, as well as figures from the Cave of Es Cuyeram, once a temple dedicated to the goddess Tanit. The city of Ibiza was founded during the 6th century BC by the Carthaginians, who are thought to have fortified the hill now known as D'Alt Vila (the old town) and to have called both town and island as *Ibasim*. There is evidence to show that agriculture was improved, tunny fishing introduced and the culture of olives and manufacture of purple dye from murex molluscs commenced. By the 3rd century BC the island was minting its own coinage.

It is claimed that Isla Conjera, off the west coast of Ibiza, was the birthplace of the Carthaginian general Hannibal – certainly the inhabitants of the Islas Planas, part of the Islas Bledas group, were known for their skill at stone slinging and a number of slingers were recruited for the armies of Hannibal in his fight against Rome. As Rome gradually became the victorious power both Ibiza and Formentera recognised her sovereignty, and became city states within the Roman Empire under the name *Pityusae*.

Other than the name *Ebysos* there is little remaining evidence of the Greeks in Ibiza, but the Romans brought prosperity to the island, now called *Ebusus*, founding saltworks at Salinas and lead mines at San Carlos. They stimulated agriculture by taking shipments of corn to Rome, minted coins, and built an aqueduct and a new citadel on the site of the old Carthaginian fortress.

With the fall of Rome Ibiza suffered the same fate as other satellite countries, being occupied throughout the centuries by various different groups. Raids by the Vandals drove many inhabitants away to seek refuge on the mainland, then in AD 426 a Barbarian tribe called the Gunderic occupied the island until the great Byzantine sailor Admiral Belisarius captured it in AD 535.

The Moors, who at first found the island useful as a base for raids on shipping and the mainland, arrived from North Africa in AD 707 and remained for more than 500 years. To them the island was *Yebisah*. The Vikings attempted an invasion in 857 followed by Charlemagne in 798–801, but the Moors managed to hold on until 1235 when Ibiza was eventually reconquered by a force under Guillem de Montgrí, Bishop of Tarragona, backed by King Jaime I of Catalonia. The Moorish influence may still be seen in the customs, architecture and traditional dress of the islanders, the Catalonian in their language, from which the Ibizan dialect is derived and in which the island is *Eivissa*.

Ibiza's return to Christian rule failed to bring peace, and the island was subject to much fighting during the period of Spanish internal strife. In 1492 the whole of Spain, including Ibiza, became united under Ferdinand and Isabella but for another two centuries attacks on the island by Barbary pirates, Moors and Turks were frequent – watchtowers were kept permanently manned, the present city walls were built and cavalry patrols were established. Even village churches were fortified.

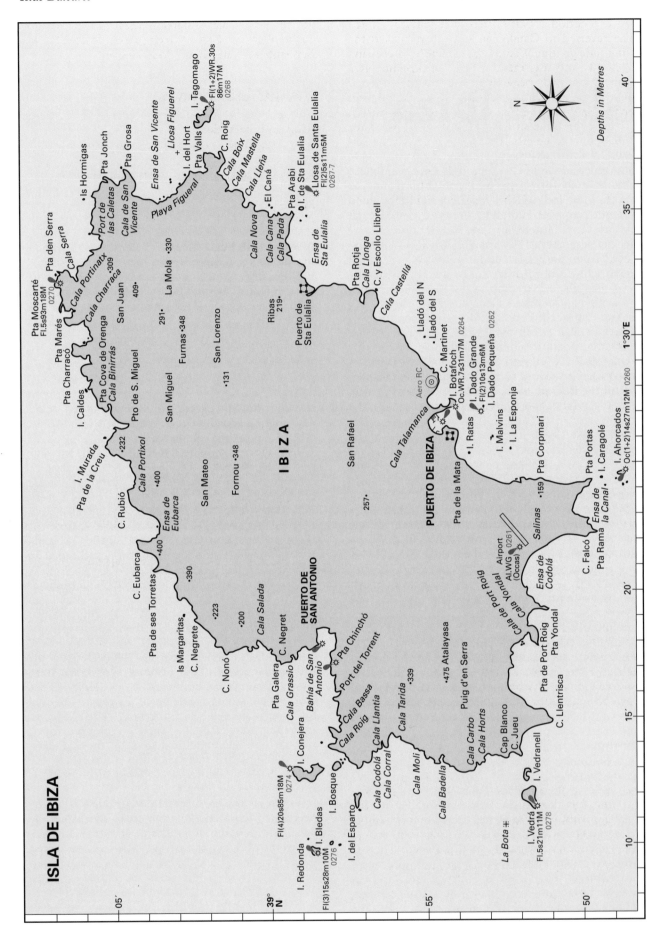

ISLA DE IBIZA

IBIZA

PUERTO DE SAN ANTONIO

PUERTO DE IBIZA

I. Redonda
Fl(3)15s28m10M
0276

I. Bledas
Fl(4)20s85m18M
0274

I. del Esparto

I. Bosque

I. Conejera

I. Vedrá
Fl.5s21m11M
0278

I. Vedranell

La Bota ⌗

Cala Codolá
Cala Corral

Cala Moli

Cala Badella

Cala Horts
Cala Carbo

C. Llientrisca

C. Jueu
Cap Blanco

Cala Roig
Cala Bassa
Cala Llantia

Cala Tarida
•339

Puig d'en Serra

•475 Atalayasa

Port del Torrent

Pta Chinchó
•Pta Chinchó

Bahía de San Antonio

Cala Grassió

Pta Galera
C. Negret

C. Negrete
•200

•223

Is Margaritas

C. Nonó

Pta de ses Torretas

•390

C. Eubarca

•400

Ensa de Eubarca

C. Rubió

•400

Cala Portixol

Pta de la Creu

I. Murada
•232

I. Caldes

San Mateo

San Miguel

Fornou •348

257•

•131

Furnas •348

291•

La Mola •330

San Lorenzo

San Juan

409•

Pto de S. Miguel

Cala Binirrás

Pta Cova de Orenga

Pta Charracó

Pta Marés

Pta Charraca

Pta den Serra

Pta Moscarté
Fl.5s93m18M
0270

Is Hormigas

Cala Serra
•Cala Serra

Pta Portinatx
•309

Cala Charraca

Port de las Caletas

Cala de San Vicente

Ensa de San Vicente

Playa Figueral

I. del Hort
Llosa Figuerel
+

Pta Valls
Pta Grosa
Pta Jonch

I. Tagomago
Fl(1+2)WR.30s
86m17M
0268

C. Roig

Cala Boix

Cala Mastella

Cala Lleñá

El Caná

Pta Arabi

Cala Pada

Cala Cana

Cala Nova

I. de Sta Eulalia
Llosa de Santa Eulalia
Fl(2)5s11m5M
0267·7

Ensa de Sta Eulalia

Puerto de Sta Eulalia

Ribas •219

Pta Rotja

Cala Llonga

C. y Escollo Llibrell

Cala Castellá

Lladó del N
Lladó del S

Aero RC

C. Martinet
C. Botafoch

I. Botafoch
Oc.WR.7s31m7M 0264

I. Dado Grande
Fl(2)10s13m6M

I. Dado Pequeña 0262

I. Ratas

I. Malvins
I. La Esponja

Cala Talamanca

Pta de la Mata

Pta Corpmari

•159

Airport
Al.WG 0261
(Occas)

Salinas

Ensa de Codolá

Cap de Yondal

Cala de Port Roig

Cala Yondal

Pta de Port Roig
Pta Yondal

C. Falcó
Pta Rama

Ensa de la Canal

I. Ahorcados
Oc(1+2)14s27m12M 0260

Pta Portas
I. Caragolé

N

Depths in Metres

39°
N

40'

35'

1°30'E

1°30'E

05'

55'

50'

10'

15'

20'

After a period as part of the Kingdom of Mallorca Ibiza reverted to Catalonian rule, then backed the losing side in the War of the Spanish Succession (1702-14) and was made a Spanish province as a result. It gradually became a cultural and economic backwater, emigration adding to a population decline begun by the Black Death 400 years earlier.

During the Spanish Civil War Ibiza declared for Franco, only to be rebuffed by the Republicans and occupied for a six-week period when considerable damage was done to churches and other buildings.

In the past Ibiza's main wealth came from the export of the 'red' salt which was particularly valued – even today over 100,000 tons are exported each year. Fruit, grain and shellfish are other exports of importance. During the last fifty years the tourist trade has expanded into a major industry and the island, which was in the past a haven for the simple life and values, has been dragged into the 20th century. In particular both Ibiza and Formentera became favourites with the so-called 'hippie' culture, a legacy still to be detected in a marked tollerance towards unusual clothes and non-mainstream lifestyles. The construction of apartment blocks for tourists continues apace, together with large numbers of tourist shops, cafés, bars, restaurants and related services.

Places of interest

The church of Nostra Señora in the small village of Jesús just north of Ibiza city contains a famous (and very beautiful) altarpiece dating back to the early 16th century.

In the northern part of the island lie Balafia, a fortified Moorish village just outside San Lorenzo, and the Es Cuyeram cave which was once a Carthaginian temple to the goddess Tanit (also accessible from the anchorage at Cala de San Vicente). If travelling by car, take the road north from Ibiza city towards San Juan Bautista and Cala Portinatx.

In the southwest, the Carthaginian and Roman remains at ses Països de cala d'Hort (near Cala Horts) make an interesting visit. Inland lies Ibiza's highest point, Atalayasa, near the village of San José. Further east, on the road to Ibiza, are the caves of Cova Santa, also accessible via a track from Cala Yondal.

Fiestas

In addition to the national holidays and *fiestas* listed in the introduction the following dates are celebrated in Ibiza: 17 January – San Antonio (San Antonio); 12 February – Santa Eulalia (Santa Eulalia del Río); 23 April – San Jorge (San Jorge); First Sunday in May – Festival of Flowers (Santa Eulalia); 24 June – San Juan Bautista (San Juan); 1-8 August – Our Lady of the Snows, patron saint of the Pitiusas Islands (Ibiza); 10 August – San Lorenzo (San Lorenzo); 15 August – Cala Llonga; 16 August – Our Lady of Carmen, sea procession (Ibiza); 24 August – San Bartolomé (San Antonio); 28 August – San Augustin (San Augustin); 21 September – San Mateo (San Mateo); 29 September – San Miguel (San Miguel).

Factual information

Magnetic variation

Ibiza – 1°45'W (decreasing 7'E annually) (1997)

Approach and coastal passage charts

Admiralty   *1701, 1702, 2834*
Spanish   *7A, 478, 479*
French   *5505, 7114*

Approach lights

0261 **Aeropuerto** 38° 52'·7N 1°22'·3E
Aero AlFl.WG.3s16m Control tower 9m
Occas. Situated 1M inland

0278 **Isla Vedrá** 38°51'·9N 1°11'·5E
Fl.5s21m11M White conical tower 3m
262°-vis-134°

0276 **Isla Bleda Plana** 38°58'·9N 1°09'·6E
Fl(3)15s28m10M White round tower 8m
349°-vis-239°

0274 **Isla Conejera** 38°59'·7N 1°12'·9E
Fl(4)20s85m18M
White tower and building 18m

0270 **Punta Moscarté** 39°07'·1N 1°32'E
Fl.5s93m18M White round tower, black diagonal stripes 52m 074°-vis-294°

0268 **Isla Tagomago** 39°02'·1N 1°39'·3E
Fl(1+2)WR.30s86m17M Grey octagonal stone tower on building 23m
043·5°-W-037°-R-043·5°
(Red sector covers Bajo de Santa Eulalia)

Radiobeacons

1033 **Cabo Martinet Aero** 38°55'N 1°28'·3E
Aerobeacon *IBZ*, 394kHz 60M (Non A2A)

Puerto de Ibiza (Eivissa)

38°54'·7N 1°26'·7E

Charts

	Approach	Harbour
Admiralty	2834	2834
Spanish	7A, 478, 479, 479A	4791
French	7114	7114

Lights

Approach

0262 **Islote Dado Grande** 38°53'·5N 1°27'·2E
Fl(2)10s13m6M
Black tower, red band, ⁏ topmark 6m
(Apparently destroyed as of May 1996)

0264 **Islote Botafoch** 38°54'·3N 1°27'·3E
Oc.WR.7s31m7M Horn(2)10s White tower
and house, grey lantern and cupola 16m
034°-R-045° (over Islas Malvins and Esponja)
045°-W-034° Obscured over Islotes Lladós
by Isla Grossa

Entrance

0264·4 **Northeast (Marina Botafoch) breakwater**
38°54'·7N 1°27'E Fl(2+1)G.11s6m6M
Green column, red band, on white base
displaying green ▲ 3m

0264·5 **Breakwater spur** 38°54'·7N 1°27'E
F.R.2m2M Red post 1m

0264·6 **Marina Botafoch, inner mole**
38°54'·7N 1°27'E F.G.2m2M Green post 1m

0265 **Southwest breakwater** 38°54'·7N 1°26'·6E
Fl.R.3s12m7M White truncated conical
tower on building, red cupola 11m
Obscured west of Islotes Malvins

0265·4 **Northeast (Marina Botafoch) breakwater**
elbow 38°54'·8N 1°26'·8E Fl.G.3s12m5M
Green column on white base displaying green ▲ 11m

0265·6 **Puerto Deportivo Ibiza Nueva, south mole**
38°54'·8N 1°26'·7E Fl(3)G.20s12m3M
Green column on white base displaying green ▲ 11m

0265·8 **Puerto Deportivo Ibiza Nueva, north mole**
38°54'·9N 1°26'·7E Fl(4)R.20s7m3M
Red tower on office building 6m

0267 **Commercial mole, southeast corner**
38°54'·8N 1°26'·5E
F.G.6m2M Green metal column 4m

0267·2 **Commercial mole, southwest corner**
38°54'·9N 1°26'·4E
F.G.6m2M Green metal column 4m

0266 **South inner mole, northeast corner**
38°54'·8N 1°26'·4E
F.R.6m3M Red metal column 4m

0266·2 **South inner mole, northwest corner**
38°54'·7N 1°26'·4E
F.R.6m3M Red metal column

Radiobeacons

1033 **Cabo Martinet Aero** 38°55'N 1°28'·3E
Aerobeacon *IBZ*, 394kHz 60M (Non A2A)

Port Communications

VHF – Pilots (*Ibiza Prácticos*) Ch 12, 13, 14, 16;
Marinas Ch 6, 9, 16.
☎/*Fax* – Port Authority 310611; Marina Botafoch
☎ 311711, 313013, 312231, *Fax* 311557; Puerto
Deportivo Ibiza Nueva ☎ 314050, 312062, *Fax*
313523; Club Náutico de Ibiza ☎/*Fax* 313363.

General

Puerto de Ibiza offers excellent facilities for yachts and a harbour which is easy to enter under most conditions and gives good shelter, though in strong east–southeast–south winds the marinas suffer from swell. It is, however, an expensive place to stay and in summer a berth may be hard to find. On occasions the harbour water becomes dirty and oily.

Sadly the description in previous editions of 'a charming little port for commercial fishing boats and yachts' is no longer true. Although a small part of the old town and citadel is still unspoilt, massive and apparently uncontrolled tourist development is taking place and changing the character of both town and harbour completely. The city has become an international tourist centre, very overcrowded in the summer, while even in winter the locals are outnumbered by foreign visitors and residents.

The city was founded during the 6th century BC by the Carthaginians, who are thought to have occupied the hill now known as D'Alt Vila (the old town) and to have referred to both town and island as *Ibasim*. On the western slopes of the hill is the Puig des Molins necropolis, a subterranean burial place which served the city from the Phoenician era (7th century BC) until Roman times. It is open to the public, together with an interesting museum. Parts of the cathedral date back to the 13th century, shortly after the island was reconquered for Spain, but the great citadel walls were built in the late 16th century and bear the arms of King Phillip II. The D'Alt Vila is well worth a visit and contains, amongst many other interesting buildings, the cathedral and the Archaeological Museum.

Fiestas are held on the Friday night of Holy Week (Good Friday), on 24 June to celebrate the king's name saint (San Juan), and 1-8 August in honour of *La Virgen de las Nieves*, patron saint of the island. On 16 August there is a sea procession as part of the *Fiesta del Virgen del Carmen*.

Approach

From south Several potential hazards litter the southern approach. As encountered these are: Islote La Esponja (10m), one mile east of Isla Sal Rossa, Malvins del Sur (20m) and Malvins del Norte (12m), 1·1 and 0·9 mile south of Pta Marloca, and Dado Grande (7m) and Dado Pequeña (9m) about 0·8 mile south of Isla Botafoch. Dado Grande is supposedly marked by a lit black and red beacon, but this has been missing since May 1996. All lie near or outside the 20m contour and in daylight can be left on either hand.

If approaching at night with the light on Dado Grande not in evidence it would be wise to pass outside all these hazards – a bearing of 345° or less on Isla Botafoch ensures safe water. Isla Botafoch shows a red sector over Esponja and the Islas Malvins, but this does not cover Dado Grande and Pequeña. If the light on Dado Grande is seen it can safely be left to starboard.

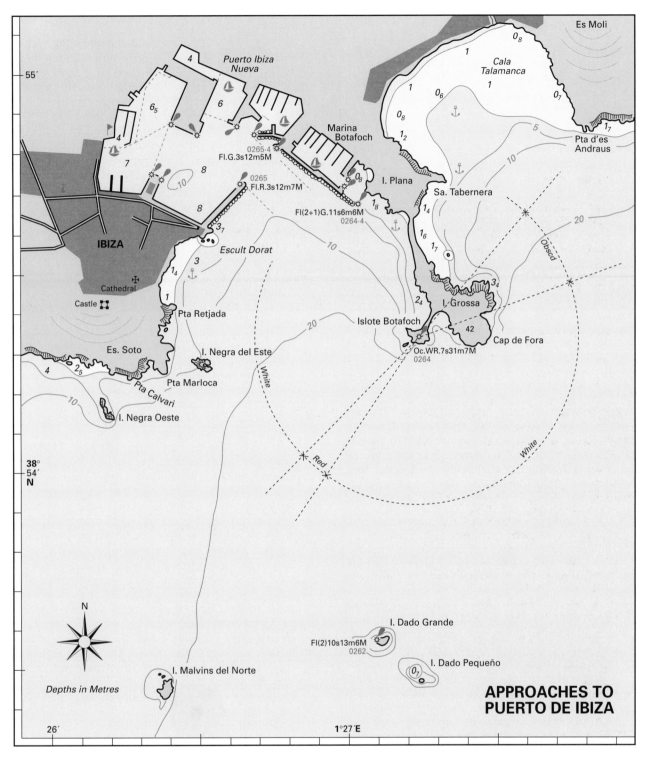

APPROACHES TO PUERTO DE IBIZA

From northeast If coastal sailing from the northeast end of the island, or approaching from the direction of Mallorca, refer to page 46 for details of the passage inside Isla Tagomago and page 48 for Isla de Santa Eulalia. After passing Puerto de Santa Eulalia, Cabo Llibrell should be given a least offing of 200m, then the two small islands Lladó del Norte (10m), and Lladó del Sur (6m) identified just under a mile northeast of Cabo Martinet. Once spotted they can safely be passed on either side. Cabo Martinet, Isla Grossa and Isla Botafoch are all steep-to, though the latter has a small offlier close inshore.

Anchorages in the approach

In fine weather it is possible to anchor 200m off the cliff due east of the cathedral in 6m over sand and weed, but it is shallow close in. Alternatively in northeasterly or easterly winds shelter can be found close in to the Isla Grossa peninsula, between Islote Botafoch and the entrance to Marina Botafoch, in 5–6m over rock and weed. Holding is reported to be poor. Both of these anchorages are made rolly by wash from ferries and other port traffic.

The approach to Puerto de Ibiza from just east of south. Islote Botafoch and lighthouse are to the right, Marina Botafoch in the centre and the south breakwater on the left.

Entrance

Large commercial ships and many ferries use the harbour – they have right of way and must not be obstructed. For this reason it is advisable to keep to the starboard side of the entrance but there are no other navigational hazards. Islote Negra del Este and Islote Botafoch are both steep-to and there are good depths (ie. more than 5m) in the entrance and throughout the commercial harbour.

Berthing

Once in the harbour there are several choices for berthing, though all are likely to be crowded in the high season:

- *Marina Botafoch* An upmarket marina (☎ 311711, 313013, 312231, *Fax* 311557) with over 400 berths, able to take yachts of up to 30m, and with excellent facilities (see below). The office staff are helpful and several speak English.

  The entrance lies outside the harbour proper, some 0·4 mile north of the Islote Botafoch from which it takes its name. Although reasonably wide, the entrance does not open up until well inside a line from Islote Botafoch to the end of the northeast (Marina Botafoch) breakwater and can therefore be difficult to identify. The fuel and reception berth is on the starboard side on entry, with the marina offices nearby. A ferry plies across the harbour into town.

- *Puerto Deportivo Ibiza Nueva* Expanding into the old commercial basin to the west has made Ibiza Nueva (☎ 314050, 312062, *Fax* 313523) the largest marina in the port with well over 500 berths for yachts of up to 40m. Facilities are good, though some of the berths are rather remote.

The dogleg entrance (see photo page 26) to the right of a large yellow building presents no particular problems and carries 3·5–4m depth. Secure on the north side of the north mole (where fuel is also available) to be allocated a berth. Again there is a ferry service into town.

- *Club Náutico de Ibiza* Situated at the head of the harbour and small compared to its neighbours, the Club Náutico de Ibiza (☎/*Fax* 313363) normally reserves twenty outside berths for visiting yachts (berths inside the harbour are private). These can be oily and are exposed to ferry wash – use *Club Náutico* lines which have car tyres as springs. Secure in any vacant berth and check at the office. The *Club Náutico* is friendly towards visitors and very convenient for the city.

- *Port Authority pontoons* Two pontoons with a mixture of permanent and visitors berths are situated in the extreme southwest of the harbour south of the *Club Náutico*. Again they are subject to ferry wash and can be oily. Water and electricity are available but there are no other facilities, however charges are low and it is just a step into the old town. A further three pontoons may be found near the root of the southwest breakwater – these were removed early in 1996 for dredging to take place and it was unclear whether they would be reinstated.

Charges *(see page 6)*

- *Marina Botafoch* High season daily rate – Band A; low season daily rate – Band C. Water and electricity extra.
- *Puerto Deportivo Ibiza Nueva* High season daily rate – Band A; low season daily rate – Band A. Water and electricity included.
- *Club Náutico de Ibiza* High season daily rate – Band C (15m), Band B (10m); low season daily rate – Band B. Water and electricity included.
- *Port Authority pontoons* High season daily rate – Band D; low season daily rate – Band D. Water and electricity extra.

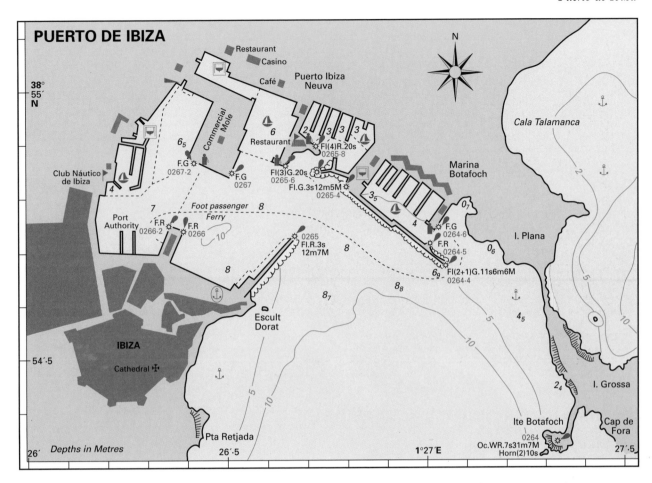

PUERTO DE IBIZA

[Map labels: Restaurant, Casino, Café, Puerto Ibiza Neuva, Commercial Mole, Restaurant, Club Náutico de Ibiza, Port Authority, Foot passenger Ferry, Escult Dorat, IBIZA, Cathedral, Pta Retjada, Cala Talamanca, Marina Botafoch, I. Plana, I. Grossa, Ite Botafoch, Cap de Fora, Depths in Metres]

[Light characters: Fl(4)R.20s 0265·8, Fl(3)G.20s 0265·6, Fl.G.3s12m5M 0265·4, F.G 0267·2, F.G 0267, F.R 0266·2, F.R 0266, 0265 Fl.R.3s 12m7M, F.G 0264·6, F.R 0264·5, Fl(2+1)G.11s6m6M 0264·4, 0264 Oc.WR.7s31m7M Horn(2)10s]

Facilities

Boatyards The biggest is situated just north of the *Club Náutico* but is actually part of the Puerto Deportivo Ibiza Nueva, as is the yard at the head of their west basin. Smaller concern at Marina Botafoch.

Travel-lift 100 tonnes and 27 tonnes at Ibiza Nueva yards, 62 tonnes at Marina Botafoch.

Slipway Close north of the *Club Náutico*.

Engineers Marina Botafoch and Ibiza Nueva boatyards, also Yates Ibiza (☎/*Fax* 190326) just north of the *Club Náutico* and Ibiza Yacht Service (☎ 310617, *Fax* 310656) at the head of the Ibiza Nueva west basin.

Official service agents include: Auto Recambios Isla (☎ 311012, 313700, *Fax* 316966) – Yamaha; Ibiza Nautica (☎ 311935, *Fax* 314076) – Ecosse, Volvo Penta; Ibiza Yachting (☎ 341159) – Johnson; Marina Marbella Ibiza SA (☎ 310811) – Mercury/ MerCruiser, Volvo Penta; Motonautica (☎ 306665, *Fax* 306662) – Honda, Mercury/ MerCruiser, Soler, Suzuki, Yanmar; Servinautic (☎ 191318, *Fax* 311963) – Mariner, MerCruiser, Volvo Penta.

Electronic & radio repairs Both marina boatyards, Nautronic at Marina Botafoch, Yates Ibiza and Ibiza Yacht Service.

Sailmaker At the Polígono Eurocentro (☎ 311660). Also services inflatable dinghies and liferafts.

Chandlery Well-stocked chandleries at the Marina Botafoch and across the road from the *Club Náutico*.

Water At all berths listed above. The water in Ibiza is of variable quality – if possible consult other yachtsmen before filling tanks.

Showers At both marinas and the *Club Náutico*.

Electricity At all berths listed above. Normally 220 volt, but 380 volts available at large yacht (25m±) berths in the two marinas.

Fuel At both marinas. Ibiza Nueva has two fuelling points (see plan).

Bottled gas Camping Gaz exchanges at chandleries or in town. It may be possible to get Calor Gas and other butane bottles refilled at Factoria Butano SA, Esquina Camina, Santa Eulalia por Jesus.

Ice In the supermarkets at the marinas and in the *Club Náutico* bar.

Yacht club The Club Náutico de Ibiza has a bar, lounge, terrace, showers and restaurant. Visiting yachtsmen are made welcome. Also clubs based at both marinas.

Banks In the town, many with credit card facilities.

Shops/provisioning Supermarkets at both marinas plus excellent choice in the town.

Market All day Friday in summer.

Hotels/restaurants/cafés, etc. Restaurants, cafés and bars at both marinas plus vast numbers in the town. Hotels of all ratings, including one in the Marina Botafoch complex.

Laundrettes At both marinas and in the town.

Hospital/medical services In the town.

Looking east over Puerto Deportivo Ibiza Neuva and Marina Botafoch, with Cala Talamanca in the background.

Looking southeast over Puerto de Ibiza on a very clear day. The old walled city is on the right, flanked by the wedge-shaped Islote Negra del Este and, further away, the twin rocks of Dado Grande and Dado Pequeño (the former missing its tower and topmark).

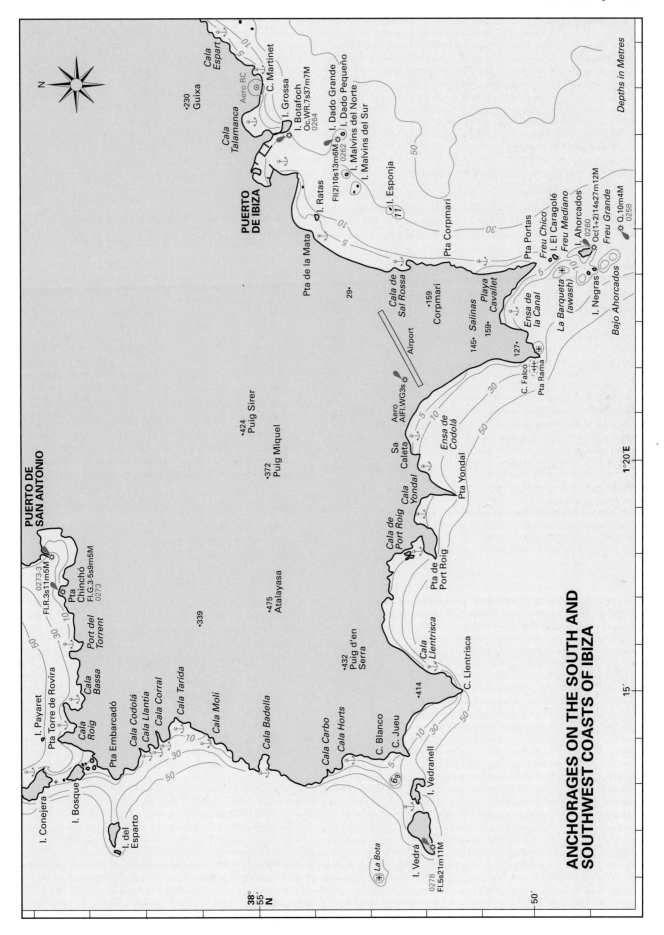

N

Depths in Metres

PUERTO DE IBIZA

Cala Espart

C. Martinet

•230 Guixa

Cala Talamanca

Aero RC

C. Grossa

I. Botafoch
Oc.WR.7s37m7M
0264

I. Dado Grande

I. Dado Pequeño

I. Malvins del Norte
Fl(2)10s13m6M
0262

I. Malvins del Sur

I. Ratas

I. Esponja

50

10

Pta de la Mata

30

5

Pta Corpmari

Pta Portas

Freu Chico

I. El Caragolé

Freu Mediano

I. Ahorcados
Oc(1+2)14s27m12M
0260

Freu Grande

Q.10m4M
0258

I. Negras

La Barqueta
(awash)

Bajo Ahorcados

Ensa de
la Canal

Pta Rama

C. Falcó

127•

145• Salinas

159•

Playa
Cavallet

159•
Corpmari

Cala de
Sal Rossa

29•

Airport

Aero
AlFl.WG3s

Sa
Caleta

Ensa de
Codolá

Pta Yondal

Cala
Yondal

Cala de
Port Roig

Pta de
Port Roig

30

50

10

5

C. Llentrisca

Cala
Llentrisca

•414

C. Jueu

C. Blanco

Cala Horts

Cala Carbo

Cala Badella

•432
Puig d'en
Serra

Cala Moli

•475
Atalayasa

•339

•372
Puig Miquel

•424
Puig Sirer

Cala Tarida

Cala Corral

Cala Llantia

Cala Codolá

Pta Embarcadó

Cala
Bassa

Cala
Roig

Pta Torre de Rovira

I. Payaret

PUERTO DE
SAN ANTONIO

Fl.R.3s11m5M
0273.3

Pta
Chinchó
Fl.G.3-5s9m5M
0273

Port del
Torrent

50

30

10

I. Conejera

I. Bosque

I. del
Esparto

La Bota

I. Vedranell

I. Vedrá
0278
Fl.5s21m11M

5

6

9

6

10

30

50

**ANCHORAGES ON THE SOUTH AND
SOUTHWEST COASTS OF IBIZA**

38°
55'
N

15'

50'

1°20'E

Communications

Car hire/taxis In the town, or arrange through marina offices.

Buses Regular services over most of the island.

Ferries Car ferries to mainland Spain and Mallorca. Frequent tourist ferries and hydrofoils to Formentera and various beaches.

Air services International airport 3½ miles south of the harbour.

Islets to the south of Puerto de Ibiza

Several small islets lie in the bay south of Puerto de Ibiza. From north to south these are: Dado Grande (Dau Gran) (7m) and Dado Pequeña (Dau Petit) (9m) about 0·8 mile south of Islote Botafoch. Dado Grande is supposedly marked by a lit black and red beacon, but this was missing in May 1996; Malvins del Norte (12m) and Malvins del Sur (20m) 0·9 and 1·1 miles south of Pta Marloca, and Islote La Esponja (10m), one mile east of Isla Sal Rossa. All lie near or outside the 20m contour and can be left on either hand.

⚓ Punta de la Mata (Playa d'en Bossa)

38°53'·8N 1°25'E

A small and shallow harbour about 1 mile southwest of Puerto de Ibiza, tucked southwest of the punta and partially enclosed by a rough breakwater and short jetty. Small fishing boats and motor boats lie to crowded moorings in 1m± over sand and weed.

It is overlooked by hotels and high-rise tourist apartments, with a main road nearby.

⚓ Calas de Sal Rossa 38°52'·4N 1°24'·4E

Two small anchorages either side of Isla Sal Rossa, open northeast–east–southeast. Anchor in 2–3·5m over weed, sand and rock. The conspicuous (28m) Torre Sal Rossa stands to the northwest.

The area is still unspoilt with only some local fishing craft and net stores ashore, but Ibiza airport is little more than a mile distant. There is a rough track to the main road.

⚓ Playa d'es Caballet (Es Cavallet)

38°50'·7N 1°24'·3E

A long sandy beach open from north through east to south. There are developments at either end, a small jetty to the north and a track to the road. Anchor in 5m or less over sand and rock.

Passages between Islas de Ibiza and Espalmador

Charts	*Approach*	*Passages*
Admiralty	*2834*	*2834*
Spanish	*7A, 478, 479*	*479A*
French	*7114*	*7114*

Lights

0260 **Isla Ahorcados (Illa des Penjat)**
38°48'·9N 1°24'·7E Oc(1+2)14s27m12M
White tower, three black bands,
on white building 22m

0258 **Bajo de'n Pou** 38°48'·4N 1°25'·2E
Q.10m4M
North cardinal beacon, ↟ topmark 9m

0254 **Los Puercos or Los Pou** 38°48'N 1°25'·3E
Fl(3+1)20s28m11M
White tower, two black bands, 27m

0256 **Isla Espardel, north point**
38°48'·4N 1°28'·7E Fl(3)7·5s37m8M
White truncated conical tower 16m

General

There are three possible passages between Isla de Ibiza and Isla de Espalmador, separated by a series of small islands and rocky banks strung along a ridge running south from Ibiza through Espalmador to Formentera. Only one passage, the Freu Grande, is usable in all conditions, though the northern Freu Mediano makes a useful short cut in good weather. Isla Ahorcados, the only island of any size between Ibiza and Espalmador, was once the site of the gallows where condemned prisoners were executed.

From west or northwest If approaching from the Spanish mainland the mountains of southern Ibiza will be first to rise above the horizon, followed by the spectacular cliffs of Isla Vedrá (lit). On closer approach the higher southern parts of Formentera will be seen, but the smaller islands of the *freus* will not become visible until much closer in, when the black and white banded lighthouses of Isla Ahorcados and Los Puercos (or Los Pou) can be identified with the lit north cardinal beacon of Bajo de'n Pou between them.

From east or southeast Approach the *freus* on a southwesterly course following the coast of Ibiza and leaving Isla Espardel (lit) to port. Two hills, Corpmari (159m) and Falcó (145m), lie near the southern extremity of Ibiza though Punta Portas itself is low. The black and white banded lighthouses of Isla Ahorcados and Los Puercos (or Los Pou) are unmistakable, with the lit north cardinal beacon of Bajo de'n Pou between them.

At night Provided the yacht's position is known and the three lights mentioned above have been identified, passage through the Freu Grande should present no problems.

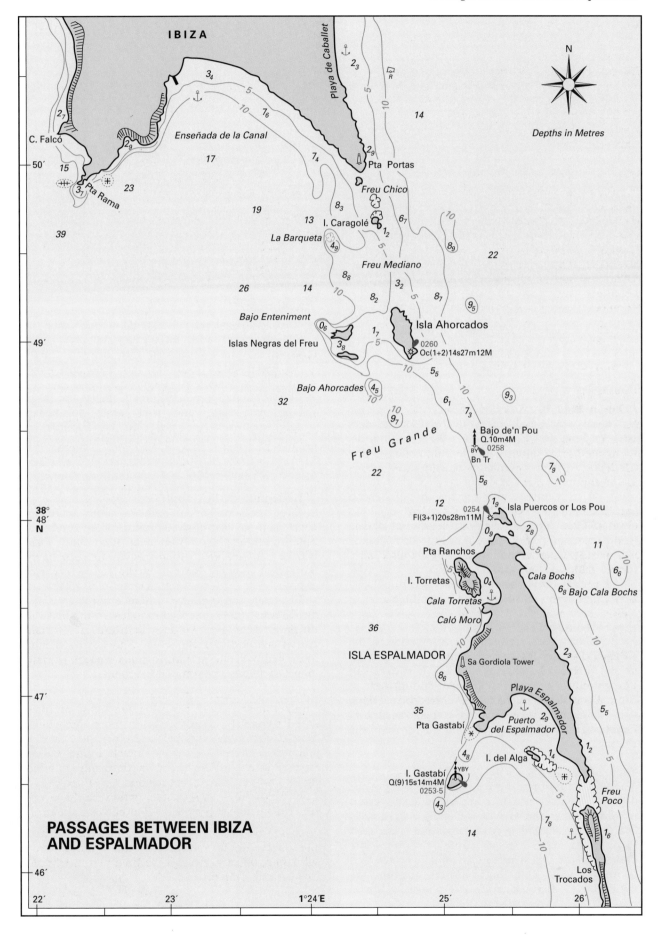

**PASSAGES BETWEEN IBIZA
AND ESPALMADOR**

Depths in Metres

IBIZA

Playa de Caballet

C. Falcó

Enseñada de la Canal

Pta Rama

Pta Portas

Freu Chico

I. Caragolé

La Barqueta

Freu Mediano

Bajo Enteniment

Islas Negras del Freu

Isla Ahorcados

0260
Oc(1+2)14s27m12M

Bajo Ahorcades

Freu Grande

Bajo de'n Pou
Q.10m4M
BY 0258
Bn Tr

Isla Puercos or Los Pou

0254
Fl(3+1)20s28m11M

Pta Ranchos

I. Torretas

Cala Torretas

Caló Moro

Cala Bochs

Bajo Cala Bochs

ISLA ESPALMADOR

Sa Gordiola Tower

Playa Espalmador

Pta Gastabí

Puerto
del Espalmador

I. del Alga

I. Gastabí
Q(9)15s14m4M
0253·5

Freu
Poco

Los
Trocados

The passages between Ibiza and Espalmador seen from the south. In the left foreground is Isla Gastabi, with Espalmador on the right. The black and white banded tower of Los Puercos (or Los Pou) lighthouse can be seen at its northern point. Isla Ahorcados lies beyond Freu Grande, with Ibiza in the distance.

Passages

Freu Grande 38°48'·6N 01°25'W

By far the widest and deepest of the three passages between Ibiza and Espalmador is the Freu Grande, between the lighthouses of Isla Ahorcados to the north and Los Puercos (or Los Pou) to the south, at just over a mile wide and 6–7m deep. Slightly to the south of its centre is the north cardinal beacon marking Bajo de'n Pou, also lit. In heavy seas keep clear of Bajo Ahorcados, 550m southwest of Isla Ahorcados, and pass just north of Bajo de'n Pou. It is the only passage recommended for use after dark, but in that case be careful to avoid the two Islas Negras del Freu, about 500m west of Isla Ahorcados, unlit, and only 2m and 4m high.

Freu Mediano 38°49'·4N 01°24'·6W

Freu Mediano lies between Isla Ahorcados to the south and Islote Caragolé, a small rock 4–7m high, to the north. Watch out for La Barqueta, an unmarked rock awash 500m west-southwest of Islote Caragolé – though often indicated by breaking seas, in calm weather it does not show clearly. Depths of 3–4m are to be found in the centre of the channel.

Freu Chico 38°49'·9N 01°24'·5W

The furthest north, narrowest and shallowest of the northern *freus*, for use only by shallow draft vessels in calm weather and with care. Depths may shoal to less than 1m. Careful eyeball navigation is required in order to avoid a rocky patch north of Islote Caragolé – a course a little north of halfway between Islote Caragolé and Punta Portas appears the optimum. La Barqueta rock (see above) is also a potential hazard when using this *freu*.

Anchorages

- *West of the passages* Ensenada de la Canal, in 2–10m over sand with rocky patches, open southeast–south–southwest (see below). Puerto del Espalmador, in 3–5m over sand and weed, open to the southwest (see page 57).
- *East of the passages* Playa d'es Caballet, in 5m or less over sand and rock open southeast–south–southwest (see page 28). Isla Espardel, in 6m± over rock, stone and weed on the west side of the island, open from south through west to north (see page 57).

⚓ Ensenada de la Canal 38°50'·5N 1°23'·2E

A large sandy bay open southeast–south–southwest with the possibility of swell from the west. Anchor to suit conditions in 2–10m over sand with rocky patches. A pier for loading salt will be seen in the northwest corner, backed by a factory complex ashore.

Relatively undeveloped ashore other than a few beach restaurants, but the beach itself – the Playa de Mitjorn – can get very crowded, due to frequent ferries and buses from Ibiza. The nearby Salinas (salt pans) are a protected area, attracting many migrating birds in spring and autumn.

Ensenada de la Canal with its salt-loading pier, seen from the northeast.

Punta Rama and Cabo Falcó 38°50'·1N 1°22'·3E
A prominent double headland with various off-lying
hazards. The isolated Bajo Morenallet lies 350m
east of Punta Rama, several islets to the south and a
wreck some 100m west of the *punta*. Allow an offing
of at least 500m.

⚓ **Ensenada de Codolá (Sa Caleta)**
38°51'·9N 1°20'·3E
A long bay open to southeast–south–southwest and
subject to swell from the west, shielded by Punta
Yondal and Cabo Falcó at either end. Anchor in
10m over sand and weed off the sand and stone
beach. The village of Sa Caleta lies at the northwest
end, backed by several tower blocks.

The centre of the bay is in line with the airport
runway, making the whole area very noisy – it is
about 1½ miles from Sa Caleta to the terminal
buildings. The southern part of the beach is backed
by salt pans.

Punta Yondal (des Jondal) 38°51'·4N 1°19'·3E
A serrated headland running out to a low
promontory with a hole through it. Rocks extend up
to 300m south of the point. Phoenician remains
have been found on the peninsula west of Sa Caleta,
including the foundations of a village dated at
around the 7th centrury BC.

⚓ **Cala Yondal (des Jondal)** 38°52'N 1°18'·9E
A wide but relatively sheltered bay lying between
Punta de Port Roig and Punta Yondal, open south
and southwest. Anchor about 100m off the beach in
6–10m over sand and weed. Beach café and other
buildings inland, and a track to the road.

Punta Port Roig (Punta Porroig)
38°51'·8N 1°17'·9E
A low flat point with a hole through it and some
scattered buildings on the summit.

⚓ **Cala de Port Roig (Cala Porroig)**
38°52'·1N 1°18'·1E
In no way a port – rather an attractive little
anchorage between Punta de Port Roig and Las
Isletas, surrounded by sloping reddish cliffs and well
protected from all winds except southwest, though
swell may enter from west and south. Anchor in
6–10m over sand, weed and rock, taking care to

The somewhat misnamed Cala de Port Roig seen from the
southwest.

avoid cables from the Spanish mainland which come
ashore in the bay.

Fishermen's huts line the eastern shore but
otherwise there are few buildings and currently no
bars or restaurants, though a small beach bar will be
found under Cabo Negret about a mile to the
northwest (best reached by dinghy). A development
is under construction on the southern headland.

⚓ **Cala Llentrisca** 38°51'·8N 1°15'·5E
A small anchorage with a stony beach tucked under
scrub-covered cliffs, open through northeast–
east–southeast and to swell from the south. Anchor
in 4–6m over sand and stone, though there are
depths of up to 23m off the entrance. Boats and
fishermen's huts line the beach, with a steep track
up to the road.

Tiny Cala Llentrisca, tucked behind the Cabo of the same name,
looking east.

Cabo Llentrisca 38°51'·4N 1°15'E
A steep, white-cliffed headland (148m) free of off-
lying dangers.

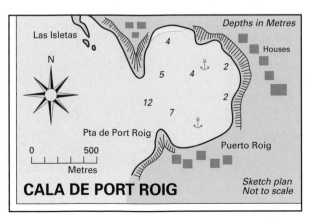

Las Isletas

N

Depths in Metres

Houses

Pta de Port Roig

Puerto Roig

0   500
Metres

CALA DE PORT ROIG

Sketch plan
Not to scale

⚓ **Isla Vedrá** 38°52'·2N 1°11'·6E

A lofty (382m), spectacular, rocky island, steep sided and steep-to, of a reddish colour. The lighthouse (Fl.5s21m11M, white conical tower 3m) is on the south coast and obscured when bearing between 134° and 262°.

There are two possible anchorages – one close north of the island in 12m, with landing feasible in a small inlet, the other off the northeast coast in 15m, just west of a group of rocks. Both have poor holding over stone and rock. Approach with care, and only in good conditions.

⚓ **Islote Vedranell** 38°52'·4N 1°12'·8E

Considerably lower (125m) and smaller than its neighbour, but equally steep-to, particularly to the south. Anchor in 12m over sand and rock close off the north coast. Again, a strictly fair weather spot.

Passages between Isla Vedrá, Islote Vedranell and Ibiza

A channel 750m wide and with a least depth of 10·8m runs between Islote Vedranell and Cabo Jueu on the mainland. A much narrower passage, some 200m wide but also carrying a good 10m, separates Islote Vedranell and Isla Vedrá. However attention must be paid to the following dangers:

- Bajo La Bota, a breaking rock 1 mile north-northwest of Isla Vedrá light
- A series of small rocky islets on the northeast and east coast of Isla Vedrá
- Bajo El Materet, 10·8m deep, 800m southwest of Cabo Blanco

A course of 125°/305° down the centre of the passage between Islote Vedranell and Cabo Jueu, keeping the point of Cabo Llentrisca equidistant between the two, clears Bajo El Materet. The inside passage is prone to sudden, strong gusts, and in heavy weather it is advisable to pass well outside Isla Vedrá and Bajo La Bota.

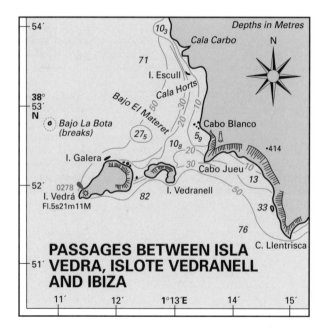

⚓ **Cala Horts (d'Hort)** 38°53'·4N 1°13'·4E

A popular anchorage in 5–10m over sand, open south–southwest–west and to swell from northwest, but sheltered by high cliffs and the two offshore islands. The long stony beach has two beach restaurants, one high-rise building and some smaller buildings, and there are daily visits by tourist boats.

Remains from the Carthaginian and Roman periods, including the foundations of a substantial villa, have been excavated at ses Païses de cala d'Hort, a short distance inland.

⚓ **Cala Carbo** 38°53'·7N 1°13'·1E

A small angled *cala* between low reddish headlands, which may be difficult to identify from offshore. Sound in carefully to anchor in 3m± over sand and weed off a fine sandy beach sporting the usual restaurant etc.

⚓ **Cala Badella (Vadella)** 38°54'·9N 1°13'·3E

A deep and attractive *cala* with an excellent beach, well protected by high wooded cliffs and offering a safe but often crowded anchorage with many permanent moorings. Open to southwest–west and swell from northwest. The northern headland

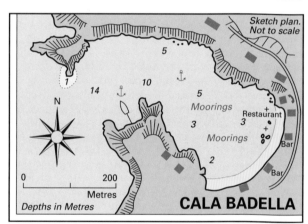

extends underwater and should be given minimum clearance of 25m, otherwise depths are considerable until well inside the *cala*. Anchor in 3–10m as space permits over sand and weed – it may be necessary to use two anchors to limit swinging. Larger yachts

Looking into Cala Badella from a little north of west. This photograph was taken in May – by July/August the bay is packed solid with moored motorboats and yachts.

sometimes moor with a line to the rocks of the southern headland. No shortage of restaurants, cafés and bars behind the beach, plus a small supermarket in the village. Daily visits in summer by tourist boats from San Antonio.

⚓ **Cala Moli** 38°55'·9N 1°13'·8E
A small *cala* with a fine sandy beach, open to southwest through northwest but otherwise well protected by high cliffs. A distinctive pink building stands on the southern headland, its curved facade supported by columns. Anchor in 5m over sand. Beach restaurant ashore, catering for the tourist boats from San Antonio, plus some new development to the north.

⚓ **Cala Tarida** 38°56'·4N 1°14'E
A long bay with sandy beaches separated by rocky outcrops, and with two low, inshore islands, Cala Tarida is easily identified by the extensive tourist developments to both north and south. Anchor in 4–5m over sand, weed and rock amongst the inevitable tourist boats, open to southwest–west–northwest. There are many beach restaurants and cafés ashore, together with some shops.

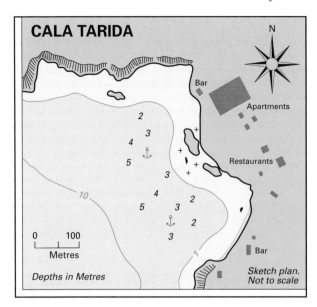

The growing resort of Cala Tarida looking northeast, with San Antonio just visible in the background.

⚓ **Cala Corral** 38°56'·8N 1°13'·8E
A rocky-sided *cala* open southwest through northwest and with small and shallow private harbour (Coralmar) tucked behind a rocky wall at its head. Anchor in 5–6m over sand and rock. A large tourist development stands behind and somewhat above the beach, itself fringed by fishermen's huts. A restaurant and supermarket will be found amongst the buildings to the north. The usual tourist boats visit daily in season.

⚓ **Cala Llantia** 38°56'·9N 1°13'·7E
A rocky-sided *cala* open southwest and west, with a beach at its head and a line of white houses on a cliff to the northwest. Anchor off the beach in 5m over sand.

⚓ **Cala Codolá (Codolar)** 38°57'N 1°13'·5E
A cliff-sided *cala* with a stony beach at its head, open southwest through northwest. Anchor in 4–6m over sand and weed near the head of *cala*, where a restaurant and beach bar will be found. Low-rise white houses line the clifftop to the north, together with a few shops. Tourist boats visit daily in season.

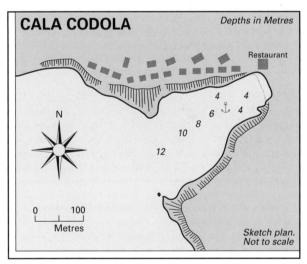

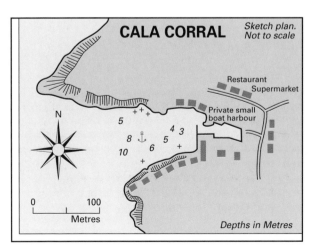

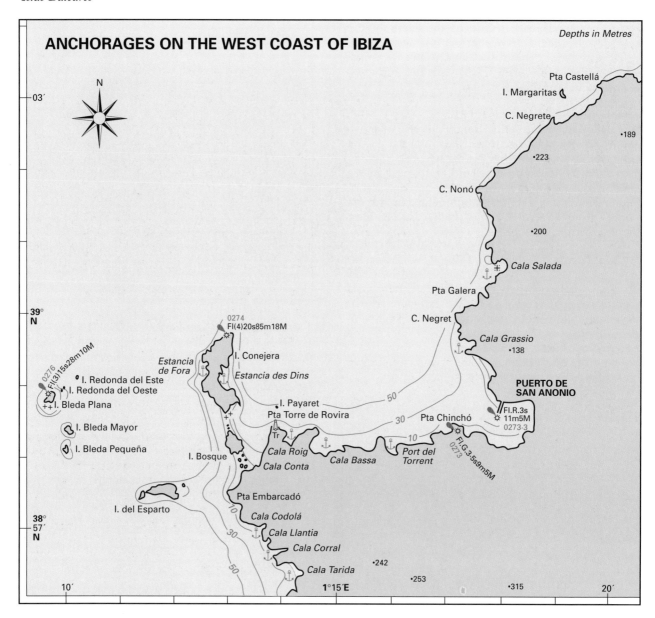

ANCHORAGES ON THE WEST COAST OF IBIZA

Passage between Isla del Esparto (Illa de s'Espart) and Ibiza

The north–south passage between Isla del Esparto (68m) and Ibiza is more than 1000m wide with a minimum depth of 30m. A small rocky islet stands just off the northeast point of the island.

Islas Bledas (Ses Bledes) 38°58'·8N 1°09'·6E

A group of five uninhabited rocky islets lying 2 miles northwest of Isla del Esparto. At their centre is Isla Bleda Plana (23m), which has off-lying rocks to the southwest. There is a lighthouse (Fl(3)15s28m10M, white round tower 8m) on the northwest side of this island, obscured when bearing between 239° and 349°. The other islands, taken from north to south, comprise:

- Isla Redonda del Este (13m), 1000m northeast of Isla Bleda Plana
- Isla Redonda del Oeste, close northeast of Isla Bleda Plana

- Isla Bleda Mayor (Na Bose) (39m), 1000m south-southeast of Isla Bleda Plana
- Isla Bleda Pequeña (Na Gorra) (29m), sometimes referred to as Porros, about 400m south of Isla Bleda Mayor and with foul ground between the two.

Explore the area with care and a bow lookout. In settled conditions it is reported possible to anchor in 5m near the lighthouse landing on Isla Bleda Plana, taking a sternline ashore.

Passage between Isla Conejera (Sa Conillera) and Isla Bosque (de Bosc)

A passage 200m wide exists between Isla Conejera (69m) and Isla Bosque (67m). It is generally deep, other than where a narrow (15m) bar carrying some 3–4m links the two islands (see plan). In good light the paler colours of the bar should be clearly visible. Rocks extend from both islands, those off Isla Conejera barely breaking while those off Isla Bosque stand well above the water (though with a few breaking outliers).

Looking southwest through the gap between Isla Conejera (right) and Isla Bosque (left), with Isla del Esparto beyond. The paler bar linking the two foreground islands can just be made out.

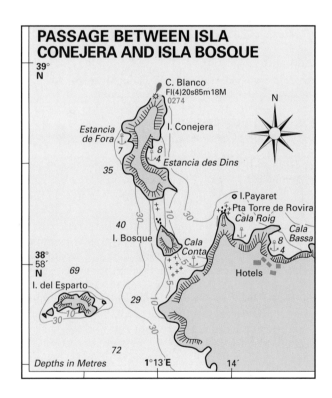

PASSAGE BETWEEN ISLA CONEJERA AND ISLA BOSQUE

39° N

C. Blanco
Fl(4)20s85m18M
0274

I. Conejera

N

Estancia
de Fora

7
8
4

35

Estancia des Dins

40

I.Payaret

Pta Torre de Rovira

Cala Roig

I. Bosque

Cala
Conta

Cala
Bassa

8
4

38°
58′
N

69

I. del Esparto

Hotels

29

10

30

72

Depths in Metres   1°13′E   14′

Take the passage in an east–west direction halfway between the two islands with a bias towards Isla Bosque. It becomes unsafe with any sea running, when it would be wise to pass outside Isla Conejera.

Passage between Isla Bosque and Ibiza

The passage between Isla Bosque and Ibiza is a mass of awash and barely-covered rocks and really only suitable for dinghies in calm conditions, though a 2m passage is said to exist.

⚓ **Estancia de Fora, Isla Conejera**
38°59′·1N 1°13′E
A small *cala* on the west side of Isla Conejera, open southwest–west–northwest and strictly a fairweather spot. Anchor in 5–7m over sand and rock.

⚓ **Estancia des Dins, Isla Conejera**
38°59′·2N 1°12′·5E
A large sandy bay on the east of the island, open to the northeast and with a 3 mile plus fetch to east and southeast. Anchor in 3m or more over sand and rock. There is a landing and miniature boat harbour at the northern end of the bay, with a track to the lighthouse (Fl(4)20s85m18M, white tower and building 18m) which stands at the north end of the island.

There are no facilities ashore, though temporary beach restaurants may be set up in summer when the island is a popular destination with tourist boats. The protected green lizard abounds.

⚓ **Cala Conta (Comte)** 38°58′N 1°13′·6E
A small *cala* on the mainland shore just north of the shoals running out to Isla Bosque, fully open northwest–north–northeast and partially open to winds from southwest and west. Anchor in 5–6m over sand, off a fine beach fringed by fishermen's huts.

⚓ **Cala Roig (Roja)** 38°58′·3N 1°14′·1E
A rocky-sided *cala* open northwest–north–northeast, not recommended unless conditions are good. The impressive Torre de Rovira, built in 1763 to protect Ibiza's west coast, stands on the headland of that name west of the *cala*. Shoals run out towards Isla Payaret some 200m northeast of the point.

⚓ **Cala Bassa** 38°58′·2N 1°14′·8E
A large and attractive *cala* with a sandy beach at its head, surrounded by pine woods and low cliffs and open to north and northeast. Anchor in 5–8m over sand. There is a landing stage used by tourist boats, several beach restaurants and cafés, and a nearby campsite. The beach is often crowded during the day, but is usually deserted by evening.

⚓ **Port del Torrent** 38°58'·2N 1°15'·9E

A large angled *cala* with low rocky sides and a sandy beach at its head, open northwest–north–northeast. Anchor in 4–6m over sand, rock and weed. Small yachts may be able to tuck into the sheltered eastern arm, though this is now partly occupied by permanent moorings – a careful watch should be kept for swimmers and water-skiers, as well as on the depth. Larger vessels should anchor further northwest (see plan) where the holding is also somewhat better, but be ready to depart at the threat of onshore winds.

The inevitable beach bars and restaurants abound, with a supermarket some 100m to the south. Hotels and apartment blocks fringe the bay to the east and south.

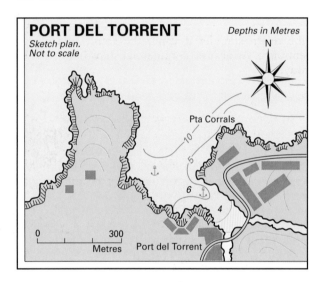

PORT DEL TORRENT
Sketch plan.
Not to scale
Depths in Metres
Pta Corrals
Port del Torrent

Punta Chinchó (Chichó) 38°58'·5N 1°17'·1E

A very low, rocky-cliffed promontory, difficult to identify except for the lighthouse on the point (Fl.G.3·5s9m5M, green column on white base displaying a green triangle). A road and buildings lie behind.

Puerto de San Antonio Abad (Sant Antoni de Portmany)

38°58'·5N 01°17'·9E

Charts

	Approach	Harbour
Admiralty	1702, 2834	2834
Spanish	7A, 478	4781
French	7114	7114

Lights

Approach

0274 **Isla Conejera** 38°59'·7N 1°12'·9E
Fl(4)20s85m18M
White tower and building 18m

0273 **Punta Chinchó** 38°58'·5N 1°17'·1E
Fl.G.3·5s9m5M Green column on white base displaying green ▲ 8m 075°-vis-275°

Entrance

0273·3 **North breakwater** 38°58'·6N 1°17'·9E
Fl.R.3s11m5M
Red column on white base displaying red ■ 9m
Club Náutico pontoons 38°58'·8N 1°18'·2E
F.R.3·5m1M Black metal posts at end of each of the five *Club Náutico* pontoons

Buoys

An unlit buoy marks the end of an outfall in the northern part of the Bahía de San Antonio.

Port Communications

VHF – Yacht harbour (*San Antonio Náutico*) Ch 9. (0830– 1330 & 1600–2100).
☎/*Fax* – Port Authority ☎ 340503; Club Náutico San Antonio ☎ 340645; *Fax* 345607.

General

A yachting and fishing harbour in a deep bay partially protected by a breakwater, San Antonio is easy to enter in almost any conditions. The original fishing village is now submerged in massive tourist development and the bay lined with high-rise apartment buildings and hotels, mainly for English tourists. However in spite of its reputation as a noisy and crowded holiday resort, San Antonio still makes a good base for exploring the western and northern coasts. Although the town itself is without charm, the bay is still surprisingly attractive and largely surrounded by rolling, tree-covered hills. The small *Club Náutico* is friendly and welcoming, with a very pleasant bar and terrace overlooking the harbour. Several of the staff speak English.

The harbour has most probably been in use since prehistoric times, and certainly since the Phoenician and Carthaginian eras. In Roman times it was called *Portús Magnus*, changed by the Ibizencos to *Portmany* (meaning 'big bay'). It is claimed that Isla Conejera ('rabbit's burrow') was the birthplace of the Carthaginian warrior Hannibal – not impossible, since the island was in the hands of the Carthaginians at the time. Certainly many of the stone slingers in his army came from the nearby Islas Bledas.

There are cave paintings of disputed date at the cave 'des Vi' near Cabo Nonó, and a subterranean chapel dedicated to Santa Inés (Santa Agnès in Ibicenco) close north of the town. The church of San Antonio de Portmany, parts of which date back to 1305, is also worth a visit.

On 17 January a *fiesta* is held in honour of San Antonio (patron saint), while on 16 July there is the *fiesta* of Our Lady of Mont Carmel with a regatta on the following Sunday. 24 August sees the *fiesta* of San Bartolomé.

Approach

From northeast and north Cabo Eubarca, which has a cone-shaped top, and Cabo Nonó, which is covered with pine woods, are high, steep headlands and easy to identify. The Islas Margaritas can be left on either side. Enter the bay of San Antonio on a southerly course, steering initally towards a group of distant mountains. When well inside the bay the head of the breakwater with its red column and white base will open up.

From west and south Isla Conejera with its conspicuous lighthouse is easily seen. In bad weather it is advisable to pass outside this island with an offing of at least 200m before setting a southeasterly course towards the harbour. In light conditions the passage between Isla Conejera and Isla Bosque can be used – see page 35. If approaching from the Iberian mainland note that the Islas Bledas lie some 2½ miles west of Isla Conejera, only the largest having a lighthouse.

Anchorage in the approach

There are several possible *cala* anchorages on the south side of the Bahía de San Antonio detailed in the preceding pages.

Entrance

Underwater obstructions extend a short distance beyond the end of the breakwater – allow an offing of at least 50m. Otherwise the entrance is wide and without hazards, though shoals run out a short way beyond Punta Chinchó and its equally inconspicuous eastern neighbour – keep an eye on the depth sounder if using the south side of the entrance. As always, commercial ships have right of way.

Berthing

The Club Náutico San Antonio currently has 350 berths on its five pontoons, though only 88 of these can take boats exceeding 10m LOA and vacant berths are seldom available in the high season.

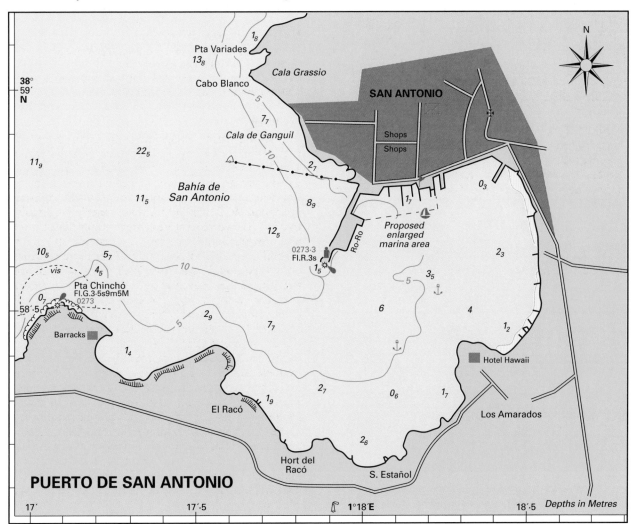

However plans have been approved to replace the current yacht harbour with a larger structure able to accommodate at least 500 yachts – see plan. Work is due to start in October 1997, with the aim of having the new pontoons completed for the 1998 season.

A small dinghy quay administered by the Port Authority exists in the extreme northeast of the bay. It is forbidden for yachts to berth alongside the breakwater.

Charges *(see page 6)*

High season daily rate – Band C; low season daily rate – Band B dropping to Band D after three days. Water and electricity included.

Anchorage

Anchor at least 400m east of the breakwater in 5m or less over mud and weed. Holding is poor in patches, with the best holding in the north of the bay. Ro-Ro ferries which berth near the root of the breakwater and on the widened area must not be impeded, and a channel must also be left for the fishing boats and tourist ferries which berth east of the Club Náutico pontoons. As much of the bay is occupied by moorings this leaves limited space for anchoring in the northern part of the bay, but even in the height of summer there is usually room to be found further south. As of 1996 no charge was made for anchoring.

Moorings

There are a few private moorings, some of which may be free. However one can never be sure of intended maximum tonnage, state of repair, or whether the owner will return at 0400! Certainly a yacht on a borrowed mooring should never be left unattended.

Facilities

Boatyards Small yard at the *Club Náutico* able to handle routine maintenance, painting etc. Other craftsmen and engineers are also available – enquire in the club.

Cranes 6·5 tonne mobile crane at the *Club Náutico*.

Engineers Enquire at the *Club Náutico*.

Chandlery On the road opposite the *Club Náutico*.

Charts The only agent for Spanish charts on the island is Valnautica SL, Ibinave, Travesia del Mar (☎/*Fax* 345251).

Water Taps on the pontoons and at the *Club Náutico*, available 1000–1300 on payment of a fee. It is very brackish and unsuitable for drinking.

Showers At the *Club Náutico*. The crews of yachts anchored off are charged a small fee.

Electricity On the pontoons.

Fuel Diesel and petrol from pumps on the breakwater. Diesel at the *Club Náutico*.

Ice From the *Club Náutico* bar.

Yacht club As already mentioned, the Club Náutico San Antonio welcomes visiting yachtsmen, including those anchored off. It has a pleasant bar/restaurant serving light meals, and an excellent view from its terrace. Several of the staff speak English.

Banks In the town, most with credit card facilities.

Shops/provisioning Wide range of shops and supermarkets in the town, several on the road leading from opposite the *Club Náutico*. Also two small supermarkets behind the prominent Hotel Hawaii on the southeast shore of the bay.

Produce market On the Carrer Vara del Rey.

Hotels/restaurants/cafés, etc. An enormous range to suit all purses.

Laundrette Several in the town, including one near the *Club Náutico*.

Hospital/medical services In the town.

The entire Bahia de San Antonio seen from the northwest, with Cala Grassio in the left foreground and Punta Chinchó on the right.

Puerto de San Antonio from the southwest, with a ferry of the Flebasa Line about to berth on the breakwater. As can be seen, the mooring area and anchorage is relatively is crowded but a fairway has been left for the tourist ferries which berth beyond the *Club Náutico* pontoons.

Communications

Car hire/taxis In the town, or arrange through the *Club Náutico*.

Buses Regular bus service to Ibiza and elsewhere.

Ferries Ferry service to the Spanish mainland.

⌁ **Cala Grassio (Gració)** 38°59'·6N 1°17'·3E

An angled *cala* surrounded by low cliffs, splitting into two branches near its head, both with sandy beaches. Open to southwest and west, plus northwest unless tucked very well in. Anchor in 4–6m over sand. The immediate surroundings are wooded, with houses and apartment blocks set further back. Both beaches are popular with tourist boats and the usual bars and restaurant will be found ashore.

⌁ **Cala Salada** 39°00'·6N 1°17'·8E

A narrow, largely unspoilt *cala* with steep rocky sides and woods above, open west and southwest (though a southerly swell may enter). The small island of S'Illeta lies close inshore to the north. Anchor in 4–8m over sand and thin weed, taking care to avoid an unmarked rock carrying some 2·8m in the north of the *cala*. Fishermen's huts line the south side where there is a small quay.

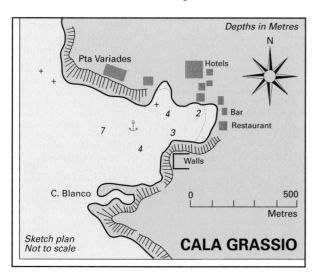

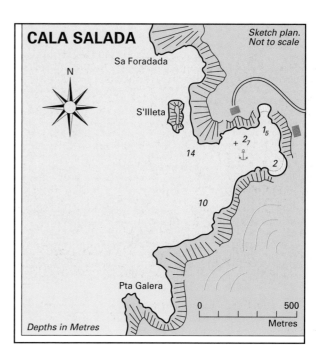

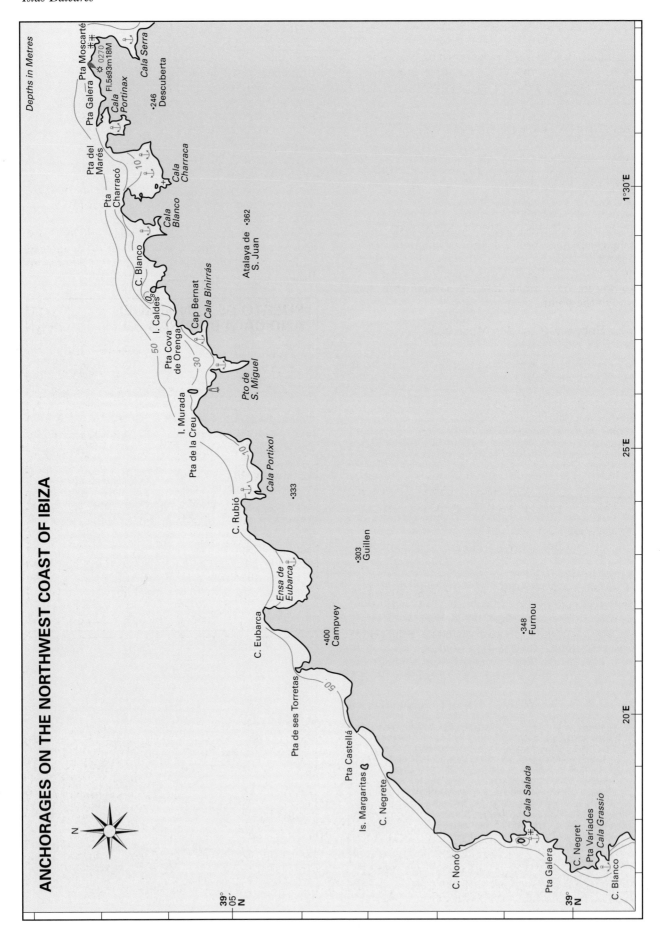

ANCHORAGES ON THE NORTHWEST COAST OF IBIZA

Depths in Metres

N

39°
05′
N

39°
N

1°30 E

25 E

20 E

Pta Moscarté
Pta Galera
Fl.5s93m18M
·0270
Cala Serra
Cala Portinax
Pta del Marés
·246 Descuberta

Pta Charracó
10
Cala Charraca

Pta Charracó
Cala Blanco

C. Blanco
·362 Atalaya de S. Juan

I. Caldes
Pta Cova de Orenga
50
30
Cap Bernat
Cala Binirrás

I. Murada
Pta de la Creu
Pto de S. Miguel

10
Cala Portixol
·333

C. Rubió

C. Eubarca
Ensa de Eubarca
·303 Guillen

·400 Campvey
·348 Furnou

Pta de ses Torretas
50

Pta Castellá
Is. Margaritas
C. Negrete

C. Nonó

Pta Galera
C. Negret
Pta Variades
Cala Grassio
Cala Salada

C. Blanco

The beaches are popular with day tourists from San Antonio, and there are the usual beach bars and restaurant. Part of the beach, marked by a line of white buoys, is marked off of swimmers – presumably more a defence against the many water-skiers than against yachts.

Islas Margaritas (Ses Margalides)
39°03'N 1°19'E
A horseshoe-shaped group of rocks with a low arch through their centre. They can be left on either side when coastal sailing, an offing of 350m ensuring good water.

Punta de ses Torretas 39°04'·1N 1°20'·8E
A relatively low promontory running out as an apparent afterthought from the surrounding 150–200m cliffs. From some directions it appears as two towers or a small fort. A natural arch runs through the point.

Cabo Eubarca (Cap des Mossons)
39°04'·6N 1°21'·8E
A high, steep-cliffed promontory topped by a regular cone (262m).

⚓ Ensenada de Eubarca (d'Albarca)
39°04'·2N 1°22'·5E
A large, high-cliffed bay with shallowish rocky sides, sheltered by Cabo Eubarca to the west and Cabo Rubió to the east and open northwest–north–northeast. The holding is mostly rock with sand patches – use with care. The *cala* itself is deserted, but there is village up the track leading inland.

Cabo Rubió 39°04'·8N 1°23'·7E
A high, steep-cliffed promontory.

⚓ Cala Portixol 39°04'·6N 1°24'E
A very small horseshoe *cala* just east of Cabo Rubió, open to north and northeast but otherwise surrounded by high cliffs. Anchor in 4–5m over sand and rock (there is a sand patch near the centre of the *cala*) off the sand and stone beach.

⚓ Puerto de San Miguel 39°05'·2N 1°26'·6E
Not a true port but a deeply indented *cala*, well protected by Isla Bosch (a rocky peninsula stretching nearly halfway across the inner entrance on the western side) and surrounded by cliffs. If approaching from the west and planning to pass inside Isla Murada, watch out for an isolated rock 1·5–2m high which lies in the passage between the island and the shore towards Punta de la Creu.

Anchor in 4–8m over sand behind the peninsula or off the larger of the two beaches, open only to north and northeast. There are some permanent moorings and a buoyed-off area reserved for the water-ski school.

The head of the *cala* is besieged by huge apartment blocks and hotels, and with a main road to Ibiza the beach is inevitably crowded in season. Beach bars and restaurants flourish.

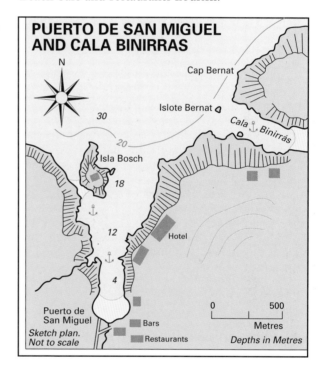

The twin *calas* of Puerto de San Miguel (right) and Cala Binirrás (left) looking southeast. Queen Victoria, alias Islote Bernat, graces the entrance to Cala Binirrás.

Puerto de San Miguel looking almost due south, fronted by Isla Bosch and its low linking isthmus. This photograph was taken in May when the beach could still be seen for bodies.

⚓ Cala Binirrás (Benirrás) 39°05'·4N 1°27'E

A small *cala* between steep cliffs, less than 1000m east of Puerto de San Miguel. The rocky, pinnacled Islote Bernat (27m) lies in the middle of the entrance, from some angles looking uncannily like the elderly Queen Victoria on her throne! It is without outliers and can safely be passed on either hand.

Anchor in 5–8m over sand near the head of the *cala*, avoiding some rocky shallows in the southeast corner, and open west through northwest to north. Although as yet undeveloped other than the obligatory bars and restaurants, the beach is often crowded.

Punta Cova de Orenga 39°05'·8N 1°27'·2E

A high, cliffed point with a cave at its foot.

Islas Caldes (d'En Calders) 39°06'·2N 1°27'·8E

A group of rocky islands close off Punta Caldes, itself between Punta Cova de Orenga and Cabo Blanco, with offliers up to 350m offshore.

Cabo Blanco 39°06'·3N 1°28'·6E

A spit is reported to stretch northeast from this headland, extending some distance offshore.

⚓ Cala Blanco 39°06'·2N 1°29'E

A small, attractive *cala* east of Cabo Blanco, open northwest through north to northeast and with two distinct 'corners'. Anchor in either corner over sand – some 5–6m will be found to the southwest with 4–5m to the southeast. Apart from two private houses the *cala* is deserted, and much of the surrounding land is private.

Punta Charracó (Xarraca) 39°06'·6N 1°29'·4E

A high (73m) cliff-edged headland, covered by trees.

⚓ Cala Charraca (Xarraca) 39°06'·2N 1°30'E

A large, square bay surrounded by forested cliffs and offering several possible anchorages open northwest– north–northeast. There are two small rock-fringed islands near the west side of the *cala* plus a rock awash in the centre of the southwestern cove – approach slowly with a lookout on the bow. The southeastern corner is without dangers. Anchor in 5–6m over stones and sand to suit wind direction.

A road runs down to the southwest corner where there are fishermen's huts, a few houses and a restaurant.

Punta del Marés 39°06'·9N 1°30'·7E

A 54m headland crowned by a 9m watchtower. The 'cliffs' are set well back from the present shoreline.

⚓ Cala Portinatx 39°06'·9N 1°30'·9E

An attractive multiple *cala* against a backdrop of wooded mountains, Cala Portinatx has seen considerable tourist development over recent years. There are three arms, each with a sandy beach crowded with visitors, pedalos, bars, restaurants and loud discos at night.

Anchor in 3–15m over sand and weed as space permits – but note that holding is patchy and very poor in places – open to northwest and north. There are some private moorings, mostly in the eastern arm, and each beach has an area roped off for swimmers.

Amongst the surrounding hotels and apartment blocks will be found many restaurants, supermarkets and other shops, plus a dive centre on the central beach where scuba bottles can be refilled.

The Torre de Portanix (or Torre de sa Plana) stands on Punta del Marés to the west of the *cala*. Like most of Ibiza's defensive towers it was built in the second half of the 18th century, but was never fitted with artillery and was later used as a dwelling.

Cala Portinatx seen from the northeast, with Cala Charraca in the background.

The eastern arm of Cala Portinatx, looking almost directly along Punta Galera. Punta Moscarté, topped by its distinctive spiral lighthouse, juts out to the left.

The southwestern arm of Cala Portinatx seen from over Punta Marés. In the high season both beach and bay become very crowded.

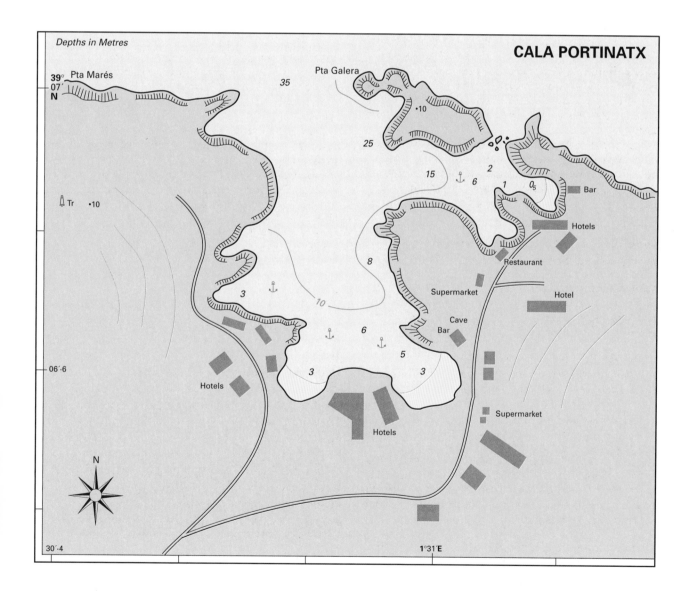

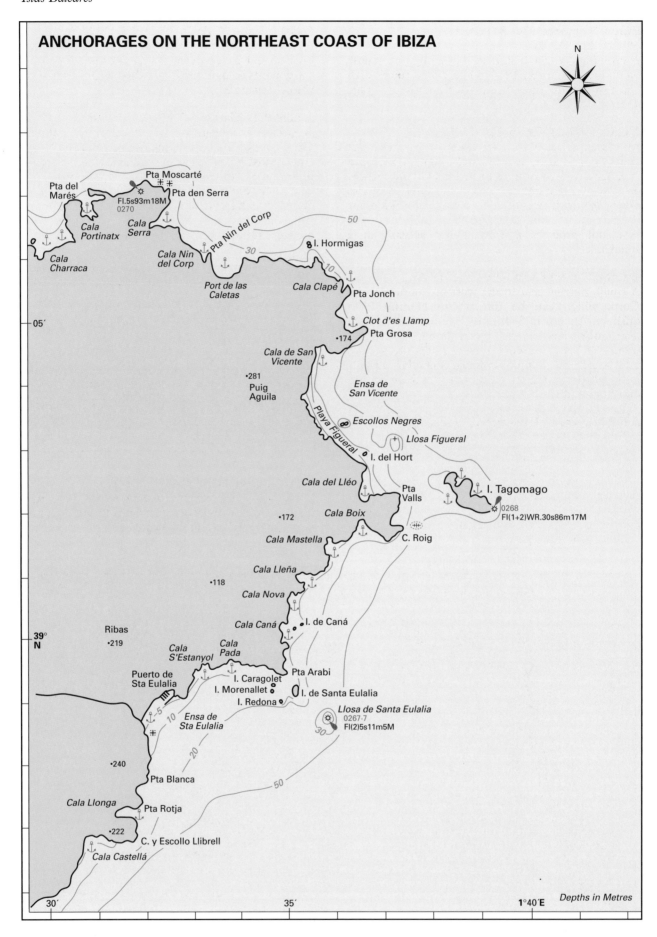

ANCHORAGES ON THE NORTHEAST COAST OF IBIZA

N

Pta del
Marés

Pta Moscarté

Fl.5s93m18M
0270

Pta den Serra

*Cala
Portinatx*

*Cala
Serra*

Pta Nin del Corp

50

*Cala Nin
del Corp*

30

*Cala
Charraca*

8 I. Hormigas

10

*Port de las
Caletas*

Cala Clapé

Pta Jonch

Clot d'es Llamp

•174   Pta Grosa

*Cala de San
Vicente*

*Ensa de
San Vicente*

•281
Puig
Aguila

Escollos Negres

Llosa Figueral

I. del Hort

Cala del Lléo

Pta
Valls

I. Tagomago

0268
Fl(1+2)WR.30s86m17M

•172   *Cala Boix*

Cala Mastella

C. Roig

Cala Lleña

Cala Nova

•118

Cala Caná

I. de Caná

Ribas   *Cala
•219   S'Estanyol*

*Cala
Pada*

Pta Arabi

Puerto de
Sta Eulalia

I. Caragolet

I. Morenallet

I. de Santa Eulalia

I. Redona

Llosa de Santa Eulalia

0267·7
Fl(2)5s11m5M

*Ensa de
Sta Eulalia*

30

20

•240

Pta Blanca

50

Cala Llonga

Pta Rotja

•222

C. y Escollo Llibrell

Cala Castellá

5

10

39°
N

30′   35′   1°40′E

05′

Depths in Metres

Punta Moscarté (des Moscarter)
39°07'·2N 1°32'·1E
A prominent rocky headland topped by a dramatic lighthouse (Fl.5s93m18M, white round tower with black diagonal stripes 52m). (See photograph page 43).

⚓ **Cala Serra** 39°06'·6N 1°32'·5E
An attractive rocky *cala* open to northeast and east and surrounded by wooded hills. Anchor in 4–5m over sand and rock close to the small stony beach, possibly taking a line to the rocks to limit swinging. Deserted until recently, a tourist development appears to be taking shape to the northwest of the *cala*, but progress is slow if not actually at a standstill.

⚓ **Cala Nin del Corp** 39°06'N 1°33'·4E
A small, narrow *cala* to the west of Punta Nin del Corp, which can be difficult to identify from offshore. Anchor in 3–4m near the head of the *cala* over rock, stones and weed open northwest–north–northeast. A second anchor or a line ashore may be needed to limit swinging. Some fishermen's huts will be found on the beach but there are no other buildings.

⚓ **Port de las Caletas (Racó de sa Talaia)**
39°05'·9N 1°33'·8E
Another misnomer, being a wide but undeveloped *cala* lying beneath high rocky cliffs and open northwest–north–northeast. Houses line the zig-zag road up from the small beach. Anchor in the western part of the *cala* close inshore in 10m over rock, stone and sand – a breaking shoal lies between this anchorage and the beach.

⚓ **Cala Clapé (Cala Jone)** 39°05'·5N 1°36'·2E
A small *cala* northwest of Punta Jonch (Punta Jone), open to northwest–north–northeast and fringed by rocks on its southern side. Anchor in the middle of the *cala* over sand.

⚓ **Clot d'es Llamp** 39°04'·9N 1°36'·4E
A coastal anchorage on the north side of Punta Grosa, useful for the crossing to and from Mallorca. Anchor inshore in 4–6m over sand and stone, open to northwest through north to east but protected from other directions by high cliffs containing some fantastic rock formations including a large stalactite cave. Landing can be difficult, but once ashore there are steps up to hotels and supermarket.

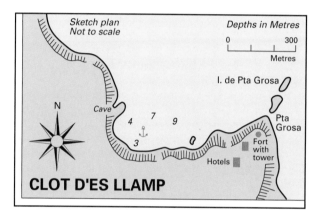

Punta Grosa 39°04'·9N 1°36'·7E
A high (174m), rocky, cliffed point with two off-lying islands. A small square fort with a distinctive single tower stands on the headland.

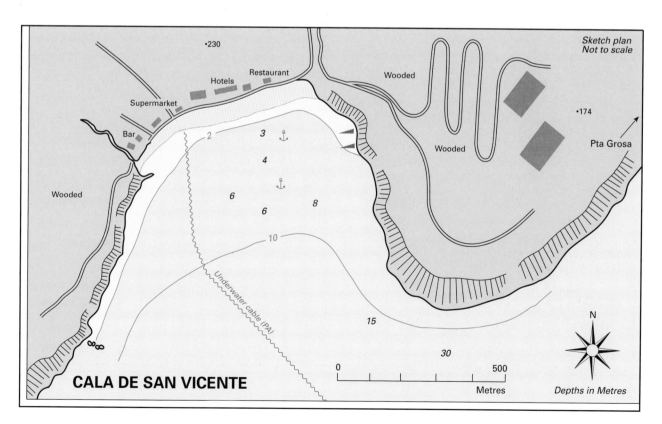

The hotel-lined beach at Cala de San Vicente, seen from east of south.

⚓ Cala de San Vicente (Sant Vicenc)
39°04'·5N 1°35'·5E

A well protected anchorage at the north end of a long bay, the Ensenada de San Vicente, open to the southeast and with some fetch from the south. Anchor close inshore in 3–6m over sand and weed, being careful to avoid an underwater cable from Palma which terminates near the road – see plan. The beach is lined by hotels and tourist apartments against a backdrop of high wooded hills. The beach is very crowded in season and the usual bars and restaurants will be found ashore.

The cave temple of Es Cuyeram, dating back to the 5th century BC and later dedicated to the Carthaginian goddess Tanit, lies in the hills to the north. Excavated in 1907, most of the artifacts have now been moved to the Archaeological Museum of Ibiza.

Playa Figueral Centred on 39°03'·4N 1°36'E

A long stony beach occupying the southern part of the Ensenada de San Vicente and with various off-lying dangers. Taken from north to south these are:

- The Escollos Negres, three small, low, black, rocky islands lying up to 0·4 mile offshore.
- Llosa Figueral (39°03'·1N 1°37'·3E), an awash black rock 0·6 mile off the beach, unmarked since the light was destroyed in 1993 but usually indicated by breaking water. Dangerous rocky shallows extend 500m to north and south. Until its destruction the light flashed Q.R.11m4M.
- Isla del Hort, 20m in height, lying 200m off the coast inshore of Llosa Figueral.

Small inshore rocky islets line much of the *playa*, in addition to the above.

⚓ Cala del Lléo (Cala San Carlos)
39°02'·4N 1°36'·8E

An open bay anchorage under high cliffs, south of Playa Figueral and northwest of Punta Valls. There are dangerous rocks on either side of the bay – approach the centre of the sandy beach on a bearing of 220° to anchor in 4–6m over sand and rock. A

few fishermen's huts will be found at the head of the *cala* with a café a short walk inland.

Punta Valls 39°02'·3N 1°37'·3E

A 67m cliffed promontory with a 9m stone tower.

Isla Tagomago 39°02'·2N 1°37'·7E

A very conspicuous island nearly 1 mile long which resembles a huge dolphin heading out to sea. The lighthouse at its southeastern tip (Fl(1+2)WR.30s 86m17M, grey octagonal stone tower on building 23m) shows red when bearing between 217° and 223·5° (over Bajo de Santa Eulalia) and is obscured from the west by a 114m hill. A large white house occupies the centre of the island.

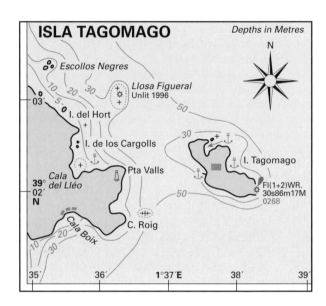

Passage between Isla Tagomago and Ibiza

A clear passage 0·8 mile wide and around 40m deep separates Isla Tagomago from Ibiza. However be aware of the unmarked wreck off Cabo Roig – see below.

⚓ Isla Tagomago, northeast anchorages
39°02'·6N 1°38'·6E and 39°02'·4N 1°38'·9E

Two small *calas* open to north–northeast–east, the northwestern tucked behind breaking rocks. Approach with care – the water is deep until very close in – to anchor close inshore in 8–10m over rock with a few sand patches.

⚓ Isla Tagomago, southwest anchorage
39°02'·2N 1°38'·4E

A small *cala* open southwest–west–northwest and susceptible to swell from north and south. Anchor close inshore in 5m over sand – a line to a rock may be required – or further off in 8–10m over weed. There are two landing places used by daily tourist boats in season, and a beach bar. A track leads up to the lighthouse.

Cabo Roig 39°01'·7N 1°37'·2E
A grey and reddish rocky, cliffed headland (138m). A dangerous wreck, awash but unmarked, lies some 350m northeast of the point. It should be given a wide berth.

⚓ **Cala Boix** 39°01'·7N 1°36'·6E
A good anchorage west of Cabo Roig, surrounded by high rocky cliffs and open southeast–south–southwest. Anchor off the sandy beach in 3–8m over sand. There is a small jetty, a beach bar and a few houses ashore, plus a track to the main road.

⚓ **Cala Mastella** 39°01'·4N 1°36'E
A pleasant little *cala* with a beach at its head, surrounded by trees and and some houses. Anchor in the centre of the *cala* in 2–4m over sand and weed with occasional rock patches. There is a beach bar and fish restaurant ashore, and the village of Ca'n Jordi about ½ mile away.

Cala Mastella (right), seen from the southeast.

⚓ **Cala Lleña (Llenya)** 39°00'·9N 1°35'·4E
A wide *cala* with an attractive beach (often crowded and featuring the usual beach bars etc.) and an outcrop of square, white hotels and apartment buildings – the Club Cala Lleña – amongst the pine trees to the south. Anchor off the beach in 5m over sand, open to east through southeast to south.

⚓ **Cala Nova** 39°00'·6N 1°35'·1E
Another wide *cala* with a long beach and pine trees, but somewhat less built up than Cala Lleña. Even so there are many beach bars etc. to cater for the tourists staying in nearby Es Caná. Anchor in 4–6m over sand, open east–southeast–south. If approaching from the south be sure to avoid the Islas des Caná, described below.

Islas des Caná 39°00'·2N 1°35'·2E
The Islas des Caná comprise Isla de Caná (2·3m) and the smaller Sa Galera, plus some off-lying rocks. Shoals run out from the headland north of Cala

Caná about halfway to the islands, and the inside passage should not be attempted without local knowledge.

⚓ **Cala Caná (Canar)** 39°00'·2N 1°35'E
A popular *cala* open east–southeast–south, with a (crowded) sandy beach and low rocky sides, surrounded by hotels and apartment blocks. There is a tiny harbour for speedboats and small fishing craft on the southern shore. Anchor off the centre of the beach in 4–6m over sand – fringing rocks covered to a depth of 2m or so extend from either side. The Islas des Caná lie some 600m offshore due east of the *cala*, but are easily seen on approach.

More hotel development takes place on the promontory just north of Cala Caná, viewed from a little east of south. Sa Galera, the smaller of the two Islas des Caná, is on the extreme right.

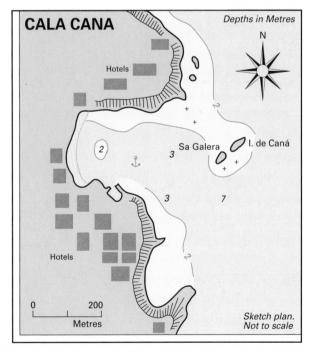

Punta Arabi 38°59'·4N 1°35'E
A low (22m) whitish rocky point surmounted by buildings and dark trees.

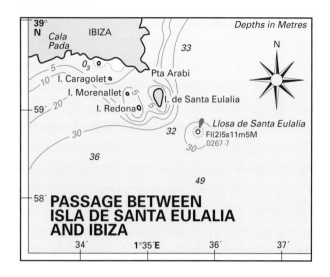

PASSAGE BETWEEN ISLA DE SANTA EULALIA AND IBIZA

Isla de Santa Eulalia 38°59'·1N 1°35'·2E

A peardrop shaped island, 37m in height and measuring some 350m along its north/south axis.

Passages between Isla de Santa Eulalia and Ibiza

The passage itself should present no problems, being at least 400m wide and with depths of more than 5m throughout. However a possible hazard is posed by four small rocky islands which straddle the western approach/exit (see plan). Taken from southeast to northwest these comprise:

- Isla Redona (22m), 400m southwest of Isla de Santa Eulalia and easily seen. Close in it is foul to east and south. It can be left on either side.
- Isla Morenallet, a low, black, rocky islet usually surrounded by breaking seas, some 650m west of Isla de Santa Eulalia and 550m northwest of Isla Redona. Easily seen in daylight but difficult to spot at night. Again it can be left on either side.
- Isla Caragolet, similar in appearance to Isla Morenallet but 450m to the northwest and about that distance offshore. On no account attempt to pass inside Isla Caragolet, due to shoals.
- A small unnamed island close inshore, which is surrounded by rocky shallows and should not be approached.

Llosa de Santa Eulalia 38°58'·8N 1°35'·7E

This rocky patch 1·7m deep lies 1000m southeast of Isla Santa Eulalia and is often marked by broken water. An isolated danger mark (Fl(2)5s11m5M, platform on column with ⸸ topmark) lies 300m from the shoal bearing 290°.

Other than a few nearby rocks the Llosa de Santa Eulalia is surrounded by clear water, and a 32m deep passage separates it from Isla Santa Eulalia. It is covered by the red sector of the Isla Tagomago light.

⚓ Cala Pada 38°59'·5N 1°33'·8E

A very small anchorage in a tiny *cala*, surrounded by trees and open southeast–south–southwest. The eastern part of the bay is reserved for boardsailors. Anchor in 3m over sand off the small beach,

avoiding the many permanent moorings. A beach restaurant lies directly behind the short wooden jetty.

⚓ Cala S'Estanyol 38°59'·5N 1°33'·3E

A small, wooded anchorage near the mouth of a river, off a sand and stone beach. Anchor in 3m over sand, stones and weed, open to east–southeast–south. Two large white hotel or apartments buildings mark the southern end of the beach.

Puerto de Santa Eulalia del Río (Santa Eulària des Riu)
38°59'N 01°32'·4E

Charts *Approach*
Admiralty *2834*
Spanish *7A,479*
French *7114*

Lights

Approach

0267·7 **Llosa de Santa Eulalia** 38°58'·8N 1°35'·7E
  Fl(2)5s11m5M Black tower, red band, ⸸ topmark
  1·7m shoal 300m away, bearing 110°

Entrance

0267·8 **Southeast breakwater** 38°59'N 1°32'·4E
  Fl(2)G.5s11m5M
  Green pyramidal column tower 6m

0267·85 **Northwest mole** 38°59'N 1°32'·4E
  Q.R.4m2M Red pyramidal column tower 3m

Port Communications

Puerto Deportivo de Santa Eulalia VHF Ch 9,
☎ 336161, 339754, *Fax* 332810.

General

Santa Eulalia marina is a large (755 berth) marina completed in 1991, with an easy approach and entrance other than in strong winds from southeast and south. The staff are helpful and several speak good English. Unfortunately the bay has been overwhelmed by hotels and other building in recent years, but still offers good if crowded sand and rock beaches. Most requirements can be met in the nearby town of Santa Eulalia del Río.

Previously a fishing village and market centre based on the fortified 16th century church at Puig de Missa, the hill above the river mouth, Santa Eulalia later became a centre for artists but is now a major tourist resort. There are many interesting buildings in the old town, plus the remains of a Roman aquaduct across the Río Santa Eulalia. The Ethnological Museum of the Pitiusan Islands is situated in the town.

Santa Eulalia's day is celebrated on 12 February, there is a Holy Week procession on the afternoon of Good Friday afternoon and a Festival of Flowers on the first Sunday in May. The *Fiesta de Jesus* is held on 8 September.

Approach

From southwest If coming from Puerto de Ibiza or Formentera be sure to identify the two small islands Lladó del Sur (6m), and Lladó del Norte (10m), which lie 0·8 and 1 mile respectively northeast of Cabo Martinet near the 30m contour. Once identified, they can safely be passed on either side. Cabo Llibrell can be rounded at 200m, after which the houses and high-rise buildings of Santa Eulalia will be seen. The harbour lies at the northern end of the town, near the middle of the wide bay.

From northeast If approaching the island from the direction of Mallorca and intending to make Puerto de Santa Eulalia the first port of call, Isla Tagomago (see page 46) may be passed on either side. However if taking the inshore passage give a wide berth to the wreck, awash but unmarked, 350m northeast of Cabo Roig. The headland itself is steep-to. Off Punta Arabi, either set a course between Isla de Santa Eulalia and Llosa de Santa Eulalia, or take one of the passages between Isla de Santa Eulalia and the mainland – for details see page 48. The harbour lies at the northern end of the town, near the middle of the wide bay.

Anchorage in the approach

There are two small *calas*, Cala Pada and Cala S'Estanyol, in the northern part of the bay (see page 48). However the anchorage most convenient for the town is that in the southwest corner of the bay, near the mouth of the Río Santa Eulalia – full details will be found directly following the harbour description. Anchoring outside the marina entrance is forbidden.

Entrance

The end of the west mole bears a round, white, three-storey tower which houses, amongst other things, the marina offices. Approach from anywhere in the bay keeping well clear of the end of the southeast breakwater, and berth alongside the fuel/reception pontoon, beneath the white tower, to be allocated a berth. There is a 3 knot speed limit within the marina. The marina entrance is kept dredged to at least 5m.

Berthing

The marina can accommodate yachts of up to 25m LOA and 4·5m draft. However like many in the Islas Baleares it is frequently full to capacity during the high season.

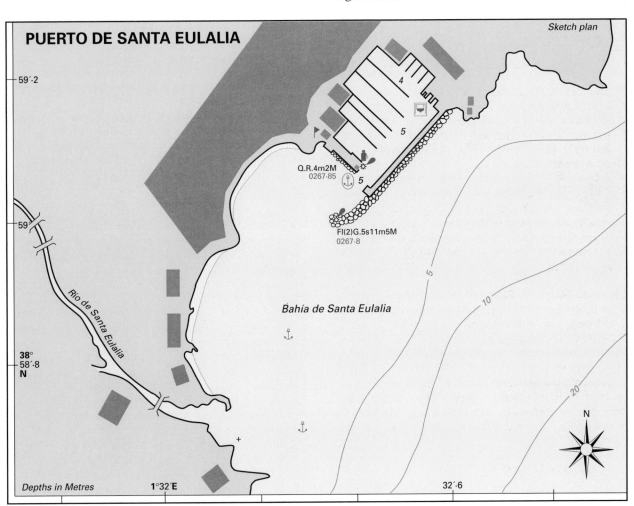

PUERTO DE SANTA EULALIA — *Sketch plan*

Q.R.4m2M 0267·85

Fl(2)G.5s11m5M 0267·8

Río de Santa Eulalia

Bahía de Santa Eulalia

Depths in Metres   1°32′E   32′·6

A motorboat swings wide of the southeast breakwater to enter the marina at Santa Eulalia del Río. The white tower containing the marina offices appears near the centre of the photograph.

Charges *(see page 6)*

High season daily rate – Band B; low season daily rate – Band C (15m), Band B (10m). Water and electricity extra.

Facilities

Boatyards Marina Río can handle all usual work including GRP repairs (☎ 330453 *Fax* 332111).

Travel-lift 60 tonnes.

Engineers At Marina Río. Boat Service Germany (☎/*Fax* 330121) is local service agent for Volvo Penta.

Chandlery In the marina complex.

Water Taps on pontoons and quays. Showers in the 'control tower' building. The water in Ibiza is of variable quality – if possible consult other yachtsmen before filling tanks.

Electricity 220v AC points on pontoons and quays.

Fuel Diesel and petrol pumps close beneath the tower on the west mole.

Ice From the marina office.

Banks In the marina complex and in town.

Shops/provisioning Shops and supermarkets in Santa Eulalia, also supermarket at the harbour.

Market All day market on Wednesdays in summer.

Hotels/restaurants/cafés, etc. Many, of all grades, including several restaurants and cafés in the marina itself.

Laundrette In the marina complex.

Hospital In the town.

Communications

Car hire/taxis Can be arranged via the marina office.

Buses Regular service to Ibiza town and elsewhere.

Ferries Tourist ferries berth outside the harbour, near the root of the west mole.

Air services Ibiza airport 15 miles.

⚓ Ensenada de Santa Eulalia (Santa Eulària)
38°58'·7N 1°32'·1E

Anchor in the southwest corner of this large bay, near the mouth of Río Santa Eulalia, in 3–5m over sand and mud and open to northeast through east to south. A sandy beach (with the inevitable bars etc.) runs northeast, with several large hotels a short distance inland. All the facilities of Puerto de Santa Eulalia are available within ½ mile. There are rocks awash near the shore south of the river mouth.

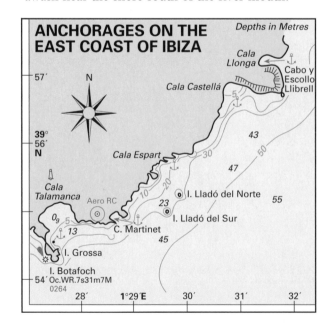

ANCHORAGES ON THE EAST COAST OF IBIZA

Depths in Metres

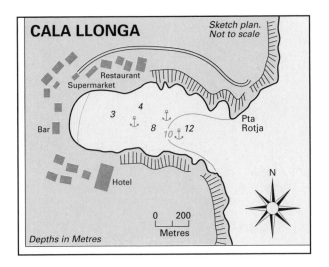

CALA LLONGA Sketch plan. Not to scale

Restaurant
Supermarket

Bar

Hotel

Pta Rotja

N

3 4
8 10 12

0   200
Metres

Depths in Metres

Punta Rotja (Roja) 38°57'·5N 1°32'E

A high (100m) red and whitish cliffed point with houses on the top.

⚓ Cala Llonga 38°57'·3N 1°31'·7E

A long, high-sided *cala* with an excellent but often very crowded beach at its head. The entrance can be difficult to spot until almost due east of the *cala*, when the huge blocks of flats and other buildings which line the wooded cliffs will be seen.

Anchor in 4–6m over sand about halfway up the *cala* and imagine how beautiful it was before the surrounding development took place. Although open only to the east and offering good protection, it can be gusty at times when westerly winds funnel down the valley. Swell from the easterly quadrant also works in, rebounding off the sides and setting yachts rolling.

Daily tourist boats visit from Santa Eulalia – another cause of rolling – and bars, restaurants and a supermarket will be found ashore. Buses run to Santa Eulalia. On 15 August Cala Llonga celebrates the anniversary of its patron saint.

Cabo y Escollo Llibrell 38°56'·8N 1°31'·8E

A high (220m) headland of whitish rock with a small outlying islet.

⚓ Cala Castellá (Sól d'En Serra)
38°56'·8N 1°30'·9E

A wide bay just south of Cabo y Escollo Llibrell, open to east through south to southwest. Anchor in 5m over sand off the long sandy beach.

⚓ Cala Espart 38°55'·8N 1°29'·7E

A small bay open east–southeast–south, with a sandy beach track to the road. Anchor in 5m over sand off the beach.

Lladó del Norte and Lladó del Sur
38°55'·1N 1°29'·8E

Two small islands, 10m and 6m high respectively, which lie 0·5 and 0·7 mile south of Cala Espart near the 30m contour. They may be left on either side.

⚓ Cala northeast of Cabo Martinet
38°54'·9N 1°28'·7E

A small unnamed *cala* on the northeast side of the cape, to be used with care. Anchor off the small beach in 5m over sand and rock, open to east–southeast–south. There is a road at the top of the cliff.

Cabo Martinet 38°54'·8N 1°28'·7E

A low headland of dark rock with trees and houses on the top. An aero radiobeacon, inconspicuous, lies 700m to the west-northwest.

⚓ Cala Talamanca 38°54'·9N 1°27'·6E

A large open *cala* with a long sandy beach at its head, open east–southeast–south and to swell from the southwest. The head of the *cala* is shallow and has some reefs – anchor with care off Punta Sa Tabernera in 3–6m over sand and weed, though with careful sounding a spot can be found further north in the middle of the *cala*. (See plan page 23).

Land in the northwest corner of the bay – from which it is about 20 minutes' walk into Ibiza or a mere 350m to the facilities of Marina Botafoch – or on the isthmus leading to Isla Grossa.

Looking eastwards up the length of Cala Llonga. This photograph was taken on a weekday in mid May, and already the beach is getting crowded.

Isla de Formentera

General description

The comparatively undeveloped islands of Formentera and Espalmador lie 2 miles south of Punta Portas on the south coast of Isla de Ibiza.

Espalmador, by far the smaller of the two and virtually deserted, is 1½ miles long and ¾ mile wide and rises to a height of 24m on its west side where there is a conspicuous tower (9·6m). It is joined to Formentera by a long sandy spit broken by a shallow rocky passage, the Freu Poco, which separates the two islands.

Formentera is 10 miles long and 8 miles wide at its extremes, but being an elongated S-shape covers an area of only 37 square miles. It comprises two high features – La Mola (192m) an island-like area to the east, and the peninsula running out to Cabo Berberia (107m) to southwest. These two higher regions are attached by a long, low neck of land.

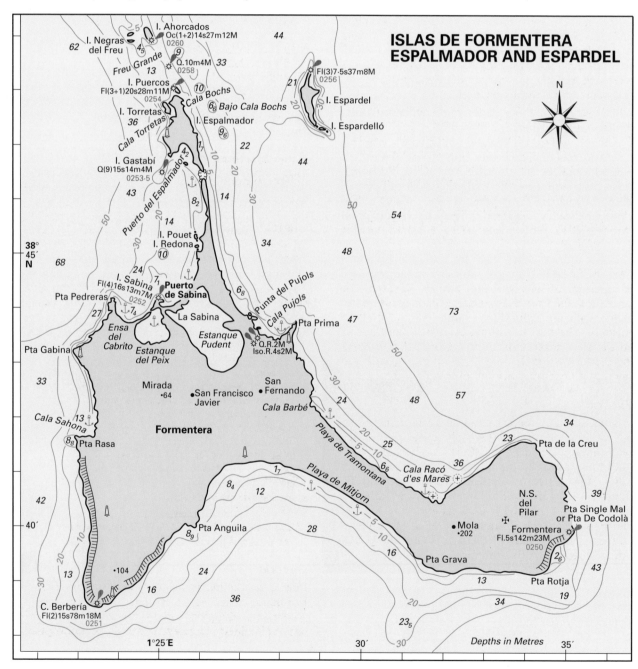

ISLAS DE FORMENTERA
ESPALMADOR AND ESPARDEL

There is a large, low-lying plain in the northern part of the island, the greater part of it occupied by lagoons and salt pans, and salt has long been a major export. Around the two high features the coast is of rocky cliffs, but in the north and northeast it is flat and sandy. Much of the island is cultivated and there are pine forests around La Mola.

There is a permanent population of around 5000 (according to some sources favoured with the longest life expectancy in Spain), most of whom are involved in some aspect of the tourist industry. Nudism has long been accepted on the beaches of Formentera, and many of the yacht crews, sailboarders and water-skiers are also unclothed.

History
The history of Formentera and Espalmador parallels that of Ibiza. The oldest evidence of human occupation is the 2000 BC megalithic tomb at Cana Costa on the eastern shore of the Estanque Pudent. In Roman times they formed part of the *Pityusae* (Pine Islands), Espalmador known as *Ophioussa* and Formentera as *Frumentum* or *Frumentaria* (a reference to the large amount of wheat it supplied), since corrupted into Formentera.

During the hundreds of years following the downfall of Rome the island became depopulated as it was frequently raided by barbarians, Moors, Saracens and even Scandinavians on their way home after taking part in one of the Crusades! It was not until 1697 that the island was repopulated, but even so was still subject to raids by pirates. The local inhabitants even turned to piracy themselves on occasion, and in 1806 captured the British 12-gun brig *Felicity* and sailed her into Ibiza.

Places of interest
San Francisco Javier is an attractive small town with a fortified church which once mounted guns on its tower – a tower from which fine views can now be enjoyed. The ravine running down to Cala Sahona on the west coast and the area around La Mola in the east are worth visiting if time permits, with the caves of d'en Xeroni also of interest.

Fiestas
In addition to the national holidays and *fiestas* listed in the introduction the following dates are celebrated in Formentera: 30 May – San Fernando (San Fernando); 24 June – San Juan (La Mola); 16 July – Our Lady of Carmen (La Sabina and Es Pujols); 25 July – St Jaime, patron saint of Formentera; 5 August – Our Lady of the Snows, patron saint of the Pitiusas Islands; 12 October – Our Lady of El Pilar (El Pilar); 3 December – San Francisco Javier (San Francisco).

Factual information

Magnetic variation
Formentera – 1°42'W (decreasing 6'E annually) (1997)

Approach and coastal passage charts
Admiralty *1701, 1702, 2834*
Spanish *7A, 478, 479, 479A*
French *5505, 7114*

Approach lights
0256 **Isla Espardel, north point**
38°48'·4N 1°28'·7E Fl(3)7·5s37m8M
White truncated conical tower 16m
0250 **Formentera (Punta Single Mal or Punta de Codolà)** 38°39'·8N 1°35'·1E Fl.5s142m23M
White tower on white building 22m
150°-vis-050°
0251 **Cabo Berbería** 38°38'·5N 1°23'·5E
Fl(2)15s78m18M White round tower 19m
234°-vis-171°
0252 **Isla Sabina** 38°44'·2N 1°25'E
Fl(4)16s13m7M
White truncated conical tower 11m
0253·5 **Isla Gastabi** 38°46'·5N 1°25'·1E
Q(9)15s14m4M
West cardinal tower, ⅄ topmark 8m

Puerto de Sabina (Port de sa Savina)
38°44'·1N 01°25'·2E

Charts *Approach*
Admiralty *2834*
Spanish *7A, 478, 479, 479A*
French *7114*

Lights
Approach
0252 **Isla Sabina** 38°44'·2N 1°25'E
Fl(4)16s13m7M
White truncated conical tower 11m
Entrance
0253 **North breakwater** 38°44'·2N 1°25'·2E
Fl.G.3s13m3M Green column on white base displaying green ▲ 6m
0253·2 **East breakwater** 38°44'·1N 1°25'·2E
Fl.R.3s5m4M Red tower 4m
Note Situated on the new east mole NOT on the old south (inner) mole

Port Communications
VHF – Marina de Formentera Ch 9.
☎/*Fax* – Port Authority ☎ 320127; Marina de Formentera ☎ 322346, 322693, *Fax* 322222.

General
Puerto de Sabina is the only harbour on Isla de Formentera and is in constant use by ferries, commercial shipping and fishing craft. Even so it has maintained its relaxed, attractive atmosphere

and is not yet overrun with tourists. The harbour is easy to approach and enter and well sheltered once inside, though the breakwaters offer little protection from the wind itself. The construction of the new Marina de Formentera, and particularly the new eastern basin known as Formentera Mar, has created considerably more space for yachts. Local facilities are reasonably good and there are more shops in the town of San Francisco Javier some two miles away.

Approach

From east If approaching from the direction of Mallorca either round Formentera on the south side, which is steep-to and offers no problems, or take the Freu Grande between Ibiza and Espalmador (see page 30), then proceed as below.

From west If approaching from the Spanish mainland follow the approach notes for the passages between Islas de Ibiza and Espalmador (see page 28), then proceed as below.

From northwest or north There are no hazards in the approach to Puerto de Sabina over an arc between Punta Pedereras (unlit) to the west and Isla Gastabi (lit) to the north. The white buildings behind the harbour show up well, as does the white tower of Isla Sabina lighthouse. Note that this lighthouse is situated near the end of a projecting rocky spur with shallow water to either side.

Anchorage in the approach

In southerly winds anchor in the bay between Isla Sabina and Punta Pedreras (Ensenada del Cabrito) in 3–5m over sand, rock and weed, open from northwest through north to northeast. In northerly winds Puerto del Espalmador would be much more sheltered – see page 57. Much of Cala Sabina to the east is occupied by the new marina.

Entrance

Entrance to the main harbour is generally straightforward, though it can become dangerous in strong northerly or northwesterly winds due to shoaling depths. Normally the greatest hazard is posed by the many ferries which enter and leave at speed. Both Marina de Formentera in the southwest corner of the basin and Formentera Mar to the east are reached through relatively narrow inner entrances.

Berthing

The two basins provide just over 200 yacht berths between them, for yachts up to 22m. There is no reception berth as such. Preferably contact the marina office on approach. Otherwise it may be necessary to occupy any convenient vacant berth until allocated a spot by marina staff.

Charges *(see page 6)*

Marina de Formentera and *Formentera Mar* High season daily rate – Band A; low season daily rate – Band D. Water and electricity extra.

Puerto de Sabina from the northeast, with the expanse of Estanque Peix behind. The photograph was taken in May 1996 when the new Formentera Mar (eastern) basin was barely finished and still almost empty. The white tower housing the marina offices can be seen near the root of the central quay.

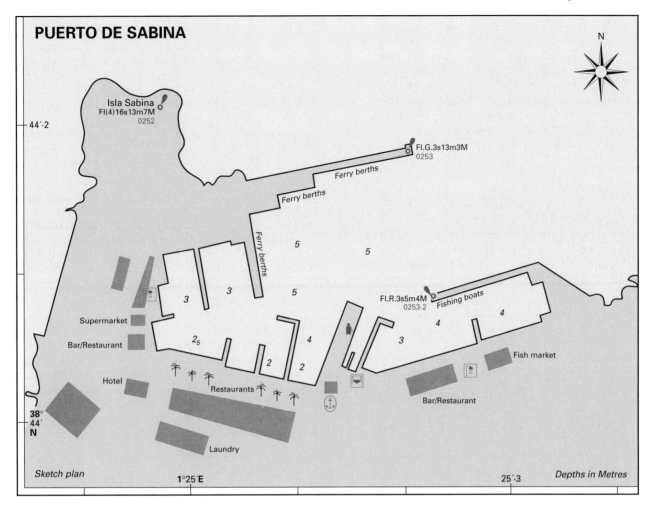

PUERTO DE SABINA

Isla Sabina
Fl(4)16s13m7M
0252

Fl.G.3s13m3M
0253

Ferry berths

Ferry berths

Ferry berths

5

5

5

3

3

5

Fl.R.3s5m4M
0253·2   Fishing boats

4

4

4

Supermarket

3

Bar/Restaurant

2₅

2

2

4

Hotel

Fish market

Restaurants

Bar/Restaurant

Laundry

Sketch plan

1°25´E

25´·3

Depths in Metres

44´·2

38°
44´
N

Facilities

Boatyards Small yard centred around the travel-lift and slipway. Enquire at the nearby marina office.

Travel-lift 35 tonne travel-lift near the marina office.

Slipway Near the marina office.

Engineers Enquire at the marina office.

Chandlery To the west of the main harbour.

Water Metered taps on pontoons and quays.

Showers Blocks serving both marina basins – a small charge is made.

Electricity 220v AC points on pontoons and quays, charged by the day.

Fuel Diesel pump on the central môle (see plan).

Ice From the supermarket.

Yacht club The Club Náutico Formentera, formerly located opposite the marina office tower, was no longer in evidence in 1996.

Banks None closer than San Francisco Javier, but several 'hole in the wall' credit card machines on the parade of shops and restaurants overlooking the harbour.

Shops/provisioning Two supermarkets near the harbour, plus more in San Francisco Javier a couple of miles inland.

Fish market Near the east basin.

Hotels/restaurants/cafés, etc. Several pleasant cafés and restaurants overlooking the harbour, with lots more throughout the rest of the island.

Laundry South of the harbour near the Estanque Peix.

Hospital/medical services Small hospital in San Francisco Javier.

Communications

Car hire/taxis Car hire from an office to the west of the main harbour. Bicycle hire is also popular and widely available.

Buses Bus service to San Francisco Javier.

Ferries Very frequent ferries (including hydrofoils) to Ibiza.

⚓ Cala Sabina 38°44'·2N 1°25'·4E

A wide *cala* close east of Puerto de Sabina, now partly taken up by the extended harbour development. Anchor in 3–5m over sand off a sand and rock beach, open to west–northwest–north. There is a restaurant in the ruined windmill at the northern end of the beach.

⚓ Islas Redona and Pouet (Ponet)

38°45'·2N 1°25'·9E

Two small islands which, together with three even smaller islets, give some shelter to a shallow (2–3m) anchorage in a sandy bay otherwise open west–northwest–north. There is a restaurant in old windmill to the south, near a landing pontoon for local tourist ferries.

Looking southeast over Islas Redona and Pouet (centre left and centre), with Punta Prima and the long Playa de Tramontana stretching away towards the wooded heights of La Mola. On the right is the Estanque Pudent and its surrounding salt pans.

⚓ **Playa Trocados (Trocadors)** 38°45'·9N 1°26'E
A long sand and rock beach open southwest through west to northwest. Anchor near the centre of the beach in 5m or less over sand – there are rocky outcrops near each end. Playa Trocados is popular with local boats and tourist ferries and can get very full in summer.

Freu Poco (Pas de Trocadors) 38°46'·5N 1°26'E
A very shallow channel separating Espalmador from Formentera, Freu Poco lies at the northern end of the Playa Trocados. It can only be transited by dinghy and sometimes it is possible to wade between the islands, though either of these would be unwise if any swell is breaking. Very much a case for eyeball navigation, best water appears to be slightly north of the halfway point between the two islands. Even so there are rocks awash – if under power, proceed at slow speed with a good lookout.

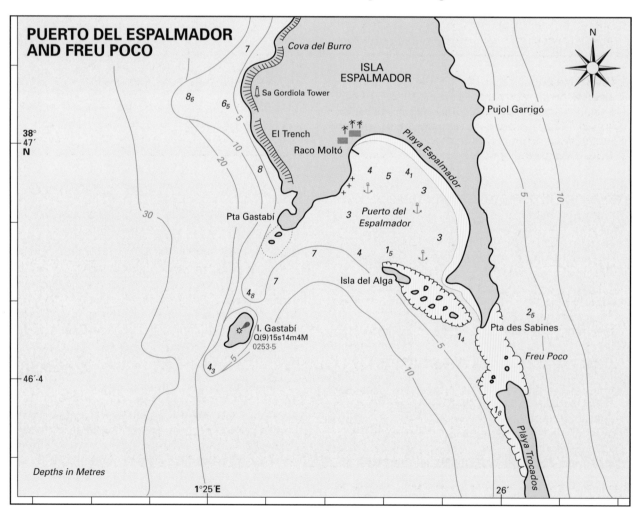

⚓ **Puerto del Espalmador** 38°46'·8N 1°25'·7E
Another misnomer – although an excellent anchorage, Puerto del Espalmador is far from a port in the accepted sense of the word. From the south, enter between Isla Gastabí (lit) and Isla del Alga. On no account attempt to cut between Isla del Alga and Espalmador itself. From north or west, enter between Punta Gastabí and Isla Gastabí, keeping at least 200m off Punta Gastabí to avoid shoals. Anchor in 3–5m over sand and weed, open to the southwest.

This popular anchorage – often containing up to a hundred yachts as well as tourist ferries and local craft – gets very ploughed towards the end of the season when holding can be poor. However it is large enough to cope with these numbers, and in mid August 1996 could still be described as 'delightful, tranquil and sheltered'. The flat and sandy island is privately owned, and though there appears to be no serious attempt to prevent visitors using the beaches the owners' privacy must be respected.

Sa Gordiola Tower (Torre Espalmador)
38°47'·2N 1°25'·1E
A large (9·6m) and very conspicuous stone tower standing near the cliff edge on the west coast of Espalmador.

⚓ **Caló Moro (Cala Morros)** 38°47'·4N 1°25'·3E
A tiny anchorage capable of taking one yacht in fair weather. Anchor in 4m over rock and sand with a line ashore, open to south–southwest–west.

⚓ **Cala Torretas** 38°47'·6N 1°25'·3E
A shallow anchorage behind Isla Torretas, suitable for shoal-draught craft and dinghies. Enter at the north end (2m) with care, watching the depth and with a lookout on the bow. Anchor off the beach in 1–1·3m over sand, open to north and west. The second and narrower southwest entrance is foul in parts and should only be used with great caution – enter about 50m from Isla Torretas.

⚓ **Isla Espardel** Bisected by 38°48'N 1°28'·7E
Mile long Isla Espardel (29m) is low to the west and cliffed to the east, with outlying rocks and islets extending 300m northwards (Piedra Espardelló

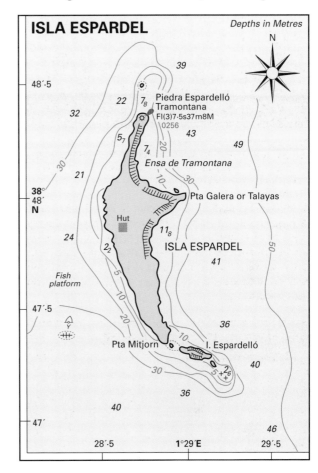

Puerto del Espalmador seen from the southwest, with Isla del Alga in the centre. Freu Poco, the shallow gap between Espalmador and Formentera, can be seen on the right.

Tramontana, awash) and 500m southeast from Pta Mitjorn to Islote Espardelló. There is no navigable passage between the latter. Anchor in 6m+ over rock, stone and weed off the western side. Landing is possible on steps to the east of lighthouse (Fl(3)7·5s37m8M, white conical tower 16m) at the north end of the island, and on the low west coast.

In 1996 a fish platform was situated off the southwest coast of Isla Espardel in approximate position 38°47'·5N 1°28'·3E. It was supposedly lit by a buoy flashing Q.Y but this has been reported unreliable.

⚓ Cala Bochs (Cala Boc or Cala Roja)
38°47'·7N 1°25'·6E
A small and very shallow anchorage near the northern end of Espalmador, open northeast–east–southeast. Anchor in 1·5m over sand off the small beach – otherwise the shore is mostly rock.

⚓ Cala Pujols 38°43'·6N 1°28'·1E
A rocky-sided *cala* on the northeast coast of Formentera, tucked between the Punta and Islas del Pujols and Punta Prima, littered with shallows and with rocks on its northwest side. Approach with care and anchor in the southeast corner in 8m over sand, northwest of the old watchtower. There is a large holiday village nearby, complete with supermarkets and restaurants. There are leading marks for the fishing boat slipway northwest of the anchorage, but these are not relevant for deep draft vessels.

⚓ Playa de Tramontana
Centred on 38°41'·4N 1°30'·2E
A long sand and rock bay (more rock than sand) stretching for 3 miles between Cala Barbé and Cala Racó d'es Mares. Anchor close inshore in 5–10m over sand, open to northwest through north to east. There are some interesting sea caves.

⚓ Cala Racó d'es Mares (Reco del Caló)
38°40'·5N 1°31'·9E
A small fishing-boat *cala*, which is open northwest–north–northeast and has steep rocky sides and a 1·5m deep rock 100m north of the entrance. There is a small jetty and a beach restaurant ashore.

Punta Single Mal (Punta de Codolà or de sa Ruda) 38°39'·9N 1°35'·1E
120m high, this headland with its tall white lighthouse (Fl.5s142m23M, white tower on white building 22m) has steep rocky cliffs, as do Punta de la Creu to the north and Punta Rotja to the south. The light is obscured when bearing between 50° and 150°.

⚓ Playa de Mitjorn (Migjorn)
Centred on 38°40'·6N 1°29'E
A 4-mile long sandy beach which is open to southeast–south–southwest. Anchor in 5m over sand and rock in settled weather only. Unsuitable for an overnight stay.

Cabo Berbería 38°38'·5N 1°23'·5E
A steep-to, rocky cliffed headland (55m) with a lighthouse (Fl(2)15s78m18M, round white tower 19m) and a watchtower 650m to the northeast. The light is obscured when bearing between 171° and 234°.

⚓ Cala Sahona (Saona) 38°41'·8N 1°23'·3E
An excellent anchorage, off a sandy beach with rocky sides, somewhat spoilt by a large hotel and other buildings ashore. Anchor off the beach in 3–5m over sand, open to west–northwest–north but protected from the south by Punta Rasa. There is a beach bar and restaurant ashore, and fishermen's huts to the south.

Looking south along the west coast of Formentera. The wide sandy bay of Cala Sahona is just left of centre with Punta Rasa to the right. The 19m lighthouse on Cabo Berbería can just be seen in the distance.

Punta Gabina (Gavina) 38°43'·2N 1°22'·9E
A 14m cliffed headland topped by a 9m tower.

⚓ Ensenada del Cabrito 38°43'·8N 1°24'·3E
An wide bay east of Punta Pedreras, open to northwest–north–northeast. Anchor in 3–5m over sand and rock with patches with weed.

⚓ Estanque Peix (Estany des Peix)
38°43'·9N 1°24'·8E (entrance)
A large saltwater lagoon with a narrow entrance carrying a scant 1m depth. Once inside depths are reported to increase, and many dinghies and other small pleasure and fishing craft are moored there. The larger Estanque Pudent (Estany Pudent) further east has no outlet to the sea.

Isla de Mallorca

General description

Isla de Mallorca is the largest island in the Islas Baleares group, being some 62 miles long and 47 miles wide. Its shape is that of a rough square, the northeast–southwest trending coasts of which are backed by jagged mountains (to the northwest) and rolling hills (to the southeast).

The mountain range that fringes the northwest-facing coast is high, culminating in the 1445m peak of Puig Mayor. This stretch of coast is very rugged, with steep rocky cliffs broken by a number of indentations, nearly all located in the northeastern section and providing some spectacular anchorages for use in settled weather. Puerto de Sóller offers the only harbour of refuge in the event of a northwest *tramontana* or *mestral* turning the entire coastline into one long leeshore.

The coast that faces northeast towards Menorca consists of two large sandy bays, each with a major harbour and a number of anchorages and smaller harbours. While not as dramatic as the northwest coast, parts are attractive and safe harbours and anchorages can be found in most conditions.

The southeast face of the square comprises the coast of the *calas*. In general this 35 mile section has low rocky cliffs with ranges of hills several miles inland. The relatively straight run of the coast is broken by numerous inlets in which lie small harbours and anchorages, the majority very attractive though too many have been marred by the building of holiday resorts. Notable on this coast is the large but relatively shallow inlet of Porto Colom, the best natural harbour and anchorage in Mallorca and possibly in the whole *Islas Baleares*.

The remaining coast, facing the southwest, is centred around the large Bahía de Palma, where the majority of the industry and population of the island is situated. Palma de Mallorca, the capital and major port, can supply most material, cultural and holiday requirements but, like any large city, it is busy, crowded and noisy. On the southeast side of this bay are high, white cliffs and on the opposite side high, rocky cliffs broken by a number of small bays and *calas*.

With the exception of the heads of the large sandy bays, deep water can generally be carried very close to the shore. Other than Isla de Cabrera and Isla Dragonera there are no offshore dangers, and the few smaller islands that exist are generally very close in.

Inland, Mallorca is unexpectedly beautiful, with large areas of fruit orchards in addition to olive groves and fields of wheat and vegetables. In the more hilly areas Moorish methods of terraced cultivation are still to be seen. The mountains of the northwest provide dramatic views and some challenging hill walks. Away from the coast – and particularly in the eastern half of the island – many of the smaller walled towns remain relatively unspoilt. One feels saddened, and at the same time relieved, that so few tourists appear to venture far beyond the nearest beach.

Two factors have tended to make the Mallorcans more cosmopolitan and subtly different from the inhabitants of the other islands in the group – firstly, wide intermarriage with the Moors, who remained in greater numbers than on the other islands, and, secondly, the rise in power and prosperity of Palma in the 14th and 15th centuries, which brought a flow of riches and contact with the outside world which the other islands lacked. Palma is still the seat of the government and parliament of the Autonomous Community of the Balearic Islands, and home to well over half of the island's current population of around 530,000 people.

History

Mallorca appears to have been inhabited for at least 6000 years, with some of the earliest human traces found in a cave near Sóller on the north coast. Later, from around 1200 BC, the bronze age *talayot* (tower) culture flourished in both Mallorca and Menorca, with sites near Artá on the east coast and Lluchmayor further south. Little is known about these early peoples, though successive invasions by Phoenicians, Carthaginians and Greeks have left some traces. According to the 1st century BC Greek writer Diodorus, the inhabitants of both Mallorca and Menorca wore few clothes and were called *gymnetes* (naked men), their islands being collectively known as *Gymnesia*.

The Romans conquered Mallorca in 123 BC and remained until the 5th century. It was known to them as *Major* – as opposed to Menorca which was called *Minor* – and these two formed, together with Cabrera, the *Insulae Baleares*. The city of Pollentia, now called Alcudia, became their capital, and they also founded the harbours of Palma and Pollensa. However the Romans used the island more as a staging post than as a permanent settlement and there are few remains of buildings to be found. A notable exception is the Roman theatre at Alcudia, easily reached from the yacht harbour. After the departure of the Romans the island entered the dark ages, over-run by the Vandals and a favoured base for pirates and Corsairs.

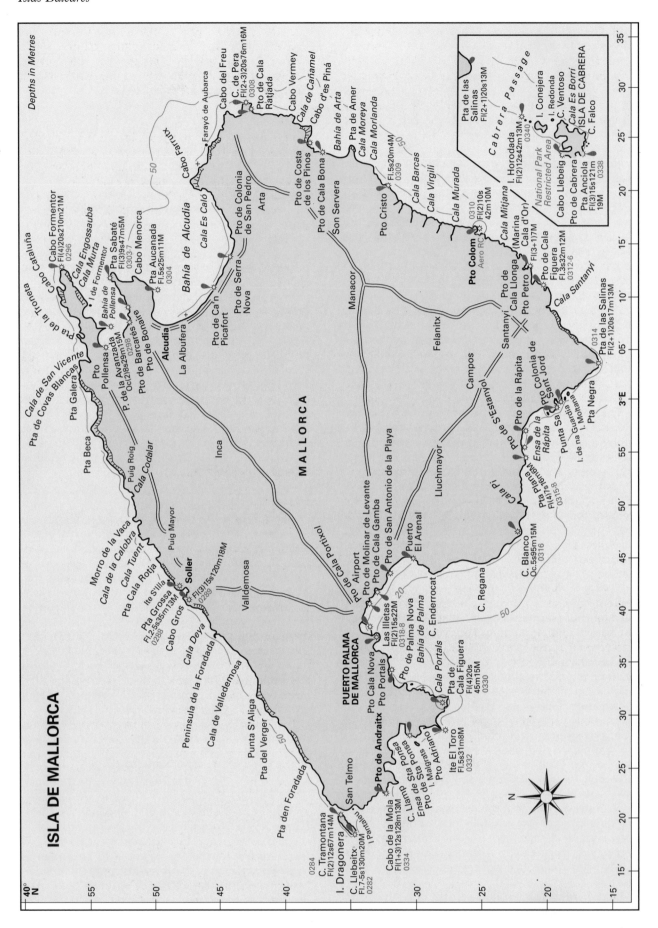

ISLA DE MALLORCA

Depths in Metres

MALLORCA

Mallorca's next taste of prosperity was under the Moors, who arrived early in the 10th century. Roman Palma was renamed *Medina Mayurqa* and grew into a bustling city of some 25,000 inhabitants, while throughout the island agriculture was improved and irrigation canals built. However almost equally little remains of this period, other than the delightful Arabian Baths and the Almudaina arch in Palma.

The destruction of Moorish Palma can fairly be laid at the door of King Jaime I (*Rey Jaime Conquistador)*, who drove the Moors out in 1229 backed by the combined armies of Catalonia and Aragon. A monument to their landing stands on the headland overlooking Puerto de Santa Ponsa on the southwest coast. With them the conquering army brought the Catalan language, which gradually evolved into the *Mallorquín* dialect spoken by many islanders today.

The 13th to 15th centuries were a golden age, with a vast increase in population and wealth. Palma, with its imposing Gothic cathedral, new castle and growing dock system, became a centre for trade inside the Mediterranean. However as Spain gradually turned her attention westward towards the New World her Mediterranean possessions became something of a backwater. Frequent attacks by pirates resulted in coastal villages and towns being rebuilt several miles inland, with only a few huts on the shore or at the harbour. In this way the damage and loss caused by surprise raids were minimised. During the next few centuries little of historical importance took place in Mallorca, other than the building of many churches and of houses for the nobility.

During the Spanish Civil War the island supported the Nationalists and suffered little damage, and greater changes have come about with the post-war advent of mass tourism. Not only are there now areas in which the ground can barely be seen for highrise hotels or the beach for sunbeds, but the many support services, from tourist shops to smart restaurants, have revived Mallorca's fortunes and changed its former agricultural based economy for ever.

Places of interest

In addition to the places of interest described in the harbour sections there are many other sites further inland which can be visited by taxi, bus or, in some cases, rail.

High in the mountains near the northwest coast is the Carthusian monastery at Valldemosa, which was once the palace of the Kings of Mallorca and has fine views. The road running east towards Sóller passes the Peninsula de la Foradada and the Son Marroig estate, once owned by Archduke Luis Salvador of Austria, before winding through Deya, famous for its associations with the writer Robert Graves. Further northeast, Lluch boasts a monastery built in the 14th century, 305m high and with excellent views.

In the southern part of the island, Campos has Roman baths and a 15th-century church while nearby Lluchmayor has prehistoric and Roman remains and is also the site of the battle where Mallorca lost her independence.

Fiestas

In addition to the national holidays and *fiestas* listed in the introduction the following dates are celebrated in Mallorca: 17 January – San Antonio (Palma); 19 January – San Sebastián (Palma); 23 April – San Jorge (Palma); Second Sunday in May – Nuestra Señora de la Victoria (Sóller); 29 June – San Pedro, sea processions (Andraitx, Alcudia); 15-16 July – Our Lady of Carmen, sea processions (Andraitx, Puerto de Sóller, Puerto de Pollensa, Porto Colom, Cala Figuera, La Rápita and elsewhere); 25 July – Santiago (Alcudia, Manacor, Sóller, Calviá); 28 July – Santa Catalina Thomás (Valldemossa, every three years); 2 August – Virgen de los Angeles (Pollensa); Sunday following 28 July – Santa Catalina Thomás (Palma); 10 August – San Cándido (Lluchmayor); 24 August – San Bartolomé (Sóller and elsewhere); 28 August – *Cavallets* of San Augustín (Felanitx); 9-16 September – Rey Jaime Conquistador (Santa Ponsa); 28 September – Vintage Festival (Binisalem); 31 December – Fiesta de la Conquista (Palma).

Factual information

Magnetic variation
Mallorca – 1°23'W (decreasing 6'E annually) (1997)

Approach and coastal passage charts
Admiralty	*1702, 1703, 2831, 2832*
Spanish	*48E, 900, 965, 970, 421, 422, 423, 424, 425, 426, 427*
French	*5505, 7115, 7116, 7118*

Approach lights

0318·8 **Puerto de Palma** 39°33'N 2°37'·5E
Fl(2)15s41m22M Square brown stone tower, visible outside Bahía de Palma 327°-040°
Racon Mo(M)22M

0330 **Punta de Cala Figuera** 39°27'·5N 2°31'·4E
Fl(4)20s45m15M Siren(2)12s Aero RC
White round tower, black diagonal stripes, on building 24m 293°-vis-094°

0334 **Cabo de la Mola** 39°32'N 2°21'·9E
Fl(1+3)12s128m12M White column, black bands, on white square tower 10m
304·4°-vis-158·2°

0282 **Cabo Llebeitx** 39°34'·5N 2°18'·3E
Fl.7·5s130m20M Masonry tower on stone building with red roof 15m
313°-vis-150°

0284 **Cabo Tramontana** 39°36'N 2°20'·4E
Fl(2)12s67m14M Round masonry tower on stone building with red roof 15m
095°-vis-230° and 346°-vis-027°

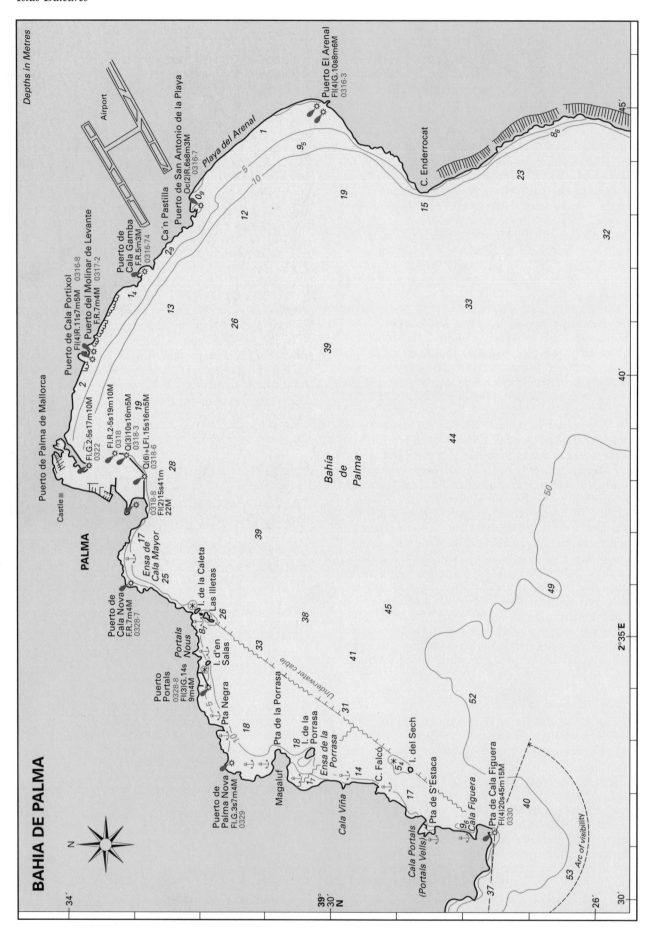

BAHIA DE PALMA

Depths in Metres

Airport

Puerto de Palma de Mallorca

Puerto de Cala Portixol
Fl(4)R.11s7m5M 0316-8

Puerto del Molinar de Levante
F.R.7m4M 0317-2

Puerto de
Cala Gamba
F.R.5m3M
0316-74

Ca'n Pastilla

Puerto de San Antonio de la Playa
Oc(2)R.6s8m3M
0316-7

Playa del Arenal

Puerto El Arenal
Fl(4)G.10s8m6M
0316-3

C. Enderrocat

PALMA

Castle

Fl.G.2.5s17m10M
0322

Fl.R.2.5s19m10M
0318

Q(3)10s16m5M
0318-3

Q(6)+Lfl.15s16m5M
0318-6

Fl(2)15s41m
22M
0318-8

Ensa de
Cala Mayor

Puerto de
Cala Nova
F.R.7m4M
0328-7

I. de la Caleta

Las Illetas

Portals
Nous

Puerto
Portals
0328-8
Fl(3)G.14s
9m4M

I. d'en
Salas

Pta Negra

Puerto de
Palma Nova
Fl.G.3s7m4M
0329

Magaluf

Pta de la Porrasa

I. de la
Porrasa

I. de la
Porrasa

Ensa de la
Porrasa

Cala Viña

C. Falcó

I. del Sech

Pta de S'Estaca

Cala Portals
(Portals Vells)

Cala Figuera

Pta de Cala Figuera
Fl(4)20s45m15M
0330

Arc of visibility

Underwater cable

Bahía
de
Palma

N

39°
30'
N

34'

45'

40'

2°35'E

26'

30'

62

0289 **Cabo Gros** 39°47'·9N 2°41'E
Fl(3)15s120m18M White tower and house,
red roof 22m 054°-vis-232°

0296 **Cabo Formentor** 39°57'·7N 3°12'·8E
Fl(4)20s210m21M
White tower and house 22m 085°-vis-006°
Note The characteristics of Cabo Formentor
are almost identical to those of Cabo Nati, Menorca

0303·7 **Punta Sabaté (Cabo del Pinar)**
39°53'·6N 3°11'·8E Fl(3)9s47m5M
White triangular tower, black band 12m

0308 **Cabo de Pera** 39°43'N 3°28'·7E
Fl(2+3)20s76m16M White tower on white
building with dark corners and red roof
21m 148°-vis-010°

0310 **Puerto Colom** 39°24'·9N 3°16'·3E
Fl(2)10s42m10M White round tower, three
black bands, on white building with red
roof 25m 207°-vis-006°

0312·6 **Torre d'en Beu** 39°19'·8N 3°10'·7E
Fl.3s32m12M White octagonal tower,
vertical black stripes 6m

0314 **Punta de las Salinas** 39°16'N 3°03'·3E
Fl(2+1)20s17m13M White tower and
building, narrow stone bands 17m
265°-vis-116° Siren Mo(S)15s3M

0316 **Cabo Blanco** 39°21'·9E 2°47'·3E
Oc.5s95m15M White tower and building 12m
296°-vis-115°

Radiobeacons

1031 **Punta de Cala Figuera** 39°27'·5N 2°31'·4E
Radiobeacon *FI*, 286·5kHz 50M (A1A)
1029 **Puerto Colom Aero** 39°25'·6N 3°15'·3E
Aerobeacon *PTC*, 401kHz 30M (Non A2A)

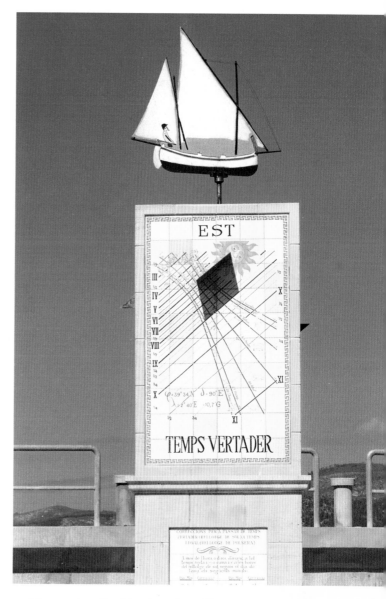

A boat under sail, a blue sky and a smiling sun – what could
sum up Mallorca better?

PUERTO DE PALMA

PALMA

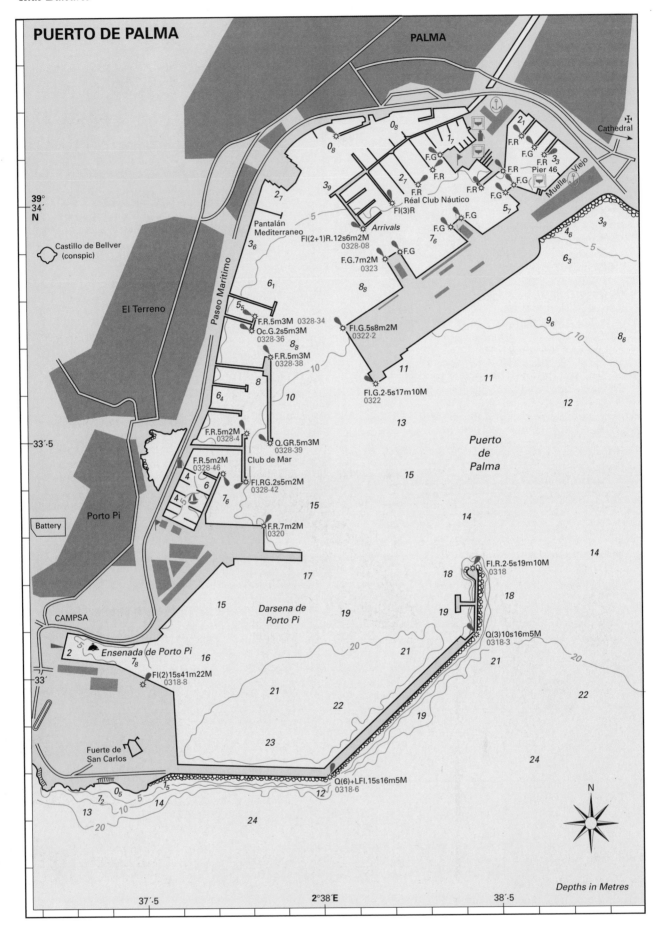

☩ Cathedral

39°
34′
N

Castillo de Bellver
(conspic)

El Terreno

Paseo Marítimo

0₈

0₈

1₇

2₁

F.R

F.G

F.G

3₃

F.R Pier 46

F.G

Muelle Viejo

3₉

2₇

3₉

2₇

F.R

F.R

F.R

F.G

Réal Club Náutico
Fl(3)R

Pantalán
Mediterraneo

5

3₆

Fl(2+1)R.12s6m2M
0328·08

Arrivals

F.G.7m2M
0323

F.G

5₇

F.G

F.G

7₆

4₆

5

6₃

6₁

8₈

9₆

8₆

70

5₅

F.R.5m3M 0328·34
Oc.G.2s5m3M
0328·36

8₈

Fl.G.5s8m2M
0322·2

11

11

12

8

F.R.5m3M
0328·38

10

6₄

10

Fl.G.2·5s17m10M
0322

13

F.R.5m2M
0328·4

Q.GR.5m3M
0328·39

15

*Puerto
de
Palma*

F.R.5m2M
0328·46

6

Club de Mar

4

4₅

7₆

Fl.RG.2s5m2M
0328·42

15

14

14

Porto Pi

Battery

F.R.7m2M
0320

17

15

Fl.R.2·5s19m10M
0318

18

18

CAMPSA

15

*Darsena de
Porto Pi*

19

19

Q(3)10s16m5M
0318·3

2

7₈

Ensenada de Porto Pi

16

20

21

21

Fl(2)15s41m22M
0318·8

21

22

22

19

Fuerte de
San Carlos

23

24

7₂

0₅

5

1₅

14

12

Q(6)+LFl.15s16m5M
0318·6

13

10

20

24

N

Depths in Metres

37′·5

2°38′E

38′·5

33′·5

33′

Puerto de Palma de Mallorca

39°33·5N 2°38'E

Charts

	Approach	Harbour
Admiralty	2832, 3036	3036
Spanish	970, 421, 421A, 4211	4212
French	7115, 7118	6775

Lights

Approach

0330 **Punta de Cala Figuera** 39°27'·5N 2°31'·4E
Fl(4)20s45m15M Siren(2)12s Aero RC
White round tower, black diagonal
stripes, on building 24m 293°-vis-094°

0316 **Cabo Blanco** 39°21'·9E 2°47'·3E
Oc.5s95m15M White tower and building 12m
296°-vis-115°

0318·8 **Puerto de Palma** 39°33'N 2°37'·5E
Fl(2)15s41m22M Square brown stone tower,
visible outside Bahía de Palma 327°-040°
Racon Mo(M)22M

Entrance

0318 **South breakwater, head**
39°33'·2N 2°38'·4E Fl.R.2·5s19m10M
Red column on white hut displaying red ■
13m F.R. on radio masts 4·5M east
and east-southeast

0318·3 **South breakwater, outer elbow**
39°33'·1N 2°38'·4E Q(3)10s16m5M
East cardinal tower 10m
Obscured inside harbour Siren Mo(P)30s4M

0318·6 **South breakwater, inner elbow**
39°32'·8N 2°38'E Q(6)+LFl.15s16m5M
South cardinal tower 8m 231°-vis-092°

0319·2 **West mole, south corner** Light withdrawn

0319 **West mole, north corner** Light withdrawn

0320 **West mole, north elbow**
39°33'·3N 2°37'·8E F.R.7m2M
Red metal column 5m

0328·46 **Club de Mar south (inner) mole**
39°33'·4N 2°37'·7E F.R.5m2M
Red metal column 4m

0328·42 **Club de Mar central mole, south head**
39°33'·4N 2°37'·8E Fl.RG.2s5m2M
Red and green metal column 4m
182°-R-290°-G-182°

0328·4 **Club de Mar central mole, north head**
39°33'·5N 2°37'·8E F.R.5m2M
Red metal column 4m

0328·39 **Club de Mar north mole, south head**
39°33'·5N 2°37'·8E Q.RG.5m3M
Red and green metal column 4m
180°-R-300°-G-180°

0322 **Northeast breakwater, southwest corner**
39°33'·6N 2°38'·1E Fl.G.2·5s17m10M
Green column on white hut displaying green ▲ 15m

0322·2 **Northeast breakwater, northwest corner**
39°33'·7N 2°38'·1E
Fl.G.5s8m2M Green column 6m

0328·38 **Club de Mar north mole, north head**
39°33'·7N 2°37'·8E
F.R.5m3M Red metal column 4m

0328·36 **Pantalán de la Cuarentena, south head**
39°33'·7N 2°37'·8E
Oc.G.2s5m3M Green metal column 4m

0328.34 **Pantalán de la Cuarentena, north head**
39°33'·8N 2°37'·8E
F.R.5m3M Red metal column 4m

0328·08 **Réal Club Náutico, south extremity**
39°33'·9N 2°38'·1E Fl(2+1)R.12s6m2M
Red support, green band 5m

0323 **Northeast breakwater spur, west corner**
39°33'·9N 2°38'·2E F.G.7m2M
Green metal column 5m

Numerous other lights exist in the northeast of the
harbour.

Puerto de Palma seen from the northeast. The pontoons of the
Réal Club Náutico can be seen on the right with the northeast
breakwater in the centre. The commanding position of Palma
Cathedral is particularly emphasised.

The entrance to Puerto de Palma looking slightly north of west, with the Club de Mar in the centre. The two Port Authority jetties can be seen on the right, behind the tip of the northeast breakwater.

Radiobeacons

1031 **Punta de Cala Figuera Lt**
   39°27'·5N 2°31'·4E
   Radiobeacon *FI*, 286·5kHz 50M (A1A)

Port Communications

VHF – Pilots (*Palma Prácticos*), Ch 6, 14, 16; Marinas, Ch 9, 16.
☎/*Fax* – Pilots ☎ 711937; Port Authority ☎ 715100, *Fax* 726948; Club de Mar ☎ 403611, *Fax* 403618; Réal Club Náutico de Palma ☎ 726848, *Fax* 718636; Pier 46 ☎ 724949, *Fax* 725208.

General

Puerto de Palma is a very large, clean, naval, commercial, fishing and yachting harbour which can be entered in all weathers and will provide good shelter. Facilities are excellent and there is an attractive town nearby with extensive shops and markets. There are two large yacht harbours, both with palatial clubhouses and all facilities, together with the smaller Pier 46 and a Port Authority quay where berthing is considerably cheaper. The harbour becomes very crowded in the season and vacant berths may be difficult to find but there are six other yacht harbours in the Bahía de Palma where berths are usually available, and many possible anchorages can be found.

The city of Palma is thought to have been founded by the Romans, who knew it as *Palmaria* and built its first city walls during the 4th century. It flourished under the Moors, who renamed it *Medina Mayurqa* and whose legacy includes the Arabian Baths and the Almudaina arch. Subsequently it became the Spanish capital of the islands and the centre of a Mediterranean trading empire, giving rise to the first proper harbour works some time in the 14th century.

First amongst Palma's treasures must be its soaring Gothic cathedral, begun in 1230 and still able to dominate the eastern part of the city. Opposite is the Almudaina palace, built by the Moors but swiftly taken over by their Christian conquerors, and behind and slightly inland the oldest – and most fascinating – part of the city, where narrow flagged alleyways lined by shops, bars and restaurants can only be explored on foot. All are within comfortable walking distance of the harbour.

Further out of the city on a hillside to the northwest stands the Castillo de Bellver, also built in the 13th century and entered by a drawbridge across the moat. As with any major city there are museums, churches and historic buildings by the score, and unless very much 'passing through' a general guide book (Appendix II, page 227) or some of the tourist information leaflets available from several offices in the city (page 11) are next to essential if much is not to be missed.

Fiestas are held on 5 January with the Procession of the Three Kings and on 17 January to celebrate the Blessing of St Anthony. Two days later are the Revels of St Sebastian. February sees Carnival week and March or April the Fair of Ramos. Religious processions are held during Easter Week, with the *fiesta* of the Angel on the first Sunday after Easter. The *fiesta* of Sta Catalina Tomás, the island's own saint, is held on the first Sunday after 28 July, with the Procession of Sta Beateta on 28 October. On 31 December the old year is rounded off with the *fiesta* of the Standard.

Approach

From west Round the very prominent Punta de Cala Figuera which has a lighthouse (Fl(4)20s45m15M, white round tower with black diagonal stripes on building 24m) and radio masts on its steep cliffs. Cross the Bahía de Palma heading northeast towards Palma Cathedral, a very large building with small twin spires. Castillo de Bellver (140m) is also conspicuous. The breakwaters will be seen on closer approach.

From east Round Cabo Blanco, which is high with steep light brown cliffs topped by a lighthouse (Oc.5s95m15M, white tower and building 12m) and an old watchtower. Follow the coast northwest until the buildings of Palma, including the Cathedral and Castillo de Bellver, described above, come into view. The breakwaters will be seen on closer approach.

At night Should present no problems, though the various navigational lights can be difficult to identify against the mass of town lights.

In fog If navigating without GPS or the equivalent, the radiobeacon and siren on Punta de Cala Figuera, the siren at the outer elbow of the south breakwater and the racon at Puerto de Palma lighthouse may be of assistance.

Anchorage in the approach

Anchor in 10–12m over mud and sand south of the northeast breakwater, exposed to the southerly quadrant. Keep well out of the channel, and display an anchor light at night.

Looking over the northeast breakwater towards the pontoons of the *Réal Club Náutico*, seen from the southeast. Pier 46's base is on the extreme right of the picture.

Entrance

Puerto de Palma is a busy harbour in which ferries and other commercial vessels have right of way. Round the end of the south breakwater with an offing of at least 100m. The Club de Mar will be seen ahead with the Réal Club Náutico de Palma to starboard behind the northeast breakwater (which should be given a similar offing).

There is a 5 knot speed limit in the harbour, decreasing to 3 knots in the marinas.

Berthing

There are five places where yachts may berth. Even so the harbour becomes crowded in the high season and it is preferable to book ahead if possible.

- *Club de Mar* A very large and well equipped marina (☎ 403611, *Fax* 403618) directly opposite the entrance, offering more than 600 berths ranging in size from 8m up to 120m. Facilities are excellent, with charges to match. There is no reception pontoon as such – call on VHF Ch 9 to be allocated a berth. Note that the marina is divided into two sections with separate entrances (see plan).
- *Réal Club Náutico de Palma* (☎ 726848, *Fax* 718636), situated in the northeast of the harbour at the root of a long mole with many side spurs berthing 250 yachts from 8m to 20m. There is a reception quay on the outside of the southwest arm (see plan), and visitors usually lie alongside or stern-to on one of the fingers in the basin to the north.
- *Pier 46* (☎ 724949, *Fax* 725208) is a relatively new concern, with offices and limited berths on the Muelle Viejo at the root of the northeast

breakwater, and another 75 berths on the Pantalán Mediterraneo off the Paseo Maritimo. Both give convenient access to the old city, and have security gates and night watchmen.

- *Port Authority jetties* Two jetties close north of the Club the Mar administered by the Port Authority (like the Paseo Marítimo berths below), but with mooring lines and a security gate provided. An official normally visits the yacht, otherwise call at the Port Authority office at 19 Muelle Viejo. In strong east or southeast winds these jetties can become untenable.
- *Paseo Marítimo* For many years yachts have moored bow or stern-to within yards of Palma's main thoroughfare. Although convenient for the town and relatively cheap, the area is noisy, dusty and without any form of security – if the crew can get aboard, so can thieves. There are no facilities and a trip line on the anchor is essential. In strong east or southeast winds the area becomes dangerous and should be vacated.

Anchoring

Anchoring is not permitted inside the harbour.

Charges *(see page 6)*

- *Club de Mar* High season daily rate – Band A (15m), Band B (10m); low season daily rate – Band B. Water and electricity extra.
- *Réal Club Náutico de Palma* High season daily rate – Band C; low season daily rate – Band C. Water and electricity included.
- *Pier 46* High season daily rate – Band C; low season daily rate – Muelle Viejo, Band B; Pantalán Mediterraneo, Band C. Water and electricity included.
- *Paseo Marítimo* and *Port Authority jetties* High season daily rate – Band D; low season daily rate – Band D. Water and electricity extra (if available).

Facilities

Palma de Mallorca has by far the best facilities for yachts in the Islas Baleares and many of the services listed below are not readily available elsewhere in the islands. Companies are normally listed alphabetically.

Boatyards Astilleros de Mallorca (☎ 710645, *Fax* 721368), a shipyard with four slipways able to take yachts up to 100m, on the Contramuelle Mollet opposite the *Réal Club Náutico*. Boat Yard Palma (☎ 718302, 718319 *Fax* 718611) and Carpinser (☎ 725079, 717384) on the Muelles Viejo and Nuevo near the root of the northeast breakwater, and several others.

Travel-lifts 150 tonne lift at Boat Yard Palma, 90 and 30 tonne lifts on the Muelle Viejo, 60 tonne lift at *Réal Club Náutico*.

Cranes 9 tonne crane at the *Réal Club Náutico*, 5 tonne crane at Club de Mar, plus many others in the commercial areas of the port.

Slipways Commercial slipway in the Dársena de Porto Pi able to handle 350 tonnes, for which a docking plan is required. Several in the shipyard east of the *Réal Club Náutico*.

Engineers C-Tec SA (☎ 405712, 405752), Marine Machine (☎ 462660, *Fax* 463693) and Talleres Guidet (☎ 718643, *Fax* 720577) can handle most types of work.

Official service agents include: C-Tec SA (see above) – Caterpillar, Man; Comercial Morey (☎ 753333, *Fax* 756149) – Mercury/MerCruiser, Suzuki; Ecosse Diesels (☎ 733957) – Ecosse Diesels; Finanzauto SA (☎ 755819, *Fax* 758966) – Caterpillar; Harald Schmidt (☎/*Fax* 780042) – Mercedes, Sole Diesel, Yanmar; Juan Frau Navarro (☎ 260599 – Yanmar; Magic Board (☎ 757426, 759363) – Ecosse Diesels; Marine Machine (see above) – Ford/Lehman, Perkins, Sabre, Volvo Penta; Mecanautica (☎ 204102) – Sole Diesel; Nautica MV SL (☎ 719131, *Fax* 719376) – Caterpillar, Volvo Penta; Náutica Seameermar (☎ 737092, 737094 *Fax* 450382) – Volvo Penta; Nautica Socias y Rosello (☎ 200511, (☎/*Fax* 207966) – Yamaha; Pressure Marine (☎ 753272, *Fax* 201316) – Mariner; Salva (☎ 730303, *Fax* 453910) – Bukh, Caterpillar, Cummins, Man; Talleres Noray (☎/*Fax* 723839) – Mercedes; Volvo Penta España SA (☎ 200000) – Volvo Penta.

Metalwork Herajes Inox SL (☎ 297232, *Fax* 755043), Ruben Doñaque (☎ 760796, *Fax* 202313) and Talleres Guidet (see above).

Hydraulics Yachtech (☎ 458942, *Fax* 732478).

Refrigeration, air conditioning and pumps Palma Yachts SL (☎ 450366, *Fax* 289099), Air Cold (☎/*Fax* 770521) and Anfra Tecnica SL (☎ 242626, *Fax* 271210).

Electronic & radio repairs, autopilots, watermakers etc. Balear Tecnologico CB (☎/*Fax* 180141), C-Tec SA (☎ 405712, 405752), Dahlberg SA (☎ 469961, *Fax* 469469), Echo Marine Services (☎ 400213, 700427, *Fax* 405873) and Vetus Mallorca (☎ 713050, *Fax* 713054).

Generators Salva (☎ 730303, *Fax* 453910).

Sailmakers and canvaswork North Sails España SA (☎ 725752, *Fax* 718374), Sails & Canvas (☎/*Fax* 733937), Velas Ferrá SA (☎ 467413, *Fax* 463982), Velería Orion (☎ 757688, 757781), Velera J Matheu (☎ 273887).

Ropes and rigging Lliñas (☎ 466686), Parts SL (☎ 732040, *Fax* 450718), The Rigging Shop (☎ 736365, *Fax* 457592), Sails & Canvas (☎/*Fax* 733937) and Yachtech (☎ 458942, *Fax* 732478).

Chandleries Yacht Centre Palma (☎ 715612, *Fax* 711246) at the Club de Mar, also Nauti Pesca (☎/*Fax* 723977), Nautica Seameermar (☎ 737092, 737094 *Fax* 450382), La Central (☎ 731838) and others. Merca Nautic (☎ 736563, 288521, *Fax* 735081) sells secondhand (as well as new) equipment.

Liferaft servicing GDR (☎ 760798, *Fax* 759688) and Nauti Pesca (☎/*Fax* 723977).

Charts Admiralty – Rapid Transit Service (☎ 403703, 403903 *Fax* 400216); Spanish – Librería Fondevila (☎ 725616, *Fax* 713326); Casa del Mapa (☎ 466061, *Fax* 771616); Valnautica SL (☎ 464990, *Fax* 465422).

Water Water points at all yacht berthing locations including the Port Authority jetties and intervals along the Paseo Marítimo.

Showers At both marinas and Pier 46. No showers on public jetties.

Electricity 220v and 380v AC available at both marinas and the two Pier 46 berthing areas. Some power points on the Port Authority jetty.

Fuel Diesel and petrol pumps at the Club de Mar and on the quay opposite Pier 46. The *Réal Club Náutico* does not have a fuel berth.

Bottled gas It may be possible to get Calor Gas and other non-standard butane bottles refilled at the CAMPSA depot south of the Club de Mar.

Ice Cube ice from the *Réal Club Náutico*, the fuel berth at the Club de Mar and many supermarkets. Block ice (not for use in drinks) from La Lonja.

Yacht clubs The Réal Club Náutico de Palma was founded nearly fifty years ago and has bars, a restaurant, bedrooms, a swimming pool, showers, repair workshops etc. The Club de Mar is a much newer 'marina' yacht club with similar facilities. Apply to the secretary before using either club.

Banks One in the Club de Mar complex, with many more throughout the city. Most (including the Club de Mar unit) have credit card facilities.

Shops/provisioning A massive PRYCA hypermarket in the Porto Pí shopping centre five minutes' walk from the Club de Mar, with another of similar size on the road to the airport. Small supermarket at Club de Mar. Wide variety of other shops, as one would expect of a major city.

Produce market At Santa Catalina, ten minutes from the *Réal Club Náutico* and Pier 46 berths.

Hotels/restaurants/cafés etc. Many hotels of all grades, likewise bars, cafés and restaurants. Of the latter, some of the most intriguing are in the old part of the city behind the cathedral. Both marinas have restaurants and indoor/outdoor bars.

Laundrettes Facilities at both marinas and others in the city.
Hospital/medical services Several in the city.

Communications

Car hire/taxis Wide choice.
Buses and trains Bus service throughout the island plus trains to Sóller (recommended) and Inca. Timetables available from tourist offices.
Ferries Car ferries to mainland Spain, Ibiza and Menorca (see page 11).
Air services Busy international airport 4 miles east of the city.

⚓ Ensenada de Cala Mayor 39°33'N 2°36'·5E

An open bay close west of Puerto de Palma, with Puerto de Cala Nova yacht harbour tucked in on its western side. Anchor in 5m+ over sand and stone about 200m northeast of the harbour entrance and well clear of the approach, open to southeast through southwest. Five underwater cables run in a south-southeasterly direction from a point near the centre of the bay. The anchorage is backed by large apartment blocks, houses and shops.

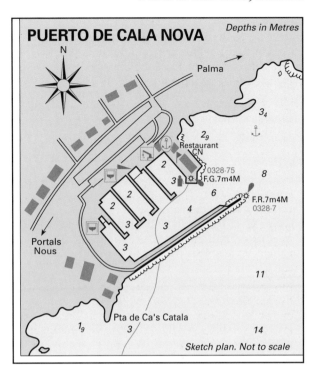

Puerto de Cala Nova

39°33'N 2°36'E

Charts   *Approach*

Admiralty   *2832,* 3036
Spanish   *970, 421, 421A, 4211*
French   *7115,* 7118

Lights

0328·7 **South breakwater** 39°33'N 2°36·1'E
    F.R.7m4M Red column 3m
0328·75 **North mole** 39°33'N 2°36'E
    F.G.7m4M Green column 3m

Port Communications

Escola Nacional de Vela Cala Nova VHF Ch 9,
☎ 402512, *Fax* 403911.

Puerto de Cala Nova from the south.

General

A small and rather shallow artificial harbour, built by the Balearic authorities as a base for the national sailing school, the *Escola Nacional de Vela*, where children and adults learn windsurfing, dinghy and keelboat sailing. Although technically a private harbour, visitors' berths are occasionally available – telephone first to check.

Cala Nova is pleasant with good facilities, though somewhat overshadowed by the high-rise buildings around it. It is easy to enter with good protection once inside, though a swell works in with strong east or southeasterly winds.

Approach

For outer approaches see Puerto de Palma, page 66.

From west After rounding Punta de Cala Figuera cross the Bahía de Palma heading northeast, leaving the low-lying Isla del Sech to port. When past Las Illetas follow the coast at 200m for one mile when Puerto de Cala Nova will easily be seen.

From east Leave Puerto de Palma's long south breakwater to starboard to enter the Ensenada de Cala Mayor. Puerto de Cala Nova will be seen in the northwest corner.

Anchorage in the approach

In the Ensenada de Cala Mayor – see above.

Entrance

Keep to the middle of the 55m-wide entrance maintaining a careful watch for sailing school craft (novices) entering or leaving. There is a 2 knot speed limit inside the harbour.

Berthing
Secure to the inside of the south breakwater unless a berth has already been allocated.

Charges *(see page 6)*
High season daily rate – Band B (15m), Band C (10m); low season daily rate – Band A (15m), Band B (10m). Water included.

Facilities
Travel-lift 35 tonne lift at the west end of the harbour.
Cranes 2·5 tonne crane.
Slipway Wide but shallow dinghy slipway backed by an area of hard standing.
Engineers Available – enquire at the *Club Náutico* or the *Escola Nacional*.
Chandlery By the harbour.
Water Taps on quays and pontoons.
Showers At the *Club Náutico*.
Electricity 220v AC points on the quays and pontoons.
Fuel For the sailing school's use only, and not on public sale.
Ice From the *Club Náutico* bar.
Yacht clubs The Club Náutico de Cala Nova has a pleasant clubhouse on the north mole with a restaurant, bar, terrace, swimming pool, showers etc.
Shops/provisioning All normal supplies are available from supermarkets and shops in Cala Nova and nearby San Augustin.
Hotels/restaurants/cafés etc. Many, of all grades, including a restaurant and bar at the *Club Náutico*.
Laundrette Near the harbour.
Hospital/medical services In Palma.

Communications
Car hire/taxis From Palma.
Buses To Palma and elsewhere.

⚓ Las Illetas 39°31'·9N 2°35'·5E
An attractive group of anchorages best viewed on the chart, surrounded by the exclusive Bendinat holiday development. There are a few dangerous rocks awash between Islote de s'Estenedor (actually a low peninsula) and Illeta, and southwest of Islote de la Caleta. Islote de s'Estenedor is a military area and landing on the beach may not be permitted. Fishing nets supported by lines of floats are sometimes laid in the approaches.

North anchorage Enter heading west or southwest to anchor in 3m over sand, open northeast through east to southeast.

Central anchorage Enter from northeast (inside Islote de la Caleta) or southeast, in which case take care to avoid Bajo Calafat and other rocks southwest of the island. Anchor in 2–3m over sand, open to northeast and southeast, off a small beach.

South anchorage A small, well protected hole between Islote de s'Estenedor and Illeta, open only to the east and to swell from northeast and southeast. Anchor in 3–5m over sand.

West anchorage The largest of the four anchorages, off a good beach (the property of the holiday complex and technically private). Enter heading northeast to anchor in 5m± over sand, open to southwest and west.

⚓ Portals Nous 39°32'N 2°34'·7E
A deeply indented *cala* surrounded by apartment blocks, close east of Islote d'en Salas. Anchor in 5m over sand open to south and southwest. There are shops, restaurants, etc. ashore.

Las Illetas from just south of east. Illeta with its ruined tower is on the left, the misnamed Islote de s'Estenedor in the centre and Islote de la Caleta on the right.

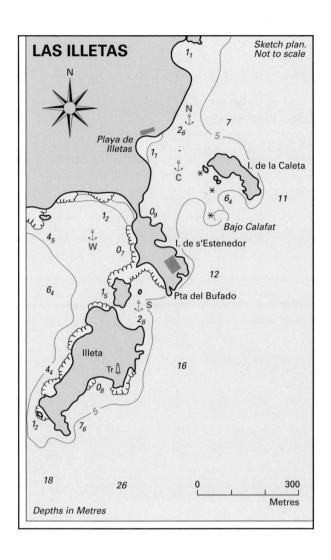

LAS ILLETAS

Sketch plan.
Not to scale

Playa de
Illetas

I. de la Caleta

Bajo Calafat

I. de s'Estenedor

Pta del Bufado

Illeta

Tr

Depths in Metres

0   300

Metres

Puerto Portals

39°31'·9N 2°34'E

Charts

	Approach
Admiralty	*2832, 3036*
Spanish	*970, 421, 421A*
French	*7115, 7118*

Lights

0328·8 **South breakwater** 39°31'·8N 2°33'·9E
Fl(3)G.14s9m4M Green column on white
base displaying green ▲ 6m
0328·85 **North mole** 39°31'·9N 2°34'E
Fl(3)R.14s9m3M Red column on white
base displaying red ■ 6m

Port Communications

Puerto Portals VHF Ch 9, ☎ 171100, *Fax* 171117.

General

Opened in 1986 Puerto Portals is, in the words of its
brochure 'modern and sophisticated' – as are many
of the 670 yachts berthed there. Like Puerto de
Palma 4 miles to the northwest it is capable of taking
superyachts up to 80m overall, and claims 4–5m
depths throughout. The immediate surroundings
include restaurants, cafés, boutiques and various
marine-related businesses, against a backdrop of
bare sandy cliffs topped by white apartment blocks
and hotels. Approach and entrance are
straightforward except with a southeasterly gale
when care must be taken.

The harbour is frequently full to capacity in
summer, and it is wise to call before arrival
(telephone or VHF) to ascertain that a berth will be
available.

Approach

For details of the outer approaches see Puerto de
Palma, page 66.

From west After rounding Punta de Cala Figuera
follow the coast north-northeast, leaving the low-
lying Isla del Sech on either side but then
maintaining an offing of about ½ mile. Isla and
Punta de la Porrassa are unmistakeable, while
Puerto Portals' orange cliffs surmounted by white
buildings can be seen from afar. In the close
approach the long south breakwater will be seen, as
will the distinctive square tower on the north mole
which houses the marina offices.

From east Round Cabo Blanco onto a northwesterly
course across the Bahía de Palma. See above for the
final approach.

Anchorage in the approach

Anchor 200m west of the tower in 5m over sand,
taking care not to impede the entrance channel.
Watch for buoys off the beach.

Entrance and berthing

Swing wide around the head of the south breakwater
onto an easterly heading, ready to berth alongside
the reception quay at the south end of the north
mole. There is a 3 knot speed limit in the harbour.

Charges *(see page 6)*

High season daily rate – Band A (15m), Band B
(10m); low season daily rate – Band B. Water and
electricity extra.

Facilities

Boatyards Mundimar Portals SA (☎ 676369, *Fax*
676409) at the northeast end of the harbour can
handle most jobs on yachts up to 80 tonnes.
Travel-lifts Two lifts (80 and 30 tonnes) in the
Mundimar yard.
Cranes 10 and 2 tonne cranes near travel-lifts.
Dinghy slip At the root of the south breakwater.
Engineers Danbrit ☎ 677201, *Fax* 677328. Official
service agents include: Danbrit – Lugger;
Motornautica Portals Nous (☎ 677795, *Fax*
677794) – Mercury/MerCruiser, Quicksilver,
Volvo Penta; Mundimar Portals SA (see above) –
Volvo Penta.
Electronic & radio repairs Danbrit ☎ 677201, *Fax*
677328.
Chandlery Multi-Marine (☎ 675662, 677229, *Fax*
677244) and Nauti Parts (☎ 677730, *Fax*
677495).

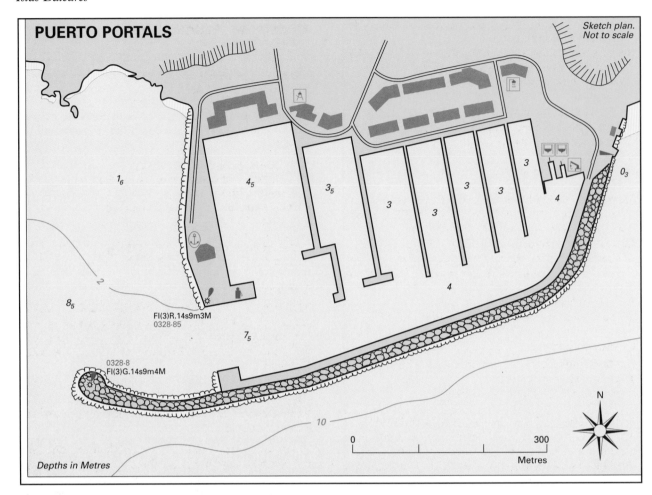

PUERTO PORTALS

Sketch plan.
Not to scale

1₆

4₅

3₅

3

3

3

3

3

0₃

4

⚓

Fl(3)R.14s9m3M
0328·85

2

8₅

7₅

0328·8
Fl(3)G.14s9m4M

10

Depths in Metres

N

0   300
Metres

Puerto Portals from the southwest. The distinctive square tower
housing the marina offices can be seen on the north mole, almost
directly above the light on the south breakwater.

Water Taps on all quays and pontoons. Check for quality before filling tanks.

Showers Two shower blocks in the marina complex, for which a key is required.

Electricity 220v and 380v AC points on all quays and pontoons.

Fuel Diesel and petrol from pumps at the head of the north mole. Direct supply to yachts over 18m requiring more than 1000 lts.

Ice At the fuel berth.

Banks Bank with credit card machine in the marina complex.

Shops/provisioning The shops on the north side of the harbour include a small supermarket. More shops in Portals Nous a short distance inland.

Hotels/restaurants/cafés etc. Many in the vicinity. There are more than twenty restaurants, cafés, bars and ice cream parlours around the harbour alone.

Laundrette In Portals Nous.

Hospital/medical services In Portals Nous and Palma.

Communications

Car hire Four car hire firms around the harbour.

Taxis Via the marina office.

Buses Bus service along the coast.

⚓ **Punta Negra** 39°31'·8N 2°33'·4E & 2°33'·1E
Anchor on either side of the headland in 2–3m over sand and stone, open on the east side to east through south, and on the west side to south and southwest. Punta Negra is remarkably unspoilt with few houses ashore.

Puerto de Palma Nova
39°31'·5N 2°32'·6E

Charts   *Approach*
Admiralty   *2832, 3036*
Spanish   *970, 421, 421A*
French   *7115, 7118*

Lights

0329 **South mole** 39°31'·5N 2°32'·6E
Fl.G.3s7m4M Green column on white base displaying green ▲ 6m

0329·2 **North mole** 39°31'·5N 2°32'·6E
F.R.6m3M Red column on white base displaying red ■ 6m
Northwest (new) mole 39°31'·5N 2°32'·6E
Characteristics unknown Red column 5m

General

This very small harbour is partially silted-up and at present can only be used by shallow draught vessels – reported depths are unreliable due to silting and periodic dredging. Harbour facilities are very limited.

Approach

For details of the outer approaches see Puerto de Palma, page 66.

From west After rounding Punta de Cala Figuera follow the coast north-northeast, leaving the low-lying Isla del Sech on either side. Round Isla and then Punta de la Porrasa, after which Puerto de Palma Nova will been seen at the north end of the long beach of the same name.

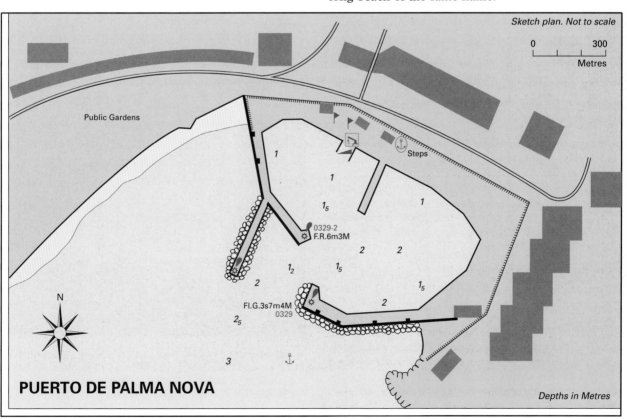

From east Round Cabo Blanco onto a northwesterly course across the Bahía de Palma. Puerto de Palma Nova will been seen at the north end of the long beach of the same name.

Anchorage in the approach

Anchor in 3–5m over sand south of the harbour, open to southeast, east and possibly northeast.

Entrance

Due to the silting problem (sand rather than mud) it would be unwise to enter the harbour in any boat drawing more than 1m without first making a recce by dinghy. The water is generally too cloudy to read depths visually. There is a 2 knot speed limit.

Berthing

Secure in an empty berth and report to the harbour office by the slipway (closed Thursday and Saturday, otherwise open 0930–1300 daily).

Facilities

Cranes 6 tonne crane beside the slipway.
Slipway In the north of the harbour, 1m depth.
Water Water taps around the harbour.
Electricity A few 220v AC points.
Fuel By can from a filling station on the road to Palma.
Yacht club The Club Náutico Palma Nova (☎ 681055) has a small clubhouse and bar near the slipway.
Banks In Palma Nova.
Provisions Supermarket and other shops nearby.
Hotels/restaurants/cafés etc. Vast numbers – Palma Nova is at the northern end of the Magaluf holiday area.
Hospital/medical services In Palma Nova and Palma itself.

Communications

Car hire/taxis In Palma Nova.
Buses Bus service along the coast.

⚓ Playa de Palma Nova

Bisected by 39°31'·3N 2°32'·5E
A long and often crowded sandy beach, broken into three by a pair of low rocky promontories each occupied by a large hotel. Anchor in 2–4m over sand open to the eastern quadrant. Behind the beaches the coast is solid with hotels, restaurants and other tourist necessities.

⚓ Playa de Magaluf

Bisected by 39°30'·5N 2°32'·4E
An anchorage off a long beach (hardly visible for sunbeds) in the northern part of the Ensenada de la Porrasa, surrounded by apartment blocks, hotels, beach cafés, shops etc. Isla de la Porrasa can be left on either side on entry, though 2·5m shoals extend northwest from the island for 200m. Anchor in 3–5m over sand, open to the east and southeast, but holding is reported to be poor. A submarine cable

runs southeast from a point just south of the centre of the bay (see plan page 62).

A huge marina with 1500 berths is supposedly planned for this bay, but in May 1996 there was no sign of any work starting and it appears unlikely to be built in the forseeable future.

Isla de la Porrasa Bisected by 39°30'·3N 2°32'·8E
A rocky, scrub-covered island 425m long, 220m wide and 36m high. The southeast point is steep-to, but the northwest end of the island has a 2·5m shoal extending 200m offshore. There is a 200m passage carrying 5–6m between Isla de la Porrasa and Punta de la Porrasa to the north. Landing is possible on the southwest coast.

Long fishing nets supported by small white or pink floats are sometimes laid near the island.

⚓ Cala Viña 39°30'·8N 2°32'·2E

A small, narrow *cala* surrounded by high-rise buildings, with a small sandy beach which is crowded in the holiday season. The inner half of the bay is roped off for swimmers. Anchor in 4–5m over sand, open to the east.

⚓ South of Cabo Falcó 39°29'·9N 2°32'·1E

Two very small *calas* lie south of Cabo Falcó (note the 0·4m shoal 100m southeast of the headland). Both anchorages are in 3m over sand, open to the eastern quadrant, with small sandy beaches and few houses.

Isla del Sech Bisected by 39°3'·N 2°3'·E
A low (10m) flat black rocky islet with 4·6m and 4m shoals extending 500m to the northeast, but with a 0·5 mile wide passage carrying more than 10m between it and the shore.

In 1996 five unlit buoys were laid up to 150m west and north of the island, marking the dive area used by the tourist submarine *Nemo I* (based in Puerto Portals). These were in place from February until October and are assumed to be laid annually.

Cala Portals seen from slightly south of east, with its tiny harbour (home to a bright orange speedboat) on the right. When this photograph was taken in May 1996 the *cala* was empty by summer standards.

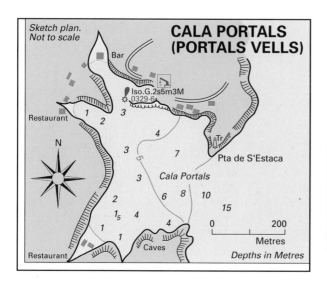

Cala Figuera, just north of the headland of that name, looking southwest. Note the fishing net supported by small pink and white floats extending from the southern shore.

⚓ Cala Portals (Portals Vells)

39°28'·5N 2°31'·5E

An attractive triple *cala* a mile north of Cabo Figuera, approached between steep-to cliffs and popular with the many tourists who visit by ferry (road access is poor). The tiny harbour (☎ 680556) is lit (Iso.G.2s5m3M, green column on white base displaying green ▲ 4m) but is shallow and can only take craft of less than 9m overall. There are water taps on the quay.

Anchor as space permits in 2–8m over sand and weed, open to east and (depending on position) either northeast or southeast, though a southerly swell may also work in. There are tombs dating back to Phoenician times cut into the caves in the southern cliffs, one of which has been turned into a small shrine (take a torch).

Several beach cafés and restaurants, some of which close for the evening after the tourists depart, overlook the bay. Parts of the beach are designated nudist areas.

⚓ Cala Figuera 39°27'·8N 2°31'·4E

A small *cala* close north of Punta de Cala Figuera. Its steep sides are wooded with few houses though development is due to take place. Anchor in 5m over sand and rock open to northeast and east.

Punta de Cala Figuera 39°27'·5N 2°31'·4E

A very prominent headland with a lighthouse (Fl(4)20s45m15M, white round tower with black diagonal stripes on building 24m) and radio masts on its steep cliffs. The light is only visible when bearing between 293° and 094° – not from within the Bahía de Palma.

Passage between Islote El Toro and Punta de sas Barbinas 39°27'·9N 2°28'·5E

A passage 200m wide and carrying 3m+ depths leads on a northwest–southeast axis between a small rock just northeast of Islote El Toro (Fl.5s31m8M, white round tower) and the double humped Islote Banco de Ibiza off Punta de sas Barbinas. This latter promontory is very low and difficult to see from a distance, which can be confusing on the approach. Best depths (4m±) are reported about two-thirds of the way from Islote Banco de Ibiza out towards the rock. (See plan page 78).

⚓ Rincón de la Fragata 39°28'·5N 2°28'·9E

An attractive but somewhat exposed anchorage close inshore at the root of the long promontory leading to Punta de sas Barbinas. The cliffs are steep-to. Anchor in 10–15m over sand and rock, open from southwest to northwest. A trip line is advisable. (See plan page 78).

Porto Adriano

39°29'·5N 2°28'·7E

Charts *Approach*
Admiralty *2832*
Spanish *970, 421, 421A*
French *7115, 7118*

Lights

Approach
0332 **Islote El Toro** 39°27'·8N 2°28'·4E
Fl.5s31m8M White round tower

Entrance
0332·5 **West breakwater** 39°29'·5N 2°28'·7E
Fl.G.3s4m1M Green column 2m
0332·6 **East mole** 39°29'·5N 2°28'·8E
Fl.R.3s2m1M Red metal post 2m

Radiobeacons

1031 **Punta de Cala Figuera** 39°27'·5N 2°31'·4E
Radiobeacon *FI*, 286·5kHz 50M (A1A)

Port Communications

Porto Adriano VHF Ch 9, 16, ☎ 102494, *Fax* 102566.

General

A large (400+ berths for yachts up to 18m) and recently completed marina beneath the holiday development of El Toro, Porto Adriano is simple to approach and enter with reasonable protection once inside, though water has been known to come over the breakwater during westerly gales. It is often very full and if possible contact should be made before arrival to check that a berth will be available. The backdrop of bare reddish cliffs, hotels and apartment buildings is somewhat barren but the marina itself quite attractive.

The diving school *Escuela Buceo* (☎ 102676, *Fax* 102701) in the marina complex covers all aspects of the sport including beginners' tuition, stocks diving equipment, and has full decompression facilities.

Approach

From northwest Round Cabo de la Mola, a high headland terminating in sheer cliffs topped by a lighthouse (Fl(1+3)12s128m12M, white column with black bands on a square white tower 10m) and Cabo Llamp (unlit). Then steer southeast across the wide mouth of Ensenada de Santa Ponsa towards Islote El Toro leaving Isla Malgrats to port. Porto Adriano will open up on rounding Punta Enguixa.

From southeast Round the very prominent Punta de Cala Figuera which has a lighthouse (Fl(4)20s45m 15M, white round tower with black diagonal stripes on building 24m) and radio masts on its steep cliffs, continuing west to leave Islote El Toro (Fl.5s31m 8M, white round tower) to starboard (or see previous page for details of the inside passage). Porto Adriano will then be visible just under 2 miles to the north, tucked well into the aptly named Cala de Peñas Rojas.

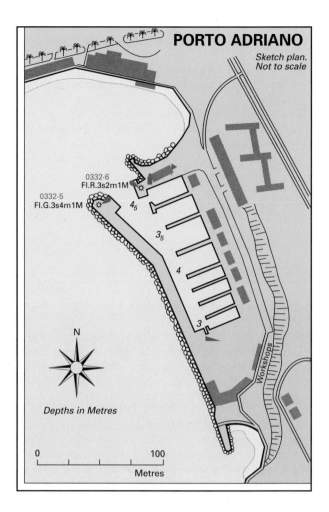

Anchorage in the approach

Anchor off the beach close north of the entrance in 3m+ over sand, open to the westerly quadrant, or see Cala de Peñas Rojas opposite.

Entrance

Entrance is straightforward, but do not cut the west breakwater too closely as stones slope downwards from its end. There is a reception pontoon at the end of the east mole, near the large brown and cream office building. There is a 2 knot speed limit in the harbour.

Berthing

Secure port side-to at the reception pontoon until a berth is allocated.

Charges *(see page 6)*

High season daily rate – Band A (15m), Band B (10m); low season daily rate – Band C (15m), Band B (10m). Water and electricity included.

Facilities

Boatyard Mar Adriano (☎ 102665) at the southern end of the harbour is able to handle all normal work.
Travel-lift 50 tonne lift in the boatyard.
Slipway In the boatyard.
Engineers At Mar Adriano (see above).

Electronic & radio repairs At Mar Adriano (see above).

Chandlery In the marina complex.

Water Water points on the pontoons and breakwater.

Showers In the marina office building.

Electricity 220v and 380v AC points on the pontoons and breakwater.

Fuel Diesel and petrol pumps at the fuel berth on the east mole (by the reception pontoon).

Ice Cube ice from bars and supermarkets.

Yacht club The Club Náutico Porto Adriano has good facilities including a large restaurant and a swimming pool.

Bank/bureau de change In the nearby holiday town of El Toro.

Shops/provisioning Small supermarket in the marina complex and another at the top of the steep hill up from the marina, but otherwise mainly tourist shops.

Hotels/restaurants/cafés etc. Restaurants and cafés overlooking the marina; hotels and more restaurants in the surrounding tourist development.

Laundrette In El Toro.

Hospital/medical services In El Toro and Palma (the latter about 8 miles by road).

Communications

Car hire/taxis Organise via the marina office.

Buses Bus service to Santa Ponsa and Palma from a stop near the top of the marina access road.

⚓ Cala de Peñas Rojas 39°29'·6N 2°28'·5E

It is possible to anchor under steep cliffs in the northwestern part of the *cala* in 5m+ over sand, open from south round to west. Watch for rocks close inshore.

⚓ Cabo Malgrats 39°30'·3N 2°27'·6E

There is a settled weather anchorage between Cabo Malgrats and Punta Negra sheltered by Isla de los Conejos. Anchor in 4–5m over rock and sand, open to south and west and to swell from northwest and southeast. The bay is surrounded by cliffs and lined with tourist developments. Although the beach is poor the area is popular with day tourist boats. In favourable conditions it is also possible to anchor south of Isla Malgrats in 10m± over rock and sand.

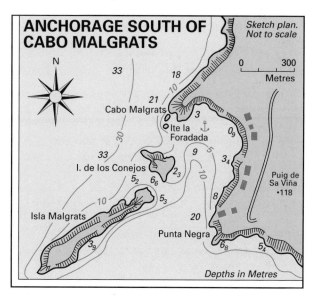

Porto Adriano looking east, with the hotels of Magaluf and the Bahía de Palma in the background.

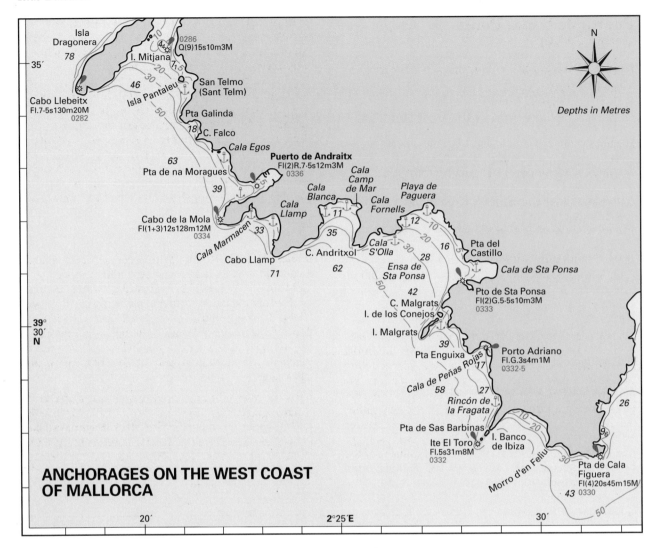

Isla Dragonera
78

−35′

Isla Mitjana
I. Mitjana
0286
Q(9)15s10m3M

San Telmo
(Sant Telm)

Cabo Llebeitx
Fl.7·5s130m20M
0282

46
Isla Pantaleu

Pta Galinda

18 C. Falco

Cala Egos

63
Pta de na Moragues

Puerto de Andraitx
Fl(2)R.7·5s12m3M
0336

Cala Camp de Mar

39

Cabo de la Mola
Fl(1+3)12s128m12M
0334

Cala Llamp

Cala Blanca

Cala Fornells

Playa de Paguera

11

33

Cala Marmacen

Cabo Llamp

C. Andritxol

Cala S'Olla

35

12 *10*

16

28

Pta del Castillo

Cala de Sta Ponsa

71

62

Ensa de Sta Ponsa

**39°
30′
N**

42

C. Malgrats
I. de los Conejos

I. Malgrats

Pto de Sta Ponsa
Fl(2)G.5·5s10m3M
0333

39

Pta Enguixa

Cala de Peñas Rojas

17

Porto Adriano
Fl.G.3s4m1M
0332·5

58

27

Rincón de la Fragata

Pta de Sas Barbinas

Ite El Toro
Fl.5s31m8M
0332

I. Banco de Ibiza

26

Morro d'en Feliu

Pta de Cala Figuera
Fl(4)20s45m15M
0330

43

50

ANCHORAGES ON THE WEST COAST OF MALLORCA

20′   *2°25′E*   *30′*

N

Depths in Metres

The long narrow Isla Malgrats, with Isla de los Conejos and Cabo Malgrats behind, seen from south-southwest. The large Ensenada de Santa Ponsa is on the left with the mountains of northern Mallorca in the distance.

Passages either side of Isla de los Conejos
39°30'·2N 2°27'·4E

Spectacular passages 100m wide exist either side of Isla de los Conejos. The southern passage has a minimum of 6m and should be taken on a northeast–southwest axis. For the northern passage, less than 5m deep, it is necessary to approach heading southeast and follow the coast of the island round to starboard at 50–60m to depart southwards, or the reciprocal. A lookout on the bow would be prudent. (See plan page 77).

Puerto de Santa Ponsa

39°30'·8N 2°28'E

Charts *Approach* *Harbour*
Admiralty *2832*
Spanish *970, 421, 421A* *3815*
French *7115, 7118* *7118*

Lights

0333 **Northwest breakwater** 39°30'·9N 2°28'E
Fl(2)G.5·5s10m3M Green column on white
base displaying green ▲ 5m
0333·2 **Punta de la Caleta** 39°30'·8N 2°28'E
Oc.R.5·2s10m3M
Red column on red base 4m

Port Communications

Club Náutico Santa Ponsa VHF Ch 9, 16, ☎ 690311,
Fax 693058.

General

On an island with many attractive harbours Santa
Ponsa (Santa Ponça) must be one of the most
picturesque in spite of the many surrounding
buildings. Long and narrow, guarded at its
northwestern end by a curved breakwater, the inlet
gives excellent protection though it can get rather
hot and airless in summer. There are 522 berths for
yachts up to 20m, but even so it is necessary to
contact the *Club Náutico* before arrival as most of the
berths are permanently occupied and there is often
no room for visitors.

Approach and entry are straightforward, but care
should be taken in strong winds from the westerly
quadrant. Space for manoeuvring larger yachts is
very restricted once inside the harbour.

The area is celebrated for the fact that the
combined fleets of Catalonia and Aragon dropped
anchor here in 1229 under the command of King
Jaime I (*Rey Jaime Conquistador*), landing an army
which eventually drove the Moors from Mallorca.

A stone cross with scenes commemorating the
event stands on Punta de la Caleta and is well worth
the short stroll for closer inspection. A *fiesta* to
celebrate the anniversary is held from 9-16
September.

Approach

From northwest Round Punta de la Mola, a high
headland terminating in sheer cliffs topped by a
lighthouse (Fl(1+3)12s128m12M, white column
with black bands on a square white tower 10m) and
Cabo Llamp (unlit). Then head east towards the
long Playa de Santa Ponsa – the tall stone memorial
to Jaime I and the breakwater below will be seen to
starboard, near the mouth of the bay, on closer
approach.

From southeast Round the very prominent Punta de
Cala Figuera which has a lighthouse (Fl(4)20s45m
15M, white round tower with black diagonal stripes
on building 24m) and radio masts on its steep cliffs,
continuing west to leave Islote El Toro (Fl.5s31m
8M, white round tower) to starboard (or see page 75
for details of the inside passage). Settle onto a

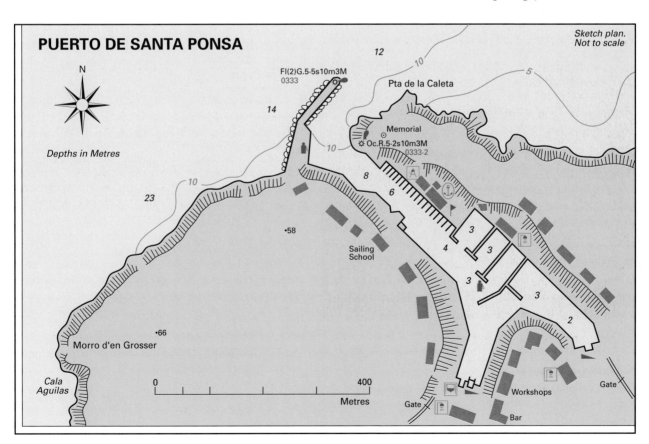

Puerto de Santa Ponsa seen from the west. The memorial to King Jaime I is clearly visible above the masts of the ketch lying alongside the breakwater.

northwest course to round Isla Malgrats (in good weather the inshore passage may be used, see page 78), then follow the coast northeast. Soon after rounding Morro d'en Grosser the tall stone memorial to Jaime I and the breakwater below will be seen to starboard.

Anchorage in the approach

See Cala de Santa Ponsa, below.

Entrance

Approach the head of the northwest breakwater on a south or southeasterly course. Enter keeping to the starboard side of the channel, ready to berth starboard-side to on the reception quay at the root of the breakwater. There is a 2 knot speed limit.

Berthing

A berth will be allocated (if available). The marina office can be contacted on VHF Ch 9, or by dialling 9 at one of the four telephone booths around the inlet (the nearest one to the reception pontoon is situated by the sailing school).

Charges *(see page 6)*

High season daily rate – Band A; low season daily rate – Band B (15m), Band A (10m). Water and electricity included.

Facilities

Boatyard At the head of the southwest arm.

Travel-lift 27 tonne lift in the boatyard.

Cranes 1·5 tonne crane at the sailing school.

Slipways Three slipways, one in each of the southern arms of the harbour and one at the sailing school.

Engineers At the boatyard and Port Fairline Santa Ponsa (☎ 690717) (official service agents for Volvo Penta).

Metalwork Metalnox SL (☎ 694011, *Fax* 695691).

Electronic & radio repairs Can be organised via the boatyard or *Club Náutico*.

Sail repairs In the block containing the *Club Náutico* and marina office.

Chandlery In the block containing the *Club Náutico* and marina office.

Water Taps on quays and pontoons.

Showers Below the *Club Náutico* and at the heads of both the southern arms.

Electricity 220v AC points on quays and pontoons. 380v AC available in the boatyard.

Fuel Pumps on the reception quay at the root of the breakwater and on one of the inner pontoons (see plan).

Ice At the fuel berth.

Yacht club The Club Náutico de Santa Ponsa (☎ 690311, *Fax* 693058) has a palatial clubhouse on the northeast side of the harbour with lounge, terrace, restaurant, bar etc.

Banks Several in Santa Ponsa.

Shops/provisioning Small supermarket near the *Club Náutico* and many shops in Santa Ponsa less than a mile away.

Hotels/restaurants/cafés etc. Many of all grades, including a restaurant at the *Club Náutico.*

Laundrette At the *Club Náutico.*

Hospital/medical services In Santa Ponsa and Palma (about 7½ miles by road).

Communications

Car hire/taxis At the marina office or in Santa Ponsa.

Buses Bus services from Santa Ponza to Palma and elsewhere.

⚓ Cala de Santa Ponsa 39°31'N 2°28'·3E

There are several good anchorages in the Cala de Santa Ponsa, a wide bay surrounded by apartments, houses and hotels. It is shallow around the sides and near the head – where there is a long but often crowded beach – with two 0·5m shoal patches (Las Secas) near the centre marked by unlit, rather inconspicuous beacons. An underwater cable runs from the southern end of the beach towards Las Secas before continuing westward.

Anchor about 200m north of Caló de Pellicer on the southern shore in 2–4m over sand, open to west and northwest, or on the north side in 4–6m over sand, open to west and southwest. Shallow draft yachts may be able to work closer in towards the head of the bay but a careful watch on the depth will be necessary.

Routine shopping requirements can be met in the tourist developments surrounding the bay, and there are many restaurants, cafés and bars. If anchored on the north side a walk out to the fortified Gothic tower and the smaller watchtower on the northern headland might be enjoyed.

CALA DE SANTA PONSA — Depths in Metres — Sketch plan. Not to scale

The wide Cala de Santa Ponsa looking east. The entrance to Puerto de Santa Ponsa is on the far right with Caló de Pellicer beyond. The Las Secas shoals are visible off the centre of the beach but the two beacons are very difficult to pick out.

⚓ Playa de Paguera 39°32'·2N 2°27'·1E

A large semi-circular bay with an excellent beach, backed by a solid mass of apartment buildings and hotels. Rocks run out some distance from the southeast side of the entrance. Anchor as space permits in 3–5m over sand, open to south and southwest. The beach gets very crowded in summer.

Playa de Paguera looking northeast. The long breaking spit on the southeast (right) side of the entrance is clearly visible. The low hooked breakwater on the left protects a shallow bathing area and should not be approached.

⚓ Cala Fornells (Puerto de Paguera) 39°32'N 2°26'·4E

An attractive anchorage, but not in any sense a port, the most sheltered part of which is occupied by moorings. Anchor as space allows in 5–10m over sand and weed, open to east and southeast plus swell from the south. A tripline is advised as there is reported to be considerable debris on the bottom. The *cala* is surrounded by wooded cliffs and a growing number of low-rise apartment buildings plus a few shops. The small sandy beach at the head of the *cala* is often crowded.

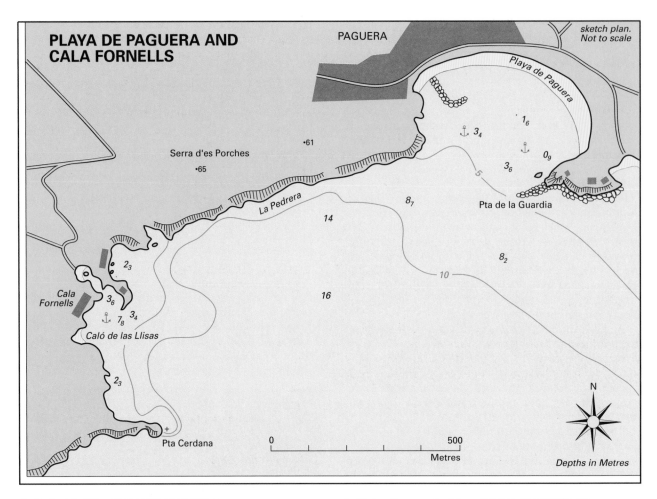

PLAYA DE PAGUERA AND CALA FORNELLS

PAGUERA

sketch plan.
Not to scale

Playa de Paguera

Serra d'es Porches
•61
•65

La Pedrera

1_6

3_4

0_9

3_6

Pta de la Guardia

8_7

14

8_2

10

16

Cala Fornells

2_3

3_6

3_4

7_8

Caló de las Llisas

2_3

+
Pta Cerdana

N

0   500
Metres

Depths in Metres

⚓ **Cala S'Olla** 39°31'·7N 2°26'E

A fascinating small *cala* between rocky cliffs, surrounded by unspoilt woodland. Approach with a lookout on the bow to anchor near the entrance in 3–5m over sand – there are several isolated rocks further in. Space is very restricted and two anchors will probably be required. Although open only to the south the *cala* would quickly become dangerous in any wind from this direction and should be vacated immediately.

⚓ **Cala Camp de Mar** 39°32'·3N 2°25'·4E

A pleasant bay which has become a popular tourist resort, partly due to a small island in its centre reached by a narrow wooden bridge and housing an outdoor bar/restaurant. There are several high-rise hotels behind the beach and more close northwest, plus a few tourist shops.

Anchor southeast of the island in 2–4m over sand and rock (shoals extend northwards from the heel of the island towards the white hotel), open to south and southwest.

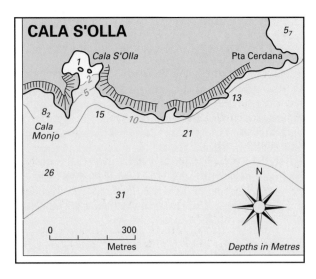

CALA S'OLLA

5_7

Cala S'Olla

Pta Cerdana

1
2
5

13

8_2

15

10

Cala Monjo

21

26

31

N

0   300
Metres

Depths in Metres

Cala Camp de Mar seen from the southwest. The shoals extending from the island towards the large white hotel left of centre can be seen quite clearly – with the least swell they would break.

⚓ **Cala Blanca** 39°32'·2N 2°24'·5E
A small *cala* with cliffed sides and a sand and stone beach, as yet undeveloped. Anchor in 2–3·5m over sand off the beach, open to east through south.

⚓ **Cala Llamp** 39°32'N 2°23'·3E
A somewhat unappealing anchorage, very open and with much development despite having no beach. Anchor close to the northeast corner in 4m over sand and stone, open south through southwest to west. (See plan page 84).

Cala Marmacen, looking north over the low neck of land leading to Cabo de la Mola. Puerto de Andraitx can be seen in the background.

⚓ **Cala Marmacen** 39°32'·2N 2°22'·7E
A spectacular anchorage surrounded by cliffs in the approach and narrow at its head. Anchor in 5m over sand and stone near the head of *cala*, open to the southern quadrant. Much new development surrounds the *cala*. (See plan page 84).

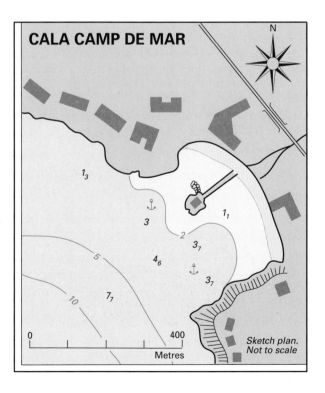

Cabo de la Mola 39°32'N 2°21'·9E
A high headland terminating in sheer cliffs topped by a rather inconspicuous lighthouse (Fl(1+3)12s 128m12M, white column with black bands on a square white tower 10m). The light is only visible when bearing between 304·4° and 158·2° and is obscured during the final approach to Puerto de Andraitx.

⚓ **Southeast of Punta del Murté**
39°32'·3N 2°22'·4E
A small anchorage under steep cliffs, suitable for use in settled southerly weather. Anchor off the beach in 3m over sand and stone, open to north and northeast. (See plan page 84).

Puerto de Andraitx
39°32'·7N 2°22'·8E

Charts	*Approach*	*Harbour*
Admiralty	*2832*	
Spanish	*970, 421*	*3814*
French	*7115, 7118*	*7118*

Lights
Approach
0334 **Cabo de la Mola** 39°32'N 2°21'·9E
Fl(1+3)12s128m12M White column, black bands, on white square tower 10m
304·4°-vis-158·2°
Entrance
0336 **Outer breakwater** 39°32'·7N 2°22'·8E
Fl(2)R.7·5s12m3M
Conical stone tower, red lantern 9m
060·1°-vis-103·9°, and inside harbour
buoy **Starboard hand buoy** 39°32'·6N 2°22'·9E
Fl(2)G.5s1M Green pillar buoy, ▲ topmark
buoy **Port hand buoy** 39°32'·7N 2°22'·9E
Fl.R.3s1M Red pillar buoy, ■ topmark
buoy **Starboard hand buoy** 39°32'·7N 2°23'E
Fl(3)G.8s1M Green pillar buoy, ▲ topmark
buoy **Port hand buoy** 39°32'·7N 2°23'E
Fl(3)R.8s1M Red pillar buoy, ■ topmark
buoy **Starboard hand buoy** 39°32'·7N 2°23'·1E
Fl(4)G.10s1M Green pillar buoy, ▲ topmark
0336·6 **North mole** 39°32'·8N 2°23'·1E
Fl(4)R.12s6m3M Red column on white hut displaying red ■ 4m
0336·8 **Inner north mole** 39°32'·8N 2°23'·2E
Fl(2+1)G.15s6m3M
Green and red column 4m
0337 **South mole** 39°32'·8N 2°23'·2E
Fl.G.2s7m3M Green column on white base displaying green ▲

Note Although the five channel buoys were in the above positions in 1996 they may be moved as necessary. The fish keeps (see photographs) are marked by one or more yellow lights (Fl.Y.4s) and several unlit reflectors, but are outside the channel.

Note Details of the light structures and characteristics on the South mole and Inner north mole appear to be confused in both BA and Spanish light lists.

Port Communications

VHF – Yacht harbour (*Andraitx Vela*) Ch 10 to avoid confusion with Puerto de Santa Ponsa.

☎/*Fax* – Port Authority ☎ 466212; Club de Vela Puerto de Andraitx ☎ 671721, 672337, *Fax* 674271.

General

A yachting and fishing harbour set in most attractive surroundings with a pleasant if slightly touristy village nearby and a larger (and much more atmospheric) town some 2½ miles inland. Inevitably a good deal of housing development is taking place around the bay, but this has not yet ruined its beauty and charm.

The harbour is easy to approach and enter and offers good protection, though strong gusts of wind can flow down from the surrounding hills. A heavy swell sets in with strong winds from southwest or west. Very occasionally the phenomenon known as *resaca* or *seiche* occurs (see page 4), particularly dangerous to yachts berthed on the quays.

In addition to the old town where there is an interesting church, a walk along the upper roads and tracks on either side of the harbour is rewarded with excellent views. *Fiestas* are held on or about 29 June, in honour of San Pedro with waterborne processions (a public holiday); 15-16 July, *Fiesta de la Virgen del Carmen*, again with waterborne processions, and the two weekends around 19-20 and 26-28 August, *S'Arracó El Santo Cristo* (also a public holiday).

Approach

From north Pass either side of Isla Dragonera (see page 88 for details of the inside passage) towards Cabo de la Mola, a high headland terminating in sheer cliffs topped by a lighthouse (Fl(1+3)12s 128m12M, white column with black bands on a square white tower 10m). The entrance to Puerto de Andraitx lies to the north of the headland and will come into view on rounding Punta de las Brescas, which has a massive housing development on its sloping face.

From southeast Cross the wide mouth of Ensenada de Santa Ponsa towards Cabo Llamp (high and pine covered) and Cabo de la Mola (see above). The entrance to Puerto de Andraitx will open on rounding the latter.

Anchorage in the approach

In northerly winds anchorage is possible in Cala Fonoy on the north side of the entrance in 2m+ over sand. In southerly winds tuck in southeast of Punta del Murté in 3m over sand and stone. These anchorages should only be used in good conditions and neither give much protection.

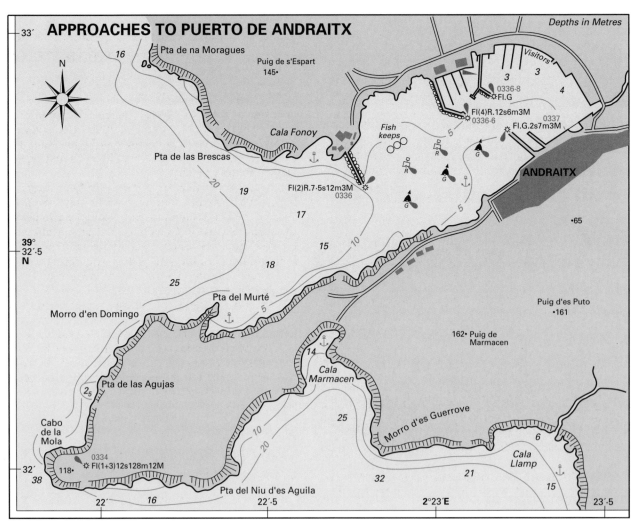

APPROACHES TO PUERTO DE ANDRAITX

The approach to Puerto de Andraitx seen from the southwest, with the abrupt cliffs of Cabo de la Mola on the right and the less obvious sloping face of Punta de las Brescas to the left.

Entrance

Approach down the centre of the bay leaving the head of the outer breakwater some 50m to port. Keep to the buoyed channel, taking care to avoid the shoal area close southwest of the south mole. There is a speed limit of 5 knots in the outer harbour decreasing to 3 knots in the inner harbour.

Berthing

If intending to stay in the yacht harbour run by the Club de Vela Puerto de Andraitx, secure to the inner side of the head of the north mole until a berth is allocated (assuming one is available – the Club de Vela has 475 berths for yachts up to 25m, but is often full). Visitors are often allocated berths on the quay in the northeast of the harbour, between the pontoons and the travel lift (which is near the end of the stone wall). Yachts lie bow or stern-to, and a mooring line is provided tailed to the quay.

Puerto de Andraitx from the southwest, with the outer breakwater on the left and the harbour laid out beyond. The five channel buoys can just be seen. The circular objects near the breakwater light are fish cages.

Alternatively the Port Authority oversees an area on the south side of the harbour, with berthing bow or stern-to along the inside of the end section of the south mole (no mooring lines, so an anchor will be needed) or on the floating pontoon just beyond it (mooring lines provided, tailed to the pontoon). About 125 Port Authority berths are available, nominally able to take yachts to 25m.

Moorings

The area between the outer breakwater and the north mole is solid with of moorings, but it is unlikely that any will be free.

Anchorage in the harbour

The most protected spot is amongst the moorings between the outer breakwater and the north mole if space can be found (a trip line will be essential), possibly moored to two anchors. Holding is reportedly very patchy.

In winds other than from the westerly quadrant it is possible to anchor southwest of the south mole in 3m+ over rock, sand and weed, taking care to avoid the shallows close in (see plan). The area is affected by wash from vessels entering and leaving the inner harbour, not least the fishing fleet who depart before dawn each morning and return in the afternoon or early evening.

Anchoring in the inner harbour is not permitted, as this could hamper the fishing boats as they leave *en masse* in the dark each morning – or even result in a yacht being run down. A few yachts may be able to tuck into the northeast corner (soft mud), but will be moved if there is any possibility of their being in the way. As of 1996 no charge was normally made for anchoring.

Formalities

The port captain's office is in the main hall of the *Club de Vela*, but he normally makes his rounds each day.

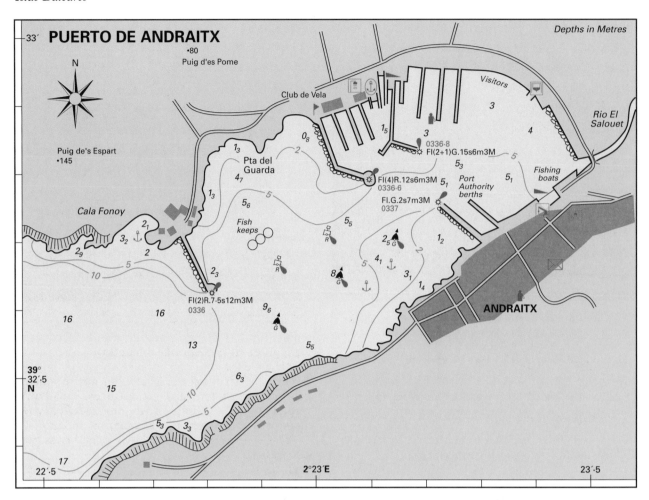

PUERTO DE ANDRAITX

Charges *(see page 6)*

- *Club de Vela Puerto de Andraitx* High season daily rate – Band B; low season daily rate – Band C. Water and electricity included. Cash only accepted.
- *Port Authority – south mole and pontoon* High season daily rate – Band D; low season daily rate – Band D. Electricity extra, water not available. Cash only accepted.

Facilities

Boatyards Repairs can be carried out at the yacht harbour – enquire at the *Club de Vela* office.

Travel-lift 50 tonne capacity lift.

Cranes 3 tonne crane in the yacht harbour.

Slipway Large slipway at the yacht harbour and another at the southeast corner of the inner harbour.

Engineers Phoenix Marine (☎ 672012, *Fax* 672966) are official service agents for Mercury/MerCruiser and Volvo Penta. Taller Nautico Toni Mas (☎ 673603, 105565, *Fax* 673603) are official service agents for Mercury/MerCruiser and Yanmar.

Electronic & radio repairs Enquire at the *Club de Vela* office.

Chandlery One at the *Club de Vela* plus a chandlery/hardware store south of the harbour.

Water On the *Club de Vela* pontoons and at the fuel berth. The quality is reported to be poor – brackish and over-chlorinated.

Showers At the *Club de Vela*, free to those staying in their marina.

Electricity 220v AC points at the *Club de Vela* and on the south mole and adjacent pontoon.

Diesel and petrol At the fuel berth on the furthest but one pontoon at the *Club de Vela*. There is a diesel pump on the fish quay but it is for fishing vessels only.

Ice From Tim's Bar close southwest of the south mole and from some supermarkets.

Yacht club The Club de Vela Puerto de Andraitx (☎ 671721, 672337, *Fax* 674271) occupies an impressive building north of the yacht harbour with lounge, bar, restaurant, swimming pool and showers.

Banks In the town south of the harbour.

Shops/provisioning Good supermarket just behind the fuel berth on the fish quay with other food shops nearby, plus many tourist shops. Two small supermarkets north of the harbour. The town of Andraitx 2½ miles inland has many more shops and a good market.

Produce/fish market Good fish market in the southeast corner of the harbour after the boats return each day. Regular Wednesday market at Andraitx, 2½ miles inland.

The inner harbour at Puerto de Andraitx seen from the southwest. The shoals extending southwest from the south mole towards the yacht anchorage show clearly.

Hotels/restaurants/cafés etc. Many around the harbour, with the southern waterfront seemingly a solid mass of cafés and restaurants.

Laundry/laundrette In the town.

Hospital/medical services In Andraitx and Palma (about 15 miles by road).

Communications

Car hire/taxis In the town or arranged through the *Club de Vela*.

Buses Frequent buses to Andraitx 2½ miles inland and several each day to Palma.

Ferries A tourist ferry makes the trip to Isla Dragonera via San Telmo.

⚓ Cala Egos 39°33'·3N 2°22'E

A small, unspoilt *cala* and beach surrounded by rocky cliffs. Anchor in 4m over sand and rocks off the beach, open to south through west.

Isla Pantaleu with the anchorage at San Telmo behind, looking slightly north of east.

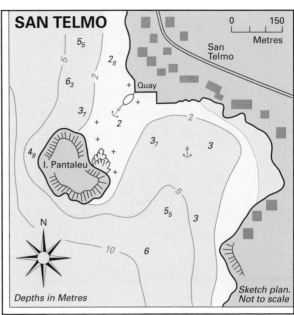

⚓ Playa de San Telmo (Sant Telm)
39°34'·7N 2°21'·1E

A pleasant bay with sandy beaches and a small, though growing, tourist resort. Isla Pantaleu (29m) 220m long by 200m wide in the mouth of the bay gives protection from the west, as does Isla Dragonera further offshore. Parts of the beach are buoyed off for swimmers.

Enter the bay from the southwest and anchor off San Telmo in 2–5m over sand, weed and clay (holding is patchy), open to southwest and with a mile or more's fetch to the northwest. The approach from the northwest is shallow, and may be obstructed by the stern anchors of tourist ferries lying bows-on at the quay as well as moored smallcraft. Several years ago plans were drawn up to construct a large yacht harbour in the bay north of Isla Pantaleu but these appear to have been dropped.

Isla Pantaleu was the first landfall of King Jaime I of Aragon on his way to liberate Mallorca from the Moors in 1229, though his troops were finally disembarked near Santa Ponsa.

Isla Dragonera and the Dragonera Passage

39°35'·3N 2°20'·5E

Charts	Approach	Passage
Admiralty	2832	
Spanish	970, 421, 427	3813
French	7115, 7118	

Lights

0282 **Cabo Llebeitx** 39°34'·5N 2°18'·3E
Fl.7·5s130m20M Masonry tower on
stone building with red roof 15m
313°-vis-150°

0284 **Cabo Tramontana** 39°36'N 2°20'·4E
Fl(2)12s67m14M Round masonry tower
on stone building with red roof 15m
095°-vis-230° and 346°-vis-027°

0286 **Isla Mitjana** 39°35'·2N 2°20'·6E
Q(9)15s10m3M West cardinal beacon 5m

General

Isla Dragonera is an island of spectacular and unique shape, being almost sheer on the northwest side and steeply sloping to the southeast. It is just over 2 miles long but only 0·6 mile wide with an old signal station and tower on Puig de Sa Popi, the pyramid-shaped 360m summit. Lighthouses (see left) mark each end of the island. There is very little ashore, but tracks link Cala Lladó to the lighthouses and the northwest coast and offer some memorable walks.

The passage between Isla Dragonera and Mallorca should present no problems to yachtsmen – the height of the surrounding hills make it appear much more alarming than it really is. The passage is funnel-shaped, opening to the south, with shoals and small rocky islets on either side of the narrows at the northern end. There are effectively two passages, either side of the 8m Isla Mitjana. The main channel is that to the west, which although wider has unmarked foul ground on both sides

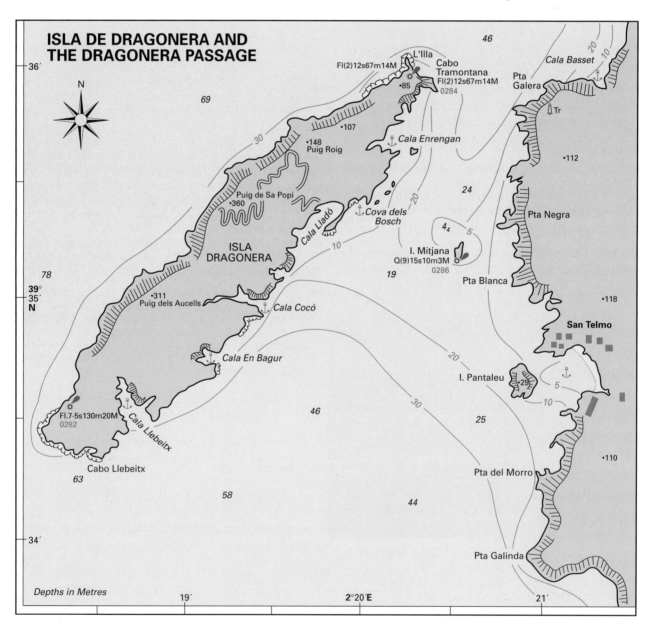

stretching some 200m from both Isla Mitjana and Isla Dragonera, leaving a passage 350m wide and 19m deep. The eastern channel, though much narrower at less than 200m, has good water (10m+) close to both Isla Mitjana and Mallorca.

Heavy gusts can descend from the high land around the passage without warning, while strong currents may flow through it in either direction after a gale, the direction dictated by the wind. Fishing nets supported by small white or pink buoys may be laid from either shore of the passage.

Approach and passages

From northeast Following the coast southwestwards from Puerto de Sóller or beyond, Isla Dragonera will be seen from afar. The Mallorcan coast is steep-to and can be followed close inshore past Punta Galera with its prominent watchtower into the north entrance to the passage. Then work 200m offshore to take the eastern passage between Isla Mitjana and Mallorca in a north–south direction, approximately down the centre. There are no further hazards once the island has been passed.

Alternatively the western passage can be used, passing equidistant between Isla Mitjana and the coast of Isla Dragonera (not the off-lying rocky islands) on a south-southwest heading.

From southeast Round Punta Galinda and then Isla Pantaleu, leaving the latter 300m to starboard. To take the eastern channel pass halfway between Isla Mitjana and the Mallorcan coast, then follow this coast past Punta Galera with its prominent watchtower into the open sea.

The western channel can be used by standing out into the centre of the passage to pass equidistant between Isla Mitjana and the coast of Isla Dragonera (not the off-lying rocky islands) on a north-northeast heading before heading northeast to round Punta Galera.

At night Transitting either passage after dark is not recommended unless the area is already familiar. It would be safer to sail the extra few miles around Cabo Llebeitx at the southwest end of Isla Dragonera.

Anchorages on Isla Dragonera

There are several possible daytime anchorages on the southeast coast of Isla Dragonera, all framed by spectacular cliffs. Without exception they are small with sand and rock bottoms, and tenable only in settled conditions. Taken from northeast to southwest they are:

⚓ **Cala Enrengan** Reasonable shelter for one yacht, open only to northeast and east. A small island lies off the southeastern promontory.

⚓ **Cova dels Bosch** A wide open, cliffed *cala*, open from east round to south and to swell from southwest. Careful eyeball pilotage is called for. There is a low, isolated rock to the east.

The central part of Isla Dragonera looking just south of west, with Cala Enrengan in the centre and the spectacular Puig de Sa Popi on the left. Part of Cala Lladó can been seen at far left.

⚓ **Cala Lladó** A narrow *cala* with a 2m rock in the centre. A stone watchtower stands on the promontory to the southeast, with a small quay (reserved for lighthouse officials and tourist ferries) opposite. Anchor in 2m+ over sand and rock, open to southeast through south to southwest.

Looking northeast into Cala Lladó. Both the watchtower and the small quay (painted with red and white chequers) show up clearly. *Photo Claire James*

⚓ **Cala Coció** Anchor close inshore under steep cliffs, open to northeast through east to southeast.

⚓ **Cala En Bagur** Again anchor close inshore under steep cliffs, open to northeast through east to southeast.

⚓ **Cala Llebeitx** Slightly larger than Cala Coció or Cala En Bagur, but still very small. Anchor under steep cliffs near the head of *cala*, open east round to south.

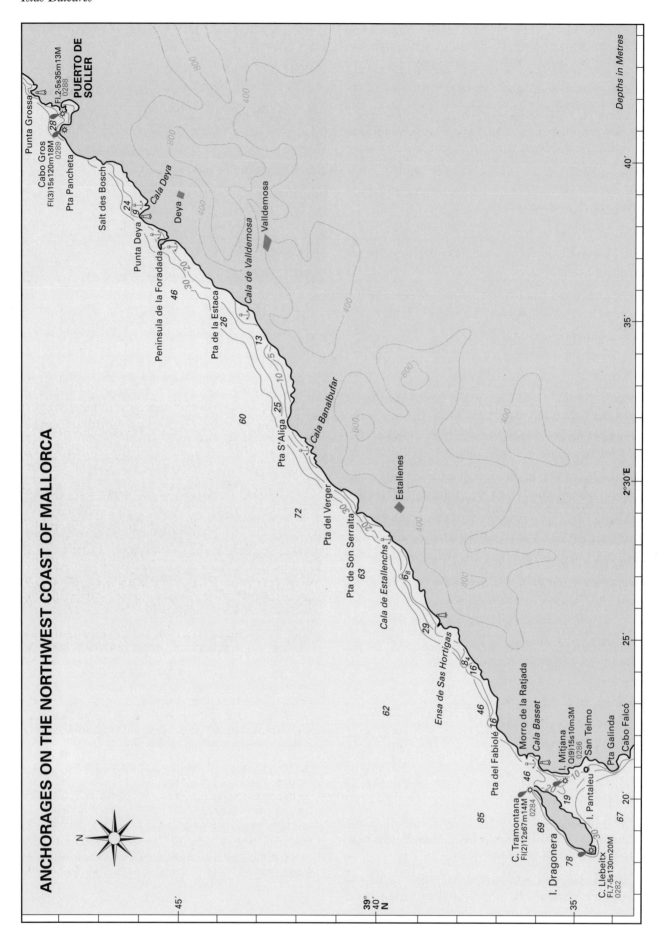

ANCHORAGES ON THE NORTHWEST COAST OF MALLORCA

Punta Grossa

PUERTO DE
SOLLER

Fl.2.5s35m13M
0288

28

Cabo Gros
Fl(3)15s120m18M
0289

Pta Pancheta

Salt des Bosch

24

Cala Deya

Punta Deya

9

Deya

Peninsula de la Foradada

46

Cala de Valldemosa

Valldemosa

Pta de la Estaca

26

30

20

13

5

Cala Banalbufar

10

25

60

Pta S'Aliga

Estallenes

Pta del Verger

72

30

Pta de Son Serralta

63

20

Cala de Estallenchs

68

62

29

Ensa de Sas Hortigas

8

16

46

16

Pta del Fabiolé

Morro de la Ratjada

Cala Basset

46

I. Mitjana
Q(9)15s10m3M
0286

San Telmo

Pta Galinda

Cabo Falcó

C. Tramontana
Fl(2)12s67m14M
0284

19

I. Pantaleu

67

20

10

30

85

69

I. Dragonera

78

C. Llebeitx
Fl.7.5s130m20M
0282

45′

39°
40′
N

35′

2°30′E

25′

40′

Depths in Metres

N

⚓ **Anchorages between Isla Mitjana and Peninsula de la Foradada**

There are four small rocky anchorages on this stretch of the northwest coast of Mallorca, only suitable for use with great care in settled conditions. The mountains and sheer cliffs which form much of the *Costa Mirador* offer spectacular scenery but also a totally unforgiving lee shore in the wrong conditions – in particular the northwesterly *tramontana* (see pages 2 and 3). The mountains and narrow valleys influence the wind in both strength and direction, and a generous offing must be allowed in these conditions.

⚓ **Cala Basset** 39°35'·9N 2°21'·3E

Close north of Punta Galera, which has a tower, small house and track to the road. Enter with a lookout forward as there are several isolated breaking rocks. Open west through north. Holding is reported to be poor.

⚓ **Cala de Estallenchs** 39°39'·7N 2°28'·3E

A very open *cala* under the village of the same name, exposed to southwest through northwest to northeast. There is a track up to the village.

⚓ **Cala Bañalbufar** 39°41'·6N 2°31'E

Another open *cala*, exposed to west through northwest to north, with a track up to the village.

⚓ **Cala de Valldemosa** 39°43'·2N 2°35'·3E

Very little shelter, but a tiny quay backed by a small village, both dwarfed by breathtaking pine-covered mountains. Worth a detour inshore if time and weather conditions permit.

Peninsula de la Foradada

39°45'·4N 2°37'·3E

Charts	Approach	Peninsula
Admiralty	2832	
Spanish	970, 427	970
French	7115	7119

General

This extraordinary L-shaped promontory 600m in length has anchorages on either side, though the most sheltered area is now full of moorings. It is possible to land in the northwest corner where there is a path up to a white house. A track inland leads to a large and conspicuous house known as Son Marroig, once owned by Archduke Luis Salvador of Austria who kept his steam yacht in the anchorage below.

West anchorage The most sheltered area, in the angle of the 'L', is now occupied by moorings – anchor as close in as these permit in 5–10m over rock and weed with a few sand patches, open (depending on

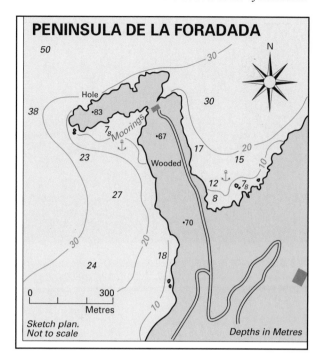

Peninsula de la Foradada seen from the southwest. The mooring bouys in the western anchorage can be seen clearly, as can the house above the anchorage and, far right, the Son Marroig estate once owned by Archduke Luis Salvador of Austria.

position) to southwest through west to northwest. Holding is generally poor. The spectacular hole through the end of the outcrop is best seen from this angle.

East anchorage This anchorage, tucked between the peninsula and the coast, is open to northwest through north to northeast. Approach from the northwest, following the coast of the peninsula, to avoid a line of breaking and submerged rocks which extend 100m or so from the mainland coast. The easternmost rock is about 100m from the anchorage. Anchor in 7–10m over rock and sand. There is a track uphill to the road.

Peninsula de la Foradada from the north. Only the size of the mountains behind – approaching 900m – makes the peninsula appear small.

⚓ **Cala Deya (Deia)** 39°45'·8N 2°38'·5E

A small, picturesque *cala* with a tiny quay at its head. Anchor near the middle in 4–6m over sand and rock, open to the northerly quadrant. There are fishermen's huts and several restaurants near the water, but little else. Deya itself, about a mile inland, is celebrated as the home of Robert Graves for many years prior to his death in 1985. It is also amongst the loveliest of Mallorca's villages and the antithesis of the Magaluf-type concrete jungle.

Puerto de Sóller

39°47'·8N 2°41'·6E

Charts	*Approach*	*Harbour*
Admiralty	*2832*	
Spanish	*970, 426, 427*	*4271*
French	*7115*	*7119*

Lights

Approach
0289 **Cabo Gros** 39°47'·9N 2°41'E
  Fl(3)15s120m18M White tower and house, red roof 22m 054°-vis-232°

Entrance
0288 **Punta de Sa Creu** 39°47'·9N 2°41'·4E
  Fl.2·5s35m13M White conical tower, three black bands 13m 088°-vis-160°

Leading lights on 126·5°
0290 *Front* 39°47'·6N 2°41'·9E Q.R.49m4M
  Aluminium ▲ on white round tower 7m
0290·1 *Rear*, 36m from front, Iso.R.4s60m4M
  Aluminium ▲ on white round tower 7m
0291 **West naval mole** 39°47'·8N 2°41'·6E
  F.R.7m3M Red post 5m
0292 **Northwest naval mole** 39°47'·9N 2°41'·7E
  F.R.6m3M Red post 5m
0293·2 **Commercial mole, head** 39°47'·9N 2°41'·8E
  F.R.6m3M Red post 5m
0293 **Commercial mole, elbow** 39°47'·9N 2°41'·7E
  F.G.6m3M Green post 5m

Port Communications
Port Authority ☎ 631699; Club Náutico de Sóller
☎ 631326.

General

A beautiful, almost circular bay lying in the midst of spectacular mountainous scenery, Puerto de Sóller is a naval, commercial and fishing harbour. The approach and entrance present no problems in normal conditions, but could become difficult and perhaps dangerous in a gale from the northwest, north or northeast. However it is the only harbour of refuge on the whole 50 mile stretch of the rugged, inhospitable northwest coast of Mallorca, although there are a number of fair weather anchorages.

Facilities for yachtsmen are somewhat limited and it is often difficult to find a vacant space on the commercial mole. There are some shops in the village but many more in the town of Sóller some 2 miles inland. Tourist development and many visitors have begun to detract from this beautiful area, but perhaps not as much as in some other places. In 1996 considerable building work was in evidence, but much of it appeared to have come to a halt unfinished.

The attractive old rural town of Sóller – the name comes from the Arabic *Sulliar* meaning 'golden valley' – was set well back from the sea as a first defence against pirate raids. It was long known for its oranges and lemons which were exported in the famous *balancelles* – small single-masted vessels. Even with the loss of that trade to Valencia the orange groves surrounding the little town remain. Sóller is linked to its port by a vintage tramway, an excursion highly recommended, as is a trip on the Victorian train which connects Sóller to Palma. Sóller claims, along with numerous other places in the western Mediterranean, to have been the birthplace of Christopher Columbus.

The *fiesta* and pageant of *Nuestra Señora de la Victoria* is held on the second Sunday in May to commemorate a victory over Moorish pirates in 1561; 15-16 July sees the *Fiesta de la Virgen del Carmen* with a waterborne procession; 25 July a *fiesta* in honour of Santiago (St James), and 24 August a *fiesta* in honour of San Bartolomé.

Approach

From northeast From Cabo Formentor, which can be recognised by its lighthouse (Fl(4)20s210m21M, white tower and house 22m), the coast is of high rocky cliffs, very rugged and broken. Careful pilotage is necessary because many of the headlands are similar. The following may be recognised: Cala de San Vicente, which has a tourist development at its head, Punta Beca with a long beak-like extension, and Morro de la Vaca, looking like the head of a cow from some directions. In the last 3 miles two conspicuous watchtowers and the small Islote S'Illa will be seen and, in the close approach, the two lighthouses at the harbour entrance. Puig Mayor

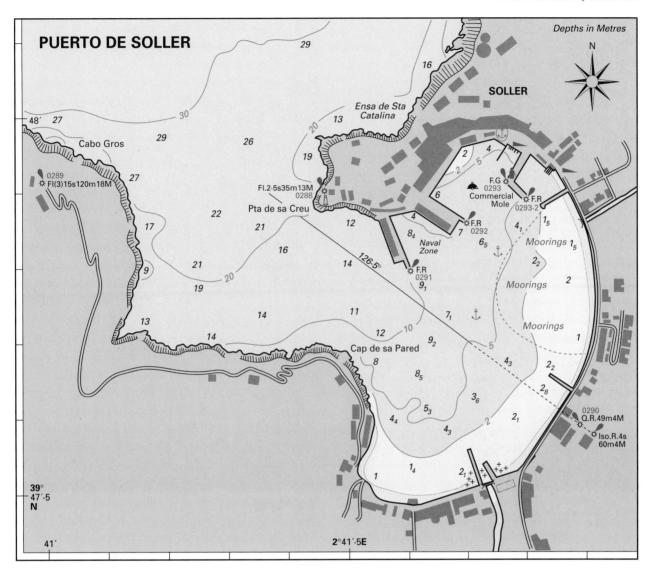

(1445m), the highest point on Mallorca with radio towers (F.R.) and two radomes on its summit, is just under 5 miles east of the entrance.

From southwest From Isla Dragonera, a large, high and conspicuous island with two lighthouses (Fl.7·5s130m20M and Fl(2)12s67m14M), the coast is very high with broken rocky cliffs backed by mountains inland. The unmistakable Peninsula de la Foradada (see page 91) will be seen if coasting close inshore, with Cabo Gros and its white lighthouse 3·8 miles beyond. Punta de Sa Creu on the east side of the entrance is considerably lower and will not open until Cabo Gros has been rounded.

Entrance

Enter on a southerly course between Cabo Gros and Punta de sa Creu, swinging southeast and then east to remain near the centre of the channel. There is a 4 knot speed limit. Keep well clear of the two naval moles if looking for a berth on the commerical mole. There is a large unlit buoy between the northwest naval mole and the north pontoon (see plan).

During the approach it may be possible to identify and use the two leading marks which are located south of the small, isolated, stone pier (see plan). They lie above the north end of a long, red-roofed white building with arches but are inconspicuous by day. The prominent red and white banded column some way up the slope to the rear is not a leading mark.

Entrance at night should not present problems in reasonable weather – follow the leading lights into the anchorage as detailed below.

Berthing

Secure stern-to on the head of the commercial mole or near the end of the pontoon to the northwest – if space permits. Only twenty or so berths are available for yachts of up to 15m, the remaining space being occupied by ferries, fishing boats and resident smallcraft. Prepare to lay two anchors in 5m over mud and sand, at least 40m from the quayside. Holding is patchy and it is essential to ensure that both anchors are well dug in. Trip lines are advised.

Both moles on the northwest side of the harbour are in the naval zone and should not be approached.

The semi-circular bay of Puerto de Sóller looking southeast. The lighthouses on Punta de Sa Creu and Cabo Gros both show up clearly, as does Sóller town in its inland basin (though it cannot be seen from sea level).

Anchorage

Anchor as space permits in 5–10m over mud and sand. Moorings extend to the 5m line, but appear too light for all but the smallest yachts. In summer the anchorage may become very full.

Formalities

The Port Captain's office is at the rear of the *lonja* (fish market) at the north end of the harbour, below the Sa Llotja des Peix restaurant.

Charges *(see page 6)*

High season daily rate – Band D; low season daily rate – Band D. Water and electricity extra. Cash only accepted.

Facilities

Boatyard No boatyard, but local craftsmen are available and should be able to carry out minor work.

Crane 1 tonne crane near the slipway.

Slipways Three small slipways either side of the commercial mole, one of which has a cradle. However there is no more than 2m depth at its foot.

Engineers Available, if more accustomed to fishing boats.

Chandlery Small chandlery/fishing tackle/hardware shop up the hill behind the commercial mole.

The quays and anchorage at Puerto de Sóller looking east. The large buoy mentioned under *Entrance* can be seen near the yacht manoeuvring off the commercial quay, which is largely occupied by ferries.

Water Water taps on the commercial mole, but only operational for a few hours each day (currently 0900–1100 weekdays). Also from a public water fountain up the hill behind the commercial mole. Reports regarding quality vary – taste before filling tanks.

Electricity 220v and 375v AC points on the commercial mole.

Fuel Diesel and petrol from pumps at the angle of the commercial mole.

Ice From the fishermen's quay, bars and supermarkets.

Yacht club There is a small *Club Náutico*.

Banks In the village and at Sóller town.

Shops/provisioning Shops and supermarkets in the village around the harbour, with a much greater selection in the town 2 miles inland.

Produce/fish market Market every morning except Sunday in Sóller town.

Hotels/restaurants/cafés etc. A growing number of hotels and many restaurants, bars and cafés.

Laundrette In the village.

Hospital/medical services In Sóller town.

Communications

Car hire/taxis In Sóller town.

Buses Bus service to Sóller and elsewhere.

Trams An elderly tram takes about 20 minutes to cover the 2 miles between Puerto de Sóller and Sóller town.

Trains Rail link from Sóller town to Palma by Victorian train (1 hour).

Ferries Tourist ferries to several of the *calas* along the coast to the northeast.

⚓ **Ensenada Sa Costera** 39°49'·8N 2°45'E

A wide, deep bay reported to be a pleasant anchorage in settled conditions. Rocks line the shore but the water is usually very clear – approach carefully with a bow lookout to anchor in 12–15m in the southwest corner, open to north and northeast. Puig Mayor (1445m), the highest point on Mallorca with radio towers (F.R.) and two radomes on its summit, lies just over 2 miles inland.

Looking directly into Cala Tuent from the northwest, with the dominating presence of Puig Mayor beyond.

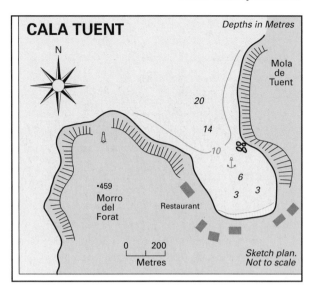

⚓ **Cala Tuent** 39°50'·6N 2°46'·4E

A small *cala* with a wide sand and stone beach, amidst spectacular surroundings 4·8 miles northeast of Puerto de Sóller. Morro de Forat close southwest has a ruined watchtower and off-lying rocks. Anchor in 5–10m over sand and rock, open to northwest and north. There are a few houses and a restaurant on the slopes overlooking the *cala* and a very winding road.

⚓ **Cala de la Calobra (Torrente de Pareis)** 39°51'·4N 2°48'·1E

A large and spectacular *cala* with several arms and a slit in the high rocky cliffs behind through which the Torrente de Pareis (more often a gentle stream) enters the sea. Anchor in 5–10m over sand and stones open to northwest and north. Tourist ferries land their passengers near the hotel overlooking the southwest beach and should not be impeded.

The Torrente de Pareis is considered one of the sights of Mallorca and is a popular destination by road and sea, resulting in the usual restaurants and beach cafés. A tunnel through the rock links the two beaches.

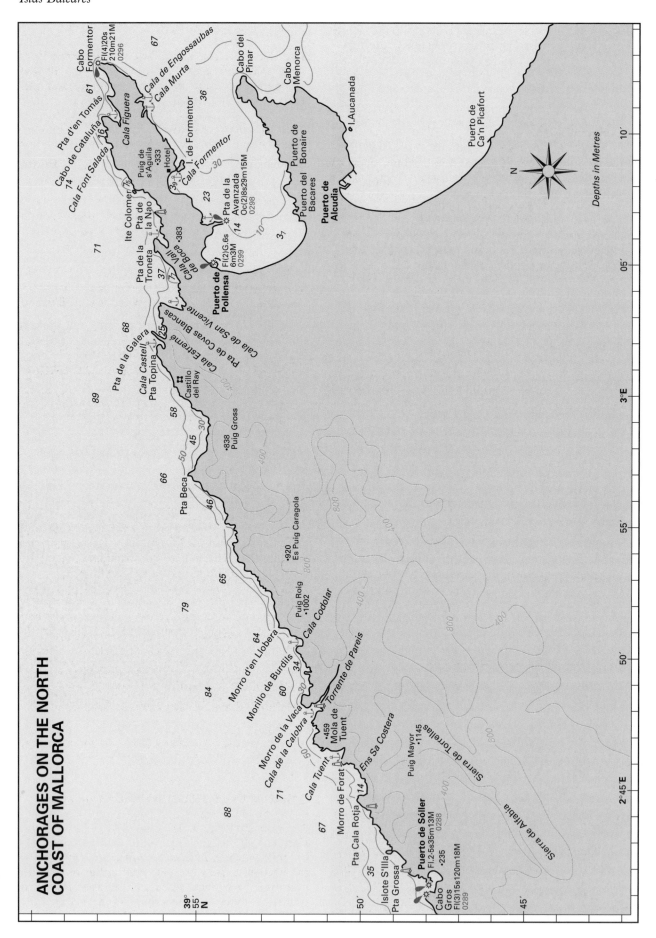

Cala de la Calobra from the northwest. The gorge of the Torrente de Pareis is just left of centre, the southwestern arm with its hotel and houses on the right.

⚓ Cala Codolar 39°51'·8N 2°50'·6E

A small *cala* surrounded by high cliffs close east of Morillo de Burdils. Anchor in 5m over sand and rock open to the northerly quadrant. There is a track up to the road but little else.

⚓ Cala Castell 39°56'N 3°02'·1E

A narrow *cala* open to the northeast, separated from Cala Estreme by Punta de la Galera, a narrow rocky peninsula. Punta Topina close west is a distinctive wedge shape when seen from the northeast. Anchor in 5m over rock in the centre of the *cala* or in 3m over sand near the beach. Rocks line the eastern side. There is a small building behind the beach at the head of the *cala*, and a road leading inland.

⚓ Cala Estremé 39°56'N 3°02'·5E

Close east of Punta de la Galera and less sheltered than its neighbour Cala Castell. Anchor over rock and sand near the small beach, open to northeast and east.

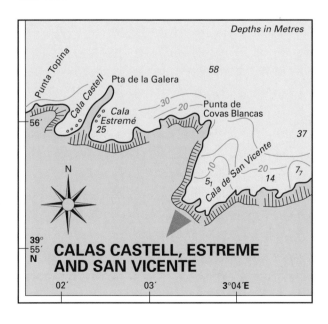

⚓ Cala de San Vicente 39°55'·4N 3°03'·6E

A large *cala* backed by holiday developments. At its head there are two sandy beaches separated by a rocky point with a hole in it, fringed by hotels and apartments plus the usual cafés and restaurants. Anchor off either beach in 5m over sand, open to north and northeast and to swell from northwest. There is a very small stone quay in the southwest corner of the western *cala*. A *fiesta* in honour of *La Virgen del Mar* is held on the first Sunday in July.

⚓ Cala Vall de Boca 39°55'·8N 3°05'·9E

A narrow *cala* with a small stony beach between high rocky cliffs. Anchor in 5m± over rock, open to north and northeast. There is a track to Puerto de Pollensa.

⚓ Cala Figuera 39°57'·2N 3°10'·7E

A large deserted *cala* 1·6 miles west of Cabo Formentor, surrounded by rocky hills and cliffs and with a small stone and sand beach at its head. Anchor in 5m over sand and rock, open to north and northeast. There is a rough road leading up from the beach but little else.

This is one of no less than three *Cala Figueras* around the coast of Mallorca, the others being at the southwest end of the Bahía de Palma and on the southeast coast near Punta de las Salinas.

Cala Figuera, just west of Cabo Formentor, seen from the northeast. The craggy Puig Fumat (334m) rises to the left of the *cala*, with more distant views over the saddle towards Pollensa.

⚓ Cala de Engossaubas (Cala En Gossalba) 39°56'·5N 3°11'·4E

A very beautiful *cala*, 1·7 miles southwest of Cabo Formentor, reasonably wide and completely unspoilt between high steep cliffs. Anchor close to the head in 2·5m over sand, or further out in 6m over weed and rock, open to southeast round to southwest though an easterly or even northeasterly swell may work in. Track up to the road.

97

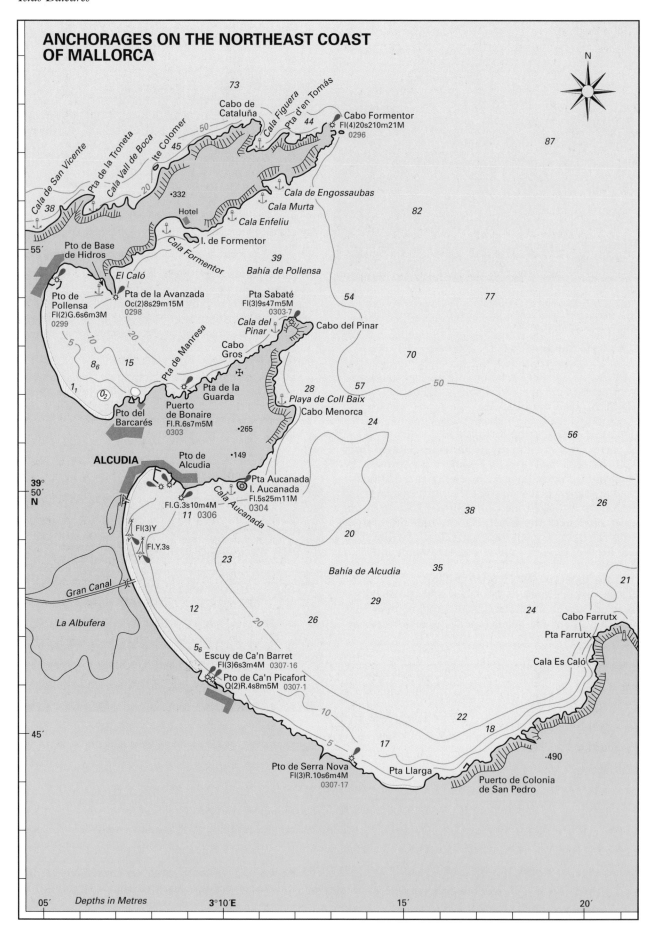

ANCHORAGES ON THE NORTHEAST COAST
OF MALLORCA

73

Cabo de
Cataluña

Cala Figuera

Pta d'en Tomás

44

Cabo Formentor
Fl(4)20s210m21M
0296

87

N

Cala de San Vicente

Pta de la Troneta

Cala Vall de Boca

Pte Colomer

50

45

82

•332

Cala de Engossaubas

Cala Murta

Cala 38

Hotel

Cala Enfeliu

I. de Formentor

Cala Formentor

55´

Pto de Base
de Hidros

El Caló

39

Bahía de Pollensa

54

77

Pto de
Pollensa
Fl(2)G.6s6m3M
0299

Pta de la Avanzada
Oc(2)8s29m15M
0298

Pta Sabaté
Fl(3)9s47m5M
0303·7

Cala del
Pinar

Cabo del Pinar

5

10

20

Pta de Manresa

Cabo
Gros

70

8₆

15

28

57

50

1₁

0₂

Pta de la
Guarda

Playa de Coll Baix

Cabo Menorca

24

56

Pto del
Barcarés

Puerto
de Bonaire
Fl.R.6s7m5M
0303

•265

•149

ALCUDIA

Pto de
Alcudia

Pta Aucanada
I. Aucanada
Fl.5s25m11M
0304

38

26

39°
50´
N

Fl.G.3s10m4M
11   0306

Cala Aucanada

20

Fl(3)Y

Fl.Y.3s

23

Bahía de Alcudia

35

21

Gran Canal

12

26

29

24

Cabo Farrutx

La Albufera

Pta Farrutx

5₆

Escuy de Ca'n Barret
Fl(3)6s3m4M   0307·16

Cala Es Caló

Pto de Ca'n Picafort
Q(2)R.4s8m5M   0307·1

20

10

22

18

45´

5

17

Pto de Serra Nova
Fl(3)R.10s6m4M
0307·17

Pta Llarga

•490

Puerto de Colonia
de San Pedro

05´   *Depths in Metres*   3°10´E   15´   20´

⚓ **Cala Murta** 39°56'·4N 3°11'E

Another pleasant, unspoilt small *cala* with rocky sides (37m) and a stony beach. There is a small castle-like rock at entrance and very clear water. Anchor in 3–5m over sand, open to east through south and possibly northeasterly swell. There is a single house ashore.

⚓ **Cala Enfeliu** 39°55'·8N 3°09'·9E

A tiny *cala* with rocky sides and a small stony beach. Enter with care to anchor in 3–5m over rock and sand, open to northeast through southeast to southwest.

⚓ **Cala Formentor (Cala Pi)** 39°55'·6N 3°08'·4E

A very popular semi-open anchorage northwest of Isla de Formentor (34m). Anchor anywhere in the bay in 3–6m in sand patches among weed – holding is very poor in the latter. The best shelter is close northwest of Isla de Formentor, off the landing stage of the large and elegant Hotel Formentor, open to south and southwest, though strong gusts from the northern quadrant may blow over the narrow peninsula. If anchored further westwards, exposure to southeast wind and swell increases. The narrow passage inside Isla Formentor carries a scant 1m.

The beaches are popular with day tourists, with speedboats, jetskis and water-skiers weaving amongst the anchored yachts. Some areas may be buoyed off for bathers. As a contrast to the five star hotel there are various beach bars and restaurants. The small jetties and quays in the northwest corner are privately owned.

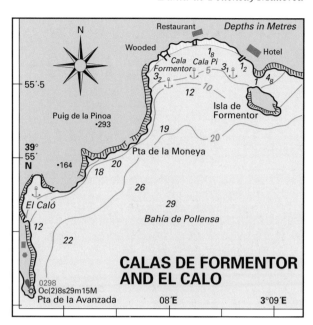

Cala Formentor looking north, with the world famous Hotel Formentor on the right.

⚓ **El Caló** 39°54'·7N 3°06'·7E

A small *cala* close east of the root of Punta de la Avanzada. Anchor in 5m± over sand, open to east through south and to northeasterly swell.

⚓ **Behind Punta de la Avanzada**
39°54'·3N 3°06'·4E

A well sheltered anchorage close west of Punta de la Avanzada (Oc(2)8s29m15M, octagonal stone tower on building 18m) and only a mile east of Puerto de Pollensa. Anchor in 3m+ over sand and weed (but allow for the fact that the bottom is uneven), open only to the south with a short westward fetch across the bay. Northeasterly swell does not appear to work around the headland, but there is considerable daytime disturbance from speedboats and jetskis and seaplanes may practice manoeuvres further out. Unfortunately the old castle on the promontory, known as La Fortaleza, is privately owned and explorations ashore may risk prosecution for trespass.

Puerto de Base de Hidros (Seaplane Base)
39°54'·5N 03°6'·1E

This small and very shallow harbour belongs to the Spanish Navy and is a busy seaplane base. For obvious reasons it does not welcome yachts.

Puerto de Pollensa

39°54'·2N 3°05'·2E

Charts   *Approach*   *Harbour*
Admiralty   *2831*
Spanish   *965, 425, 426*   *3842*
French   *7116*   *7119*

Lights

Approach

0296 **Cabo Formentor** 39°57'·7N 3°12'·8E
   Fl(4)20s210m21M
   White tower and house 22m 085°-vis-006°

0303·7 **Punta Sabaté (Cabo del Pinar)**
   39°53'·6N 3°11'·8E Fl(3)9s47m5M
   White triangular tower, black band 12m

0298 **Punta de la Avanzada** 39°54'·1N 3°06'·7E
   Oc(2)8s29m15M Octagonal stone tower on
   building 18m 238°-vis-276°

Entrance

0299 **Northeast breakwater, head**
   39°54'·2N 3°05'·2E Fl.G.3s6m3M
   Green truncated conical tower 5m

0299·5 **Northeast breakwater, elbow**
   39°54'·3N 3°05'·3E
   Fl.Y.5s3m2M Yellow post 2m
   (Reported in 1996 to be Fl(2)R.4s)

0299·7 **Southwest mole** 39°54'·2N 3°05'·2E
   Fl.R.2s2m2M Squat red column 1m

0300 **Fuel berth, south head**
   39°54'·2N 3°05'·2E
   Fl(2)R.7s2m2M Squat red column 1m
   Synchronised with 0300·2

0300·2 **Fuel berth, north head**
   39°54'·3N 3°05'·2E
   Fl(2)R.7s2m2M Squat red column 1m
   Synchronised with 0300

0301 **Yacht club spur** 39°54'·3N 3°05'·1E
   Fl(2)G.6s5m3M
   Green truncated conical tower 4m

Port Communications

VHF – Real Club Náutico de Pollensa VHF Ch 9.
☎/*Fax* – Port Authority ☎ 864635 *Fax* 864636; Real
   Club Náutico de Pollensa ☎ 864635; *Fax* 864636.

General

A good sized yacht and fishing harbour (420 berths)
which was extended a few years ago and where two
new Port Authority pontoons were being installed in
1996, Puerto de Pollensa is at the head of a beautiful
wide bay surrounded by spectacular mountains.
The approach and harbour are both somewhat
shallow, but should present no problems other than
in strong winds with an easterly component. The
bay is open to the sea from northeast through east to
southeast, and with heavy winds or swell from these
directions the head of the bay is best avoided. The
anchorage behind Punta de Avanzada (see page 99)
provides a sheltered alternative, though during gales
from the northern quadrant violent gusts may be
experienced without warning.

Puerto de Pollensa from the southeast. An area adjoining the
south mole is enclosed in order to install two new pontoons,
almost certainly accounting for the discolouration of the water.

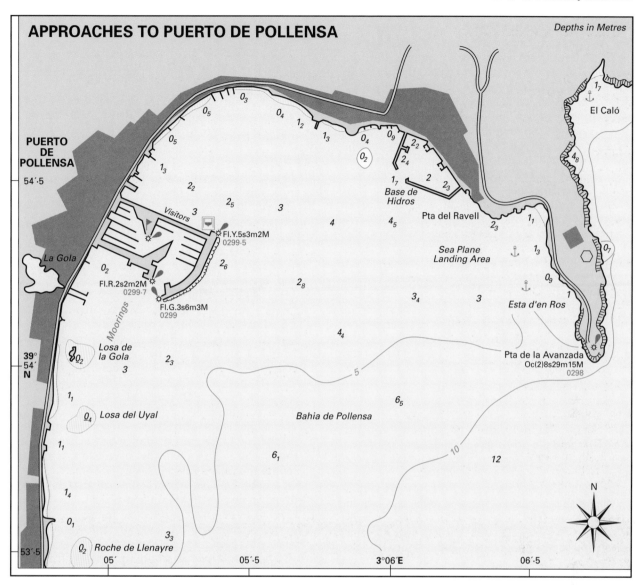

APPROACHES TO PUERTO DE POLLENSA

Depths in Metres

PUERTO DE POLLENSA

La Gola

Visitors

Fl.Y.5s3m2M 0299·5

Fl.R.2s2m2M 0299·7

Fl.G.3s6m3M 0299

Moorings

Losa de la Gola

Losa del Uyal

Roche de Llenayre

Base de Hidros

Pta del Ravell

Sea Plane Landing Area

Esta d'en Ros

Pta de la Avanzada Oc(2)8s29m15M 0298

Bahia de Pollensa

El Caló

N

The area around Puerto de Pollensa is mainly tuned to the needs of package tourists, though broader shopping requirements can also be met. However Pollensa town – built, like Sóller, some distance inland from its harbour – is much more attractive with good shops and some interesting old buildings. Its name comes from the Latin 'Pollentia' meaning powerful, though it is now agreed that the famous Roman Pollentia was actually sited near Alcudia.

There are good walks around the harbour, particularly among the hills to the north with some dramatic views over the north coast of Mallorca. Two recommended hikes are across the Peninsula de Formentera to Cala de San Vicente and further northeast to Cala Vall de Boca.

Fiestas are held on 17 January (San Antonio) and 20 January (San Sebastian) with the usual processions; on Good Friday; in mid July, with the week-long *Fiesta de la Virgen del Carmen*; and on 2 August in honour of *Nuestra Señora de los Angeles*, incorporating a mock battle between Moors and Christians.

Approach

From south Cross the wide Bahía de Alcudia towards Cabo del Pinar and Punta Sabaté – conspicuous, with high rocky cliffs (Fl(3)9s47m5M, white triangular tower, black band 12m). Cabo de Formentor will be seen beyond. Round Punta Negra onto a westerly course towards Punta de la Avanzada (Oc(2)8s29m15M, octagonal stone tower on building 18m), after which Puerto de Pollensa will open up.

From north Round the almost vertical rocky cliffs of Cabo de Formentor (Fl(4)20s210m21M, white tower and house 22m), then follow the coast southwest past the lower Punta de la Avanzada. Puerto de Pollensa will be seen once past this headland.

Note There is considerable seaplane activity in the Bahía de Pollensa associated with the naval harbour behind Punta de la Avanzada. It hardly needs saying that both seaplanes and their tenders should be given a generous berth at all times.

Anchorage in the approach

See Anchorage behind Punta de la Avanzada, page 99. Alternatively anchor in the bay northeast of the harbour in 2–3m over sand and weed (though some patches carry less than 2m – a careful watch on the depth is necessary while manoeuvring), open to east and southeast with a limited fetch. Holding is good once the anchor has dug in.

Less protection can be had south of the harbour towards the two training walls (see plan) in 2m+ over sand, mud and weed open to southeast and south. There are some moorings in this area, and in 1996 the wreck of a 15m yacht was reported as covered by a scant 1m.

In strong southeasterlies best shelter will be found close west of Puerto de Bonaire, some 3½ miles across the bay, in 4–6m over sand.

Entrance

Approach the head of the northeast breakwater from east or southeast, leaving it 30–40m to starboard on entry. There are shoals close southwest of the entrance (see plan). The fuel berth at the end of the southwest mole doubles as reception quay. There is a 4 knot speed limit.

Berthing

The *Club Náutico* visitors' berths are on the OUTSIDE of the north quay, exposed to northeast and east. Mooring lines are provided, tailed to the quay.

Inside the harbour there is a Port Authority quay on the north side of the southwest mole, and visitors may also use the outer section of the nearby pontoon (see plan). All the berths have mooring lines provided, and water and electricity are available.

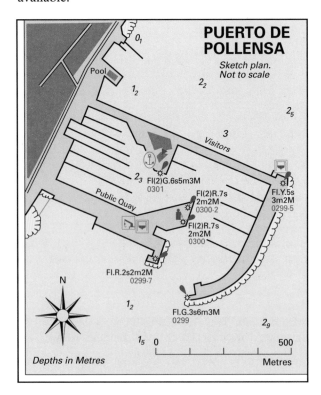

PUERTO DE POLLENSA

Sketch plan. Not to scale

Pool

3 Visitors

Fl(2)G.6s5m3M
0301

Public Quay

Fl(2)R.7s
2m2M
0300·2

Fl.Y.5s
3m2M
0299·5

Fl(2)R.7s
2m2M
0300

Fl.R.2s2m2M
0299·7

N

Fl.G.3s6m3M
0299

0   500

Depths in Metres   Metres

Charges *(see page 6)*

- *Real Club Náutico de Pollensa* High season daily rate – Band B; low season daily rate – Band B (15m), Band C (10m). Water and electricity included.
- *Port Authority quay* High season daily rate – Band D; low season daily rate – Band D. Water and electricity extra.

Facilities

Boatyards Astilleros Cabanellas on the southwest mole can handle all normal work.

Travel-lift 50 tonne lift at the northeast breakwater elbow.

Cranes 1 tonne crane on the northeast breakwater and 4 tonne crane at the boatyard.

Slipways Small slipway in the interior of the harbour and larger one, with cradle able to take vessels to 21m, at the boatyard.

Engineers At the boatyard. Motonautica Bonaire (☎ 530462, 892301, *Fax* 530466) are official service agents for Mercury/MerCruiser, Sole Diesel, Tohatsu, Volvo Penta and Yamaha.

Sailmaking & repairs Wilson Yachts (☎ 864067, *Fax* 864059); Plana Velámenes (☎/*Fax* 866061).

Chandleries Náutica Brúixola SL (☎ 531193, *Fax* 534818) and others.

Water Water points on quays and pontoons. The drinking fountain/tap behind the beach north of the harbour (between the two palm trees) is reported to supply particularly good water.

Showers At the *Club Náutico* (free to visitors using their berths, otherwise a small fee). A shower block is to be built for those on the public quay.

Electricity 220v AC points on all quays and pontoons, plus some 380v points.

Fuel Diesel and petrol pumps on the head of the southwest mole.

Ice At the fuel berth, the *Réal Club Náutico* bar and a shop opposite the harbour.

Yacht club The Club Náutico de Puerto de Pollensa (☎ 86463, *Fax* 864636) has a smart, modern clubhouse on the northeast breakwater with lounge, terrace, bar, restaurant, swimming pool and showers.

Banks In Puerto de Pollensa and Pollensa town.

Shops/provisioning Two supermarkets and other specialist food shops able to supply all normal requirements.

Produce market Open air market on Wednesday morning in Puerto de Pollensa and Sunday in Pollensa town.

Hotels/restaurants/cafés etc. Many – Pollensa is a popular tourist resort. Restaurant and bar at the *Club Náutico*.

Laundrette Near the harbour.

Hospital/medical services In Puerto de Pollensa and Pollensa town 3 miles inland.

Communications

Car hire/taxis In Puerto de Pollensa and Pollensa town.

Buses Frequent service to Pollensa town, several times daily to Palma.

Puerto del Barcarés

39°51'·85N 03°07'·2E

General

Puerto del Barcarés, ☎ 531867, is a tiny harbour limited to small fishing boats and yachts drawing less than 1m and in no way a port, though in the right conditions it would be possible to anchor off and visit by dinghy. The single light (Q.G.6m3M, green column on white base displaying green ▲ 5m) did not appear to be functioning in May 1996. There are no facilities other than a water tap on the quay.

Approach

Punta del Barcarés lies near the southwest corner of the Bahía de Pollensa, west of Punta de Manresa and some 3 miles southeast of Puerto de Pollensa. There are shoals in the approach, including the 1½m Losa del Barcarés 400m northeast of the entrance and an unnamed breaking patch southeast of Islote del Bacarés (itself only a low rocky ledge).

Anchorage in the approach

Anchor north of Islote del Bacarés in 2–5m over sand and weed, open to west through north to northeast.

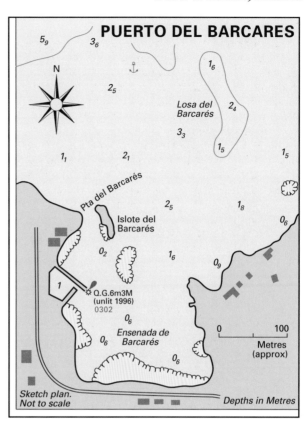

Entrance and berthing

Swing wide of the unnamed shoal mentioned above to round the north mole at slow speed. The entrance itself is no more than 6m wide and 1m deep. Secure in a vacant berth, ready to move if necessary. There is a dinghy slipway opposite the entrance.

Puerto de Bonaire

39°52'·1N 03°08'·7E

Charts

	Approach
Admiralty	2831
Spanish	965, 425, 426, 3841
French	7116

Lights

Approach

0296 **Cabo Formentor** 39°57'·7N 3°12'·8E
Fl(4)20s210m21M
White tower and house 22m 085°-vis-006°

0303·7 **Punta Sabaté (Cabo del Pinar)**
39°53'·6N 3°11'·8E Fl(3)9s47m5M
White triangular tower, black band 12m

Entrance

0303 **North breakwater** 39°52'·1N 3°08'·7E
Fl.R.6s.7m5M Red column on white base 4m

0303·2 **West mole** 39°52'·1N 3°08'·7E
Fl(2)G.12s5m5M
Green column on white base 4m

Port Communications

Marina de Bonaire VHF CH 9, ☎ 546955, *Fax* 548564.

The minature Puerto del Barcarés from the northeast. Islote del Barcarés lies in the right foreground with disturbed water marking the shoal to its southeast.

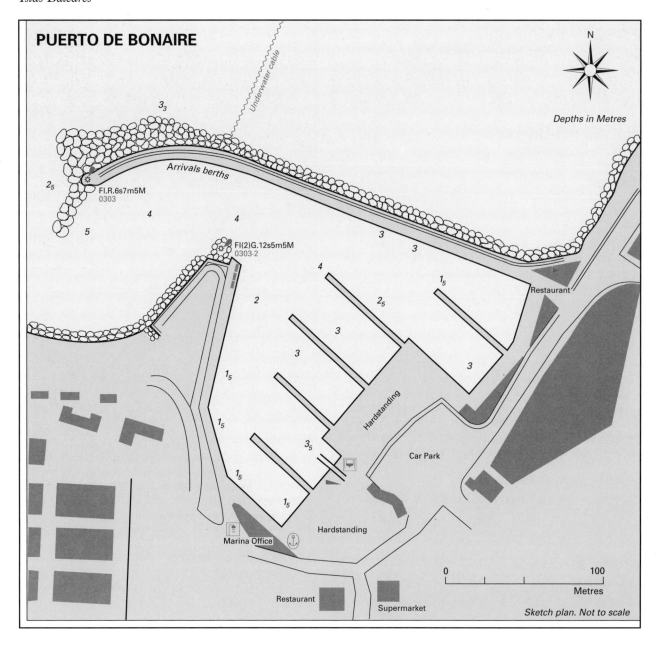

PUERTO DE BONAIRE

N

Depths in Metres

3₃

Underwater cable

Arrivals berths

2₅

Fl.R.6s7m5M
0303

4

4

3

3

5

4

Fl(2)G.12s5m5M
0303·2

4

1₅

Restaurant

2

2₅

3

3

3

1₅

Hardstanding

1₅

Car Park

3₅

Marina Office

1₅

Hardstanding

1₅

Restaurant

Supermarket

0   100
Metres

Sketch plan. Not to scale

General

Formerly known as Port del Cocodrilo, Puerto de Bonaire is an attractive, purpose-built yacht harbour amongst pleasantly wooded surroundings, believed to be on the site of one of the original Phoenician landing places – a small enclosed bay ½ mile east of Punta de Manresa. There are excellent walks in the area and good views from Punta de Manresa, while the old Roman city of Alcudia is just over a mile away.

The harbour is simple to approach and enter and offers excellent shelter, particularly since the north breakwater was extended in 1996 to form a hook. Construction was begun back in 1973, but lack of finance held up progress and the harbour was not completed until the 1980s. Most of the 324 berths for yachts up to 17m are permanently occupied. Unlike many similar harbours in the Islas Baleares there is no commercial or fishing usage.

Approach

From south Cross the wide Bahía de Alcudia towards Cabo del Pinar and Punta Sabaté – conspicuous, with high rocky cliffs (Fl(3)9s47m5M, white triangular tower, black band 12m). Round Punta Negra to follow the south coast of the Bahía de Pollensa past Cabo Gros and Punta de la Guarda. Puerto de Bonaire lies 0·5 mile further west.

From north Round the almost vertical rocky cliffs of Cabo de Formentor (Fl(4)20s210m21M, white tower and house 22m), then steer southwest towards Punta de Manresa, a low, dark rocky point surmounted by a castle. Puerto de Bonaire lies 0·5 mile east of this headland.

Anchorage in the approach

Anchor in the bay west of the harbour entrance in 5m± over sand, open to the northern quadrant.

Puerto de Bonaire looking east. As can be seen the north breakwater has been extended well beyond its light, but otherwise approach and entry are straightforward.

Entrance

The entrance is relatively narrow with a distinct dog-leg. Approach on a southerly course, slowly closing the coast west of the north breakwater until the west mole comes into view. Then swing east and northeast to remain in the centre of the channel. If entering at night (quite feasible in settled conditions) note that the light on the north breakwater is, at the time of writing, some distance from the end of the rubble breakwater. A bow lookout with a strong torch is recommended. The reception quay is to port immediately inside the entrance.

Berthing

Berth at the reception quay until directed elsewhere by marina staff, preferably having already called on VHF Ch 9.

Charges *(see page 6)*

High season daily rate – Band C; low season daily rate – Band B (15m), Band C (10m). Water and electricity included. Cash only accepted.

Facilities

Boatyards Workshops near the marina office. Motonautica Bonaire ☎ 530462, *Fax* 530466.

Travel-lift 30 tonne lift in the south part of the harbour.

Slipway Next to the travel-lift.

Engineers Engineering workshop near the marina office and Motonautica Bonaire (see above).

Electronic & radio repairs Enquire at the marina office.

Chandlery Next to the marina office.

Water Taps on quays and pontoons.

Showers Near the marina office.

Electricity 220v AC points on quays and pontoons.

Fuel No fuel available in 1996. The nearest pumps are at Puerto de Pollensa, about 3½ miles across the bay.

Ice From the bar/restaurant at the root of the north breakwater.

Banks In Alcudia.

Shops/provisioning Small supermarket just south of the harbour (opposite a restaurant) and many shops in Alcudia a mile southwest.

Restaurants/cafés etc. Bar/restaurant at the root of the north breakwater and another south of the harbour. Others in the vicinity.

Laundrette By the shower block.

Hospital/medical services In Alcudia.

Communications

Car hire/taxis From Alcudia. Enquire at the marina office.

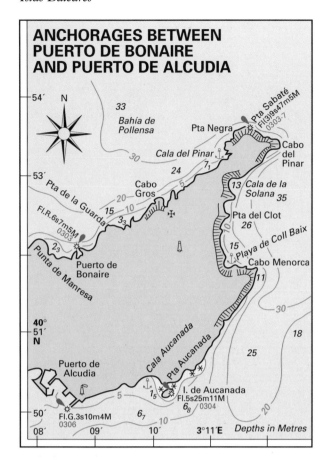

ANCHORAGES BETWEEN PUERTO DE BONAIRE AND PUERTO DE ALCUDIA

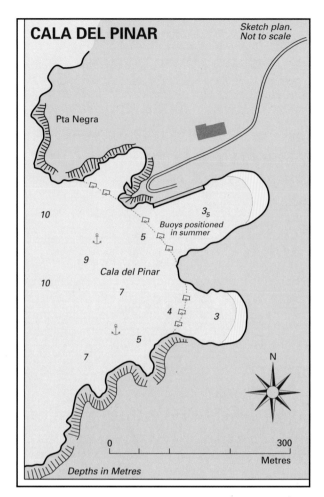

CALA DEL PINAR

Sketch plan. Not to scale

⚓ Cala del Pinar (Ses Caletas)
39°53'·3N 03°11'·3E

An anchorage behind Punta Negra consisting of a double *cala* plus a smaller one to the north. Unfortunately Cabo del Pinar is a military area with landing in the *calas* forbidden and access sometimes restricted by buoys. Anchor in 5–7m (less if it is possible to enter the *calas*) over sand and weed, open to southwest through west to north. Holding is patchy. It is a popular place for day visitors from Pollensa and can become crowded.

⚓ Playa de Coll Baix 39°51'·9N 03°11'·4E

An open anchorage beneath dramatic cliffs off a small sand and stone beach. Anchor in 5m over rock, sand and stones, open to north through northeast to east and to swell from the southeast. There is a track to the road but nothing else.

⚓ Cala Aucanada 39°50'·3N 03°09'·9E

A wide but shallow bay 600m west-northwest of Isla Aucanada (Fl.5s25m11M, white tower and house 15m). The surrounding land is generally flat – quite a contrast if coming from the north.

Approach from the south or southwest to anchor in 1·5m+ over sand, open to the southern quadrant. The beach close northwest of the island is fringed by reefs and the narrow passage between the island and Punta Aucanada very shallow. There is a road down to the point and a few houses.

Playa de Coll Baix, looking westward from near Cabo Menorca.
Photo Claire James

Puerto de Alcudia

39°50'·3N 03°08'·2E

Charts

	Approach	Harbour
Admiralty	2831	2831
Spanish	965, 425, 426, 3841, 3843	3845
French	7116	7119

Lights

Approach

0304 Isla Aucanada 39°50'·2N 3°10'·3E
Fl.5s25m11M White tower and house 15m
F.R. on chimney 4M west-southwest

Commercial harbour

0306 Southeast (commercial) breakwater
39°50'N 3°08'·5E Fl.G.3s10m4M
Green column on white base displaying green ▲ 5m
buoy **Port hand buoy** 39°50'N 3°08'·3E
Fl(2+1)R.12s5M Red pillar buoy, ■ topmark
Note A STARBOARD HAND buoy if entering the
marina (Work in progress 1996)
0306·5 North quay, southeast corner
39°50'·1N 3°08'·4E Fl(2)R.7s4m2M
Red pyramidal tower 3m

Note In 1996 a number of Fl.Y. buoys marked work in
progress in the commercial harbour.

Marina and fishing harbour

0306·6 Southwest (marina) breakwater
39°50'·3N 3°08'·2E
Fl.R.3s5m3M Red pyramidal tower 4m
0307 North mole 39°50'·4N 3°08'·2E
Fl(2)G.7s4m3M Green pyramidal tower 3m

Note At night the outer approach to the marina
currently lies between two RED lights. Unlit buoys
may also lie in the approach.

Port Communications

VHF – Pilots (*Alcudia Prácticos*) Ch 11, 13, 14, 16;
Marina (*Alcúdiamar*) Ch 9.
☎/*Fax* – Pilots ☎ 890180, ☎/*Fax* 890179; Port
Authority ☎ 545076; Alcúdiamar ☎ 546000-4,
Fax 548920.

General

Alcúdiamar, a large, well-equipped but rather
shallow marina able to accommodate over 700
yachts of up to 25m, lies northwest of a small
commerical port handling cargo ships and ferries
(where harbour works were in progress in 1996)
with a small naval zone sandwiched between the
two. The marina is easy to approach and enter
and well sheltered once inside, though public
access to the many restaurants and cafés on the
west breakwater mean that security is virtually nil.
It shares its area with an old fishing harbour but

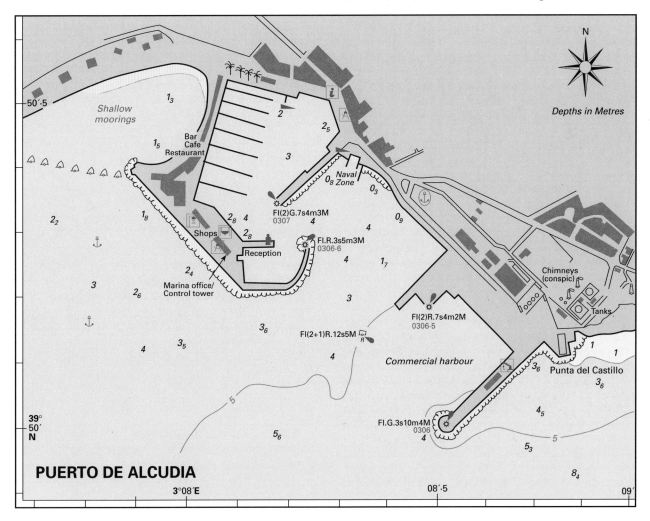

Alcúdiamar marina from a little east of south. The commercial harbour is out of the picture to the right. In the background lies the Bahía de Pollensa with the Peninsula de Formentor on the skyline.

this is no longer busy. The Bahía de Alcudia is a popular tourist area, doubtless largely due to its good beaches which are crowded during the holiday season.

Both the port and the old town a mile inland date back to Phoenician times, the latter a typical settlement site on a hilly peninsula served by two harbours on opposite sides of the isthmus. In due course the Romans took it over, calling the area Pollentia (powerful) and making it the capital of the island, however the Vandals occupied the town after the fall of Rome and destroyed most of the Roman buildings. Little evidence is left of the Moorish occupation except the name, *Al Kudia*, which means 'the hill'. After the Christian re-conquest walls were built around the town, and sections of these can still be seen together with the remains of the Roman theatre. In addition to the theatre (on the road between the harbour and the town), St Martin's cave, the castle and the museum are worth visiting.

For those who are interested in birds the Albufera Nature Reserve behind the beach to the southwest is a most important site. Follow the coast road south for about 3 miles, cross the Gran Canal and the entrance to the park is clearly labelled. There is an entry fee, but bird hides etc. are provided.

Fiestas are held on 29 June, in honour of San Pedro with land and sea processions, on 2 July the *Romería a la Virgen de la Victòria* includes a pilgrimage to the Santuari de la Victòria on a peak 3 miles away, and on 25 July a *fiesta* in honour of Santiago (St James), the patron saint of the town, includes a parade on horseback.

Approach

From south The high headland of Cabo de Pera (Fl(2+3)20s76m16M, white tower on white building with dark corners and red roof 21m) and the even higher (272m) Cabo del Freu, which has a long low rocky projection at its foot, are both unmistakeable. Follow the coast northwest towards Cabo Farrutx, passing the islet of Farayó de Aubarca (23m high and about 750m offshore) *en route*. There is good water on either side of the island.

On rounding Cabo Farrutx (unlit, though there are red lights on Puig Tudosa 1·5 miles to the south) the Bahía de Alcudia opens up, with Puerto de Alcudia in the northwest corner. Pass OUTSIDE Isla Aucanada (Fl.5s25m11M, white tower and house 15m) and leave the head of the southeast breakwater at least 50m to starboard. The two tall chimneys near the root of the breakwater are conspicuous.

From north Cross the Bahía de Pollensa and round first the steep reddish-cliffed Cabo del Pinar and then the even higher, but not so prominent, Cabo Menorca. Follow the coast (now becoming low and flat) at 500m to pass OUTSIDE Isla Aucanada and proceed as above.

Note The approach and entrance to the yacht harbour are relatively shallow and can be dangerous in heavy seas from east and southeast. The area is silting up and charted depths should not be relied upon.

Submarines occasionally exercise in the Bahía de Alcudia and its approaches. Commercial ships may be anchored south of the harbour.

Anchorage in the approach

Anchor southwest of the marina in 2–4m over sand and weed, open to southeast and south, keeping well clear of the entrance.

Entrance

By day Leave the head of the southeast (commercial) breakwater a good 50m to starboard and keep well clear of any harbour works still in progress. (In 1996 the end of the central quay was being demolished and the quay along the shore widened). Approach the head of the southwest (marina) breakwater on a northerly course, leaving it 20–30m to port.

A line of either green or yellow buoys are claimed to mark the entrance channel but were not in place in 1996. Depths in the entrance are no more than 3m. There is a 3 knot speed limit.

By night Note that the outer approach to the marina lies between two RED lights – the Port hand buoy (Fl(2+1)R.5M) and Southwest (marina) breakwater (Fl.R.3s5m3M) detailed on page 107.

Berthing

There is a reception area on the south side of the fuelling quay, but it is preferable to contact the marina office on VHF Ch 9 before arrival so that a permanent berth can be allocated. Anchoring is not allowed inside the yacht harbour.

Charges *(see page 6)*

High season daily rate – Band B; low season daily rate – Band A. Water and electricity included.

Facilities

Boatyards Construcciones Navales Benassar SA (☎/*Fax* 546700) and Astilleros Domingo Marti CB (☎ 548415). Some jobs are also handled by Náutica Mahon (☎ 546750, *Fax* 546754).
Travel-lift 80 tonne lift on southwest breakwater.
Crane 8 tonne mobile crane.
Slipway Small slipway in shallow (0·7m) water on the north side of the yacht harbour.
Engineers Náutica Mahon (see above) and Motonáutica Alcudia (☎ 546130) who are official service agents for MerCruiser, Tohatsu, Volvo Penta, Yanmar. Both in the marina complex.
Electronic & radio repairs Náutica Mahon (see above) and others.
Sailmaker Plana Velámenes (☎/*Fax* 866061).
Rigging Yacht-Rigger, (☎ 908 435975).
Chandleries Enmartor (☎ 548415), EMO's Ship-Shop (☎/*Fax* 547110) and others.
Water Water taps on quays and pontoons, and at the fuelling berth.
Showers On the southwest breakwater.
Electricity 220v AC at all berths plus 380v AC at berths over 14m.
Fuel Diesel and petrol pumps on the inner arm of the southwest breakwater.

Bottled gas Calor Gas cylinders can be refilled at the gas bottling plant in Alcudia town.
Ice From the fuel berth.
Yacht club The Club Amigos de Alcudia has bar, restaurant and showers.
Banks In Puerto de Alcudia and Alcudia town.
Shops/provisioning Small supermarket on the southwest breakwater, many more in Puerto de Alcudia and Alcudia town.
Produce market Sunday and Tuesday mornings in Alcudia town.
Hotels/restaurants/cafés etc. Many hotels lining the bay, and nearly as many restaurants and cafés lining the marina.
Laundry In the marina.
Hospital/medical services Medical services via marina office, hospital in Alcudia town.

Communications

Car hire/taxis In both Puerto de Alcudia and Alcudia town. Taxi rank at root of southwest breakwater.
Buses Bus service to Alcudia town, Palma and elsewhere.
Ferries Regular service to Ciudadela in Menorca and Port Vendres in France.

Puerto de Ca'n Picafort

39°46'·1N 3°09'·6E

Charts	*Approach*
Admiralty	*2831*
Spanish	*965, 425, 426, 3841, 3843*
French	*7116*

Lights

Approach

0307·16 **Escuy de Ca'n Barret** 39°46'·2N 3°09'·5E
  Fl(3)6s3m4M East cardinal post on wide yellow base, ♦ topmark
  Note Reported to be Fl(3)10·5s in 1996

Entrance

0307·1 **East breakwater** 39°46'·1N 3°09'·6E
  Q(2)R.4s8m5M Red metal column 4m
0307·15 **West mole** 39°46'·1N 3°09'·5E
  Fl(2)G.6·5s5m5M Green metal column 4m

Beacons

Seventeen pairs of tall day-marks, about 1000m apart and numbered from north to south, were erected along the coast from a point just south of the Gran Canal to northeast of Colonia de San Pedro. Though some pairs are now missing the remaining beacons are still useful navigationally.

Beacon Nos 1 and 2 mark an area of obstructions 1·5 miles northwest of the harbour. Beacon No 4 (which is white with a red top, but does not display its number) is located just west of the entrance to C'an Picafort. Some of the remaining beacons are white, others natural stone.

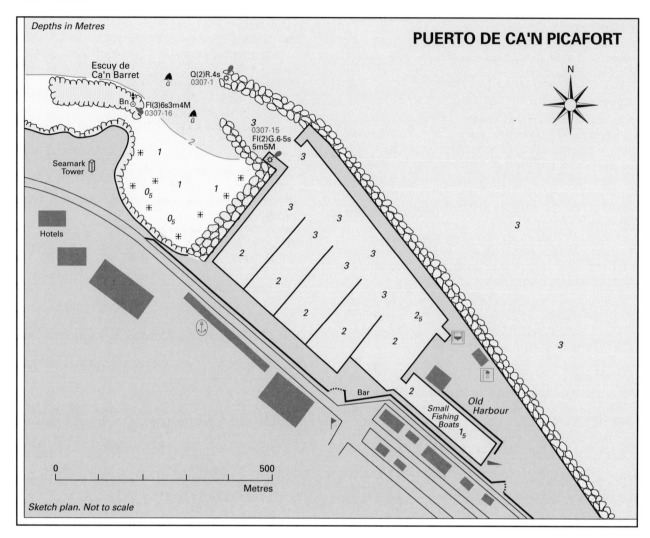

PUERTO DE CA'N PICAFORT

Depths in Metres

Escuy de Ca'n Barret

Q(2)R.4s 0307·1

Bn Fl(3)6s3m4M 0307·16

3 0307·15 Fl(2)G.6·5s 5m5M

Seamark Tower

Hotels

Bar

Small Fishing Boats

Old Harbour

0 — 500 Metres

Sketch plan. Not to scale

Port Communications

Harbour Authority ☎/*Fax* 850010; Club Náutico C'an Picafort ☎/*Fax* 850185.

General

C'an Picafort is a fairly small yacht harbour able to take 464 boats up to 12m, built onto a small, old fishing harbour. Approach is straightforward, but entrance would be dangerous with even moderate seas from the eastern quadrant due to shoaling water and its proximity to the shore. The harbour is backed by a popular tourist resort of fairly recent origin, the first hotel having been built in 1933 when building controls were lifted. The excellent beaches on either side of the harbour become crowded in the season.

The name 'Picafort' is from the Spanish 'hew strongly', presumably referring to the cutting of stone from nearby quarries, though the Necropolis de Son Real (a Bronze Age cemetery dating back to 700 BC) is only ten minutes' walk along the shore to the southeast. The *fiesta* of *Mare de Deu d'Agost* is held on 15 August each year.

Approach

For outer approaches see Puerto de Alcudia, page 108.

From south Round the high (432m) Cabo Farrutx on to a course just south of west – Puerto de C'an Picafort lies 9 miles away, near the southern end of the hotels which line much of the Bahía de Alcudia. There is a day-mark (see Beacons, page 109) close to the harbour entrance but it may be lost against the high-rise buildings behind.

From north After rounding Cabo Menorca head south-southwest across the Bahía de Alcudia – Puerto de C'an Picafort lies 6 miles away, identified as above.

Anchorage in the approach

The bottom is rocky near the harbour. Anchor in 5m over sand, 700m from the shore and some 1000m northwest of the harbour with the two No 3 beacons in line, open to northeast and east. Sound carefully.

Entrance

A dangerous breaking reef, Escuy de Ca'n Barret, marked by an east cardinal beacon (Fl(3)6s3m4M, BYB post on wide yellow base, ♦ topmark) lies 300m west-northwest of the entrance.

Approach the head of the northeast breakwater on a southerly course at slow speed, watching the depth-sounder. In 1996 two green buoys indicated the west side of the channel – in some years red buoys have also been laid. Round the breakwater at about 20m and turn sharply to port to line up for the centre of the entrance, where at least 3m should be found. The west mole now has a right-angled extension, but the light has not been moved. In any case, entrance after dark is not recommended.

Berthing

Secure to the inner side of the northeast breakwater until a berth can be allocated. The harbour office will be found near the root of the west mole. High season charges Bands C or D.

Facilities

Boatyards Basic boatyard services near the travel-lift.
Travel-hoist 20 tonne lift beside the old harbour.
Cranes 8 tonne mobile crane.

Slipway Small slipway with 1½m at the head of the old harbour.
Water Taps on quays and pontoons. Check quality before filling tanks.
Showers Shower block near the travel-lift.
Electricity 220v AC points on quays and pontoons, 380v on hardstanding.
Fuel No fuel pumps as of 1996. A service station a mile to the southwest may be able to deliver by tanker lorry.
Ice Available from bars and the *Club Náutico*.
Yacht club The Club Náutico de Ca'n Picafort (☎/*Fax* 850185) has a lounge and bar.
Banks In the town.
Shops/provisioning Many shops and supermarkets in the town. Market on Tuesday afternoons in Calle Cervantes.
Hotels/restaurants/cafés etc. Many hotels, restaurants and cafés in the town. Outdoor bar near the old harbour.
Laundry In the town.
Hospital/medical services Doctor in the town, otherwise in Alcudia.

Communications

Car hire/taxis In the town.
Buses Bus service to Alcudia, Palma and elsewhere.

Puerto de C'an Picafort looking just east of south. The Escuy de Ca'n Barret reef and beacon show clearly, with No 4 day-mark to the right. A small speedboat is entering the harbour.

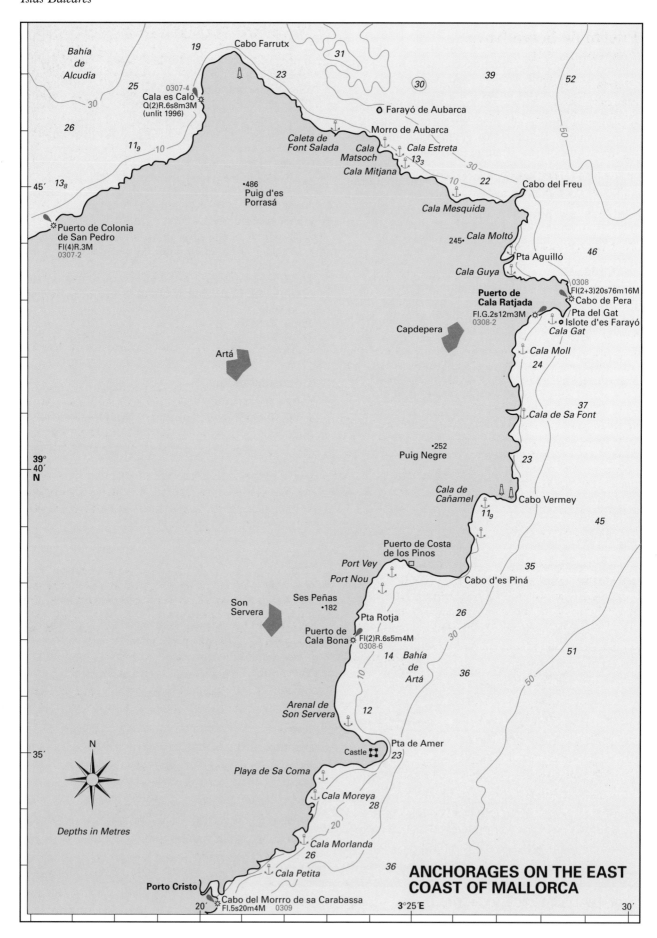

Bahía de Alcudia

19 Cabo Farrutx

31

25

30

26

30

11₉ 10

0307·4
Cala es Caló
Q(2)R.6s8m3M
(unlit 1996)

39

52

○ Farayó de Aubarca

50

Morro de Aubarca

Caleta de Font Salada

Cala Matsoch *Cala Estreta* 13₃

Cala Mitjana

30 22

10

Cabo del Freu

45′ 13₈

Puerto de Colonia de San Pedro
Fl(4)R.3M
0307·2

•486
Puig d'es Porrasá

Cala Mesquida

245• *Cala Moltó*

46

Pta Aguilló

Cala Guya

0308
Fl(2+3)20s76m16M
Cabo de Pera

Puerto de Cala Ratjada
Fl.G.2s12m3M
0308·2

Capdepera

Pta del Gat
○ Islote d'es Farayó
Cala Gat

Artá

Cala Moll

24

37

Cala de Sa Font

•252
Puig Negre

23

39°
40′
N

Cala de Cañamel

11₉

Cabo Vermey

45

Puerto de Costa de los Pinos

Port Vey

35

Port Nou

Cabo d'es Piná

Son Servera

Ses Peñas
•182

26

Pta Rotja

Puerto de Cala Bona
Fl(2)R.6s5m4M
0308·6

30

14 *Bahía de Artá*

36

51

60

Arenal de Son Servera

12

10

35′

N

Pta de Amer

Castle 23

Playa de Sa Coma

Cala Moreya

28

20

Depths in Metres

Cala Morlanda

26

36

Cala Petita

Porto Cristo

20′ Cabo del Morrro de sa Carabassa
Fl.5s20m4M 0309

3°25′E

ANCHORAGES ON THE EAST COAST OF MALLORCA

30′

Puerto de Serra Nova

39°44'·5N 3°13'·5E

Charts *Approach*

Admiralty *2831*
Spanish *965, 425, 426, 3841, 3843, 3844*
French *7116*

Lights

0307·17 **Northeast breakwater** 39°44'·4N 3°13'·5E
  Fl(3)R.10s6m4M Red column 2m
0307·19 **West mole** 39°44'·4N 3°13'·4E
  Fl(4)G.12s3m3M Green column 2m

Port Communications

Club Náutico Serra Nova, ☎ 850630 or 294100, where
  harbour officials may (with luck) be found.

General

Puerto de Serra Nova is another tiny harbour which
hardly rates 'port' status. It was built as the first
stage of a large yacht harbour to complement the
'urbanisation' of Son Serra Nova, but both harbour
and development have ground to a halt and as of
1996 there appeared to be little prospect of further
expansion. Currently the harbour and surroundings
are bleak and facilities very limited.

Approach is straightforward but would be
dangerous with heavy seas from the northern
quadrant. Entrance is limited to small vessels no
more than 9m in length and drawing less than 2m.

Approach

For outer approaches see Puerto de Alcudia, page
108.

From south Round the high (432m) Cabo Farrutx
and follow the coast westwards at 500m past
Colonia de San Pedro. Puerto de Serra Nova lies 3
miles beyond, at the northern end of an area of
scattered houses backed by pine forest.

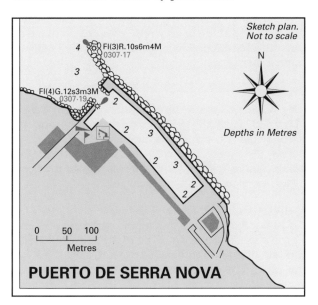

PUERTO DE SERRA NOVA

Puerto de Serra Nova from north-northwest. The very narrow
entrance shows clearly. Had the original plans ever been
completed the harbour would have extended over at least ten
times this area.

From north After passing Cabo Menorca head south
across the Bahía de Alcudia to close the coast close
northwest of the harbour, which lies at the northern
end of an area of scattered houses backed by pine
forest. The surrounding countryside is generally flat.

Anchorage in the approach

Anchor in 5m over sand about 400m from the shore
north of the harbour entrance, open to northwest
through north to northeast.

Entrance

Approach the head of the northwest breakwater at
slow speed on a southwesterly course. The entrance,
which lies a short distance beyond, is narrow – 10m
or less – and room to manoeuvre once inside very
restricted. In bad weather the entrance can be
closed by a metal barrier.

Berthing

Secure in a vacant slot as available and await
allocation of a berth. The harbour shoals towards its
head.

Facilities

Crane 3 tonne crane at the *Club Náutico*
Slipway At the *Club Náutico*.
Water Water taps around the harbour.
Electricity 220v AC points around the harbour.
Fuel No fuel available.
Yacht club The Club Náutico Serra Nova has a small
  clubhouse with bar near the west mole.
Shops/provisioning The nearest shops are in the
  village of Son Serra 1¼ miles inland.
Hotels/restaurants/cafés etc. Bar at the *Club Náutico*
  and a café or two in the 'urbanisation'. No hotels
  or restaurants nearby.

Communications
Car hire/taxis Taxi from C'an Picafort by telephone.
Buses Bus service along the main road a mile inland.

Puerto de Colonia de San Pedro
39°44'·3N 3°16'·6E

General
A very cramped old fishing harbour, packed solid
with small motorboats and quite unsuitable for
anything exceeding 5m overall or needing more than
1m depth. However in settled southerly conditions
it might be possible to anchor off and visit by
dinghy. There is a light (Fl(4)R.3M, red column on
white base displaying red ■ 3m) on the northwest
mole and in 1996 work was taking place close east,
also lit (Fl.Y.6m1M, yellow post). It was not clear
whether this was a harbour extension or to protect a
bathing zone.

The area was inhabited as far back as Neolithic
times – the Talayotic settlement of Sa Canova 1½
miles inland off the road to Artá is the best
preserved example of its type in Mallorca – and later
became part of the Moorish estate of Farrutx. As
such it was the last stronghold to fall to Jaime I
during the Christian re-conquest and Jaime II
turned the area into a royal hunting reserve. In 1868
San Pedro de Artá was established, and there have
been few changes since its area was defined twelve
years later. It is tempting to suppose that both the
tiny harbour and the wooden barrier which closes it
against bad weather have similarly ancient origins.

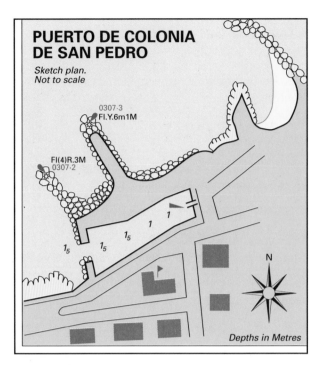

PUERTO DE COLONIA DE SAN PEDRO
Sketch plan.
Not to scale

0307·3
Fl.Y.6m1M

Fl(4)R.3M
0307·2

N

Depths in Metres

Approach
For outer approaches see Puerto de Alcudia, page
108.

Puerto de Colonia de San Pedro lies 4·6 miles
southwest of Cabo Farrutx, at the point where the
higher land slopes down onto the plain. On closer
approach the small village of Colonia de San Pedro,
which has a tall church spire and No 14 sea-mark
beacon on its east side, will be seen.

Anchorage in the approach
The bottom is largely rock and weed and holding is
poor. A member of the crew should remain aboard,
and a trip line is adviseable.

Entrance and berthing
See previous caution regarding size limitations. If
entry is feasible, approach the head of the northwest
mole at slow speed – the entrance is no more than
5m wide and there is very little room to manoeuvre
once inside. Secure in any vacant berth, ready to
move if necessary.

Facilities
The Club Náutico de Colonia de San Pedro
(☎ 751337 or 589147) across the road from the
harbour has a bar and restaurant. There are several
hotels, restaurants and cafés and a few shops in the
village, and a water tap near the slipway at the head
of the harbour. Fuel is not available.

Cala Es Caló 39°46'·5N 3°20'E
An isolated anchorage 1·2 miles southwest of Cabo
Farrutx set against a dramatic rocky backdrop, Cala
Es Caló offers a useful anchorage if waiting to round
the cape. There is a short mole but no harbour as
such and the single light (Q(2)R.6s8m3M, grey
round tower on square base 7m) did not appear to
be functioning in May 1996. There are no facilities
and only a track ashore.

The tiny and crowded Puerto de Colonia de San Pedro looking
northeast. The new mole (with sand 'tail') under contruction in
1996 may herald an extension to the harbour.

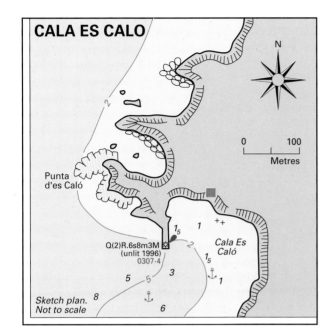

CALA ES CALO

Punta d'es Caló

Q(2)R.6s8m3M (unlit 1996) 0307·4

Cala Es Caló

Sketch plan. Not to scale

0   100
Metres

⚓ **Caleta de Font Salada** 39°46'N 3°23'·2E
One of several similar *calas* in a large shallow bay. Anchor off a white sandy beach in 4–6m over sand, open northwest through north to northeast. A track leads to a road some distance inland.

Farayó de Aubarca 39°46'·3N 3°24'·5E
A small nobbly islet, 23m high and some 750m offshore, off the headland of Morro de Aubarca which is topped by a watchtower. There is good water on either side – the inshore passage carries 20m or more and is free of dangers.

⚓ **Calas Matsoch, Estreta and Mitjana**
Around 39°45'·5N 3°24'·8E
Three small open anchorages off narrow white sand and stone beaches backed by sand dunes. Anchor in 3–5m over hard sand, open northwest through north to east. All three can be reached by road and are frequented by tourists, and Cala Mitjana has a beach café.

⚓ **Cala Mesquida** 39°44'·8N 3°26'·1E
An open anchorage off a long white sandy beach with a growing tourist resort behind. Anchor in 2–5m over sand open to north, northeast and east and to swell from northwest. Water and basic provisions are available.

⚓ **Calas Moltó and Guya (Calas Molta and de S'Agulla)** 39°43'·6N 3°27'·3E
Two *calas* either side of a narrow rocky promontory terminating in Punta Aguilló, Calo Moltó has a very small beach and no facilites whereas Calo Guya has

Approach from west or northwest to anchor in 5–6m over sand, weed and stones south or southeast of the molehead, open to west and northwest with some fetch from southwest and south. Holding is poor in places. The short mole has underwater projections near its head and its east (inner) side is sometimes used by fishing vessels which must not be obstructed. Nets may also be laid in the vicinity.

There are good walks in the surrounding hills, and for the fit the climb to the top of Atalaya de Morey (432m) overlooking Cabo Farrutx is rewarding. The Cueva (cave) des Vells Marins some 600m south of the anchorage is also worth visiting.

Cala Es Caló seen from the southwest, with two yachts rafted at anchor. Atalaya de Morey towers over the anchorage – it is mislabelled on BA 2831.

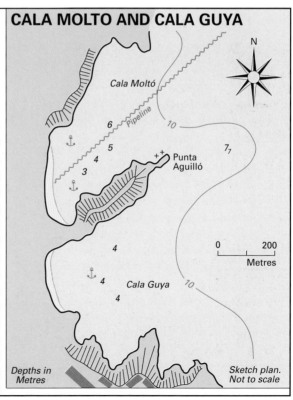

CALA MOLTO AND CALA GUYA

Cala Moltó

Pipeline

Punta Aguilló

Cala Guya

Depths in Metres

Sketch plan. Not to scale

0   200
Metres

a much longer sandy beach which is popular with holidaymakers. There is a small but growing tourist development on its southern shore.

Anchor in 3–5m over sand off either beach, taking particular care in Cala Moltó to avoid a pipeline running northeast towards Menorca. Cala Moltó is open to the northeast, Cala Guya to northeast and east.

Cabo de Pera, Mallorca's most easterly headland, seen from the southeast.

⚓ **Cala Gat (Cat)** 39°42'·8N 3°28'·3E

A deeply indented *cala* between Punta del Gat and Islote d'es Farayó to the east and Puerto de Cala Ratjada to the west, with cliffed and wooded sides and overlooked by several houses including the conspicuous Palacio Torre Ciega on a hill 200m to the west. Anchor in 3–5m over sand, weed and rock open southwest to southeast. Although there is a channel carrying 4m inside the island it is not recommended without local knowledge. Foul ground extends some distance to the south of the island.

Puerto de Cala Ratjada
39°42'·7N 3°27'·9E

Charts	*Approach*	*Harbour*
Admiralty	*2831*	
Spanish	*965, 424, 425*	*4241*
French	*7116*	*7119*

Lights
Approach
0308 **Cabo de Pera** 39°43'N 3°28'·7E
Fl(2+3)20s76m16M White tower on white building with dark corners and red roof 21m 148°-vis-010°
Entrance
0308·2 **Breakwater head** 39°42'·6N 3°27'·9E
Fl.G.2s12m3M Green column on white base displaying green ▲ 3m
0308·3 **Breakwater spur (fishermen's quay)**
39°42'·7N 3°27'·9E F.G.6m3M
Green post 5m
0308·32 **West mole** 39°42'·7N 3°27'·9E
F.R.6m3M Red post 5m
0308·34 **Northwest mole** 39°42'·7N 3°27'·9E
F.R.6m3M Red post 5m

Port Communications
Puerto de Cala Ratjada ☎ 563007; Club Náutico de Cala Ratjada ☎/*Fax* 564019.

General
Once a little fishing harbour but now a thriving (and rather pleasant) tourist resort with a strong German influence. The vast majority of local boats are small and the *Club Náutico* pontoons can only take craft up to 12m or so. However yachts up to 20m can lie alongside the breakwater, outside the harbour proper but well sheltered in most conditions. Menorca is only 21 miles to the east making Puerto de Cala Ratjada a popular destination or departure point for the inter-island passage.

Approach is straightforward but the entrance to the inner harbour is narrow and the harbour congested with fishing craft. Strong winds from between east and south create a heavy swell in both entrance and harbour, and the outside berths might become untenable.

Little of the original town has survived the tourist building boom, but both Artá 5 miles inland and Capdepera 1½ miles away have retained many of their old buildings, the latter including an interesting castle with particularly good views. The Cuevas (caves) de Artá at Cabo Vermey are well worth visiting and the garden museum of Sa Torre Cega has an interesting collection of sculptures. An enclave of Moors remained in this area much longer than elsewhere and the local people show more traces of Moorish descent than do those in other parts of the island. They also practise the old Moorish art of *palmetto* (palm work).

A *fiesta* is held at Puerto de Cala Ratjada in mid August in honour of San Roc, patron saint of the

PUERTO DE CALA RATJADA

town – events include sailing races. On 24 August Capdepera honours its patron saint, San Bartolomé, this time with horse races amongst the revelry.

Approach

From south The coast is very broken, with high rocky cliffs backed by even higher tree-covered hills. Cabo Vermey is high (252m sloping down to 185m) and has a rounded profile of reddish rocks with two towers on the top. Puerto de Cala Ratjada lies 4·4 miles north of this headland and about 0·8 mile west of Cabo de Pera (Fl(2+3)20s76m16M, white tower on white building with dark corners and red roof 21m).

From north Cross the wide Bahía de Alcudia towards Cabo Farrutx, a high sloping promontory (unlit, though there are red lights on Puig Tudosa 1·5 miles to the south). Follow the coast southeast to Cabo del Freu, a low, narrow, pointed promontory, also unlit, passing Farayó de Aubarca islet (23m high and about 750m offshore) *en route*. There is good water on either side of the island.

Cabo de Pera 2·1 miles south-southeast of Cabo del Freu is easily identified by its lighthouse. Follow its steep rocky cliffs southwest to round Islote d'es Farayó off Punta del Gat, after which the harbour will be seen 0·7 mile to the west.

Anchorage in the approach

Anchor 500m southwest of the end of the breakwater in 5m over sand, open to east through southeast to south. Closer to the entrance the bottom is of rock, stone and weed and unsuitable for anchoring. There are a few sand patches opposite the breakwater head (see photograph) in 2–5m, but they may be occupied by moorings.

Entrance

Round the end of the breakwater at 30–40m to seek a berth on the inner side. There is a 3 knot speed limit. A rock carrying less than 3m has been reported 90–100m south-southwest of the breakwater head.

Sea levels

The level of the water increases by about 0·5m with onshore winds and decreases by the same amount with offshore winds.

Berthing

Visitors normally berth on the inner side of the breakwater, lying alongside rather than stern-to because of the poor holding. In the summer rafts may be four or five deep. Yachts are no longer allowed to secure to the sides of the breakwater spur

Puerto de Cala Ratjada from slightly west of south. Yachts can be seen alongside the outer part of the breakwater – the inner harbour is almost solid with local craft. A fishing boat and a couple of tourist ferries are on the move, possibly waiting for fuel.

(fishermen's quay), even on the south side which in any case has rocks along its base and some timber projections. Should it be necessary to lay an anchor be certain to use a tripping line – the bottom is very rough, consisting of broken rocks with many crevices and holes. Smaller yachts may occasionally be found a berth on the pontoons off the *Club Náutico*. Enquire at their office on the west side of the harbour.

If arriving between Friday evening and Sunday evening it may be possible to moor alongside a fishing boat in the eastern arm of the harbour – but note that most depart at 0600 on Monday morning.

Charges *(see page 6)*

High season daily rate – Band C; low season daily rate – Band C. Water and electricity extra.

Facilities

Boatyards No boatyard as such, though basic repairs can be carried out.

Crane 10 and 7·5 tonne cranes by the *Club Náutico* on the west side of the harbour.

Slipways The slipway for fishing craft in the northeast corner of the harbour may be available for yachts. In 1996 there were two rather rough cradles, maximum draught 2m. Other slipways around the harbour.

Engineers To service the fishing vessels.

Chandlery Small chandlery/hardware store on the east side of the harbour.

Water Water points on all quays and pontoons.

Showers At the *Club Náutico*.

Electricity 220v AC points on the pontoons and at visitors' berths on the inner side of the breakwater.

Fuel Diesel from pumps at the head of the breakwater spur (fishermen's quay), not open on Sundays and public holidays. Petrol from a garage ¾ mile northwest of the harbour.

Ice There is an ice factory at the back of the town just south of the Plaza.

Yacht club The Club Náutico de Cala Ratjada (☎/*Fax* 564019) is small, but has showers and a bar.

Banks In the town, with credit card facilities.

Shops/provisioning Several supermarkets and specialist food shops in the town, with more in Capdepera about 1½ miles away.

Markets Saturdays in Puerto de Cala Ratjada, Wednesdays in Capdepera.

Hotels/restaurants/cafés etc. Many of all grades, with the harbour apparently beseiged by cafés and restaurants.

Laundry In the town.

Hospital/medical services In the town.

Communications

Car hire/taxis In the town.

Buses Bus service to Capdepera and thence to Palma etc.

Ferries Tourist ferries make daily trips to a number of popular beaches in the area.

⚓ **Cala Moll** 39°42'N 3°27'·4E

A wide bay off a popular sandy beach ¾ mile southwest of Puerto de Cala Ratjada, Cala Moll has low rocky sides and is largely surrounded by buildings. Anchor about 150m off the beach in 2·5 m over sand, open to northeast through east to southeast. The small Islote Forana lies to the southeast and should be left on the landward side.

⚓ **Cala de Sa Font (Cala de San Geroni)** 39°41'N 3°27'·3E

A sizeable, attractive *cala* with a fine – and often crowded – sandy beach and some apartment buildings nearby. Anchor off the beach in 5m over sand and stone, open to northeast through southeast. Some facilities ashore, otherwise less than 2 miles by road to Capdepera.

Cala de Cañamel (left) and Cabo Vermey from south-southwest, with Cabo de Pera in the background.

Cala de Sa Font from the southeast. The angular white hotel to the left of the beach is conspicuous from offshore.

⚓ **Cala de Cañamel** 39°39'·4N 3°26'·6E

Rather an open anchorage in a bay just south of Cabo Vermey (reddish, with little vegetation) and the famous Cuevas (caves) de Artá. The sandy beach at the head of the *cala* is backed by hotels and

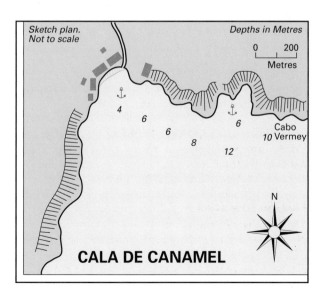

apartments, but a good deal of greenery has been retained. A river flows through the beach on its northern side. Anchor in 3–5m of very clear water over sand, open to east, southeast and south. The bottom shelves gradually and in heavy weather waves break some distance offshore. There are some shops in the tourist complex, including a small supermarket.

A second anchorage, with less swell but with room for only two boats, will be found in a very small *cala* halfway to Cabo Vermey, open to south and southeast. A spherical yellow buoy (Fl(5)Y.20s) is positioned 1·4 miles east of the cape itself.

Puerto de Costa de los Pinos

39°38'·2N 3°24'·8E

General

A very small, shallow harbour – or more accurately a broad quay with short protective extension – built as an amenity for guests of the four-star Hotel Golf Punta Rotja (☎ 567600), Puerto de Costa de los Pinos offers little shelter and can take only the smallest craft. The bay is often used for waterskiing etc., but nevertheless makes a pleasant anchorage.

Approach

The harbour and anchorage lie close west of Cabo d'es Piná (Cabo d'es Ratx), itself some 5·4 miles south of Cabo de Pera and 3·6 miles north of Punta de Amer. The square, white hotel overlooking the harbour will be seen for many miles.

Anchorage in the approach

Anchor in 2–4m over sand and weed west of the molehead, open south round to east. The bottom is uneven with some rocks and a careful watch on the depthsounder will be necessary.

Sketch plan. Not to scale

Depths in Metres

0   200

Metres

4   6
6   6
8   6
12   Cabo
10 Vermey

N

CALA DE CANAMEL

The grandly named Puerto de Costa de los Pinos, part of the Hotel Golf Punta Rotja complex.

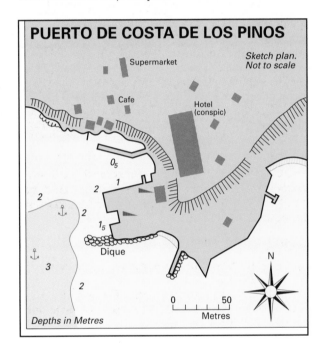

Entrance and berthing

Approach the northwest corner of the quay sounding continuously and secure as space permits. There are a few projecting underwater rocks. Officials may appear, otherwise visit the hotel reception desk.

Facilities

Two small dinghy slipways and water tap on the quay. Supermarket behind hotel and choice of restaurants and cafés.

⚓ Port Vey (Vell) and Port Nou

39°37'·9N 3°24'·2E

Not ports at all, but coastal anchorages off a long sandy beach between Puerto de Costa de los Pinos and Puerto de Cala Bona. Anchor in 3–4m over sand and weed open to northeast through east to south. A few houses, hotels, shops and cafés line the road behind the beach.

Puerto de Cala Bona

39°36'·9N 3°23'·7E

Charts *Approach*
Admiralty   *2831*
Spanish   *965, 424*
French   *7116*

Lights

0308·6 **South breakwater** 39°36'·9N 3°23'·7E
Fl(2)R.6s5m4M Red column on white base displaying red ■ 2m

0308·7 **North breakwater** 39°36'·9N 3°23'·7E
Fl.G.3s5m3M Green column on white base displaying green ▲ 2m

0308·8 **South inner mole** 39°36'·9N 3°23'·6E
F.R.4m2M Red column on white base displaying red ■ 3m

Port Communications

Puerto de Cala Bona ☎ 820419.

General

Originally a small fishing harbour with an even tinier inner harbour, Puerto de Cala Bona has been improved by the construction of two outer breakwaters. Even so it is not large with a total of 136 berths and facilities are limited. The approach is straightforward but should not be attempted in strong onshore winds. The harbour is home to a number of glass-bottomed and other tourist excursion boats.

Approach

From south Punta de Amer is a low, rocky-cliffed promontory with a small castle on its summit. The wide Bahía de Artá stretches northwards from it as far as Cabo d'es Piná and the harbour is located near its centre, at the northern end of the heavily built up area.

From north The high, rounded profile of Cabo Vermey, which has reddish rocks, is recognisable as is the dark, cliffed Cabo d'es Piná. South of Cabo d'es Piná lies the wide Bahía de Artá, with Puerto de Cala Bona near its centre, at the northern end of the heavily built up area.

Anchorage in the approach

There are sand patches off the harbour entrance in 5m+, but it would be distinctly exposed.

Entrance

There are a number of rocky breakwaters close south of the harbour, established to retain sand on the beaches – ensure that the harbour entrance is identified beyond all doubt. Enter at slow speed on a southwesterly course. Once inside there is little room to manoeuvre and parts are shallow.

Puerto de Cala Bona from the southeast. Part of one of the sand retaining breakwaters can be seen on the left.

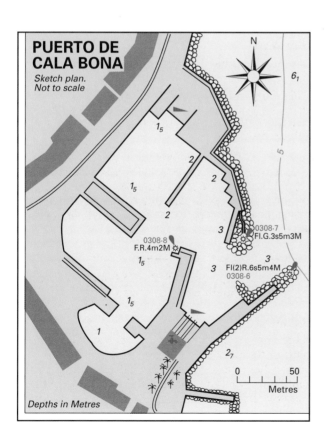

PUERTO DE CALA BONA

Sketch plan.
Not to scale

N

6₁

5

1₅

2

2

2

1₅

2

0308·7
Fl.G.3s5m3M

3

0308·8
F.R.4m2M

1₅

3

3

Fl(2)R.6s5m4M
0308·6

1₅

1

2₇

0   50
Metres

Depths in Metres

Berthing

Secure bow or stern-to on the inside of the south breakwater. This position is exposed to wind or swell from east or northeast but well protected from the southerly quadrant.

Facilities

Slipways Three around the harbour, but little more than dinghy size.

Water In containers from the fishermen's co-operative near the old inner harbour, or from one of the bars or restaurants.

Electricity A few 220v AC points around the harbour.

Fuel No fuel pumps. There is a service station outside the town.

Ice From the fishermen's co-operative or from one of the bars or restaurants.

Banks To the south of the harbour and in Son Servera, 2 miles inland.

Provisions Shops and supermarkets to the south of the harbour, more in Son Servera.

Market Friday market in Son Servera.

Hotels/restaurants/cafés etc. Many around the harbour.

Hospital/medical services In Son Servera, 2 miles inland.

Communications

Car hire/taxis In the town.

Buses Bus service to Son Servera and beyond.

⚓ **Arenal de Son Servera** 39°35'·6N 3°23'·3E
A long sand and stone beach immediately north of
Punta de Amer. Anchor in 5m over sand and rock
near the southern end of the Cala Millor holiday
development, open to north, northeast and east and
to swell from southeast. There are numerous
restaurants and cafés ashore plus a few shops.

⚓ **Playa de Sa Coma** 39°34'·5N 3°22'·8E
A wide and often crowded sandy beach close south
of Punta de Amer, with a reasonably restrained
development behind. Anchor in 2–4m over sand,
with some rock and weed further out, open to
southwest through south to east.

⚓ **Cala Moreya** 39°34'·1N 3°22'·6E
A sandy bay close south of Playa de Sa Coma but
surrounded by the much denser development of the
S'Illot holiday town. Anchor in 2–4m over sand,
open southeast through northeast.

⚓ **Cala Morlanda** 39°33'·4N 3°22'·3E
A double *cala* at the south end of the S'Illot holiday
development but still largely unspoilt, with rocky
sides and two small stony beaches. Anchor in 4–5m
over sand, open to east and southeast.

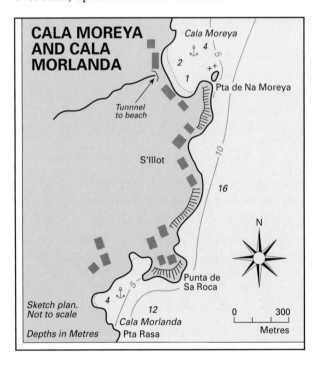

⚓ **Cala Petita** 39°32'·9N 3°21'·4E
A narrow, dog-legged *cala* with space for no more
than two boats, enclosed by rocky cliffs and with
nothing ashore beyond a rough track. Anchor in
3–6m over sand and rock in the centre of the *cala*
using two anchors to restrict swinging room, open to
east and southeast. There are a number of isolated
rocks awash just off the small beach.

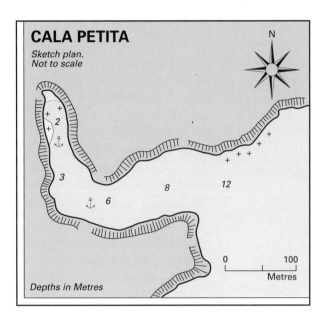

Porto Cristo (Cala Manacor)
39°32'·3N 3°20'·5E (entrance)

Charts	Approach	Harbour
Admiralty	2831	
Spanish	900, 424	4241
French	7116	7119

Lights

0309 **Cabo del Morro de sa Carabassa**
    39°32'·2N 3°20'·5E Fl.5s20m4M
    White tower, black vertical stripes 6m
0309·4 **Northeast mole** 39°32'·5N 3°20'·3E
    Fl(2)R.6s5m3M Red octagonal column 2m

Port Communications

VHF – Puerto de Porto Cristo VHF Ch 16. Club
    Náutico de Porto Cristo VHF Ch 9.
☎/*Fax* – Puerto de Porto Cristo ☎ 820419; Club
    Náutico de Porto Cristo ☎ 821253, *Fax* 820650.

General

A long and well sheltered inlet with several dog-legs,
which has managed to retain a good deal of its
charm despite the many new buildings associated
with a growing tourist resort. The town and beach
become crowded in the summer but few visitors
walk round to the yacht pontoons on the south side
of the channel. (Conversely it is a long, hot walk
loaded with shopping, unless the dinghy is used).
Approach and entrance present no problems other
than in strong onshore winds, but the harbour is
often full in summer and berths cannot be reserved
in advance.
   The area is famous for the caves discovered by
MEA Martel in 1896, and for an unsuccessful
landing by Communist forces during the Civil War.
There are two monuments to this landing, one near
the root of the northeast mole and another at the
northwest end of the town. The area was also
favoured by the kings of Mallorca for their summer

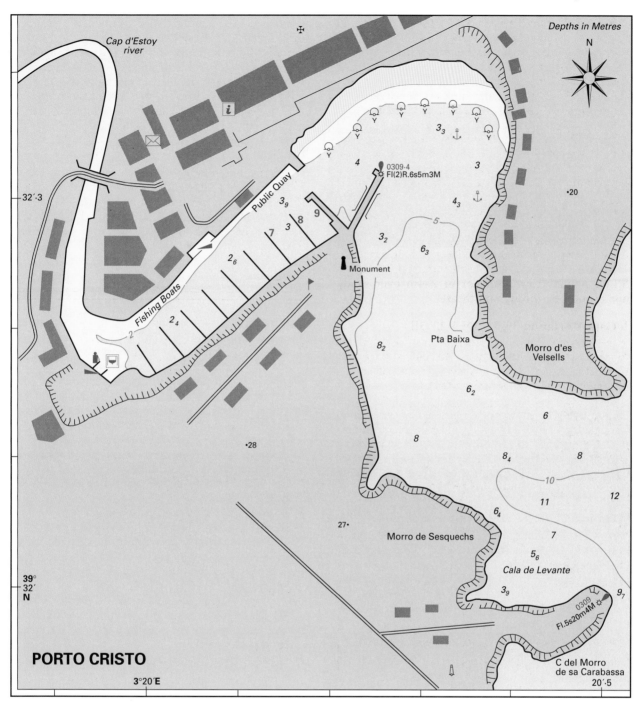

holidays. The spectacular Cuevas del Drach (Caves of the Dragon) and Cuevas del Hams south of the town should not be missed (open 1000 to 1700). There is also a wildlife park nearby, and good views of the coast from the tower southwest of the lighthouse. The *Fiesta de la Virgen del Carmen*, with waterborne processions, is held on 16 July.

Approach

From south The coast from Porto Colom is of low rocky cliffs which are broken by many *calas*, all very similar and difficult to identify. However, at Porto Cristo the conspicuous lighthouse tower with black and white vertical stripes is easily seen.

From north Cross the wide Bahía de Artá which terminates on its south side at Punta de Amer, relatively low but prominent. Porto Cristo lies 4 miles to the southwest and can be identified as above.

Anchorage in the approach

It is possible to anchor under the cliffs on the east side of the channel opposite the monument, or further north outside a line of yellow buoys marking the bathing area, in 3–5m over sand, mud and weed. Both spots can be rolly, due either to swell or to wash from passing speedboats, and may be affected by a circular current in low pressure weather. Anchoring in the harbour itself is not permitted.

The entrance to Porto Cristo seen from the southeast. In spite of the poor photograph the very clean nature of the bottom can be clearly seen.

Entrance

The entrance channel is both wide and deep. Keep to the centre or slightly to starboard before rounding the northeast mole into the yacht harbour (this mole is not completely solid but includes a bridge near the shore). Strong currents can occur when the river Cap d'Estoy is in spate and in heavy weather a strong surge may build up. In pleasanter conditions it is not unusual to find swimmers and snorkellers virtually under the bow! A series of yellow buoys with a connecting line lies some way off the bathing beach. There is a 3 knot speed limit.

Berthing

The *Club Náutico* reserves its three easternmost pontoons (7-8-9) for visiting yachts. Moorings and lazy lines are provided and it is claimed that a berthing master is always on duty. However the harbour is often full in summer – it is advisable to call on VHF Ch 9 to check whether a berth will be

Porto Cristo harbour looking southwest, taken in May 1996 when the *Club Náutico* pontoons were relatively empty.

available, even though they cannot be reserved before arrival. The visitors pontoons have 3m or more at the outer ends, shoaling towards the quay.

If there is no space available at the *Club Náutico* it may be possible to lie stern-to on the Port Authority quay opposite, southwest of the beach. An anchor will be needed, which should be equipped with a tripping line.

Charges *(see page 6)*

- *Club Náutico Porto Cristo* High season daily rate – Band B; low season daily rate – Band B. Water and electricity included.
- *Public quay* High season daily rate – Band D; low season daily rate – Band D. Water and electricity extra.

Facilities

Boatyards Jaume Vermell Nautica (☎ 822022, *Fax* 822021) at the southwest end of the harbour has most facilities including a very protected winter lay-up area.

Travel-lift 50 tonne lift in the boatyard.

Crane 12·5 tonne crane in the boatyard.

Slipways Small slipways on both sides of the harbour.

Engineers At the boatyard. Marina Marbella Balear SA (☎ 820653) are official service agents for Mercury/MerCruiser and Volvo Penta.

Chandlery Two well stocked chandleries either side of the channel north of the boatyard.

Water Water points on the quay, pontoons and at the *Club Náutico*.

Showers At the *Club Náutico*.

Electricity 220v AC points on quays and pontoons.

Fuel Diesel and petrol from pumps next to the travel lift.

Ice Delivered to the quay daily, also from the *Club Náutico* bar.

Yacht club The Club Náutico de Porto Cristo (☎ 821253, *Fax* 820650) has a smart clubhouse with bar, restaurant, swimming pool, terrace, showers etc.

Banks Several in the town, mostly with credit card facilities.

Shops/provisioning Shops of all types in the town including several small supermarkets, but a long walk round from the yacht pontoons (unless the dinghy is used).

Produce/fish market Sunday market in Porto Cristo, Monday in Manacor 6 miles inland.

Hotels/restaurants/cafés etc. Many hotels, mostly quite small, and a large number of restaurants, cafés and bars.

Laundrettes In the town and at the *Club Náutico*.

Hospital/medical services Medical services in Porto Cristo, hospital in Manacor 6 miles inland.

Communications

Car hire/taxis In the town.

Buses Regular service to Manacor, Palma etc.

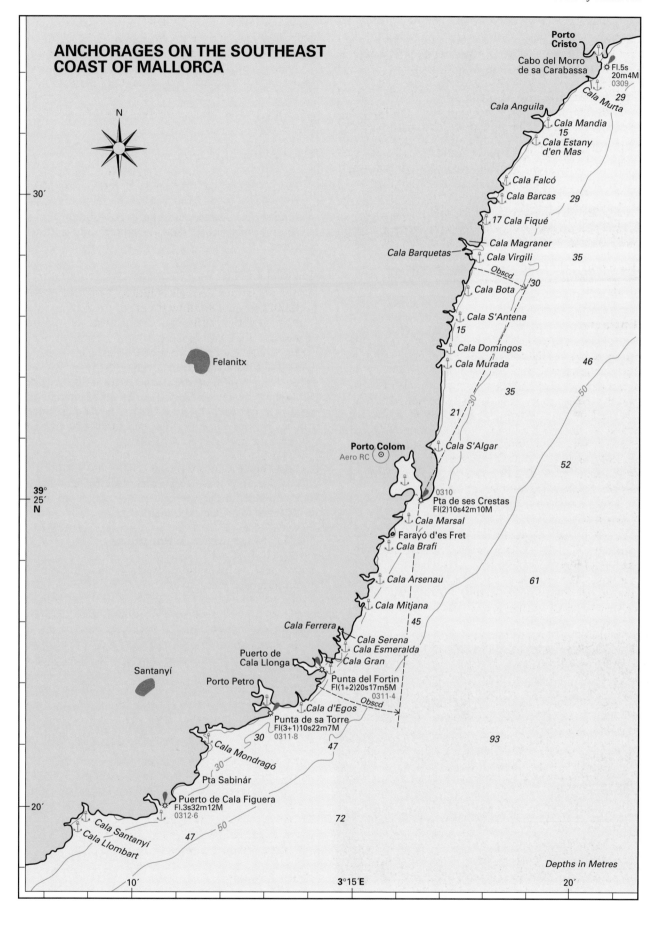

ANCHORAGES ON THE SOUTHEAST
COAST OF MALLORCA

N

Porto
Cristo

Cabo del Morro
de sa Carabassa

Fl.5s
20m4M
0309

Cala Murta

29

Cala Anguila

Cala Mandia
15

Cala Estany
d'en Mas

Cala Falcó

Cala Barcas

29

17 Cala Fiqué

30′

Cala Magraner

Cala Barquetas

Cala Virgili

35

Obscd

Cala Bota

30

Cala S'Antena

15

Felanitx

Cala Domingos

Cala Murada

46

35

50

21

Cala S'Algar

52

Porto Colom
Aero RC

30

39°
25′
N

0310

Pta de ses Crestas
Fl(2)10s42m10M

Cala Marsal

Farayó d'es Fret

Cala Brafi

Cala Arsenau

61

Cala Mitjana

45

Cala Ferrera

Cala Serena

Cala Esmeralda

Puerto de
Cala Llonga

Cala Gran

Porto Petro

Punta del Fortin
Fl(1+2)20s17m5M

0311·4

Obscd

Santanyí

Cala d'Egos

Punta de sa Torre
Fl(3+1)10s22m7M
0311·8

93

30

Cala Mondragó

47

30

Pta Sabinár

20′

Puerto de Cala Figuera
Fl.3s32m12M
0312·6

72

Cala Santanyí

Cala Llombart

47

50

Depths in Metres

10′

3°15′E

20′

125

⚓ **Cala Murta** 39°32'N 3°20'·1E

A narrow *cala* between steep rocky sides, with some new buildings to the north. Anchor in 3–5m over sand, open to east and southeast.

⚓ **Calas Anguila and Mandia** 39°31'·3N 3°19'·1E

A small double *cala* with sandy beaches and many tourists. A holiday development, Porto Cristo Nova, lies on the north side and there are others to the south. Anchor off either beach in 3–5m over sand, open to northeast through east to southeast. Several restaurants and cafés.

⚓ **Cala Estany d'en Mas** 39°31'N 3°18'·9E

A small *cala* with rocky sides, the northern almost completely covered with low-rise buildings. Anchor in 2–4m over sand off the crowded beach, open to east and southeast. Beach bars and restaurant.

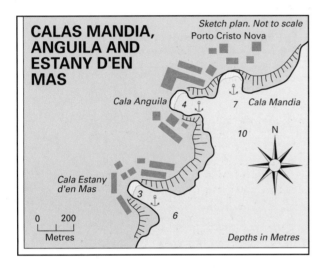

⚓ **Cala Falcó** 39°30'·3N 3°18'·2E

A very open, totally deserted *cala*, with a track to the Cuevas del Pirata about a mile inland. Anchor in 2–5m over sand off the small stony beach, open to the eastern quadrant.

Cala Barcas seen from a little north of east.

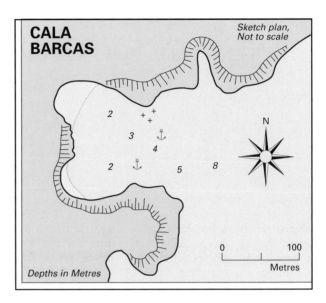

⚓ **Cala Barcas** 39°30'N 3°17'·9E

A wide, square, undeveloped *cala*, the two sandy beaches at its head separated by a stretch of dark rocks. There is a shallow rocky outcrop projecting from the cliffs to the north, which have many sea caves. Keep to the centre of the entrance to anchor off either beach in 3–5m over sand, open to northeast and east. There is only a very rough track ashore, but the *cala* is popular with tourist boats and can become crowded in summer.

⚓ **Cala Fiqué (Cala Serrat)** 39°29'·7N 3°17'·7E

More accurately three very small, deserted *calas* with rocky headlands between. Anchor in 3–5m over sand, open to the eastern quadrant.

⚓ **Calas Magraner and Barquetas**
39°29'·1N 3°17'·4E

Twin *calas* with sandy beaches, offering good protection near their heads. Anchor in 2–4m over sand, open to east and southeast. Other than a small grey hut on the northern headland there are no

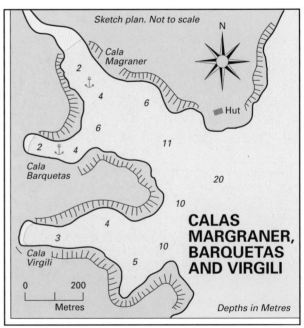

buildings, and the development shown behind the *calas* on several local maps does not appear to have taken place. Tracks from the road bring some summer tourists.

⚓ Cala Virgili 39°29'N 3°17'·4E
A small *cala* with rocky cliffs and a small sandy beach, close south of Calas Magraner and Barquetas. Anchor in 3–5m over sand in the middle of the *cala*, open to northeast and east. Again, there is a track inland but no buildings.

⚓ Cala Bota 39°28'·5N 3°17'·3E
A small undeveloped *cala*, its mouth partially obstructed by a breaking rocky shoal running out from the southern cliffs, Cala Bota should be approached with extreme care. Enter from the northeast with a lookout on the bow, to anchor in 4–5m over sand and weed open to east and southeast.

⚓ Cala S'Antena 39°28'N 3°17'E
A small *cala* between high rocky sides, with some sizeable sea caves and a high-rise tourist complex to the south. Anchor off the beach in 3–5m over sand, open to the eastern quadrant.

⚓ Cala Domingos 39°27'·5N 3°16'·8E
A double *cala* with two fine – and frequently crowded – sandy beaches, inevitably surrounded by tourist development. Anchor in 3–5m over sand, open to northeast through east to southeast. There are several large hotels close north, and the southern arm is backed by a restaurant with a distinctive conical roof.

⚓ Cala Murada 39°27'·3N 3°16'·8E
A curved *cala* with a sandy beach at its southern end and dense housing on the point – once again the beach is often crowded. Anchor off the beach in 3–5m over sand and weed, open to northeast and east. Protection is best close to the beach, where there is a bar/restaurant.

Cala Murada looking slightly south of west.

⚓ Cala S'Algar 39°25'·8N 3°16'·6E
A large open *cala* with rocky sides and a very small stony beach, a mile north of the entrance to Porto Colom. Anchor in 3–5m over sand and weed, open to northeast and east. There is a road across the headland to Porto Colom where supplies are available.

Porto Colom
39°25'N 3°16'·2E (entrance)
39°25'·4N 3°15'·8 (public pontoons)

Charts	*Approach*	*Harbour*
Admiralty	*2831*	
Spanish	*900, 423, 424*	*4241*
French	*7116*	*7119*

Lights
Approach
0310 **Punta de ses Crestas (Punta de la Farola)**
39°24'·9N 3°16'·3E Fl(2)10s42m10M
White round tower, three black bands,
on white building with red roof 25m
207°-vis-006°

Entrance
0310·4 **Punta de sa Batería** 39°25'·0N 3°16'·1E
Fl(4)R.11s12m4M Red column on white
base displaying red ■ 7m
buoy **Port hand buoy** 39°25'·1N 3°16'·1E
Fl.R.3s1M Red pillar buoy, ■ topmark
buoy **Starboard hand buoy** 39°25'·2N 3°16'·1E
Fl.G.4s1M Green pillar buoy, ▲ topmark
buoy **Port hand buoy** 39°25'·2N 3°15'·9E
Fl(3)R.8s1M Red pillar buoy, ■ topmark
buoy **Starboard hand buoy** 39°25'·2N 3°16'E
Fl(2)G.6s1M Green pillar buoy, ▲ topmark
buoy **Starboard hand buoy** 39°25'·3N 3°15'·9E
Fl(3)G.8s1M Green pillar buoy, ▲ topmark
0311 **West mole** 39°25'·3N 3°15'·8E
Fl(2)R.7s5m3M Red column on white base
displaying red ■ 2m
0311·2 **Yacht harbour south mole** 39°25'·4N 3°15'·8E
Oc.R.6s2M Red column
(Reported in 1996 to be Iso.4s)

Radiobeacons
1029 **Puerto Colom Aero** 39°25'·6N 3°15'·3E
Aerobeacon *PTC*, 401kHz 30M (Non A2A)

Buoys
In addition to the above starboard hand buoys, ten unlit white buoys with green triangular topmarks indicate the starboard side of the dredged channel into the yacht harbour, and two white buoys with red triangular topmarks mark a shoal near the root of the yacht harbour south mole. A line of yellow buoys marks the swimming area off the beach at Arenal Gran.

Port Communications
VHF – Puerto de Porto Colom VHF Ch 16. Club Náutico de Porto Colom VHF Ch 9.
☎/*Fax* – Puerto de Porto Colom ☎ 824695; Club Náutico de Porto Colom ☎ 824658, *Fax* 825399.

General

Undoubtedly the best natural harbour and anchorage on Mallorca, where up to 100 yachts could anchor in shelter, Porto Colom is large and well-protected with a deep and narrow entrance, though much of the interior is relatively shallow (under 2·5m). The Club Náutico de Porto Colom operates a small yacht harbour in the northwest corner, but visitors normally either anchor or lie stern-to one of the Port Authority pontoons recently built between the yacht harbour and the west mole. Approach and entrance are straightforward and excellent shelter obtained once inside, but the entrance could be difficult in strong winds from south or southeast.

There is a good deal of low-rise housing, particularly to the south of the harbour, but overall Porto Colom is still surprisingly undeveloped. The Monastery of San Salvador 4 miles inland is interesting and has a fine view, as has the ruined Castillo de San Tueri 3½ miles inland. However neither can be approached direct and some form of transport will probably be needed. A *fiesta* in honour of the *Virgen del Carmen* is held on 16 July, when the local fishing boats parade around the harbour dressed overall.

Approach

From south The coast from Porto Petro and beyond is of low rocky cliffs broken by many *calas*. The distinctive lighthouse on Punta de ses Crestas (Fl(2)10s42m10M, white round tower with three black bands on white building with red roof 25m) on the east side of the entrance can be seen from many miles, though if sailing close inshore the light itself will be obscured when bearing more than 006°. There is a small islet, Farayó d'es Fret (11m), 0·8 mile southwest of the entrance.

The conspicuous banded lighthouse on Punta de ses Crestas guards the eastern side of the entrance to Porto Colom. In this photograph, taken from just north of west, a fourth band is also seen.

From north The coast from Porto Cristo also consists of low rocky cliffs broken by many *calas*. Unless very close inshore (obscured when bearing less than 207°) the lighthouse on Punta de ses Crestas (see above) will be seen from many miles. The entrance itself does not open until around this headland.

Note In December 1996 a 'dangerous shipwreck' was reported 0·5 mile southeast of the entrance at 39°24'·5N 3°16'·5E.

Entrance and buoyed channel

The entrance is deep and unobstructed, other than a small rocky islet against the eastern shore. As the harbour widens out, follow the buoyed channel to remain in depths of 4–5m. Unlit fish cages may be anchored to the east of the channel.

Much of the harbour is shallow and all manoeuvring outside the buoyed channel should be done with one eye on the depth-sounder and one hand on the engine controls, particularly since some of the banks appear to be unusually steep-sided.

Berthing

Secure bow or stern-to the OUTSIDE of the yacht harbour south mole, or to one of the two Port Authority pontoons close south of it. The former has no more than 2·2m at its outer end and all three shoal towards the shore. Lazy lines are tailed to both mole and pontoons. None of these berths are viable in strong southeasterly winds.

Moorings

There are a few private moorings in the harbour but they are of unknown provenance and in any case are unlikely to be free.

Anchorages

Most yachts anchor off the town, southeast of the west mole and boatyard, with shoal draft vessels using the Ensenada de la Basa Nova. Holding is variable in mud and weed, and plenty of scope is required. There is better holding (and cleaner water) off Arenal Gran to the east over mud and sand outside a line of yellow buoys marking the swimming area, but southerly or southeasterly swell affects the area.

In 1996 a small charge was made for anchoring (less than 1000 ptas, apparently covering several days) which included use of the showers beside the harbour authority office.

Charges *(see page 6)*

- *Club Náutico de Porto Colom* High season daily rate – Band B; low season daily rate – Band B. Water and electricity included.
- *Port Authority pontoons* High season daily rate – Band D; low season daily rate – Band D. Water and electricity extra. Cash only accepted.

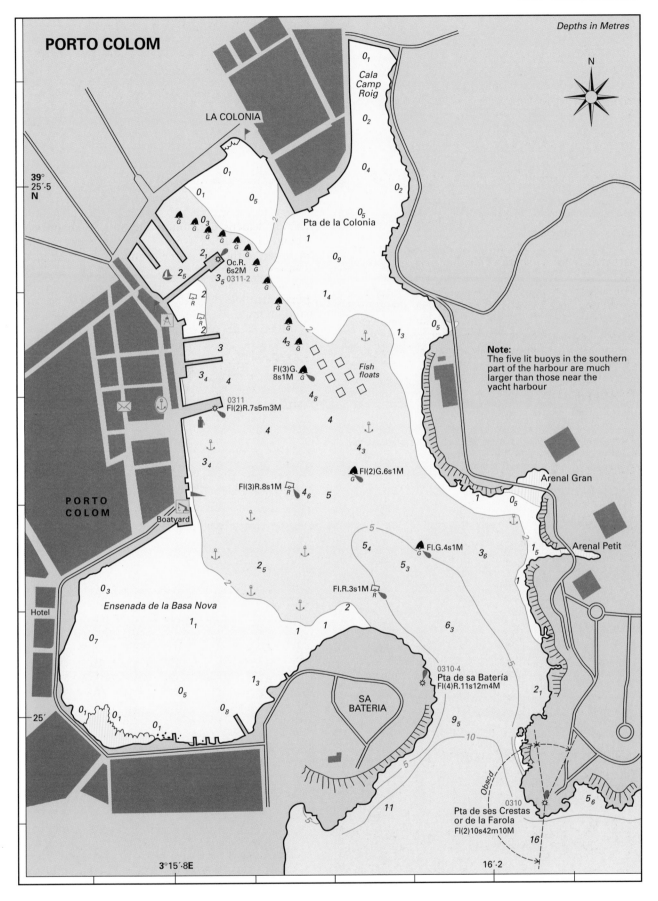

PORTO COLOM

Depths in Metres

N

39°
25'·5
N

LA COLONIA

Cala
Camp
Roig

0_1

0_2

0_4

0_2

Pta de la Colonia

0_5

0_1

0_1

0_5

0_3

G

G

2_1

Oc.R.
6s2M

2_5

3_5 0311·2

2

R

2

R

2

3

3_4

4

1

0_9

1_4

2

2

1_3

0_5

Note:
The five lit buoys in the southern
part of the harbour are much
larger than those near the
yacht harbour

4_3

Fl(3)G.
8s1M G

4_8

Fish
floats

4

0311
Fl(2)R.7s5m3M

4

3_4

4_3

4

Fl(2)G.6s1M

Arenal Gran

1

0_5

Fl(3)R.8s1M 4_6

R

5

**PORTO
COLOM**

Boatyard

2_5

5_4

5_3

Fl.G.4s1M
G

3_6

1_5

Arenal Petit

2_1

Fl.R.3s1M
R

6_3

0_3

Ensenada de la Basa Nova

1_1

1

1

2

Hotel

0_7

1_3

0_5

SA
BATERIA

0310·4
Pta de sa Batería
Fl(4)R.11s12m4M

9_5

10

0_1

0_1

0_8

0_1

11

5

Obscd

0310

Pta de ses Crestas
or de la Farola
Fl(2)10s42m10M

16

5_6

3°15'·8E

16'·2

25'

The entrance to Porto Colom, seen from east of south. It is, without doubt, the best natural harbour and anchorage on Mallorca.

The west mole, two public pontoons and *Club Náutico* yacht harbour at Puerto Colom. The shoals marked by the small white buoys show up clearly.

Facilities

Boatyards A boatyard on the corner north of the Ensenada de la Basa Nova capable of straightforward work in wood or GRP.

Cranes 10+ tonne and 5 tonne mobile cranes at the boatyard.

Slipway Slipway (1·5m) at the boatyard and several others around the harbour.

Engineers At the boatyard.

Chandlery Near the *Club Náutico*.

Water Taps on yacht harbour mole and pontoons, on Port Authority pontoons and near the Port Authority office. Also a tap by the fuel berth, for which a charge is made. In 1996 yachtsmen were warned NOT to drink the water, which in any case tasted very bad.

Showers By the Port Authority office just north of the west mole, and at the *Club Náutico*.

Electricity 220v AC points on yacht harbour mole and pontoons, and on the public pontoons.

Fuel Diesel from pumps on the south side of the west mole (claimed to have 4m alongside). Petrol from a garage near the root of the mole.

Ice From the *Club Náutico* and from the above filling station.

Yacht clubs The Club Náutico de Porto Colom (☎ 824658, *Fax* 825399) at the northwest corner of the harbour has a bar, lounge, terrace and showers. The Club Náutico de Pescadores is northeast of the harbour.

Shops/provisioning Two supermarkets near the Ensenada de la Basa Nova, south of the yacht pontoons. Many other shops in the town.

Hotels/restaurants/cafés etc. The usual range of hotels, restaurants, cafés and bars.

Hospital/medical services Medical services in the town, hospital in Manacor 11 miles away.

Communications

Post office A mobile post office visits a site near the Port Authority office (see plan) between 1150 and 1220, weekdays only. Times appear to change periodically.

Car hire/taxis In the town.

Buses Bus service to Felanitx, Manacor and beyond.

⚓ Cala Marsal and Caló d'en Manuell
39°24'·7N 3°15'·8E

A double *cala* with rocky cliffs close south of Porto Colom, Cala Marsal has a sandy beach at its head which is crowded in the summer. Anchor in 3–5m over sand off the beach, open to northeast and east, or tuck into Caló d'en Manuell which has a sand and rock bottom, open to the southeast. Both *calas* are surrounded by apartment blocks and hotels.

Cala Marsal (with beach) and the smaller Caló d'en Manuell, seen from east-southeast.

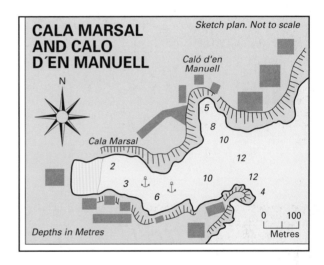

⚓ Cala Brafi 39°24'·3N 3°15'·5E

A small, narrow, dog-legged *cala* between rocky cliffs, with a stone boathouse at its head but no other buildings nearby. Anchor in 3–4m over sand, stone and weed, open to east and southeast.

The small (11m) islet of Farayó d'es Fret lies close northeast of the *cala*. It consists of a flat shelf of rock just above sea-level, with a narrow, vertical-sided rock on the top. Doubtless in time erosion will displace this and convert it into a dangerous breaking ledge.

⚓ Cala Arsenau (Cala sa Nau or Cala de Ras)
39°23'·7N 3°15'·2E

A narrow, angled *cala* offering relatively good protection, particularly near its head where there is a sandy beach, boathouse and café. Anchor in 3–6m over sand and weed open to east and (depending on position) northeast – one option is to take a sternline ashore to the northern bank behind the central promontory. In settled conditions Cala Arsenau makes a feasible overnight anchorage. There are breaking rocks close to the headland north of the *cala*.

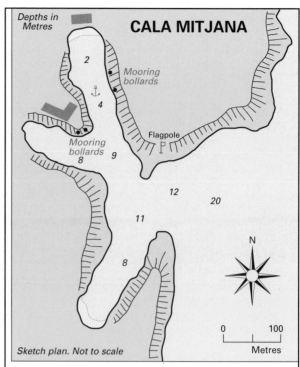

Cala Arsenau looking west, with a tourist ferry leaving at speed. This is one of the few *calas* in the area suitable for an overnight stay in the right conditions.

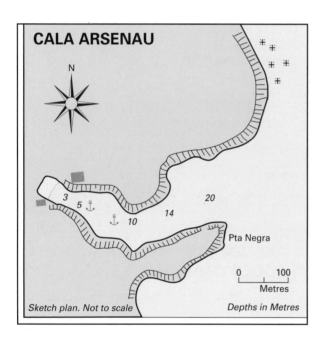

Cala Mitjana, arguably one of Mallorca's most attractive anchorages, seen from the southeast.

⚓ **Cala Mitjana** 39°23'·2N 3°15'E

A very attractive treble *cala* with two sandy beaches and room for at least ten yachts. A tall white flagstaff (often with flags) stands on the north side of the entrance and a pink-roofed building occupies the central headland. Swing wide of the rocky promontory below the flagstaff – the turn is very blind.

Anchor in 5m or less over sand and weed in the northern arm, setting a second anchor to limit swinging room, or take a line to the bollards set into the cliffs (see plan). This spot offers all-round protection though swell from the eastern quadrant would probably work in. The anchorage below the central headland is open to east and southeast.

⚓ **Calas Serena, Ferrera and Esmeralda** 39°22'·6N 3°14'·5E

A treble *cala* with sandy beaches surrounded by hotels and apartments, with a prominent squarish island off the northern headland and breaking rocks to the south. There is an isolated shoal patch carrying 3·5–4m in the centre of the entrance.

Anchor in 3–6m over sand and weed open (depending on position) to southeast and either east or south. Supermarkets and other shops nearby plus innumerable restaurants and cafés.

Calas Ferrera and Esmeralda, with Cala Serena almost hidden on the right, seen from the southeast.

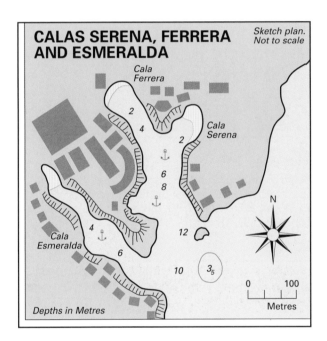

Puerto de Cala Llonga
(Marina Cala d'Or)
39°22'·2N 3°14'·2E

Charts	*Approach*	*Harbour*
Admiralty	*2831*	
Spanish	*900, 423*	*4231*
French	*7116*	*7119*

Lights

0311·4 **Punta del Fortin** 39°22'·1N 3°14'·1E
  Fl(1+2)20s17m5M
  Round white column on square white base,
  both with vertical black stripes 6m
0311·45 **Cala Llonga north side**
  39°22'·2N 3°13'·9E Fl.G.5s9m5M
  Green column on white base 6m
0311·5 **Marina south mole** 39°22'·2N 3°13'·7E
  Fl(2)R.6s5m5M Red column 3m

Buoys

In May 1996 four port hand and eight starboard hand buoys marked the channel to the marina and a shoal opposite. None were lit. A yellow buoy previously positioned 250m east of the lighthouse on Punta del Fortin was not in place.

Port Communications

VHF – Marina (Puerto Deportivo Marina) Ch 9.
☎/Fax – Marina Cala d'Or ☎ 657070, Fax 657068.
  Club Náutico de Cala d'Or ☎ 657069.

General

A single entrance from the sea leads to three *calas* – Cala Gran, Cala d'Or and Cala Llonga. Confusingly, the Marina Cala d'Or is located in the southernmost, Cala Llonga, rather than in Cala d'Or itself. Before the developers moved in these were some of the most beautiful *calas* on the coast of Mallorca, and even with the growth of new villas, hotels and apartments they still retain a good deal of their charm.

The 380 berth Marina Cala d'Or is well protected, with good facilities and helpful staff, but is not cheap. It is often full in summer and a call on VHF Ch 9 prior to arrival would be wise. Approach and entrance are straightforward and good shelter obtained, though in an east or southeast wind a heavy swell enters all three *calas*.

The old fort on the headland is worth the walk, when the unusual Punta de Fortin light structure can also be studied. A *fiesta* with waterborne processions is held on 15 August in honour of the area's patron saint, Santa Maria del Mar.

Approach

From south Low rocky cliffs broken by two small *calas* extend northwards from Porto Petro. The low, square pinkish-brown fort on Punta del Fortin with its nearby lighthouse (Fl(1+2)20s17m5M, round white column on square white base, both with vertical black stripes 6m) are easily identified.

133

**PUERTO DE CALA LLONGA
(MARINA CALA D'OR),
CALA D'OR AND CALA GRAN**

From north There are five small *calas* in the low rocky cliffs that extend from Porto Colom southwards. Again the fort and lighthouse are easy to identify.

Anchorages in the approach

- *Cala Gran* Anchor in 5–6m over sand and weed in the middle of the *cala*, opposite a small squarish *cala* on the starboard side, open to the south and to swell from southeast and east. There is a fine sandy beach which is buoyed off for bathing.
- *Cala d'Or* This *cala* is sometimes closed in the summer by means of buoys, when anchoring is prohibited. Otherwise anchor in the centre of the *cala* in 3–5m over sand and weed patches off a small sandy beach, open to east and southeast and to swell from the east. This is the least sheltered of the three *calas*.
- *Cala Llonga* Anchor in the entrance to Caló d'es Pous in 2·5m over sand and weed, well out of the marina approach channel, open to the east.

Entrance

The outer entrance is straightforward with good depths. After passing the light structure on the north side of the entrance to Cala Llonga (Fl.G.5s9m5M, green column on white base 6m) and crossing the 5m contour the buoyed channel into the marina will open up. A minimum depth of 2·5m should be found in the channel.

Berthing

Secure temporarily to the fuelling berth at the end of the marina south mole, having preferably already called on VHF Ch 9. In this case a berth may be allocated over the radio.

Charges *(see page 6)*

High season daily rate – Band B (15m), Band A (10m); low season daily rate – Band A. Water and electricity included.

Facilities

Boatyards Small repairs to GRP and wood hulls can be handled by the marina boatyard. Outside contractors are not allowed to work in the marina without permission.

Travel-lift 50 tonne lift at the marina plus a new one at the head of the *cala*.

Crane 5 tonne crane.

Engineers Workshops in the marina boatyard.

Sail repairs Can be arranged via the marina office.

Chandlery In the marina complex.

Water On the pontoons and the marina south mole.

Showers In the marina complex and the *Club Náutico*.

Electricity 220v AC points on all pontoons, some 380v points.

Fuel Fuelling berth at the end of the marina south mole.

Cala Llonga and the Marina Cala d'Or on the left, with Cala d'Or itself on the right. The camera is looking northwest.

Ice From the supermarket.

Yacht club The Club Náutico de Cala d'Or (☎ 657069) has a clubhouse on the northeast side of Cala Llonga with bar, lounge, terraces and showers.

Banks Several in the nearby tourist complex.

Shops/provisioning Supermarket and other shops nearby, with more at Porto Petro about 1 mile away.

Produce market Wednesday and Saturday mornings in Santanyí, about 7 miles away by road.

Hotels/restaurants/cafés etc. Many hotels of all grades, plus restaurants, cafés and bars.

Laundry In the nearby tourist complex.

Medical services In Cala d'Or and Santanyí, about 7 miles away by road.

Communications

Car hire/taxis In the town.

Buses Bus service to Santanyí, Palma etc.

⚓ **Cala d'Egos** 39°22'N 3°14'·1E

A twisty, rocky-cliffed *cala*, surrounded by mainly detached houses plus a large hotel overlooking the beach at its head. Anchor in 3–5m over sand and weed, open to southeast and south.

⚓ **Cala del Llamp** 39°21'·6N 3°13'·6E

A small *cala* between rocky cliffs on the northeast side of the entrance to Porto Petro. Anchor near the head in 3m over stone and weed, open to southeast and south. The area is occupied by detached houses, many with large gardens and pools.

Cala d'Or on the left and Cala Gran on the right, looking northwest.

Porto Petro

39°21'·5N 3°13'E (entrance)

Charts *Approach* *Harbour*
Admiralty *2831*
Spanish *900, 423* *4231*
French *7116* *7119*

Lights

0311·8 **Punta de sa Torre** 39°21'·4N 3°13'E
  Fl(3+1)10s22m7M
  White tower on square base with two
  vertical black stripes 9m
0311·9 **Yacht harbour south mole**
  39°21'·7N 3°12'·8E
  Fl.R.3s7m5M Red column 3m
0312·3 **Punta Sa Plaja** 39°21'·8N 3°12'·8E
  Q.G.6m3M Green column on white base
  displaying green ▲ 4m
0312·2 **Yacht harbour hammerhead, north end**
  39°21'·8N 3°12'·8E Fl(2)R.6s6m3M
  Red column on white hut displaying red ■ 5m
0312·25 **Yacht harbour hammerhead, south end**
  39°21'·7N 3°12'·7E
  Fl(2)G.7s4m2M Green post 3m
0312 **Yacht harbour south inner mole**
  39°21'·7N 3°12'·7E Q(4)R.12s6m3M
  Red column on white hut displaying red ■ 5m

The entrance to Porto Petro looking northwest. Cala d'els
Homos Morts and Cala de Sa Torre are on the left, Porto Petro
yacht harbour in the centre with Cala dels Mats opposite, and
Cala del Llamp to the right.

Port Communications

VHF – Yacht harbour (Real Club Náutico Porto Petro)
  Ch 9.
☎/*Fax* – Puerto de Porto Petro ☎ 657012; Real Club
  Náutico Porto Petro ☎ 657657, *Fax* 659216.

General

A small but attractive yacht and fishing harbour
occupying only one corner of a good-sized *cala*
amidst relatively undeveloped surroundings, Porto
Petro yacht harbour can berth 230 or so boats up to
15m. In the past depth was a problem with much of
the yacht harbour having less than 2m, but dredging
is reported to have approximately doubled previous
figures (and charges have increased to match). A
new mole has been built northeastwards from the
rocky headland south of the harbour, increasing the
number of deeper berths and blocking any
southeasterly swell. There is a sailing school and a
branch of the Club Méditerranée in the *cala* and
facilities for visitors are improving. However the
small yacht harbour is frequently crowded in
summer and a preliminary call on VHF Ch 9 is
advisable.

A visit to the old town of Santanyí some 5½ miles
inland should prove interesting and a market is held
there on Wednesday and Saturday mornings. A
'petit train' runs between Cala d'Or, Porto Petro
and Cala Mondrago.

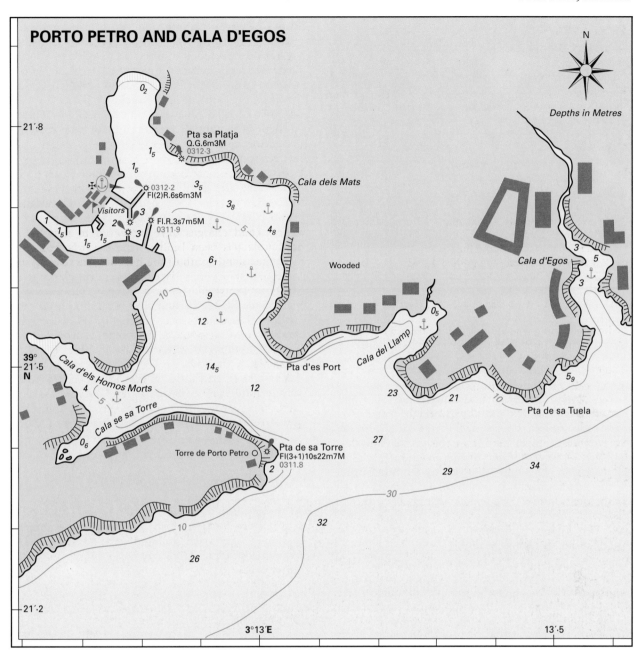

PORTO PETRO AND CALA D'EGOS

Fiestas are held on 25 July in honour of San Jaime, with horseback processions, and on 30 November in honour of San Andrés.

Approach

From south Porto Petro lies 9·5 miles northeast of Punta de las Salinas (Fl(2+1)20s17m13M, white tower and building, narrow stone bands 17m), much of it being rough cliffs with few *calas* of any size until Calas Llombarts and Santanyí are reached. From Puerto de Cala Figuera with its conspicuous lighthouse (Fl.3s32m12M, white octagonal tower with vertical black stripes 6m) the coast is of low rocky cliffs. There is one small bay and a large deep *cala* before Porto Petro is reached. The Torre de Porto Petro and lighthouse (Fl(3+1)10s22m7M, white tower on square base with two vertical black stripes 9m) are obscured from west of south, and the entrance will be visible before they are seen.

From north From Cala Llonga and its low, square pinkish-brown fort and nearby lighthouse (Fl(1+2)20s17m5M, round white column on square white base, both with vertical black stripes 6m) the coast is of low rocky cliffs broken by two small *calas*. The Torre de Porto Petro is very conspicuous from this direction, as is the lighthouse described above.

Entrance

The *cala* entrance is wide and unencumbered. Buoys are sometimes laid in the approach to the yacht harbour, otherwise remain near the middle of the *cala* until the south mole is abeam before swinging to pass between it and the hammerhead. On no account venture beyond the north end of the hammerhead as depths shoal rapidly. There is a 3 knot speed limit.

137

Porto Petro yacht harbour, looking just north of west. Many of the features mentioned in the text can be made out, including the shoals close north of the hammerhead mole.

Berthing

There is no designated reception quay, and both sides of the south mole are sloped. Preferably contact the harbour office on VHF Ch 9 prior to arrival, otherwise look for a vacant berth on the visitors' quay (see plan) and enquire at the *Club Náutico*. 3m should be found between the outer and inner south moles, 2·5–3m against the south arm of the hammerhead and 2·5m in the visitors' berths opposite. Otherwise watch the depth-sounder whilst manoeuvring. The angle enclosed by the north arm of the hammerhead is reserved for fishing and commerical tourist boats and the shallow inner harbour is private.

Anchorages in the approach

There are several possible anchorages – in Cala d'els Homos Morts and Cala de Sa Torre (4–6m over sand and weed, open to the east), in the main part of the *cala* (4–12m over sand, stones and weed open to the southeast), Cala dels Mats (3–5m over sand and weed, open to the south) or, for very shallow craft, off the beach north of the yacht harbour. All anchorages may be affected by swell from south, southeast or east and a trip line is recommended because the bottom is foul in places. As of 1996 there was no charge for anchoring.

For Cala del Llamp see page 135.

Charges *(see page 6)*

High season daily rate – Band B (15m), Band A (10m); low season daily rate – Band A. Water and electricity included. Not all credit cards are accepted.

Facilities

Boatyard Basic work on engines, woodwork and GRP possible. Enquire at the *Réal Club Náutico*.
Slipway Shallow slipway north of the hammerhead mole.

Water On the quays and a tap on the hammerhead mole. A deposit is normally required before the hose is connected, but it may be possible to fill the odd container *gratis*.
Showers At the *Réal Club Náutico*. A small charge is made if not berthed in the yacht harbour.
Electricity 220v AC on quays plus a few 380v points. A deposit is normally required before the cable is connected.
Fuel No fuel available.
Ice From a café near the root of the mole.
Yacht club The Réal Club Náutico Porto Petro (☎ 657657, *Fax* 659216) has a small clubhouse on the quay overlooking the yacht harbour.
Banks In Cala d'Or and Santanyí, the latter about 5 miles away by road.
Shops/provisioning Small supermarket nearby plus other shops in the village able to meet all day-to-day requirements.
Produce market Wednesday and Saturday mornings in Santanyí.
Hotels/restaurants/cafés etc. A couple of hotels and several restaurants, cafés and bars.
Laundry In Cala d'Or.
Medical services In Cala d'Or and Santanyí, the latter about 5 miles away by road.

Communications

Car hire/taxis Enquire at the *Réal Club Náutico*.
Buses Bus service to Santanyí, Palma etc.

⚓ **Cala Mondragó** 39°21'N 3°11'·5E
A wide, attractive and largely unspoilt *cala* between low rocky cliffs, Cala Mondragó has four arms, two of which are buoyed off in summer for swimmers. Anchor in 4–8m over sand and some weed, open to east and southeast. There are café/bars on both the tourist beaches.

Cala Mondragó with its fine beaches seen from southeast. The line of buoys marking the bathing area can just be seen.

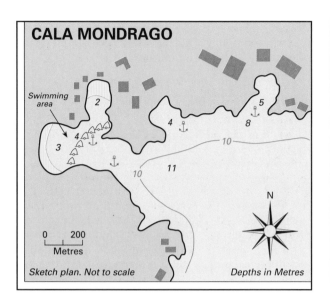

CALA MONDRAGO

Swimming area

2

5

8

4

3 4

10

10 11

N

0 200
Metres

Sketch plan. Not to scale

Depths in Metres

Looking straight into Puerto de Cala Figuera from the southeast. Both lights listed in the text can be seen, together with three yachts berthed stern-to at the mole.

Puerto de Cala Figuera

39°19'·8N 3°10'·5E

Charts	*Approach*	*Harbour*
Admiralty	*2831*	
Spanish	*900, 423*	*4231*
French	*7116*	*7119*

Lights

0312·6 **Torre D'en Beu** 39°19'·8N 3°10'·7E
Fl.3s32m12M
White octagonal tower, vertical black stripes 6m
0313 **Molehead** 39°20'N 3°10'·3E
Fl(2)R.6s6m3M Red column on white base
displaying red ■ 5m

Port Communications

Puerto de Cala Figuera ☎ 645242.

General

A very small, attractive harbour devoted to fishing and a small day tourist trade. There is little space for yachts in the sheltered areas although five berths are reserved for visitors stern-to at the short mole. These would become untenable with much wind or swell from east, southeast or south, as would the anchorage further out. For this reason the *cala* is only suitable for a night stop in very settled weather. The approach is straightforward but the entrance can be difficult to locate as it is narrow and lies between cliffs. Facilities are very limited.

A visit to the old town of Santanyí 2½ miles inland should prove worthwhile. The shopping there is reasonably good and a market is held on Wednesday and Saturday mornings. The *cala* itself is interesting to explore by dinghy. Puerto de Cala Figuera is one of many harbours in Mallorca to honour *Nuestra Señora del Carmen* on 16 July with a *fiesta* including waterborne processions.

Approach

From south Puerto de Cala Figuera lies 7 miles northwest of Punta de las Salinas (Fl(2+1)20s 17m13M, white tower and building, narrow stone bands 17m), much of it being rough cliffs with few *calas* of any size until Cala Llombart is reached. The entrance to Cala Figuera can be identified in the close approach by the lighthouse (Fl.3s32m12M, white octagonal tower with vertical black stripes 6m) in front of a brownish stone watchtower on the northeast side of the entrance.

From north From Porto Petro the coast is of low, broken rocky cliffs with a wide, deep indentation at Cala Mondragó. If sailing close inshore the lighthouse and tower at Cala Figuera are screened by hills and not visible until the closer approach.

PUERTO DE CALA FIGUERA

N

Moorings

Fishing boats

0.9

Depths in Metres

20´

0.9 1.6 2 3.1

2.8 Fl(2)R.6s
6m3M

4

Fisherman's
Quay Visitors

10

12

17

Torre
D'en Beu

39°
19'·8
N

18 20

26

Fl.3s32m12M
0312·6

10·2 3°10'·5E

Entrance

The red column on the end of the molehead can be seen from outside the entrance. Follow an S-shaped course, remaining near the centre of the *cala* and swinging wide of the foul ground extending from the two rocky points (see plan). The wind can be fluky between the high cliffs and the seas heavy and confused, making it difficult for craft with limited auxiliary power. There is a 3 knot speed limit.

Berthing

Five berths are reserved for visiting yachts on the southeast side of the mole, laying an anchor ahead and taking a stern line ashore. Holding is poor with weed on soft, shallow, muddy sand over rock, and plenty of scope is required. There are some underwater projections off the mole itself. This position is completely exposed to onshore winds from between east and southeast which bring in a nasty swell and the *cala* is therefore only suitable as a night stop in very settled conditions.

Yachts are not normally permitted to berth at the fishermen's quay inside the mole, though from Friday evening to Sunday evening it may be possible to lie alongside a fishing boat – which will probably wish to leave at 0600 on Monday morning. A small yacht can sometimes find a slot in the narrow northern arm. The western arm is very tight and is further obstructed by lines across the harbour.

Moorings

There are a few moorings in the northern arm but they are private and usually occupied.

Anchorage

Anchor in the middle of the *cala* well clear of the mole in 4–8m over muddy sand and rock, possibly with a line ashore to limit swinging, open to east and southeast. If space and draught permit anchorage may be found north of the mole, but this area is usually taken up by large fishing boats. Holding is reported to be poor in places.

Facilities

Crane 5 tonne crane on the fishermen's quay.
Slipway Small slipway at the head of the western arm.
Water Tap at the (wholesale) fish market near the root of the mole.
Electricity Not available.
Fuel Diesel from a pump near the root of the mole. Petrol by can from a filling station at Santanyí some 2½ miles inland.
Ice From one of the restaurants.
Banks In Santanyí.
Shops/provisioning Provisions Supermarket 10 minutes' walk up the hill south of the harbour. A few small shops provide everyday requirements, with many more shops in Santanyí.

Hotels/restaurants/cafés etc. A few hotels, several restaurants and some café/bars near the harbour.
Medical services In the village and at Santanyí, 2½ miles inland.

Communications

Car hire/taxis In Santanyí.
Buses Summer service to Santanyí and beyond.

⌀ Cala Santanyí 39°19'·8N 3°08'·9E

A 'developed' *cala* surrounded by houses and hotels, its sandy beach roped off for swimming. There is a small tower on the east side of entrance and a small island on west side, plus some breaking rocks inshore. Anchor in the middle of the *cala* in 5–10m over sand, open to east and southeast. In addition to the many swimmers there is a windsurfing school.

⌀ Cala Llombart 39°19'·5N 3°08'·6E

A double *cala*, though the northern arm is much the smaller, with rocky sides and a roped-off beach to the south. There is foul ground off the headland between the two. Anchor in 4–6m over sand and weed, open to east, southeast and possibly south.

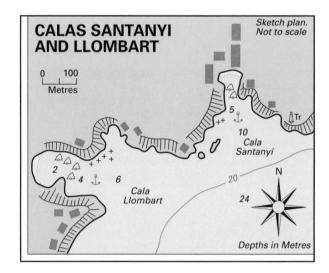

Cala Llombart from the southeast. The 'double' cliffs, falling sheer to a rubble platform just above sea level, are typical of much of the surrounding coastline.

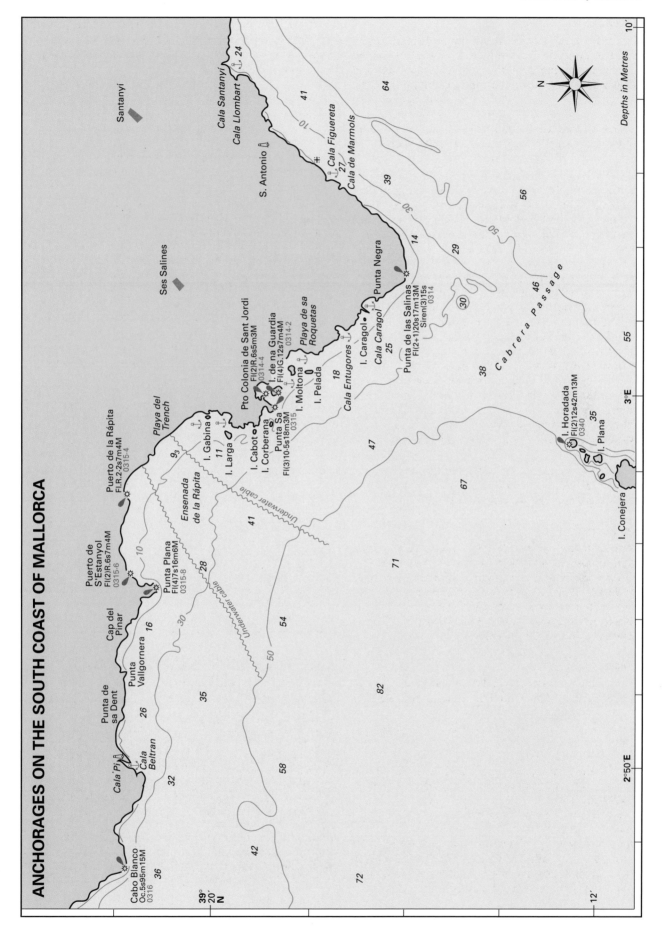

ANCHORAGES ON THE SOUTH COAST OF MALLORCA

Depths in Metres

N

Cabo Blanco
Oc.5s95m15M
0316

Punta de
sa Dent

Cala Pi

Cala
Beltran

Punta
Vallgornera

Cap del
Pinar

Punta Plana
Fl(4)7s16m6M
0315·8

Puerto de
S'Estanyol
Fl(2)R.6s7m4M
0315·6

Puerto de la Rápita
Fl.R.2.2s7m4M
0315·4

Playa del
Trench

Ensenada
de la Rápita

I. Gabina

I. Larga

I. Cabot

I. Corberana

Punta Sa
Fl(3)10·5s18m3M
0315

Pto Colonia de Sant Jordi
Fl(2)R.6s5m3M
0314·4

I. de na Guardia
Fl(4)G.12s7m4M
0314·2

I. Moltona

I. Pelada

Playa de sa
Roquetas

Cala Entugores

I. Caragol

Cala Caragol

Punta de las Salinas
Fl(2+1)20s17m13M
Siren(3)15s
0314

Punta Negra

Santanyí

Ses Salines

S. Antonio

Cala Santanyí

Cala Llombart

Cala Figuereta

Cala de Marmols

Cabrera Passage

I. Horadada
Fl(2)12s42m13M
0340

I. Plana

I. Conejera

39°
20'
N

2°50'E

3°E

10'

12'

Underwater cable

Underwater cable

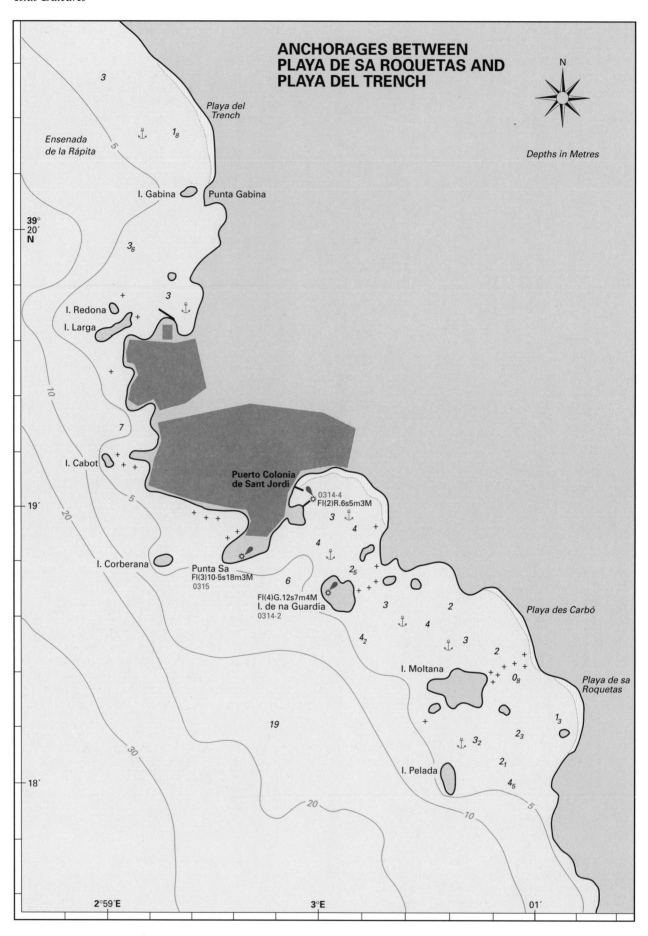

ANCHORAGES BETWEEN
PLAYA DE SA ROQUETAS AND
PLAYA DEL TRENCH

N

Depths in Metres

Playa del
Trench

Ensenada
de la Rápita

I. Gabina   Punta Gabina

39°
20′
N

I. Redona

I. Larga

I. Cabot

Puerto Colonia
de Sant Jordi

0314·4
Fl(2)R.6s5m3M

19′

I. Corberana

Punta Sa
Fl(3)10·5s18m3M
0315

Fl(4)G.12s7m4M
I. de na Guardia
0314·2

Playa des Carbó

I. Moltana

Playa de sa
Roquetas

I. Pelada

18′

2°59′E   3°E   01′

⚓ **Cala Marmols** 39°17'·3N 3°05'·6E
A small and completely deserted *cala* between rocky cliffs, just over 2 miles north of Punta Salinas. Anchor in 3–6m over sand, open from east round to south.

⚓ **Punta de las Salinas** 39°16'N 3°03'·5E
A low, flat, wooded promontory edged by stony beaches and marked by a conspicuous lighthouse (Fl(2+1)20s17m13M, white tower and building with narrow stone bands 17m).

Punta de las Salinas with its 'helter-skelter' lighthouse seen from the west on a blowy day.

⚓ **Cala Caragol** 39°16'·8N 3°02'·6E
A wide bay one mile northwest of Punta Salinas and backed by pine woods, Cala Caragol has a particularly fine beach bounded to the southeast by the low rocky Punta Negra and to the northwest by Islote Caragol. Anchor in 2–5m over sand and weed, open southeast through south and southwest to west. The bay is often full of yachts during summer, but otherwise appears little visited. There are a few houses and a rough road.

⚓ **Cala Entugores** 39°17'·4N 3°01'·8E
Much smaller and narrower than its neighbour, Cala Entugores has no beach and is very shallow. Enter carefully watching the depth-sounder – it is reported to shoal to below 2·5m not far from the entrance. Anchor as depth dictates open to south, southwest and west.

⚓ **Playa de sa Roquetas** 39°18'·3N 3°01'·1E
⚓ **Playa des Carbó** 39°18'·6N 3°00'·8E
Two indentations on a long sandy beach, separated by a sand spit running out towards Isla Moltona. Isla de na Guardia lies at the northwestern limit of the two beaches with Puerto Colonia de Sant Jordi beyond, and Isla Pelada at the southern end. Keel yachts should not attempt to pass inside either Isla Moltona or Isla de na Guardia (see also photograph page 145).

Anchor in the northern bay (Playa des Carbó) in 3–4m over mainly sand, open to the southwest and to swell from west, south and southeast, or further south (Playa de sa Roquetas) in 2–4m over sand and weed open to south, through southwest to west. There can be considerable disturbance from jet-skis and small speedboats in both anchorages.

Puerto Colonia de Sant Jordi (Puerto de Campos)
39°19'N 3°00'E

Charts   *Approach*
Admiralty   *2832*
Spanish   *900, 422, 423, 422A*
French   *7115,* 7116

Lights
Approach
0315 **Punta Sa** 39°18'·8N 2°59'·7E
    Fl(3)10·5s18m3M
    White round tower, three black bands 12m
0314·2 **Isla de na Guardia** 39°18'·7N 3°00'E
    Fl(4)G.12s7m4M White tower, green top 5m
Entrance
0314·4 **Southeast breakwater** 39°19'N 3°00'E
    Fl(2)R.6s5m3M
    Red column on white base 3m
0314·5 **Marina east mole** 39°19'N 3°00'E
    F.R. Red column on white base 3m
0314·6 **Marina north mole** 39°19'N 2°59'·9E
    Fl.G.3s4m3M
    Green column on white base 3m

Port Communications
Puerto Colonia de Sant Jordi ☎ 655148, *Fax* 656019.

General
A smallish fishing and yachting harbour, much of it shallow and occupied by local craft. The old central quay has been demolished to make way for three new pontoons, already fully occupied, but there is still a very genuine fishing presence with nets being mended on the quayside. Facilities are limited but do include fuel, water and reasonable shopping. The approach is between low islands, some unmarked, and care is necessary.

Tourist ferries taking visitors to Cabrera berth inshore of the fuelling pontoon and leave the harbour at speed, apparently with no real lookout. This is a particular hazard if coming in by dinghy. For details of Isla and Puerto de Cabrera see pages 161 onwards.

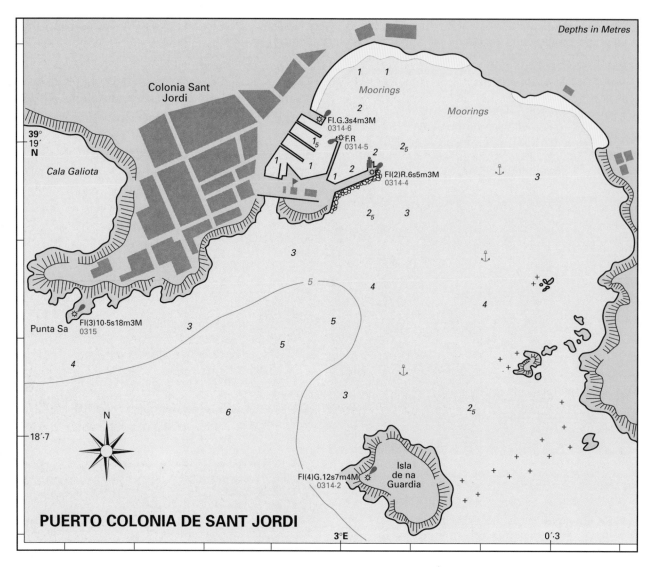

PUERTO COLONIA DE SANT JORDI

Approach

From west From Cabo Blanco, a high promontory of steep light brown cliffs topped by a lighthouse (Oc.5s95m15M, white tower and building 12m) and an old watchtower, the coast is of low rocky cliffs with a long sandy bay, Playa del Trench, followed by more low rocky cliffs and the houses and apartment blocks of Colonia de Sant Jordi. Punta Sa may be identified by its conspicuous lighthouse (Fl(3)10·5s18m3M, white round tower with three black bands 12m) on the very end of the headland, though it is partially hidden if viewed from further north. The low and inconspicuous Isla Corberana some 550m offshore presents a potential hazard, particularly when sailing at night, though there is good water on either side.

From east Round the low, tree-covered Punta Salinas with its lighthouse (Fl(2+1)20s17m13M, white tower and building with narrow stone bands 17m) and follow the coast past several sandy bays and low inconspicuous islands until south of the lighthouse on Punta Sa (see above). On no account attempt to pass inside either Isla Moltona or Isla de na Guardia.

Anchorage in the approach

The northeastern part of the bay between the harbour entrance and Isla de na Guardia is occupied by moorings – anchor further southwest in 3–5m over sand and weed, open to southwest and south but with partial shelter from the southeast. Areas of the bottom are foul and a tripline is advisable.

Entrance

From a point south of the lighthouse on Punta Sa, enter the bay on a northeasterly course leaving Isla de la Guardia to starboard. Depths shoal as the harbour is approached – sound carefully. Note that the end of the southeast breakwater projects some distance beyond the light structure (though entry at night is not recommended).

Berthing

Much of the inner harbour has depths of less than 1·5m, though the fuel berth and the southern side of the marina south mole are reported to have 2m. Secure at the fuel berth and consult harbour staff.

Puerto Colonia de Sant Jordi looking southwest, with Punta Sa on the left (the lighthouse can just be made out on the headland) and Isla Corberana behind.

Charges *(see page 6)*

High season daily rate – Band A (15m), Band B (10m); low season daily rate – Band C. Water and electricity extra.

Facilities

Boatyard Small yard west of the *Club Náutico*.

Slipways Two, both very shallow.

Engineer At the boatyard.

Water Taps on quays and pontoons, and at the fuel berth.

Electricity 220v AC on quays and pontoons.

Fuel Diesel and petrol pumps inside the end of the south breakwater, but no more than 2m depth. Access can be difficult due to nearby tourist boats.

Ice From the fuel berth.

Yacht club The Club Náutico de Sant Jordi has a small clubhouse at the south end of the harbour.

Banks In the town.

Shops/provisioning Supermarket and other shops in the town.

Hotels/restaurants/cafés etc. A few of each, including a bar at the south end of the harbour.

Laundry In the town.

Medical services Simple medical services available.

Communications

Car hire/taxis In the town.

Buses Bus service to Ses Salinas and on to Palma etc.

Looking southeast over Colonia Sant Jordi towards Punta Salinas. Isla Cabot is on the right of the picture with Isla Corberana behind, the lighthouse on Punta Sa can be made out, and the three islands of Isla de na Guardia, Isla Moltona and Isla Pelada lie off the Playas des Carbó and de sa Roquetas.

⚓ Ensenada de la Rápita, southeast corner
39°19'·7N 2°59'·4E

A well sheltered anchorage close north of the headland on which Colonia Sant Jordi stands, and south of the Playa del Trench. Anchor in 3m or more over sand and weed northeast of an old and ruinous quay, open to northwest (short fetch) and west. There is a fine beach to the east and a large

145

ENSENADA DE LA RAPITA

hotel near the root of the quay, generating the inevitable jet-skis and small speedboats.

⚓ **Bay south of Isla Gabina** 39°20'N 2°59'·5E
Similar to the above, but with much less shelter from the southwest. However there is also less disturbance from jet-skis and speedboats.

⚓ **Playa del Trench** 39°20'·8N 2°59'E
An open bay anchorage off a fine sandy beach. Anchor in 3m+ over sand and weed, open to south through southwest to northwest. A submarine cable runs in a west-southwesterly direction from Punta de sas Covetas at the north end of the beach.

Puerto de la Rápita
39°21'·8N 2°57'·4E

Charts *Approach*
Admiralty *2832*
Spanish *900, 422, 423*
French *7115*

Lights
Approach
0315·8 **Punta Plana** 39°21'·2N 2°54'·9E
 Fl(4)7s16m6M White tower, black bands, on building 12m
Entrance
0315·4 **Southwest breakwater** 39°21'·8N 2°57'·4E
 Fl.R.2·2s7m4M
 Red column on white base 6m
0315·3 **East breakwater** 39°21'·8N 2°57'·4E
 Fl(2)G.9s8m4M
 Green column on white base 6m

Port Communications
Club Náutico de la Rápita VHF Ch 9, ☎ 640001, *Fax* 640821.

General
Puerto de la Rápita is a large and modern artificial yacht harbour with more than 450 berths and excellent facilities, situated at the northwest end of the long Playa del Trench. It is easy to enter and offers good protection once inside, though a heavy swell from southeast or south could make the final approach dangerous due to shoaling water. In 1996 development of the land behind the marina was still in its very early stages, however the white sand beach to the southeast already had its share of tourists and sunbeds.

For those interested in ancient history and archaeological remains, this area is littered with interesting 'finds' such as Capicorp Vey, a prehistoric village, Sollerich (a burial cave) and Son Herue, a Bronze Age burial site. A *fiesta* in honour of *Nuestra Señora del Carmen* is held on 16 July.

Puerto de la Rápita is a favourite departure point for Isla de Cabrera 12½ miles to the south and the marina staff are happy to help visitors apply for the necessary permit. For details of Isla and Puerto de Cabrera see pages 161 onwards.

Approach
From west From Cabo Blanco, a high promontory of steep light brown cliffs topped by a lighthouse (Oc.5s95m15M, white tower and building 12m) and an old watchtower, the coast is of low rocky cliffs until Punta Plana (Fl(4)7s16m6M, white tower with black bands on building 12m) is rounded. Passing Puerto de S'Estanyol in the northwest corner of the bay, a northeast course should be set towards the far end of the houses of La Rápita. On closer approach the harbour breakwater will be seen with an old watchtower (18m) behind.

From east Round the low, tree-covered Punta Salinas with its lighthouse (Fl(2+1)20s17m13M, white tower and building with narrow stone bands 17m) and follow the coast past several sandy bays and low inconspicuous islands. Allow Punta Sa (Fl(3)10·5s18m3M, white round tower with three black bands 12m) an offing of at least ½ mile in order to clear Isla Corberana, then steer north-northwest into the wide Ensenada de la Rápita towards the houses of La Rápita. On closer approach the harbour breakwater will be seen with an old watchtower (18m) behind.

Anchorage in the approach
Anchor in 4–5m over sand 200–300m east or southeast of the harbour entrance, open from southeast round to southwest.

Entrance
The entrance presents no problems and normally Puerto de la Rápita would be easy to enter by day or night, though a heavy swell from southeast or south could make the final approach dangerous due to shoaling water. However in 1996 the southwest breakwater was being extended, leaving the port

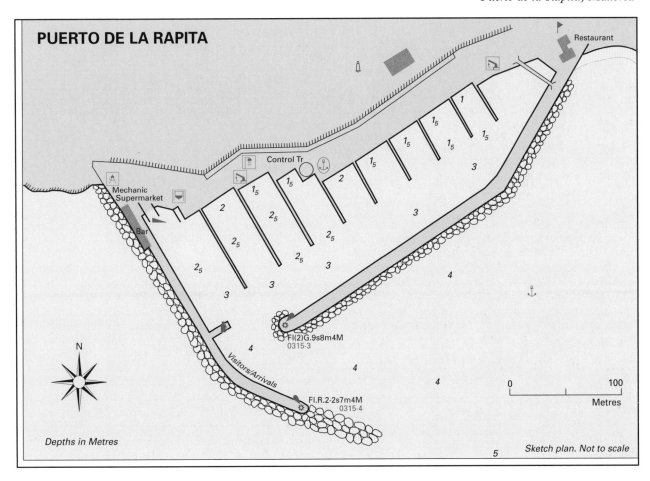

PUERTO DE LA RAPITA

Restaurant

Control Tr

Mechanic
Supermarket

Bar

Visitors/Arrivals

Fl(2)G.9s8m4M
0315·3

Fl.R.2·2s7m4M
0315·4

N

Depths in Metres

Sketch plan. Not to scale

0   100
Metres

Puerto de la Rápita looking almost due north. The marina
control tower is in the centre of the picture with the old
watchtower mentioned in the text on its right.

hand light well short of its end. A very small (and presumably temporary) red light was displayed on a post near the end. It would be wise for visitors' to avoid first time entry at night until the work is completed. There is a 2 knot speed limit in the harbour.

Berthing

Secure stern-to at the reception quay inside the southwest breakwater until allocated a berth. Alternatively call the marina office on VHF Ch 9 before arrival.

Charges *(see page 6)*

High season daily rate – Band A; low season daily rate – Band B. Water and electricity extra.

Facilities

Boatyard In the northwest area of the marina.
Travel-lift 50 tonne lift in the boatyard area.
Crane 7 tonne crane at the northeast end of the harbour.
Slipway The wide slipway at the northeast end of the harbour has been rendered inaccessible by a fixed walkway.
Engineers Cosme Oliver (☎ 640199, *Fax* 640021) at the west end of the harbour are official service agents for Caterpillar, Honda, Perkins, Tohatsu, Vetus, Volvo Penta and Yamaha.
Chandlery Two at the west end of the harbour.
Water Taps on pontoons and quays, and at the visitors' quay. However it is sometimes brackish – check before filling tanks. It has been reported that the water at the fuel berth is of better quality.
Showers Several blocks opposite the control tower.
Electricity 220v AC and some 380v AC points on quays and pontoons, and at the visitors' quay.
Fuel Diesel and petrol at the fuel berth.
Ice From a machine near the marina supermarket.
Yacht club The Club Náutico de la Rápita (☎ 640001, *Fax* 640821) has a large and well appointed clubhouse with a bar and terrace restaurant at the east end of the harbour.
Bank In the town.
Shops/provisioning Small supermarket at the west end of the harbour, more shops in the town ½ mile away.
Hotels/restaurants/cafés etc. A few hotels and several restaurants in the town, plus a restaurant at the *Club Náutico* and a café/bar at the west end of the harbour.
Medical services In the town.

Communications

Car hire/taxis Consult the marina office.
Buses Bus service to Palma etc.

Puerto de S'Estanyol (El Estañol)

39°21'·7N 2°55'·3E

Charts

	Approach
Admiralty	*2832*
Spanish	*900, 422, 423*
French	*7115*

Lights

Approach
0315·8 **Punta Plana** 39°21'·2N 2°54'·9E
Fl(4)7s16m6M White tower, black bands, on building 12m

Entrance
0315·6 **South breakwater** 39°21'·7N 2°55'·3E
Fl(2)R.6s7m4M
Red column on white base 6m
0315·7 **North mole** 39°21'·7N 2°55'·2E
Fl.G.2·5s8m3M Black post 7m

Port Communications

Club Náutico de S'Estanyol VHF Ch 9, ☎ 640085, *Fax* 640682.

General

A small, square, artificial harbour close east of Punta Plana, occupied by fishing boats and a few yachts under 12m or so. Approach and entrance are not usually difficult but would be dangerous in strong winds and swell from southeast or south due to shallow water in the approach. Facilities are fair and everyday shopping requirements can be met in the strip of coastal development which joins up with La Rápita to the east.

Ambitious plans to more than double the size of the harbour by means of a new breakwater have been under discussion for several years. Although work had not started by February 1997 it appeared increasingly likely that, if funds could be raised, the expansion might yet take place.

Approach

From west From Cabo Blanco, a high promontory of steep light brown cliffs topped by a lighthouse (Oc.5s95m15M, white tower and building 12m) and an old watchtower, the coast is of low rocky cliffs until Punta Plana (Fl(4)7s16m6M, white tower with black bands on building 12m) is rounded. Puerto de S'Estanyol lies 0·6 mile northnortheast of the headland past a small, low-lying island which should be left to port.

From east Round the low, tree-covered Punta Salinas with its lighthouse (Fl(2+1)20s17m13M, white tower and building with narrow stone bands 17m) and follow the coast past several sandy bays and low inconspicuous islands. Allow Punta Sa (Fl(3)10·5s18m3M, white round tower with three black bands 12m) an offing of at least ½ mile in order to clear Isla Corberana, then steer northwest into the wide Ensenada de la Rápita, heading for a

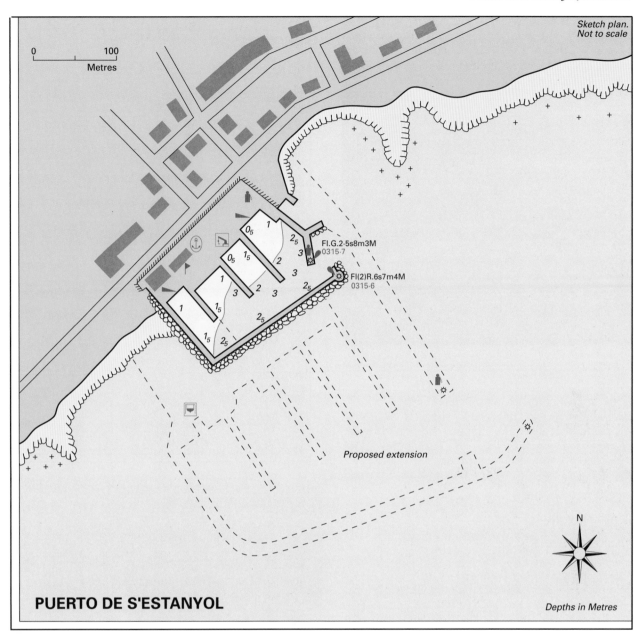

Sketch plan.
Not to scale

0 — 100
Metres

Fl.G.2·5s8m3M
0315·7

Fl(2)R.6s7m4M
0315·6

Proposed extension

N

PUERTO DE S'ESTANYOL

Depths in Metres

position just inside the low-lying Punta Plana. Puerto de S'Estanyol lies 0·6 mile north-northeast of the headland.

Entrance

Approach the eastern corner of the harbour heading northwest to round the head of the south breakwater at slow speed. The entrance is narrow and may be partially blocked by moored boats. There is a 2 knot speed limit. Note that the close approach and entrance are shallow, making it dangerous in heavy swell from south or southeast.

Berthing

Secure to the inner side of the south breakwater as space permits and visit the harbour office for allocation of a berth. Depths are 2·5–3m near the breakwater head shoaling to 2m or so at the elbow.

Charges *(see page 6)*

High season daily rate – Band B; low season daily rate – Band C. Water and electricity included.

Facilities

Crane 12·5 tonne crane.
Slipway Near the root of the north mole.
Engineer Motor mechanic available.
Water Taps on quays and pontoons.
Showers In west corner of the harbour.
Electricity 220v AC points at foot of lamp-posts and at normal supply points.
Fuel Diesel pump at the head of the north mole, petrol pump at its root (ie. by can only).
Ice From the bar.
Yacht club The Club Náutico S'Estanyol (☎ 640085, *Fax* 640682) has a small clubhouse with restaurant, bar, terrace and two tennis courts.

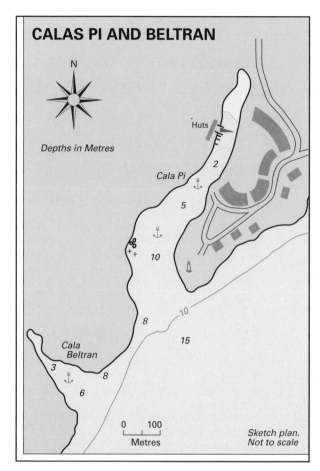

The small harbour of Puerto de S'Estanyol (with Punta Plana in the distance), looking west.

Bank In La Rápita, about 1½ miles away.

Shops/provisioning Everyday supplies from a supermarket and other shops in the nearby town.

Hotels/restaurants/cafés etc. A few hotels and restaurants and several café/bars.

Hospital/medical services In Lluchmayor, 8 miles inland.

Communications

Car hire/taxis Consult the harbour office.

Communications Bus service to Palma etc.

⚓ Cala Pi 39°21'·8N 2°50'·2E

A beautiful and very popular *cala* between high cliffs, but extremely narrow and often crowded (avoid weekends when charter yachts are setting out or returning). There is a conspicuous stone tower on the headland southeast of the entrance. Anchor in 2–8m over sand and some weed, open to the south and to swell from southeast and east, either using a stern anchor or taking a line ashore to restrict swinging. There are fishermen's huts and a rough slipway by the sandy beach at the head of the *cala*, and a small tourist development with cafés and restaurants etc. to the east.

⚓ Cala Beltran 39°21'·6N 2°50'E

A small *cala* between rocky cliffs just west of Cala Pi, where it is possible to anchor in 3–5m over sand open to east and southeast.

Looking into Cala Pi from the south, with the smaller Cala Beltran on the left. The tower mentioned in the text is much more prominent from sea level.

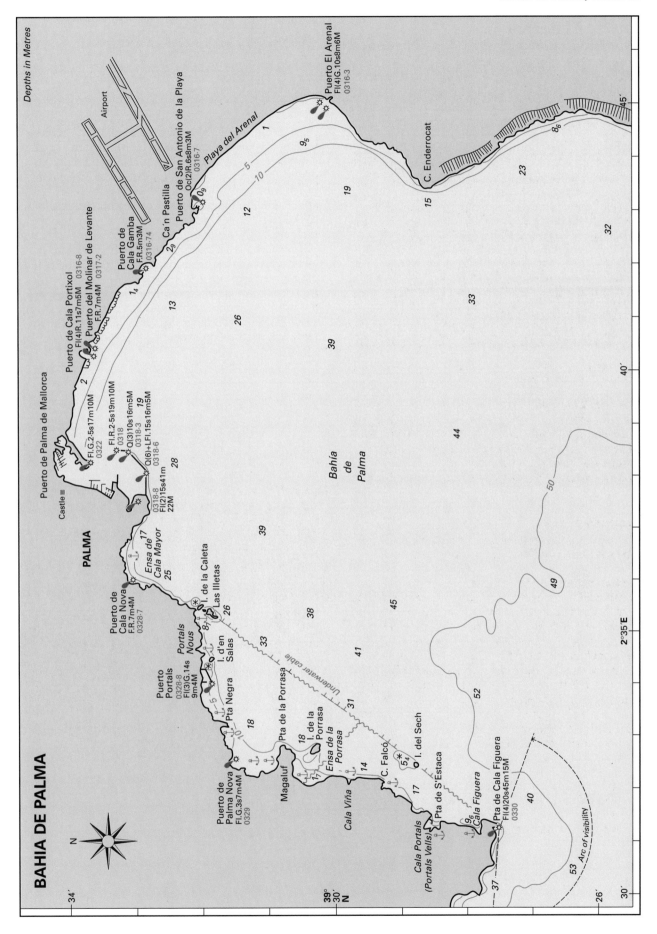

Depths in Metres

BAHIA DE PALMA

N

PALMA

Puerto de Palma de Mallorca

Castle

Puerto de Cala Nova
F.R.7m4M
0328-7

Puerto de Cala Portixol
Fl(4)R.11s7m5M 0316-8
Puerto del Molinar de Levante
F.R.7m4M 0317-2

Puerto de Cala Gamba
F.R.5m3M
0316-74

Ca´n Pastilla
Puerto de San Antonio de la Playa
Oct(2)R.6s8m3M 0316-7

Airport

Puerto El Arenal
Fl(4)G.10s8m6M
0316-3

Playa del Arenal

C. Enderrocat

Fl.G.2.5s17m10M
0322
Fl.R.2.5s19m10M
0318
Q(3)10s16m5M
0318-3
Q(6)+LFl.15s16m5M
0318-6
Fl(2)15s41m
22M 0318-8

Ensa de Cala Mayor
I. de la Caleta
Las Illetas

Portals Nous
I. d'en Salas
Pta Negra

Puerto Portals
0328.8
Fl(3)G.14s
9m4M

Pta de la Porrasa

Magaluf
I. de la Porrasa
Ensa de la Porrasa

Puerto de Palma Nova
Fl.G.3s7m4M
0329

Underwater cable

Bahía de Palma

C. Falcó
I. del Sech

Cala Viña
Pta de S'Estaca

Cala Portals
(Portals Vells)

Cala Figuera
Pta de Cala Figuera
Fl(4)20s45m15M
0330

Arc of visibility

Puerto El Arenal

39°30'·2N 2°44'·9E

Charts *Approach*
Admiralty   *2832*, 3036
Spanish   *970, 421, 421A*
French   *7115*, 7118

Lights

0316·3 **Northwest breakwater** 39°30'·2N 2°44'·9E
Fl(4)G.10s8m6M Green column on white
base displaying green ▲ 4m

0316·55 **Northeast breakwater** 39°30'·3N 2°44'·9E
Oc(4)R.15s7m4M Red post 4m

0316·6 **Northeast breakwater spur**
39°30'·2N 2°45'E Fl(2)R.8s8m6M
Red column on white hut displaying red ■ 6m

0316·4 **Central mole, northeast head**
39°30'·2N 2°44'·9E Fl.G.3s8m6M
Green column on white hut 7m

0316·5 **Central mole, west head**
39°30'·2N 2°44'·9E
Fl.R.3s4m3M Red column 3m

Port Communications

Club Náutico El Arenal VHF Ch 9, ☎ 440142, 440267
  Fax 440568.

General

A large, modern yacht harbour with over 600 berths for yachts up to 25m and with 3m+ depths throughout, built alongside a small old harbour which has been improved. It is located at the southeast end of the 2·4 mile Playa del Arenal, one of the finest sandy beaches in Mallorca – inevitably lined with a solid wall of high-rise hotel and apartment buildings. However to the south a low rocky coast is backed initially by large houses and, further on, by unspoilt open country.

The harbour offers first class facilities including a lovely clubhouse with restaurant and pool and is far enough away from the tourist areas not to suffer from traffic or other noise. Approach and entrance are normally without problem, but heavy winds and swell from the southwest quadrant could render the close approach and entrance dangerous.

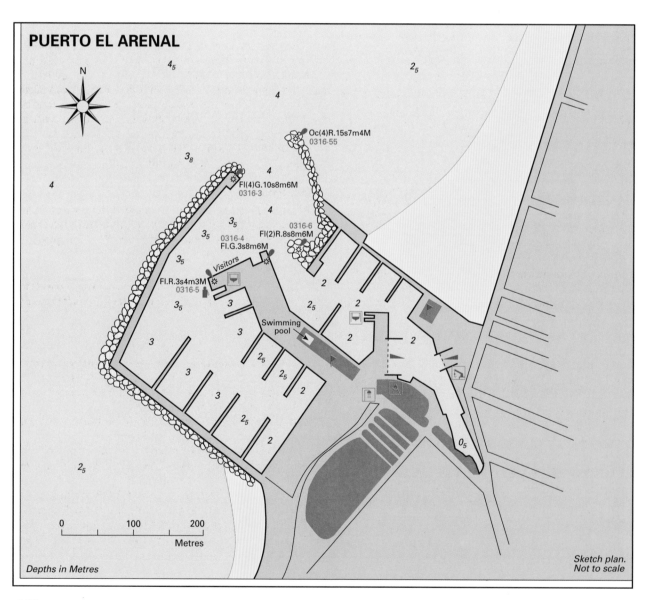

The excellent yacht harbour at Puerto El Arenal seen from the northwest. The *Club Náutico* building – and its swimming pool – can be seen on the central mole.

Puerto El Arenal is one of many suitable departure points for Isla de Cabrera and the *Club Náutico* are happy to help visitors apply for the necessary permit. For details of Isla and Puerto de Cabrera see page 161 onwards.

Approach

From west Round the very prominent Punta de Cala Figuera which has a lighthouse (Fl(4)20s45m15M, white round tower with black diagonal stripes on building 24m) and radio masts on its steep cliffs. Cross the Bahía de Palma heading just north of east towards Cabo Enderrocat, with a tower on its summit, at the northern end of a line of high cliffs. El Arenal lies 2 miles northeast of this headland, at the southeast end of a sandy beach backed by solid high-rise development.

From east Round Cabo Blanco, which is high with steep light brown cliffs topped by a lighthouse (Oc.5s95m15M, white tower and building 12m) and an old watchtower. Follow these cliffs north-northwest to round Cabo Enderrocat, which has a tower on its summit. El Arenal 2 miles northeast of this headland, at the southeast end of a sandy beach backed by solid high-rise development.

Anchorage in the approach

Anchor either side of the harbour in 3m+ over sand and weed, open southwest through west to northwest.

Entrance

The entrance is easily seen and without hazards, other than those posed by (or to) stray bathers, snorkellers, sailboards and pedalos. In previous years a line of buoys off the northeast breakwater has indicated the channel, but these were not in place in 1996 (presumably made redundant by the recent dredging). 4–5m should now be found in the entrance and 3m throughout the yacht harbour. There is a 2 knot speed limit.

Berthing

Visitors lie bow or stern-to against the head of the central mole, between the slipway and the fuel berth. Lazy lines are provided, tailed to the quay.

Charges *(see page 6)*

High season daily rate – Band B (15m), Band C (10m); low season daily rate – Band A. Water and electricity extra.

Facilities

Boatyard Layup area on the central mole with some services available. Fully fledged boatyards in Palma. For repairs and general maintenance Renav is recommended locally.

Travel-lift 50 tonne lift at the west end of the central mole. Smaller lift in the old harbour.

Crane 3 tonne mobile crane in the old harbour.

Slipways Two slipways in the old harbour and one on the end of the central mole.

Engineers Available through the *Club Náutico*.

Chandlery Just outside the main gate to the harbour.

Water Water points on the pontoons and quays.

Showers At the east and southeast corners of the harbour area.

Electricity 220v AC available on all quays and pontoons plus some 380v points.

Fuel Diesel and petrol from pumps at the west end of the central mole.

Ice From the *Club Náutico* bar.

Yacht club The Club Náutico El Arenal (☎ 440142, 440267, *Fax* 440568) has an elegant clubhouse with restaurant, TV room, bar, terraces and large swimming pool, ☎ 264019. The old clubhouse to the northeast also has a restaurant and is used by fishermen and dinghy sailors.

Banks In the town.

Shops/provisioning Everyday supplies from nearby shops and supermarkets with many more in Palma 6 miles away. Hypermarket less than 5 miles away on the road between Palma and the airport.

Markets A market is held in the town on Tuesday and Friday, with a clothes market on Thursday.

Hotels/restaurants/cafés etc. More than 100 hotels along the beach, plus many restaurants, cafés and bars.

Medical services In the town. Hospital in Palma 6 miles away.

Communications

Car hire/taxis In the town.

Buses Frequent bus service to Palma.

Ferries From Palma to the other islands and mainland Spain.

Air services Busy international airport 3½ miles away.

⚓ Bahía de Palma, northeast side

In settled weather it is possible to anchor off the shore virtually anywhere between El Arenal and Palma itself – the coast is in the main gently sloping, with wide sandy beaches. Anchor to suit draught, open to south or southeast through southwest to west. The beaches are solid with sunbeds and tourists and the road behind is, for the most part, lined with wall-to-wall apartment buildings and hotels.

Puerto de San Antonio de la Playa (Ca'n Pastilla)

39°32'N 02°43'·1E

Charts

	Approach
Admiralty	*2832*, 3036
Spanish	*970, 421, 421A*
French	*7115*, 7118

Lights

0316·7 **Southwest breakwater** 39°31'·9'N 2°43'·1E
   Oc(2)R.6s8m3M Red column 6m

0316·72 **East breakwater** 39°32'N 2°43'·1E
   F.G.6m3M Green column on small building 5m

Port Communications

Club Marítimo San Antonio de la Playa VHF Ch 9,
   ☎ 263512, *Fax* 261638.

General

A good-sized yacht harbour with nearly 400 berths, handy for the airport (though paying the price with a good deal of aircraft noise) and with better than average facilities. It is easy to approach and enter in normal conditions though with strong onshore winds and swell it could become dangerous due to shallows in the close approach.

Puerto de San Antonio de la Playa lies very close to the large tourist resort of Ca'n Pastilla with its many high-rise hotels and apartment blocks, and is occasionally referred to by this name. An excellent, but crowded, sandy beach stretches for over 2 miles to the southeast.

Approach

From west Round the very prominent Punta de Cala Figuera which has a lighthouse (Fl(4)20s45m15M, white round tower with black diagonal stripes on building 24m) and radio masts on its steep cliffs. Cross the Bahía de Palma on a northeast course – planes taking off and landing from Palma airport give a good indication of the position of this harbour. In the closer approach the long sandy Playa del Arenal, which is backed by a line of high-rise buildings, will be seen. Near the northwest end of this beach is a separate group of high-rise buildings with the harbour in front. The small, low Islote Galera which has reefs extending 100m southwest lies 0·5 mile northwest of the harbour entrance.

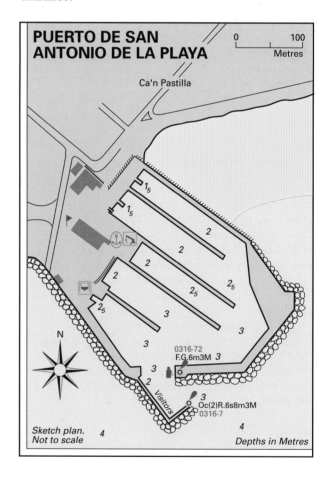

Puerto de San Antonio de la Playa seen from the southeast, with Cala Estancia just beyond. In the distance are the buildings of Palma.

From east Round Cabo Blanco, which is high with steep light brown cliffs topped by a lighthouse (Oc.5s95m15M, white tower and building 12m) and an old watchtower. Follow these cliffs north-northwest to round Cabo Enderrocat, which has a tower on its summit. Puerto de San Antonio de la Playa lies almost due north about 3·3 miles distant. See previous page for the closer approach.

Anchorage in the approach

Anchor southeast of the entrance in 5m over sand, open to south through southwest to west.

Entrance

A northward extension to the end of the southwest breakwater has improved protection, particularly at the visitors' quay, but has turned the entrance into an S-bend. Observe the 2 knot speed limit.

Cala Estancia, a shallow, semi-enclosed swimming area and dinghy harbour lies immediately northwest of the harbour. It would be possible (though difficult) to confuse the two, but with depths of 1·5m and shoaling the consequences would be dramatic.

Berthing

Preferably call ahead on VHF Ch 9 to check that a berth will be available. Otherwise secure to the inner side of the southwest breakwater and visit the harbour office at the *Club Maritimo* building. There is no more than 2·5m at the visitors' quay, shoaling to 1·5m in places.

Charges *(see page 6)*

High season daily rate – Band B (15m), Band C (10m); low season daily rate – Band A (15m), Band B (10m). Water and electricity included.

Facilities

Boatyard On the west side of the harbour, equal to most work. Otherwise large boatyards in Palma.

Travel-lift 60 tonne lift in the boatyard.

Cranes 6 tonne mobile crane and several smaller ones.

Slipway Small slipway near the *Club Maritimo* building.

Engineers At the boatyard.

Electronic & radio repairs At the boatyard.

Sailmaker Several in Palma.

Chandlery Near the harbour. Several large chandleries in Palma.

Water Taps on all quays and pontoons, including the visitors' quay.

Showers Below the *Club Maritimo* building.

Electricity 220v AC points on all quays and pontoons, including the visitors' quay. 380v AC in the boatyard.

Fuel Diesel and petrol from pumps at the head of the east breakwater. (The green column marking the starboard side of the entrance emerges from the fuel cabin's roof).

Ice From the bar.

Yacht club The Club Marítimo San Antonio de la Playa (☎ 263512, *Fax* 261638) has a large clubhouse with restaurant, bar terrace, showers, etc.

Banks In Ca'n Pastilla, directly behind the yacht harbour.

Shops/provisioning Many shops and supermarkets nearby, with more in Palma 3½ miles away. Hypermarket about 2 miles away on the road between Palma and the airport.

Market Tuesdays and Thursdays in C'an Pastilla.

Hotels/restaurants/cafés etc. Dozens of hotels in the vicinity. Restaurant at the *Club Maritimo* and many more restaurants, cafés, and bars in the town.

Laundrette In C'an Pastilla.

Medical services In C'an Pastilla. Hospital in Palma 3½ miles away.

Communications

Car hire/taxis In the town.

Buses Frequent bus service to Palma.

Ferries From Palma to the other islands and mainland Spain.

Air services Busy international airport 3½ miles away.

⚓ **Cala Estancia** 39°32'·1N 2°42'·8E

A small *cala* just west of Puerto de San Antonio de la Playa. Semi-protected by two short breakwaters it is shallow (1–1·5m) and open to the south. A particularly large hotel overlooks it from the west and there is a busy road nearby.

Puerto de Cala Gamba

39°32'·9N 2°41'·8E

Charts

	Approach
Admiralty	*2832, 3036*
Spanish	*970, 421, 421A, 4211*
French	*7115, 7118*

Lights

0316·74 **Southwest breakwater** 39°32'·9N 2°41'·8E
F.R.5m3M Red post 3m

0316·76 **East breakwater** 39°32'·9N 2°41'·8E
F.G.4m3M Green post 3m

Buoys

A tall, solid, black and white buoy with an × topmark (Fl.Y.3s3M) 650m south of the harbour entrance marks the water inlet for a power station. A west cardinal beacon with ⚡ topmark (Fl(9)15s5m5m) marks the end

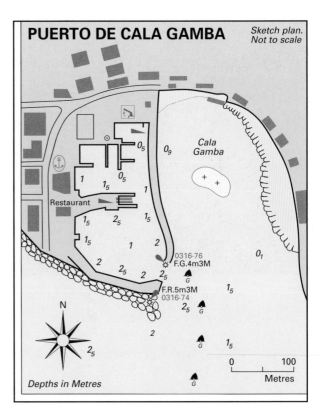

of a short breakwater 550m northwest of the harbour, with a second west cardinal beacon, also (Fl(9)15s5m5m), a further 600m to the northwest. All three must be passed on the seaward side. Four small conical green buoys mark the entrance channel to the harbour.

Port Communications

Club Náutico Cala Gamba VHF Ch 9, ☎ 261849, *Fax* 491900.

General

The addition of new breakwaters and pontoons has turned this pleasant little fishing harbour into a flourishing yacht harbour with 275 berths, but both depth and facilities are still limited. Much of the harbour carries less than 2m, though 2·5m may be found against parts of the southwest breakwater. It cannot be entered with any swell from southeast, south or southwest due to very shallow water in the approach, but otherwise approach and entry offer no difficulties. The noise generated by the nearby Palma airport is considerable.

Approach

For outer approaches see Puerto de San Antonio de la Playa, page154.

From west Puerto de Cala Gamba lies 1·3 miles northwest of Puerto de San Antonio de la Playa and slightly north of the airport main runway. The black and white buoy and the chimneys of the power station mentioned above may also be seen.

From east Steer north-northwest from Cabo Enderrocat, being certain to leave both Islote Galera, 0·5 mile northwest of Puerto de San

Puerto de Cala Gamba from the southwest with the four green buoys marking the entrance channel can just visible. More obviously, Palma airport's main runway is on the far right.

Antonio de la Playa, and the black and white buoy mentioned previously to starboard.

Anchorage in the approach

Anchor in 4m over stones 400m south of the entrance and some 250m north of the black and white buoy, open from southeast through southwest to northwest. Holding is poor.

Entrance

Approach cautiously heading northeast – though dredged from time to time the entrance channel is narrow and subject to silting – swinging north and then northwest to enter the harbour.

Berthing

Seek a vacant berth as draft permits and visit the *Club Náutico* office for allocation of a visitor's berth.

Charges *(see page 6)*

High season daily rate – Band B; low season daily rate – Band C. Water and electricity included.

Facilities

Boatyard Local craftsmen can carry out simple work. Fully equipped boatyards in Palma.

Cranes 5 tonne and 1 tonne cranes near the root of the east breakwater.

Slipway A slipway on the central mole and another in the northeast corner.

Water Taps on quays and pontoons.

Showers At the *Club Náutico*.

Electricity 220v AC points on quays and pontoons.

Fuel Not available.

Ice From the *Club Náutico* bar.

Yacht club The Club Náutico Cala Gamba (☎ 261849, *Fax* 491900) has a clubhouse overlooking the harbour with restaurant, bar, showers etc.

Banks Nearby.

Shops/provisioning Some small shops nearby, supermarkets and more shops a little further inland and all the resources of Palma 2½ miles away. Hypermarket on the road between Palma and the airport.

Hotels/restaurants/cafés etc. Numerous hotels, restaurants, cafés and bars nearby.

Hospital/medical services In Palma, 2½ miles away.

Communications

Car hire/taxis Locally or in Palma.

Buses Frequent bus service to Palma.

Ferries From Palma to the other islands and mainland Spain.

Air services Busy international airport 2 miles away.

Puerto del Molinar de Levante (Caló d'en Rigo)
39°33'·5N 2°40'·6E

Charts

	Approach	Harbour
Admiralty	*2832*, 3036	*3036*
Spanish	*970, 421, 421A, 4211*	*4212*
French	*7115*, 7118	*6775*

Lights

0317·2 **Southwest breakwater** 39°33'·6N 2°40'·6E
F.R.7m4M Red post 4m

0317 **Southeast mole** 39°33'·5N 2°40'·6E
F.G.7m4M Green post 4m

Port Communications

Club Marítimo Molinar de Levante ☎ 249460.

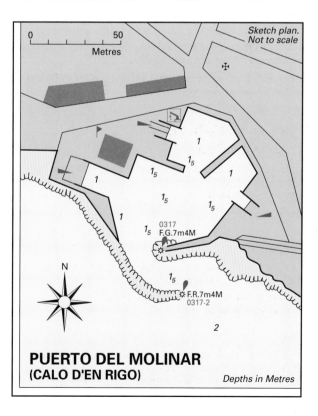

PUERTO DEL MOLINAR
(CALO D'EN RIGO)   *Depths in Metres*

The very small harbour of Puerto de Molinar de Levante, looking northeast. Even a slight southeasterly swell is causing waves to break across the entrance.

General

A very small fishing harbour built in Caló d'en Rigo, only suitable for craft drawing less than 1m and under 9m in length and almost exclusively occupied by *llauds* and small speedboats. Facilities are limited to everyday requirements. Approach and entrance are easy but would be dangerous with swell from the southern quadrant. The surrounding area is, as yet, relatively unspoilt with some attractive older houses and a lofty brick church directly behind the harbour.

Approach

See Puerto de Cala Portixol, opposite. Puerto del Molinar de Levante lies 0·3 mile to the southeast.

Anchorage in the approach

Anchor in 2·5m over sand and mud 400m southeast of the harbour entrance, open southeast through southwest to northwest.

Entrance

Approach the east side of the harbour at slow speed, watching the depth carefully, until the entrance opens up to port.

Berthing

Seek a vacant berth and visit the *Club Náutico* office for allocation of a visitor's berth.

Facilities

Crane On the north side of the harbour.
Slipways Three slipways around the harbour.
Chandlery Small chandlery shop nearby.
Water Water taps around the harbour.
Electricity 220v AC points around the harbour.
Fuel Not available.
Ice From the *Club Marítimo* bar.

Yacht club The Club Marítimo Molinar de Levante (☎ 249460) has a clubhouse with restaurant and bar on the west side of the harbour.
Banks In El Molinar.
Shops/provisioning Shops and supermarkets in El Molinar.
Hotels/restaurants/cafés etc. Wide selection nearby.
Hospital/medical services In Palma, 1½ miles away.

Communications

See Puerto de Cala Portixol, below.

⚓ **Cala Portixolet** 39°33'·6N 2°40'·4E
A shallow and somewhat bleak anchorage, with the rocky breakwaters of Puerto de Cala Portixol on one side and a road backed by houses at the head. Anchor in 1·5m over sand open to the southern quadrant.

Puerto de Cala Portixol

39°33'·6N 2°40'·2E

Charts	*Approach*	*Harbour*
Admiralty	*2832, 3036*	
Spanish	*970, 421, 421A, 4211*	*4212*
French	*7115, 7118*	*6775*

Lights

0316·8 **Southwest breakwater** 39°33'·6N 2°40'·2E
  Fl(4)R.11s7m5M Red column on white base displaying red ■ 6m
0316·82 **Southeast breakwater** 39°33'·6N 2°40'·2E
  Fl(3)G.9s7m5M Green column on white base displaying green ▲ 6m
0316·83 **Southwest inner mole** 39°33'·7N 2°40'·2E
  F.R.7m2M Red column on white base displaying red ■ 4m
0316·84 **Southeast inner mole** 39°33'·7N 2°40'·2E
  F.G.7m2M Green column on white base displaying green ▲ 5m
0316·9 **Yacht harbour mole** 39°33'·7N 2°40'·2E
  F.R.6m4M Red column 4m
0316·86 **Fishermen's mole** 39°33'·7N 2°40'·2E
  F.G.5m4M Green metal column 4m

Port Communications

Puerto de Cala Portixol ☎ 715100; Club Náutico Portixol ☎ 415466.

General

An old fishing harbour in a semi-circular cove, converted into a combined fishing and yachting harbour by the addition of extra breakwaters and other facilities, Puerto de Cala Portixol is claimed to provide berths for over 1000 craft. However the largest are no more than 12m and the majority under 10m, and no space is reserved for visitors. Much of the harbour carries less than 2m. Traffic noise from the nearby motorway is distinctly audible.

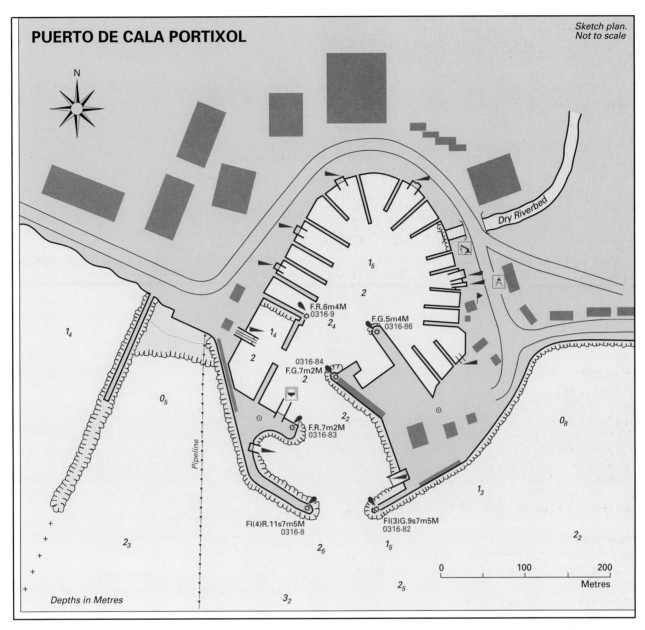

As with the harbours to the southeast, approach and entrance are straightforward other than in heavy swell from the southern quadrant, when shoals in the approach could render it dangerous.

Approach

From west Round the very prominent Punta de Cala Figuera which has a lighthouse (Fl(4)20s45m15M, white round tower with black diagonal stripes on building 24m) and radio masts on its steep cliffs. Cross the Bahía de Palma heading northeast towards Palma Cathedral, a very large building with small twin spires. From a position 0·8 mile off Puerto de Palma south breakwater the very much smaller breakwaters of Puerto de Cala Portixol will be seen 1·5 miles ahead.

From east Round Cabo Blanco, which is high with steep light brown cliffs topped by a lighthouse (Oc.5s95m15M, white tower and building 12m) and an old watchtower, and set a course northwest until the buildings of Palma, come into view. Puerto de Cala Portixol will be seen to starboard when still a mile short of the entrance to Puerto de Palma.

Anchorage in the approach

See Cala Portixolet, opposite.

Entrance

Approach and enter on a northerly course between the outer breakwaters and then the inner moles to enter the main harbour. There is a 2 knot speed limit.

Berthing

Local yachts berth on the west side of the harbour just inside the inner mole, but it is unlikely that there will be a space available.

Puerto de Cala Portixol from southwest with the sprawling suburbs of Palma in the background.

Facilities

Boatyard Simple work possible. Fully equipped boatyards in Palma.

Cranes 4 tonne crane to the northeast of the harbour.

Slipways Nine, mostly very small.

Chandlery Two chandlery/fishing tackle shops on the road opposite the harbour gate.

Water Water taps around the harbour.

Showers At the *Club Náutico*.

Electricity 220v AC points around the harbour.

Fuel Not available.

Ice Ice machine at the *Club Náutico*.

Yacht club The Club Náutico Portixol (☎ 415466) has a pleasant clubhouse on the east of the harbour with restaurant, bar, terrace etc.

Banks In Palma.

Shops/provisioning Some shops nearby, with a vast range in Palma 1½ miles away.

Hotels/restaurants/cafés etc. Many in the area.

Hospital/medical services In Palma.

Communications

Car hire/taxis In Palma.

Buses Frequent bus service to Palma.

Ferries From Palma to the other islands and mainland Spain.

Air services Busy international airport 3 miles away.

Isla de Cabrera

General description

This rugged and hilly island with numerous off-lying islets was declared a National Maritime–Terrestial Park in April 1991. As such access is restricted and a permit must be obtained before visiting (see below). The main island measures some 3 miles in each direction, indented by several deep bays and rising to 172m at Alto de Picamoscas. There is an excellent sheltered bay on the northwest side, known as Puerto de Cabrera despite having no port facilities beyond a couple of short jetties. Anchoring is forbidden but fifty visitors' moorings have been laid. Access to the many other small, secluded anchorages is also restricted.

The only other island in the group of any size is Isla Conejera, measuring about 1 mile by 0·6 mile and separated from Isla de Cabrera by a channel 0·7 mile wide and more than 20m deep. Seven smaller islands lie north of Isla de Cabrera with others close inshore to the south. In general Isla de Cabrera and its islets are all steep-to, and in most places deep water runs close inshore.

History

It is probable that Isla de Cabrera (Goat Island) and Isla Conejera (Rabbit Island) were inhabited in prehistoric times – traces of an ancient building have been identified at Clot des Guix, and Roman and Byzantine ceramics and coins have also been found. The castle overlooking Puerto de Cabrera is thought to date back to the end of the 14th century and was probably built as a defence against pirates. During the Peninsular Wars some 9000 French prisoners were interned on the island, where nearly two-thirds died of disease and starvation. They are buried near the castle and a memorial was erected in 1847 in the centre of the island.

Prior to World War I the island was privately owned, but was requisitioned by the Spanish government in 1915 to prevent it falling into enemy hands. A small army garrison was established which still exists and at various times the area has been used as a gunnery range. Landing on any of the smaller islands could be DANGEROUS, due to the presence of unexploded shells or other ammunition (as well as being contrary to the rules of the Park).

Wildlife

There are several species of fauna, flora and lizards unique to the archipelago, which is also a haven for seabirds including the rare Audouins gull (see page 12) and birds of prey such as osprey and both peregrine and Eleonora's falcon. The surrounding waters are home to fish, turtles, dolphins, whales and a variety of corals. Booklets describing the history and wildlife of the Cabrera group are available in several languages from the Cabrera National Park Office (see below).

Permits

The National Park is administered by ICONA, the *Instituto Nacional para la Conservación de la Naturaleza*, whose head office is at Calle Ciudad de Queretaro s/n, 07007 Palma de Mallorca. Permits, which are dated and can be applied for between three and ninety days in advance, are issued by the Cabrera National Park Office at Plaza España 8, 07002 Palma (☎ 725010, 725384, *Fax* 725585), closed at weekends and bank holidays. Most nearby yacht clubs, marina offices and harbour masters can provide a blank *Solicitud de Autorizacion* and, when completed, will fax it through (a small fee is sometimes charged for this service, though the permit itself is free). Details of the yacht (registration document), skipper (passport and certificate of competence), owner and number aboard are required. A scuba diving permit is available from the same office, though fishing is strictly prohibited. Animals may not be landed from boats and all rubbish must be taken back aboard.

No more than fifty yachts can use the harbour at any one time and visits are limited to one night in July and August, two nights in June and September and seven nights at other times. The permit is dated, and only valid for the date(s) shown, but if not all the buoys are occupied it may be possible to remain an extra night. (Equally, if all fifty buoys are already allocated a last minute application may be refused). Weekends are inevitably in greatest demand.

Each permit is accompanied by a map with details of permitted daytime (1000–1900) anchorages – currently two areas in the entrance to Puerto de Cabrera and Cala Es Borri on the east coast – and prohibited areas, which at present include Cala Ganduf, Cala Anciola, Cala Es Codolar and others on the south coast, Cala La Olla and Cala Emboixar. Even so brief details of these *calas* are included below in case the restrictions are lifted. There is a 5 knot speed limit in the entire Maritime Park area and a 2 knot speed limit in the harbour.

The boundary of the National Park is indicated by five pillar buoys, all lit and with × topmarks, in positions 39°13'·5N 2°58'E (Fl.Y.2s5M); 39°13'·5N 3°00'E (Fl(2)Y.5M); 39°06'·5N 3°00'E (Fl.Y. 2s5M); 39°06'·5N 2°53'·5E (Fl(2)Y.5M); and 39°10'N 2°53'·5E (Fl(3)Y.5M).

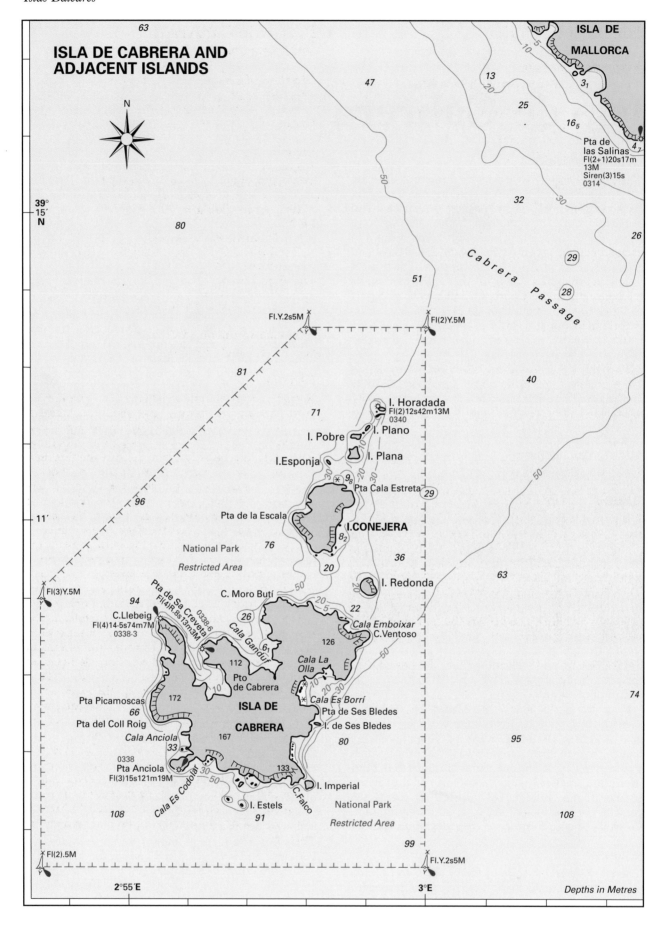

ISLA DE CABRERA AND ADJACENT ISLANDS

N

63

ISLA DE
MALLORCA

47

13

25

3₁

16₅

Pta de
las Salinas
Fl(2+1)20s17m
13M
Siren(3)15s
0314

4₇

**39°
15′
N**

80

32

30

26

29

Cabrera Passage

51

28

Fl.Y.2s5M

Fl(2)Y.5M

40

81

71

I. Horadada
Fl(2)12s42m13M
0340

I. Pobre

I. Plano

I.Esponja

I. Plana

9₈

Pta Cala Estreta

29

96

Pta de la Escala

I.CONEJERA

82₂

11′

National Park

Restricted Area

76

36

50

Fl(3)Y.5M

20

C. Moro Butí

I. Redonda

63

20

Pta de Sa Crevera
Fl(4)R.8s13m3M

94

0338·6

22

Cala Emboixar
C.Ventoso

C.Llebeig
Fl(4)14·5s74m7M
0338·3

26

Cala Garduf

6₁

126

112

Cala La
Olla

50

Pto
de Cabrera

Pta Picamoscas

172

10

**ISLA DE
CABRERA**

Cala Es Borrí

74

66

Pta del Coll Roig

167

Pta de Ses Bledes

I. de Ses Bledes

Cala Anciola

33

80

95

0338
Pta Anciola
Fl(3)15s121m19M

30

133

50

I. Imperial

108

Cala Es Codolar

I. Estels

91

C.Falco

National Park

Restricted Area

108

Fl(2).5M

99

Fl.Y.2s5M

2°55′E

3°E

Depths in Metres

Factual information

Magnetic variation
Cabrera – 1°21'W (decreasing 6'E annually)

Approach and coastal passage charts
Admiralty   *2831, 2832*
Spanish   *423, 422A, 4221*
French   *7115, 7116*

Approach lights
0338 **Punta Anciola** 39°07'·8N 2°55'·4E
  Fl(3)15s121m19M Red and white
  chequered tower on white building 21m
  277·5°-vis-169°
0338·3 **Cabo Llebeig** 39°09'·7N 2°55'·1E
  Fl(4)14·5s74m7M Black and white
  chequered angular tower 7m
0340 **Isla Horadada** 39°12'·5N 2°58'·8E
  Fl(2)12s42m13M White round tower, five
  black bands, on white round house 13m
  047°-vis-001°

The Cabrera group from the northeast. Isla Horadada with its distinctive banded lighthouse is nearest to the camera.

Puerto de Cabrera
39°09'·3N 02°55'·8E

Charts	*Approach*	*Harbour*
Admiralty	*2831*, 2832	
Spanish	*423, 422A, 4221*	4222
French	*7115*, 7116	*7119*

Lights
Approach
0338·3 **Cabo Llebeig** 39°09'·7N 2°55'·1E
  Fl(4)14·5s74m7M Black and white
  chequered angular tower 7m
Entrance
0338·6 **Punta de Sa Creveta** 39°09'·3N 2°55'·8E
  Fl(4)R.8s13m3M Red and white chequered
  angular tower 5m
0339 **Jetty** 39°09'·1N 2°56'·1E
  Fl(2)R.10·5s5m3M
  Column on angular red tower 4m

Port Communications
Park Information Office VHF Ch 9.

General
A large natural harbour which can be entered under virtually any conditions and shelter obtained, though it can become dangerous in strong northwesterlies when a swell also rolls in. Gusts blowing down into the harbour from the surrounding hills can also be fierce. However in normal conditions it is one of the few truly peaceful spots in the Balearics, without jet-skis, water-skiers and speedboats, though tourist ferries from Palma and Colonia de Sant Jordi arrive daily in the summer.

There are a few houses near the south mole, some used by the owners of the sheep and pigs pastured on the island. These keep the vegetation down and until recently many fine walks could be enjoyed over deserted countryside. Unfortunately this is no longer the case and yachtsmen, having landed at the main jetty, are only allowed to walk unsupervised along the foreshore. All other walks (minimum of four people) are conducted by Park Rangers at designated times available from the Park Information Office. The walk up the steep track leading to the castle ruins will be rewarded with spectacular views and it is also possible to visit the memorial to the French prisoners of war.

The Cuevas Azul (Blue Caves) in Cala Ganduf some 600m south-southwest of Cabo Moro Butí are also most attractive but are only accessible by sea. Anchoring in the *cala* is not permitted, but at some 1·4 miles from the buoys in Puerto de Cabrera a visit by sailing or outboard-powered dinghy is feasible.

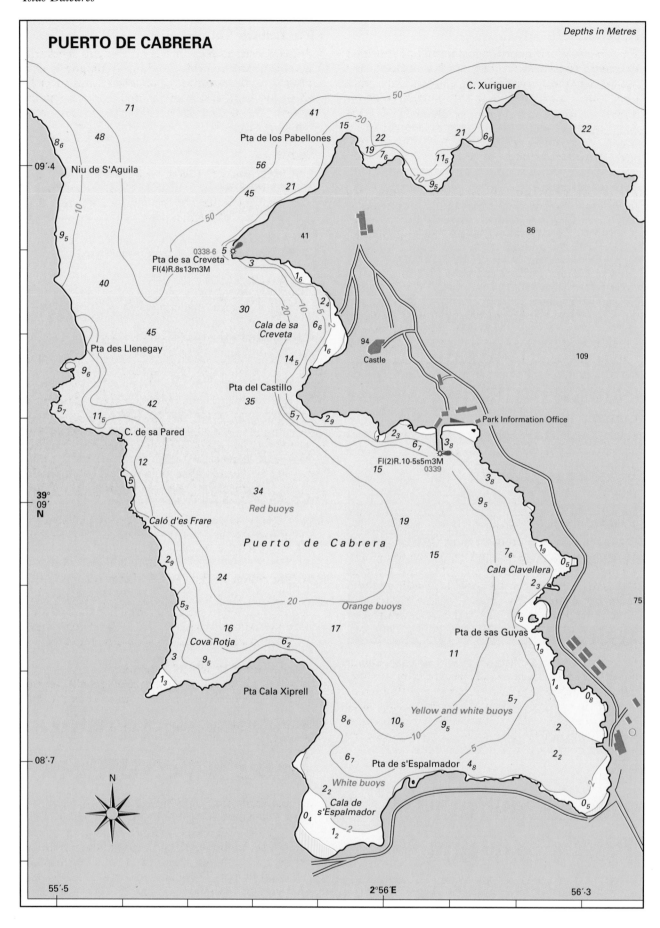

PUERTO DE CABRERA

Depths in Metres

C. Xuriguer

71

48

8₆

09′·4 Niu de S'Aguila

Pta de los Pabellones

41

15 20

22

19 7₆

21 6₆

22

56

21

11₅

9₅

10

45

50

9₅

40

41

86

0338·6 5

Pta de sa Creveta
Fl(4)R.8s13m3M

3

1₆

2₄

30

Cala de sa Creveta

6₆

2

5

10

20

45

Pta des Llenegay

14₅

1₆

9₆

94

Castle

109

5₇

42

Pta del Castillo

35

11₅

C. de sa Pared

5₇

2₉

1

2₃

6₇

Park Information Office

3₈

12

15

Fl(2)R.10·5s5m3M
0339

3₈

5

34

9₅

39°
09′
N

Red buoys

Caló d'es Frare

19

Puerto de Cabrera

7₆

1₉

0₅

15

2₉

Cala Clavellera

2₃

24

75

5₃

20

Orange buoys

1₉

16

17

Pta de sas Guyas

1₉

Cova Rotja

6₂

11

1₉

3

9₅

1₄

0₈

1₃

5₇

Pta Cala Xiprell

2

8₆

10₅

Yellow and white buoys

9₅

2₂

6₇

10

5

08′·7

6₇

Pta de s'Espalmador

4₈

0₅

N

White buoys

2₂

2

*Cala de
s'Espalmador*

0₄

1₂

2

55′·5

2°56′E

56′·3

Approach

From north When approaching from this direction the chain of islands running north/south does not appear separated from Isla de Cabrera itself until quite close. Leave these islands to port, heading for a position slightly east of Cabo Lleibeig (Fl(4)14·5s 74m7M, black and white chequered angular tower 7m). The entrance lies close under this headland, with Punta de Sa Creveta (Fl(4)R.8s13m4M, red and white chequered angular tower 5m) to the east.

From west The hills of Isla de Cabrera can be seen from some distance away, with the line of smaller islands running towards the north visible on closer approach. Set course to round Cabo Lleibeig, the northwest tip of the island, after which the entrance will open up beyond.

From east or northeast The hills of Isla de Cabrera can be seen from some distance away, with the line of smaller islands running towards the north visible on closer approach. Pass either side of Isla Redonda to round Cabo Moro Butí and cross the wide and deep Cala Ganduf towards Cabo Xuriguer and Punta de los Pabellones. The entrance will open up on rounding Punta de Sa Crevata beyond.

Currents

Strong wind-induced currents may be experienced around the islands, the direction and strength dependent on that of the wind.

Entrance

The entrance, which is deep but relatively narrow, lies between Cabo Llebeig and Punta de Sa Crevata. Wind conditions in both the entrance and harbour can be very fluky due to the high surrounding hills. Mooring buoys lie south of a line between Cabo de sa Pared and Punta del Castillo. As well as the 5 knot speed limit in the entire Maritime Park area there is a 2 knot speed limit in the harbour itself.

Moorings

Secure to one of the fifty visitors' moorings, colour coded according to yacht size (up to 12m – white; 12–15m – yellow; 15–20m – orange; 20–30m – red) for which no charge is made. The smaller sizes tucked into Cala de s'Espalmador are the most sheltered but also furthest from the main (northeast) jetty, the only place where landing is permitted.

Berthing

Lying alongside the jetty is only possible with a military permit or in an emergency.

Anchoring

Anchoring in the harbour is forbidden.

Formalities

A guard visits each yacht every evening to check that a valid permit is held. Landing by dinghy is only allowed at the main jetty, and the permit must be shown at the Park Information Office on coming ashore. Scuba permits should also be presented before diving.

Facilities

The army *cantina* welcomes visitors and has a bar, though food is not available. Small quantities of non-drinking water can usually be collected from the *cantina*. (Take containers).

Puerto de Cabrera from a little west of north. The landing jetty is hidden behind the hill on which the castle sits, but some of the visitors' buoys can just be seen.

Anchorages in the Isla de Cabrera group

A number of the anchorages listed below are currently closed to yachts, indicated by the omission of a preceding ⚓ symbol. These brief details are included in case restrictions should be lifted.

Cala Ganduf 39°09'·2N 2°56'·8E

A protected but rather deep anchorage with several separate indentations, open to northeast and north.

Passage between Isla de Cabrera and Isla Redonda

An 800m wide passage with a minimum depth of 21m. Take in a northwest–southeast direction.

⚓ Cala Emboixar 39°09'·6N 2°58'·3E

An attractive anchorage in a small bay under cliffs, with a rocky ledge looking like a breakwater to the northwest. Anchor on the west side of the bay in 5m over stone, rock and weed, open to north through northeast to east. There are two small beaches, one rocky and one of sand.

Cala Emboixar from just north of east, with Cala Ganduf and Cabo Llebeig in the background.

Cabo Ventoso (Cap Ventós) 39°09'·5N 2°58'·7E
A high (88m), steep, rocky-cliffed promontory with good water at its base.

Cala La Olla 39°09'·1N 2°58'E
An interesting anchorage amidst wild scenery at the mouth of the eastern of two small *calas*, themselves at the northern end of a wide bay. Anchor in 5m over sand, rock and stone open to southeast round to southwest. Several islets lie close to the west.

⚓ Cala Es Borrí 39°08'·7N 2°57'·5E
Anchoring is currently permitted in the central and southern parts of the wide bay mentioned above – Cala Es Borrí is actually the small inlet at its southwest corner. Yachts may only anchor in the bay between 1000 and 1900, and no more than twenty boats can be present at any one time.

Cala Es Borrí (left) and Cala La Olla (right) seen from the southeast.

Anchor as space permits in 5m+ over sand and rock, open to the eastern quadrant and to swell from the south. There is a fine sandy beach in Cala Es Borrí itself.

Passage between Islote Imperial and Isla de Cabrera
A 100m wide, 18m deep, passage between dramatic cliffs, sailed in a northeast–southwest direction. Not for use in bad weather.

Islotes Estels 39°07'·3N 2°56'·4E (Southernmost) Five scattered, rocky islands up to 750m off the south coast of Isla de Cabrera.

Punta Anciola 39°07'·8N 2°55'·3E
A rounded headland connected to Isla Cabrera by a low, narrow neck. The paintwork on its lighthouse (Fl(3)15s121m19M, red and white chequered tower on white building 21m) may well be unique.

Punta Anciola with its extraordinary lighthouse, looking southeast.

North of Punta Mal Entrador
39°09'·1N 2°55'·2E
A small bay where it is possible to anchor in 5m± over rock and stone, open to the western quadrant. This anchorage is in an area currently reserved for scuba diving.

Cala Galiota 39°09'·2N 2°55'·3E
An attractive anchorage under high cliffs in 5m± over rock and stone at head of the *cala*, open to west and northwest. This anchorage is in an area currently reserved for scuba diving.

Cabo Llebeig 39°09'·7N 2°55'·1E
A large (60m) conspicuous rocky hummock with a not very prominent lighthouse (Fl(4)14·5s74m7M, black and white chequered angular tower 7m).

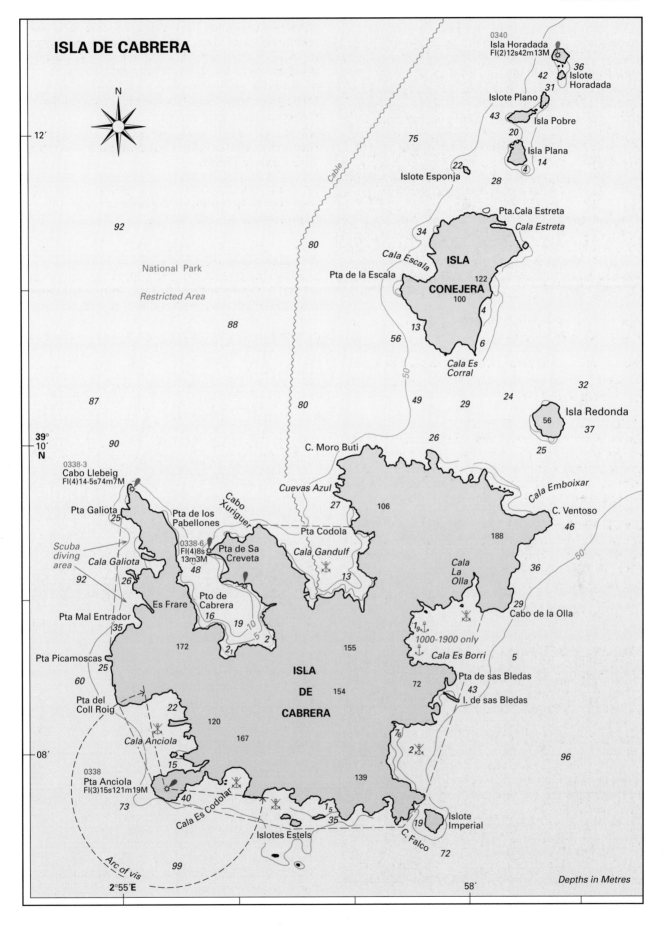

ISLA DE CABRERA

N

12′

National Park

Restricted Area

**39°
10′
N**

92

87

90

0338·3
Cabo Llebeig
Fl(4)14·5s74m7M

Pta Galiota
25

*Scuba
diving
area*

Cala Galiota

92   26

Pta Mal Entrador
35

Pta Picamoscas
25

60

Pta del
Coll Roig

0338
Pta Anciola
Fl(3)15s121m19M
40

73

Pta de los
Pabellones

Cabo
Xuriguer

0338·6
Fl(4)8s
13m3M
48

Pta de Sa
Creveta

Es Frare

Pto de
Cabrera
16

19
10
5   2

2₁

172

120

Cala Anciola

15

Cala Es Codolar

Islotes Estels

Arc of vis

99

75

Islote Esponja

80

88

80

C. Moro Buti

Cuevas Azul

27

Pta Codola

Cala Gandulf
13

26

106

155

ISLA
DE
CABRERA

154

167

139

1₅
35

C. Falco

19

0340
Isla Horadada
Fl(2)12s42m13M

42   36
Islote
Horadada
31

Islote Plano
43   Isla Pobre
20
Isla Plana
14
4

22
28

Pta.Cala Estreta
34   *Cala Estreta*

Cala Escala   **ISLA**
Pta de la Escala   **CONEJERA**
122
100
4
13
56   6

*Cala Es
Corral*

49   29   24   32

Isla Redonda
56   37

25

Cala Emboixar

C. Ventoso
46
188

36

*Cala
La
Olla*

29   Cabo de la Olla
1₉
1000-1900 only
Cala Es Borri   5
72   Pta de sas Bledas
43
I. de sas Bledas

7₆

2₄

96

Islote
Imperial
72

58′

Depths in Metres

2°55′E

The smaller islands of the Isla de Cabrera group

Isla Redonda Centred on 39°10'·2N 2°58'·6E
A roughly circular island some 450m in diameter and 57m high. No anchorages, but there is reported to be a possible landing on the southwest side.

Passage between Isla Redonda and Isla Conejera
A 1000m wide passage with a minimum depth of 20m. Take in a southwest–northeast direction.

Isla Conejera (Illa des Conills)
Centred on 39°11'·1N 2°57'·9E
The second largest island at 1 mile long by 0·6 mile wide and reaching 131m high. There are possible landing places reported on the east coast and three *cala* anchorages:

Cala Es Corral, Isla Conejera
39°10'·6N 2°57'·9E
Two small *calas* side by side at south end of the island, to be used only with great care. There are two small off-lying islets on either side. Anchor near the head in 5m over rock and stone, open to southeast through south to southwest.

Cala Escala, Isla Conejera 39°11'·2N 2°57'·6E
A rather open anchorage in 5m over rock and stone on the east side of bay, open to west and northwest and to swell from the north.

Cala Estreta, Isla Conejera 39°11'·4N 2°58'·3E
A very small *cala* some 60m wide and 200m long, with room for a single yacht using lines ashore. Anchor in 5m over rock and stone open to northeast and east.

Passage between Isla Conejera and Islote Esponja or Isla Plana
A passage 400m wide, with a minimum depth of 11m if midway between Isla Conejera and the two smaller islands. Take in a west–east direction.

Islote Esponja 39°11'·8N 2°58'E
200m by 40m, and 23m high, Islote Esponja is steep-to and almost inaccessible.

Isla Plana 39°11'·9N 2°58'·4E
400m by 125m, 26m high.

Passage between Isla Plana and Isla Pobre
A 150m wide passage with depths shoaling to 2·5m.

Isla Pobre 39°12'·1N 2°58'·5E
400m by 100m, 27m high. There is a possible landing but no anchorages.

Passage between Isla Pobre and Islote Plano
Foul.

Islote Plano (Illot Plá) 39°12'·2N 2°58'·6E
200m by 100m, 27m high.

Passage between Islote Plano and Islote Horadada
A passage 200m wide with 12m minimum depth. Take in a west–east direction.

Islote Horadada (Illot Foradada or Foradat)
39°12'·3N 2°58'·8E
100m by 80m, 12m high.

Passage between Islote Horadada and Isla Horadada
Foul.

Isla Horadada (Illa Foradada or Foradat)
39°12'·5N 2°58'·8E
210m by 120m and 42m high, with a lighthouse (Fl(2)12s42m13M, white round tower with five black bands on white round house 13m) on its summit.

Isla de Menorca

General description

Twenty miles east-southeast of Mallorca, Menorca is the most easterly of the Islas Baleares and is 26 miles long and 11 miles wide, with its longitudinal axis running in a west-northwest–east–southeast direction. It is not as mountainous as the other two main islands, being for the most part a low plateau with a few small hills near the north coast and the lone Monte Toro (358m) near the centre of the island. This 'mountain' can be seen from afar and makes a useful landmark.

Geologically the island consists of two parts: that north of a line drawn from near Cala Morell to Mahón is the oldest part of the Islas Baleares and was joined to Corsica, mainland Europe and Catalonia some 570 to 225 million years ago. The southern part of the island was created between 136 and 65 million years ago by a process of overlaying and folding, part of the upheaval which formed the Alps. Menorca was also the first of the Baleares to become separated as an island, but this was much later. It lies in the path of the northwesterly *tramontana* or *mestral* and is sometimes referred to as the 'Windy Isle'. The north coast is dangerous when this wind is blowing and should be given a wide berth.

Viewed from offshore many parts of Menorca have a barren appearance, perhaps partly due to the rocky cliffs, despite a considerable amount of arable and wooded land behind the coast. However these cliffs are broken by innumerable *calas* which offer many attractive anchorages. A few have been marred by tourist development but generally to a lesser extent than those on the neighbouring islands.

Puerto de Mahón (Maó) on the east coast is the major port and can be entered under most conditions. On the west coast lies the much smaller – and often very crowded – Puerto de Ciudadela, which offers shelter in all conditions other than westerly or southwesterly gales. The remaining harbours should not be entered with strong onshore winds and are mostly very uncomfortable, if not downright dangerous, at such times. Cala de Addaya is a notable exception, offering excellent shelter once inside though the entrance itself may become impassable.

Menorca has noticeably fewer tourist developments than the other Islas Baleares, and where such facilities exist they generally cater more for the 'quality' than the 'quantity' market. It is certainly less commercialised than the other islands. Mahón is, to a certain extent, an exception because it has been an important naval base for many years and has absorbed the influences, habits and behaviour of the various occupying forces – including the British who were there for much of the 18th century. The island population is currently some 60,000, of whom more than a third live in either Mahón or Cuidadela. Local industries of long standing include leatherwork – mainly shoes – jewellery, and the production of a hard mature cheese which is enjoyed throughout Spain.

Although not as spectacularly beautiful as much of Mallorca, Menorca has its own attractions and has much to offer those who prefer to avoid major centres of tourism.

History

Menorca has the greatest concentration of prehistoric remains in the entire Mediterranean, including what is claimed to be the oldest building in Europe. There are a number of Neolithic caves and villages on the island and many megalithic monuments such as *talayots* (towers), *navetas* (burial mounds) and *taulas* (T-shaped monuments) – probably built for religious and funerary purposes by the Bronze Age civilisation which inhabited the land before the Iberians established themselves. Unfortunately very little has been discovered about this Bronze Age tribe, or about the construction and use of the 400 or so large buildings and monuments which are scattered around the island.

In due course, as in large parts of the Mediterranean basin, Menorca saw successive waves of invasion and colonization by Phoenicians, Carthaginians, Greeks, Romans, Vandals, Byzantines, Visigoths and Moors. During the occupation by the Carthaginians the towns of *Maguén* (Mahón) and *Yamma* (Ciudadela) were founded, though doubtless both inlets had been used by seafarers since time immemorial. The period of Roman occupation from 123 BC to AD 427 was relatively peaceful and prosperous, Mahón becoming *Municipio Flavio Magontano* and Ciudalela *Iamnona*. Amongst other legacies, the Romans built the island's first road system.

The successive waves of invasion and colonization by Vandals, Byzantines and Visigoths left fewer permanent traces. After many years of raids the island was finally occupied by the Moors in about 913. They remained until driven out by King Alfonso III of Aragon in 1287, by which time Menorca was the last Muslim territory in eastern Spain, although in theory it had owed allegiance to the crown of Aragon since 1232. The common prefix 'Bini', as in Binidalí and Binibeca, is from the Arabic, meaning 'belonging to the son of'.

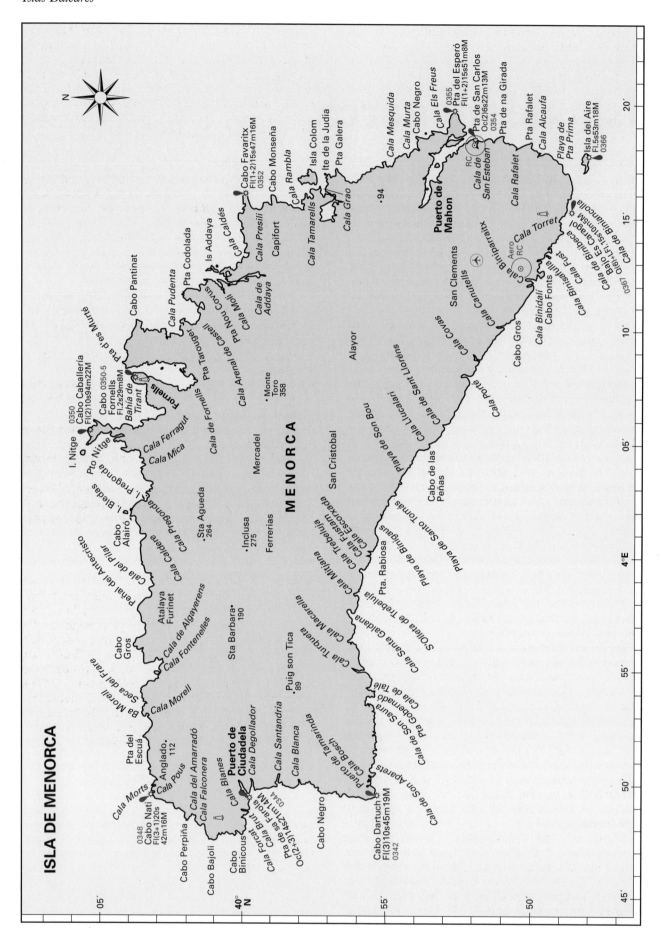

ISLA DE MENORCA

MENORCA

The following centuries were difficult for the islanders, with devastating pirate raids, droughts and epidemics. In 1535 Mahón lost much of its population to a raid by the Turkish pirate Barbarrossa, in 1558 it was the turn of Ciudadela, which withstood a nine day siege before being overrun and almost completely destroyed by a force of 15,000 Turks.

Due to the strategic position of Mahón as a naval base in the western Mediterranean it was coveted by all maritime nations, and Menorca changed hands frequently. In 1708 it was occupied by the British, who had supported the Carlist cause in the War of the Spanish Succession, and in 1713 the island was officially ceded by the Treaty of Utrecht (as was Gibraltar). One of their most lasting legacies was the road built by the Goveror, Sir Richard Kane, from Ciudadela to Mahón – the first good road linking the two towns since Roman times – and his moving of the capital from Cuidadela to Mahón in 1722. The island remained in British hands for more than forty years, during which Mahón grew as a fortified naval base and the island prospered.

In 1756 a French army landed near Ciudadela and marched across the island to lay siege to the fortress of San Felipe, near Mahón, which was eventually forced to surrender. It was following this episode that the unfortunate Admiral Byng was executed by firing squad at Portsmouth, on the quarterdeck of HMS *Monarque*, for failing to engage the French fleet and thereby lift the siege. This provoked Voltaire's famous quip: '*Dans ce pays-ci, il est bon de tuer de temps en temps un amiral pour encourager les autres.*' However the French only held the island until 1763 when it was returned to Britain by the Treaty of Paris.

Richelieu, who had commanded the successful French invasion in 1756, had a sauce called *mahon-ésa* – based on the local *alioli* sauce – served at the victory banquet in Paris. This delicacy, which his chef had invented while on the island, has become the ubiquitous 'mayonnaise'.

In 1782 a Franco-Spanish force once more laid siege to the garrison, which after another heroic resistance was forced to surrender. Not surprisingly one of the first things the victors did was to demolish the fortress, first built in the 1500s as a defence against Corsairs. Sixteen years later the British recaptured the island but had to return it to Spain in 1802 under the Treaty of Amiens. A direct result of this ongoing rivalry was the construction of forts and other large defensive works in and around the port of Mahón, many which are still to be seen. A further effect was the transfer of the island's capital from Ciudadela to Mahón, where all naval and military force was concentrated.

Under Spanish rule the island reverted to a simple pastoral and fishing existence, though in 1830 the French were permitted to establish a base at Mahón for use during their campaign in Algeria. The limited opportunities and employment for young people during the 19th century encouraged emigration, particularly to the west coast of America. During the Spanish Civil War Menorca remained in the hands of the Republicans and much damage was done to the island's churches.

Only recently has any attempt been made to cater for the tourist trade, but today considerable development can be seen in this direction, bringing not only income but outside influences and values into the lives of the islanders.

Places of interest

In addition to the places of interest described in the harbour sections there are many other sites inland which can be visited by taxi, bus or on foot. One is Monte Toro, near the village of Es Mercadal, both for the panoramic view and the restored 17th century monastry. Of the many Megalithic remains, the following are easy to reach from the two main harbours:

- 1 mile south of Mahón, the *taula* and *talayot* of Trapuco
- 2 miles southwest of Mahón, the *talayot* of Torellonet (near the airport)
- 5 miles west of Mahón, the Torralba group of *taulas*
- 3 miles east of Ciudadela, the *naveta* at Nau d'es Tudóns, claimed to be the oldest building in Europe
- 4 miles east of Ciudadela, the *poblado* and *taulas* of Torre Llafuda.
- 4 miles south of Ciudadela, the *talayot* of Son Olivaret

The Euro-Map of Mallorca, Minorca, Ibiza published by GeoCenter International shows many of the historic and prehistoric sites, as does a multi-lingual map available locally.

Fiestas

In addition to the national holidays and *fiestas* listed in the introduction the following dates are celebrated in Menorca: 19 March – San José (San José); first Sunday in May – pilgrimage to Es Mercadal; 15-16 June – Our Lady of Carmen, sea procession (Mahón); 23-24 June – San Juan (Ciudadela); 9 July – *Fiesta Patriótica* (Ciudadela); 3rd week in July – San Martin (Es Mercadal); 24-25 July – Santiago (Villa Carlos and Es Castell); last week in July – San Antonio (Fornells); 2nd weekend in August – San Lorenzo (Alayor); 24-25 August – San Luis (San Luis); 7-8 September – Nuestra Señora de Gracia (Mahón).

Factual information

Magnetic variation
Menorca – 1°W (decreasing 6'E annually)

Approach and coastal passage charts
Admiralty *1703, 2833*
Spanish *48E, 6A, 428A*
French *5505, 7117*

Approach lights
0355 **Punta del Esperó** 39°52'·7N 4°19'·7E
Fl(1+2)15s51m8M White round tower, two
black bands, on white building 11m
0354 **Punta de San Carlos** 39°52'N 4°18'·5E
Oc(2)6s22m13M White round tower, three
black bands, on square white base 15m
183°-vis-143° RC
0366 **Isla del Aire** 39°48'N 4°17'·7E
Fl.5s53m18M White tower, black bands,
on white building 38m 197°-vis-111°
0367 **Bajo d'en Caragol** 39°48'·6N 4°15'·3E
Q(6)+LFl.15s10m5M
South cardinal beacon with ⚑ topmark 10m
0342 **Cabo Dartuch (D'Artruix)**
39°55'·4N 3°49'·5E Fl(3)10s45m19M
White tower, three black bands,
on white building 34m 267°-vis-158°
0348 **Cabo Nati** 40°03'·2N 3°49'·5E
Fl(3+1)20s42m16M White tower, aluminium
cupola, on white building with red roof 13m
039°-vis-162°
OBSCURED from east of north-northeast
Note The characteristics of Cabo Nati are almost
identical to those of Cabo Formentor, Mallorca
0350 **Cabo Caballería** 40°05'·4N 4°05'·6E
Fl(2)10s94m22M White tower and building
15m 074°-vis-292° Racon
0352 **Cabo Favaritx** 39°59'·8N 4°16'·1E
Fl(1+2)15s47m16M White tower, black
diagonal stripes, on white building 28m

Radiobeacons
1027 **Mahón** 39°52'N 4°18'·4E
Radiobeacon *MH*, 292kHz 100M (A1A)
Located 152m 258° from San Carlos light
1028 **Isla de Menorca Aero** 39°50'·4N 4°12'·8E
Aerobeacon *MN*, 344kHz 60M (Non A2A)

Puerto de Mahón (Maó)
39°52'·1N 4°18'·6E

Charts	*Approach*	*Harbour*
Admiralty	*2833*	*2833*
Spanish	*6A, 428A*	*4281*
French	*7117*	*7117*

Lights
Approach
0366 **Isla del Aire** 39°48'N 4°17'·7E
Fl.5s53m18M White tower, black bands,
on white building 38m 197°-vis-111°
0355 **Punta del Esperó** 39°52'·7N 4°19'·7E
Fl(1+2)15s51m8M White round tower, two
black bands, on white building 11m
0352 **Cabo Favaritx** 39°59'·8N 4°16'·1E
Fl(1+2)15s47m16M White tower, black
diagonal stripes, on white building 28m
Entrance
0354 **Punta de San Carlos** 39°52'N 4°18'·5E
Oc(2)6s22m13M White round tower, three
black bands, on square white base 15m
183°-vis-143° RC
buoy **Laja de San Carlos** 39°52'N 4°18'·7E
Fl.R.5s3M Red pillar buoy, ■ topmark
buoy **Laja de Fuera** 39°52'·2N 4°18'·7E
Fl.G.5s3M Green pillar buoy, ▲ topmark
buoy **Punta San Felipet** 39°52'·3N 4°18'·4E
Fl(2)G.7s3M Green pillar buoy, ▲ topmark
buoy **Laja del Moro** 39°52'·3N 4°18'·3E
Fl(2)R.7s3M Red pillar buoy, ■ topmark
0356 **Punta del Lazareto** 39°52'·6N 4°18'·2E
Fl(3)G.9s13m4M Green column on white
base displaying green ▲ 9m
0359 **Isla Cuarentena or Plana** 39°53'N 4°18'E
Fl(4)G.11s9m1M Green column, white top
and base 6m
0358 **Punta de Na Cafayes** 39°53'N 4°17'·7E
Fl(3)R.9s8m3M Red column on white hut
displaying red ■
0360 **Punta de Villacarlos** 39°53'·1N 4°17'·4E
Fl(4)R.11s10m3M Red column on white hut
displaying red ■ 4m
0361 **Isla del Rey or del Hospital, south side**
39°53'·2N 4°17'·3E Fl.G.5s13m3M
Green column on white hut displaying green ▲ 13m
0361·4 **Isla del Rey, north side (Punta Sa Cova)**
39°53'·3N 4°17'·3E
Oc.R.4s16m3M Red tower 6m
0361·6 **Punta de Sa Bassa** 39°53'·4N 4°17'·4E
Oc.G.4s9m3M Green ▲ on green metal
tripod on white hut 3m
0362 **Punta de Cala Figuera** 39°53'·5N 4°16'·6E
Fl.R.5s7m4M Red ■ on red metal post 5m
0362·4 **Isla Pinta, south side**
39°53'·6N 4°16'·3E Fl(2)G.7s4m3M
Green ▲ on green metal post 3m
F.R. on tower 650m north–northwest
0362·5 **Isla Pinta, west side**
39°53'·6N 4°16'·2E Fl(3)G.9s4m3M
Green ▲ on green metal post 3m
0363 **Naval base, east jetty**
39°53'·6N 4°16'·2E Oc(2)G.6s4m1M
Green ▲ on green metal post 3m

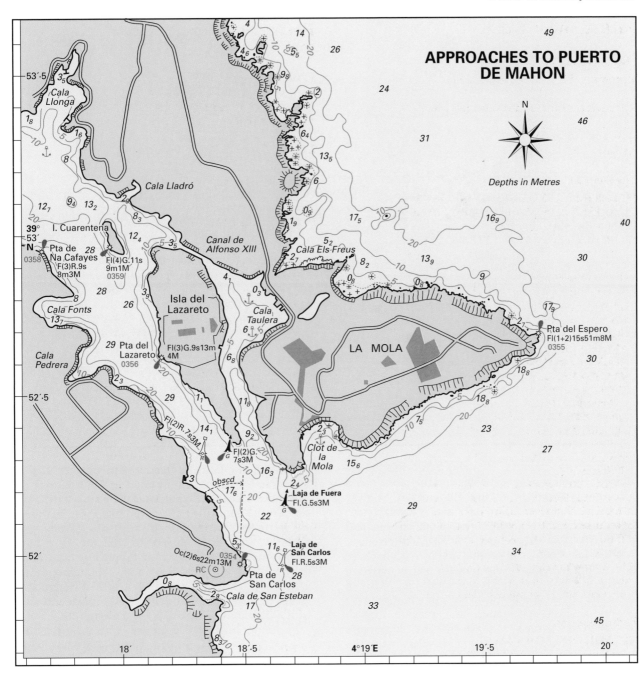

APPROACHES TO PUERTO DE MAHON

Depths in Metres

0363·2 Naval base, central jetty
39°53'·6N 4°16'·1E Q.G.4m1M
Green ▲ on green metal post 3m

0363·4 Naval base, west jetty
39°53'·7N 4°16'·1E Fl(4)G.11s4m1M
Green ▲ on green metal post 3m

Radiobeacons

1027 Mahón 39°52'N 4°18'·4E
Radiobeacon *MH*, 292kHz 100M (A1A)
Located 152m 258° from San Carlos light

1028 Isla de Menorca Aero 39°50'·4N 4°12'·8E
Aerobeacon *MN*, 344kHz 60M (Non A2A)

Port Communications

VHF – Pilots (*Mahón Prácticos*) Ch 12, 14, 16, 20, 27;
yacht berthing (*Ribera del Puerto*) Ch 9.
☎/*Fax* – Pilots ☎ 362666, 367254; Port Authority
☎ 363066, *Fax* 363101; Ribera del Puerto
☎ 354844, *Fax* 354327; 215 SA ☎ 350013,
Fax 365095; Club Maritimo de Mahón ☎ 365022,
Fax 360762; Pedro's Boat Centre (Port d'Hivernada)
☎ 366968, 366714 *Fax* 362455; Club Náutico de
Villacarlos ☎ 365884.

General

An attractive and interesting commercial, naval,
fishing and yachting port up a long deep *cala*. The
whole area is steeped in history – elements of it
British. The approach and entrance are
straightforward and entry can be made in storm
conditions, with good shelter available once inside.
There are excellent facilities for yachtsmen
including a first class, if expensive, yacht club.

The ancient *Portús Magonis* was once thought to
have been called after Mago, the younger brother of

173

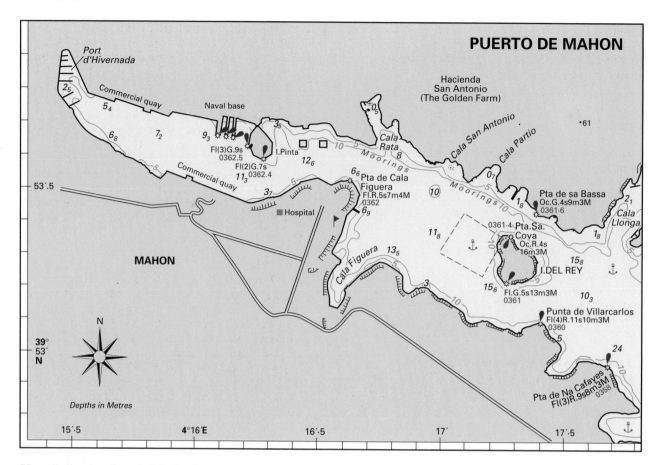

PUERTO DE MAHON

Hannibal, who founded it in about 206 BC. There is, however, no evidence for this and the name could also have come from the Phoenician *maguén* meaning 'shield' or 'fortress', which would have been equally apt. Due to its excellent harbour and its position in the centre of the Mediterranean Mahón has been a prize that many nations have coveted, and traces of the long British occupation during the 18th century are unmistakable. Many of the older streets and houses with sash windows have a very English appearance, and various English words have gained a place in the *Menorquín* language. There is even a gin distillery near the harbour. The island changed hands six times between 1708 and 1802 (see page 171), and each time it was Mahón that was the prize.

During the last period of British occupation Lord Nelson, who was in temporary command of the Mediterranean Fleet, spent a few days at the Golden Farm on the north side of the harbour sometime between 12 and 22 October 1799. Local tradition declares (without evidence) that Lady Hamilton was a guest in the house at the same time. Villa El Fonduco, near the southeast side of Cala Figuera and now a hotel, was the residence of Lord Collingwood when Flag Officer in Mahón during the early 19th century.

Amongst places of interest near Mahón the Golden Farm (so called because of its yellow colour) should be visited for the view – the house is privately owned and not open to the public. The church of Santa María with its superb early 19th century organ and the Casa Mercadel Museum are in the town itself. For those interested in the underwater world there is an aquarium near the ferry wharf. The old fortifications around the mouth of the harbour are worth exploring, though much of La Mola is a military area and closed to the public. The prehistoric *taula* and *talayot* at Trepuco about a mile to the south are typical of many throughout the island – if prepared to stroll a little further, the village of San Luis, founded by the French and still with a definite Gallic feel, is on the same road.

Fiestas are held on 5–6 January with the arrival by boat of *Los Reyes Magos* (the Three Wise Men) with toys for the children, followed by a procession. On Good Friday there is a procession and medieval parade. On 15-16 June a sea procession is held in honour of Our Lady of Carmen, and on 7-8 September the *fiesta* of Nuestra Señora de Gracia includes processions, music, sailing races and other sports. In the third week of September a fair is held to showcase local products.

Approach

From south The tall lighthouse on Isla del Aire (Fl.5s53m18M, white tower with black bands on white building 38m) is easily identified and the island can safely be left on either side (see page 181). The few hazards between Isla del Aire and Puerto de Mahón will be avoided by taking a line at least 250m off Punta Rafalet and Punta de Na Girada. The lighthouse (Oc(2)6s22m13M, white tower with three black bands on square white base

15m) and nearby radio towers on Punta de San Carlos are also conspicuous, and the high (78m) peninsula of La Mola ahead easily recognised. The harbour entrance lies between the two.

From north From Cabo Favaritx (Fl(1+2)15s47m 16M, white tower with black diagonal stripes on white building 28m) southwards the coast is very broken – Isla Colom may be recognised if sailing inshore. The high peninsula of La Mola (78m) with buildings on its summit and a lighthouse on Punta del Esperó (Fl(1+2)15s51m8M, white tower with two black bands on white building 11m) are conspicuous from this direction. The entrance to Puerto de Mahón lies just beyond.

Currents

There is normally a southwest-going current past the entrance to Puerto de Mahón. North or northeasterly winds increase its speed while winds from south or southwest either slow or reverse the flow.

Anchorages in the approach

Just south of the entrance lies Cala de San Esteban (see page 179), north of it are Clot de la Mola and Cala Taulera. Clot de la Mola is a small horseshoe bay with 10m over rock and stone, exposed to east-southeast through south to south-southwest.

Cala Taulera, in contrast, is a long narrow inlet between La Mola and Isla del Lazareto, offering total protection in 6m or less over sand though shallow along its northern edge. If coming from the east, turn in close past Laja de Fuera buoy to avoid the spit running out from the south end of Isla del Lazareto – this is NOT marked by the next buoy (Punta San Felipet) which is close off the island itself. The *cala* can easily accommodate twenty or thirty yachts at anchor, and is popular with both visitors and locals even though a charge is sometimes made. Avoid the western side of the *cala* as this is used, at speed, by the tourist boats. An artificial channel, the Canal de Alfonso XIII (sometimes referred to as the Canal del Lazareto), provides a 'back door' into the harbour and is said to carry 3m. The electricity cable marked on BA 2833 as crossing this channel at a height of 15m has now been removed.

Entrance

Enter Puerto de Mahón on a northwesterly course between the high peninsula of La Mola to starboard and the low rocky-cliffed Punta de San Carlos to port. Lit buoys mark the channel, which is used by commercial vessels of some size and should offer a yacht no difficulties, day or night, provided the buoyage is complied with. However note that Mahón is a naval, ferry and commercial port and that these vessels have right of way over yachts and small craft. There is an 8 knot speed limit.

Sea levels

The sea level falls prior to and during strong winds from southwest, west and northwest.

The entrance to Puerto de Mahón looking northwest. The red Laja de San Carlos pillar buoy is clearly visible, the green Laja de Fuera rather less so. Isla del Lazareto divides the entrance, with Cala Teulera on its right.

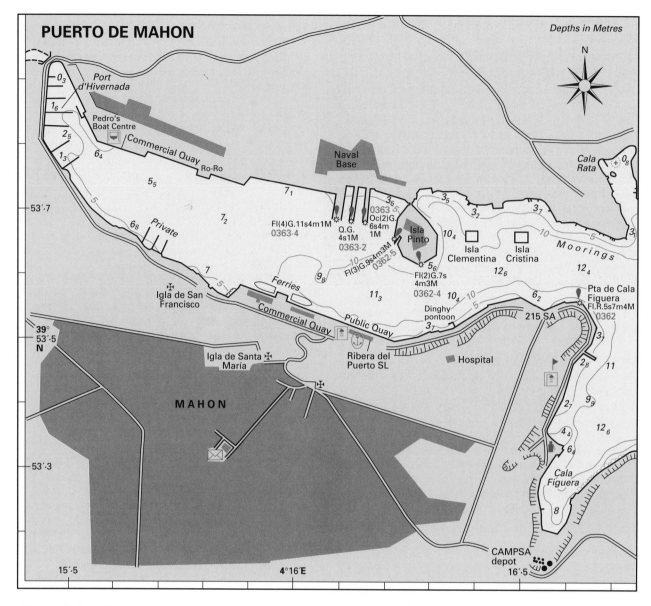

PUERTO DE MAHON

Depths in Metres

Charted depths

Depths in Puerto de Mahón are reported as being up to 2m less than shown on the 1994 edition of BA 2833. The new edition published in 1997 shows the amended depths.

Berthing

Other than the few visitors' berths offered by the *Club Marítimo* and 215 SA, nearly all yacht berthing in Puerto de Mahón is controlled by Ribera del Puerto SL. The new Port d'Hivernada yacht harbour at the head of the estuary offers an alternative but is some distance from the city.

- *Ribera del Puerto SL* (☎ 354844, *Fax* 354327) Licenced by the harbour authorities to administer visitors berths and moorings. They have three principal berthing areas:
- Stern-to on the quayside just east of their office (see plan);
- Two floating 'islands', Isla Clementina and Isla Cristina, moored between Punta de Cala Rata and Isla Pinto. They can take 25 and 18 yachts

respectively, moored stern-to (buoys or lazy lines are provided). A rubbish collection service is provided, and water and electricity are available. There is a dinghy landing stage east of the Ribera del Puerto office (a floating restaurant is currently moored to the end of the pontoon);

- Two pontoons in Cala Llonga, able to take 36 yachts of up to 14m. Rubbish collection is laid on and water, electricity and showers are available.
- *215 SA* (☎ 350013, *Fax* 365095) has some stern-to berths (with lazy lines) outside their office just west of Punta de Cala Figuera (see plan).
- *Club Marítimo* Situated on Punta de Cala Figuera, the *Club Marítimo de Mahón* (☎ 365022, *Fax* 360762) has a number of stern-to berths (with lazy-lines) either side of their jetty in Cala Figuera. However the vast majority are occupied by locally-owned boats and there is seldom room for visitors. Anchoring is no longer allowed in the *cala*.

Cala Llonga, on the north side of the estuary, where Ribera del Puerto has two pontoons and a number of yellow visitors moorings. A large housing development was planned for the hillside but much of it has yet to be built.

- *Port d'Hivernada* (☎ 366968, 366714 *Fax* 362455), a new yacht harbour in the extreme west of Puerto de Mahón which became operational late in 1996. When fully complete it will offer more than 100 berths for craft up to 15m, though many of the slots will be much smaller and in shoal depths. Water and electricity are installed on the pontoons.
- *Public quay* There are two areas on the public quay (see plan) where yachts are currently allowed to raft up much as they please. Water and electricity are available and a charge is made.

Mooring buoys

Private moorings occupy most of the northern shore, with some visitors moorings (bright yellow) in Cala Llonga, around Cala Partio and off Cala Rata extending westwards toward Isla Clementina. All

The view northeast across Puerto de Mahón, with Isla Pinto on the left and the Isla Clementina floating island in the centre (a second 'island' has since been installed). Cala Rata is on the right with the Golden Farm on the hillside beyond.

are administered by Ribera del Puerto SL. A rubbish collection service is provided and there is a dinghy landing stage east of the Ribera del Puerto office (a floating restaurant is currently moored to the end of the pontoon).

Anchorages

- In Cala Taulera just inside the entrance to the harbour – see *Anchorages in the approach* – for which a charge is sometimes made.
- In the designated anchorage close west of Isla del Rey (see plan). Again there is a fee, but this includes rubbish collection and use of a dinghy landing stage in Cala Figuera.
- In the mouth of Cala Llonga, outside the moorings. A marina may be built in the *cala* and if/when work starts anchoring will be prohibited.
- In Cala Fonts, for a brief shopping visit. Anchor close to the head of the *cala* in 15m.

Note In 1996 one yacht reported being charged 5000 ptas for a single night at anchor – several times the correct fee. Ask to see official identification/authorisation if in doubt.

Prohibited anchorages

Anchoring is not permitted northwest of two white buoys positioned northeast of Isla Pinto.

Charges *(see page 6)*

- *Ribera del Puerto* (Quay) High season daily rate – Band D; low season daily rate – Band C (15m), Band D (10m). Water and electricity extra.
- *Ribera del Puerto* (floating islands, pontoons, buoys and anchorage) High season daily rate – Band D; low season daily rate – Band D. Water and electricity (on islands and pontoons) extra.
- *215 SA* High season daily rate – Band B (15m), Band C (10m); low season daily rate – Band B. Water and electricity included.
- *Club Marítimo de Mahón* High season daily rate – Band B; low season daily rate – Band C. Water included.
- *Port d'Hivernada* High season daily rate – Band B; low season daily rate – Band C. Water and electricity included.
- *Public quay* High season daily rate – Band D; low season daily rate – Band D. Water and electricity extra.

Facilities

Boatyards Major repairs to wood, GRP and aluminium hulls can be undertaken by local yards. Both Ribera del Puerto and 215 SA are willing to assist in arranging repairs or maintenance. Pedro's Boat Centre, opposite the new Port d'Hivernada marina, has a large area of hardstanding.

Travel-lift Two travel-lifts, 50 and 35 tonne capacity, at Pedro's Boat Centre.

Cranes 215 SA has a 12 ton crane, the *Club Marítimo* 10 and 2 tonne models. Also a mobile crane at Pedro's Boat Centre and several more on the commercial quays.

Looking southwest across Puerto de Mahón towards the commercial quay, with the Ribera del Puerto and 215 SA berthing areas in the left foreground. On the right are Isla Clementina, Isla Pinto, the naval base and, at the head of the harbour, the new Port d'Hivernada still under construction in May 1996.

Slipway There is a slipway on the west side of Cala Figuera, 20 tonnes and 14m maximum. Enquire at Ribera del Puerto or 215 SA regarding its use.

Engineers Many around the harbour, including the English-run Marine & Auto Power (☎ 354438) and MenMar (☎ 354835. *Fax* 353350).

Official service agents include: 215 SA (☎ 350013, *Fax* 365095) – Volvo Penta; Auto Recambios Union (☎ 360113) – Yamaha; Motonautica Menorca (☎ 368917, *Fax* 352725) – Detroit diesel, Honda, Man, Mariner, Perkins; NauticCentreMenorca (☎ 360550, *Fax* 351250) – Ecosse, Mercury/MerCruiser, Solé diesel, Yanmar; Nautic Reynes (☎ 350567, 365952, *Fax* 353498) – Force, Mariner, Mercury/MerCruiser, Yanmar; Pedro's Boat Centre (☎ 366968, 366714 *Fax* 362455) – Mercury/MerCruiser.

Electronic & radio repairs Enquire at Ribera del Puerto or 215 SA.

Sailmaker At the *Club Marítimo*.

Chandlery Well stocked chandlery opposite the *Club Marítimo*, plus several at the west end of the commercial quay. Some items from 215 SA. It is possible to berth for an hour or so near the chandleries on the commerial quay to load heavy items.

Charts From the chandlery opposite the *Club Marítimo* and possibly others. However there is no official Spanish chart agent in Menorca.

Water At the *Club Marítimo*; on the quay near both the 215 SA and Ribera del Puerto offices; at the western end of the commercial quay (coin-operated); on Isla Clementina and its sister island; on the pontoons in Cala Llonga; on the pontoons at Port d'Hivernada (intended); from the Club Náutico de Villacarlos at the head of Cala Fonts. Water is metered other than on the commercial quay where it is coin-operated. The minimum charge can be quite high for small quantities.

Showers At the *Club Marítimo*, Ribera del Puerto building and 215 SA. Also on the pontoons in Cala Llonga and on Isla Clementina (outdoor shower). Doubtless showers will also be provided at Port d'Hivernada.

Electricity At the 215 SA berths, on Isla Clementina and the pontoons in Cala Llonga, and promised for Port d'Hivernada. There is a 220v AC supply point in the *Club Marítimo* but cables may not cross the road.

Fuel Diesel and paraffin from the CAMPSA depot on the west side of Cala Figuera (where bunkering facilities are also available). At first sight the CAMPSA depot does not look like a fuel station. Diesel and petrol from the *Club Marítimo*.

Bottled gas Camping Gaz is readily available in chandleries and hardware stores. It may be possible to get Calor and other non-standard bottles filled at the CAMPSA depot – ask at Ribera del Puerto, 215 SA etc.

Ice From the *Club Marítimo* and 215 SA as well as nearby bars and supermarkets.

Yacht clubs The Club Marítimo de Mahón (☎ 365022, *Fax* 360762) has a large clubhouse overlooking Cala Figuera with bars, restaurants, lounge, terrace and showers. Visiting yachtsmen are welcome. The Club Náutico de Villacarlos (☎ 365884) at the head of Cala Fonts is a smaller concern, offering a bar and water point but no berths.

Banks Several banks in the town, mostly with credit card facilities.

Shops/provisioning Small supermarket behind the Ribera del Puerto office. Larger one near the CAMPSA depot and another just up the hill from Cala Fonts. The largest supermarkets are on the industrial estates outside the town. General shops of every description are to be found in Mahón.

Produce/fish market Excellent produce and fish markets near the large church of Santa María, open every morning except Sunday.

Hotels/restaurants/cafés etc. At least a dozen hotels, a wide selection of restaurants and many quayside bars and cafés. Bar/restaurant at Cala Llonga.

Launderette Several in the town, also at the *Club Marítimo* and in the Ribera del Puerto building.

Hospital In the town.

Looking west into Cala Pedrera (left) and Cala Fonts (centre) where the Club Náutico de Villacarlos is situated. Isla del Rey is on the right.

Communications

Car hire/taxis Numerous car hire and taxi companies.

Buses Bus service to Cuidadela and elsewhere.

Ferries To Palma and mainland Spain.

Air services Smallish international airport, with services direct to major capitals, less than 3 miles southwest of Mahón.

⚓ Cala de San Esteban (Sant Esteve)

39°51'·9N 4°18'·4E

A narrow but deeply indented *cala* surrounded by a fringe of houses, just south of Puerto de Mahón and easily identified by Punta de San Carlos lighthouse, two radio masts and a large house all close north of the entrance. Depths of 2m or more can be carried almost to its head – favour the deeper north side and sound carefully as the bottom is rocky. Close to the entrance the *cala* is open northeast to southeast, further in more protection is gained from the northeast and east.

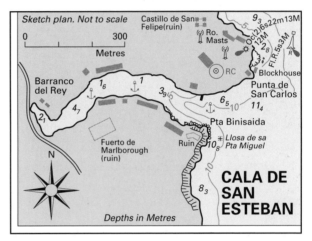

⚓ Cala Rafalet 39°50'·5N 4°18'·1E

One of the most beautiful of the islands' small *calas*, narrow with steep rocky cliffs and ideal for a fantastic yacht photograph. Investigate by dinghy first and approach with great caution to anchor in 4–6m, open to the easterly quadrant. The narrow

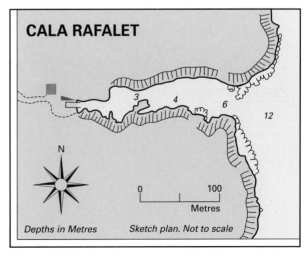

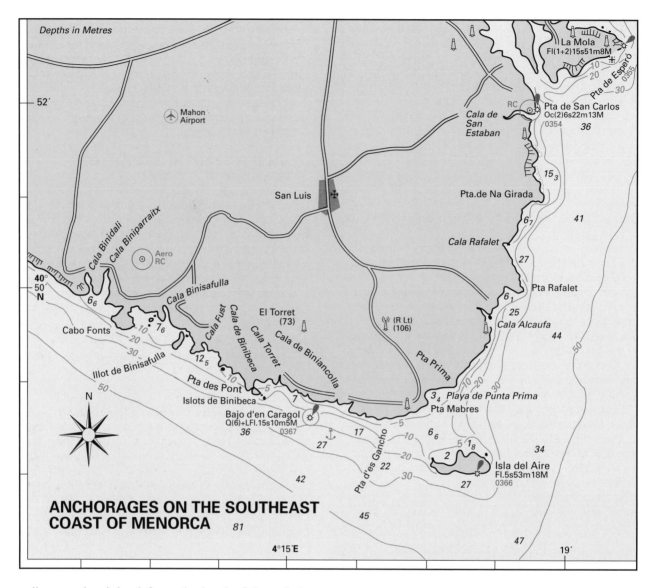

Depths in Metres

ANCHORAGES ON THE SOUTHEAST
COAST OF MENORCA

valley running inland from the head of the *cala* is most attractive and shows signs of ancient cave dwellers. There is a track to the main road and a housing estate on the high ground several hundred metres to the south. A *talayot* lies 1½ miles to the northwest.

⚓ **Cala Alcaufa (d'Alcaufar)** 39°49'·7N 4°17'·9E
One of the first *calas* to be developed, with many houses on the northern side but virtually nothing to the south, and easy to identify by virtue of a large pale stone tower just south of the entrance. Enter leaving Illot d'es Torn to starboard and anchor in 2–4m over rock and sand open to the southeast. Holding is reported to be poor. There are many moorings and space to anchor is restricted – it may be necessary to moor fore and aft or take a line ashore. There are a few shops, restaurants and bars in the village.

Looking westward into Cala Alcaufa, with the smaller Cala Roig on the left. The tower stands out almost white in the sunshine.

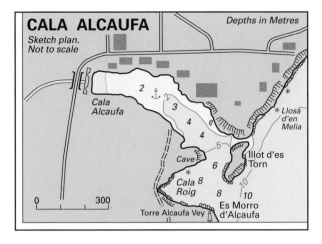

CALA ALCAUFA
*Sketch plan.
Not to scale*

Depths in Metres

Cala
Alcaufa

Llosa
d'en
Melia

Cave

Illot d'es
Torn

Cala
Roig

0   300

Torre Alcaufa Vey

Es Morro
d'Alcaufa

⚓ **Playa de Punta Prima (Ensenada Arenal de Alcaufa)** 39°48'·9N 4°17'·1E

A somewhat exposed anchorage in a wide bay off a superb sandy beach which gets crowded in season. Anchor in 2m+ of turquoise water, open to east through southeast to southwest, but somewhat protected from the south by Isla del Aire. The bay is backed by houses and apartment blocks together with the usual shops, bars and restaurants. A submarine cable runs in southeasterly direction from a point near the head of the bay.

The British landed here under Admiral Sir John Leake and General Stanhope when they captured the island in 1708. Later it was used again by Spanish troops under the Duc de Crillon landing in 1781 to recapture the island.

☼ F.R.
Ro Mast
(160)

To San Luis

Pta Prima

Depths in Metres

N

Torre Alcaufa
Nou

Playa de
Punta Prima

Pta d'es
Gancho

Pta
Mabres

Underwater
cable

Escollo
del
Aire

Pta Llebeig

I. del Aire

Pta
Mitans

Fl.5s53m18M
0366

**PLAYA DE PUNTA PRIMA
AND ISLA DEL AIRE**
Sketch plan. Not to scale

0   500

Metres

⚓ **Isla del Aire** Bisected by 39°48'·1N 4°17'·4E

A low, flat, island just over 1000m long by 400m wide but much of it less than 4m high, with a couple hillocks (18m) and (20m) to the southeast, one topped by a lighthouse (Fl.5s53m18M white tower, black bands, on white building 38m).

Anchor in a bay on the northwest side of the island in 2–4m over sand, weed and some rocks, about 150m west of the landing pier from which there is a track to the lighthouse. Watch for rocky pinnacles and use a trip line. The island is uninhabited – other than by rabbits and a unique race of black lizards (*lacerta lilfordi*) – but is visited by tourist boats during summer. It is said that the lizards particularly enjoy tomatoes and will approach quite close if pieces are offered.

Admiral Byng's unsuccessful battle against the French fleet under Galissonnière took place off Isla del Aire in May 1756. Byng failed to close and engage the enemy, and the following day withdrew his fleet to Mallorca and thence to Gibraltar. He was court-martialled and executed, as Voltaire said '*pour encourager les autres*'.

Passage between Isla del Aire and Menorca

An unimpeded passage 1000m wide exists between Isla del Aire and Menorca with a minimum central depth of 6·6m. Yachts drawing 2·5m or less can follow the Menorcan coast at 200m. The sandy bottom can usually be seen quite clearly.

⚓ **Cala de Biniancolla** 39°48'·7N 4°15'·8E

A small *cala* with low rocky sides and a village at its head, suitable for small yachts only. A large, conspicuous, apartment block stands behind the hamlet and can be seen from afar. If approaching from the west give the rocky Bajo Es Caragol (see below) a generous berth, and enter with care to avoid the outlying rocks on either side. Anchor in sand, rock and weed in 3m±, open to south and southwest. There are restaurants and cafés in the village.

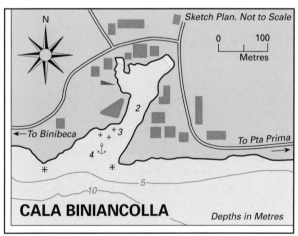

N

Sketch Plan. Not to Scale

0   100
Metres

To Binibeca

To Pta
Prima

CALA BINIANCOLLA

Depths in Metres

Bajo Es Caragol 39°48'·6N 4°15'·3E

A breaking, rocky bank about 800m southwest of Cala de Biniancolla, marked by a south cardinal beacon (Q(6)+LFl.15s10m5M with ▼ topmark) at its NORTHWEST corner. Although there is good water about halfway between the beacon and the shore, the *baja* should be given a generous berth as rocks extend up to 100m east and south.

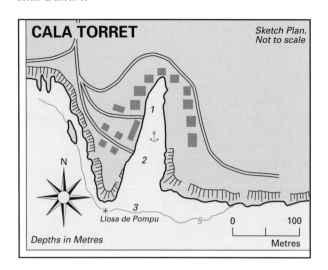

Cala de Binibeca seen from the southwest, with Punta des Pont and the Illots de Binebeca in the foreground.

⚓ **Cala Torret** 39°49'N 4°14'·8E

A small, developed *cala* surrounded by houses, only suitable for smaller yachts in good weather. The El Torret tower on the skyline about ¾ mile northeast is a useful mark, as is a line of arched doorways along the west side of the *cala*. Enter with care and anchor in the middle of the *cala*, open southeast through to southwest. The usual cafés, restaurants and small shops will be found ashore.

⚓ **Cala de Binibeca (Binibequer)**
39°49'N 4°14'·5E

A large, well-known 'developed' *cala* tucked behind Punta des Pont and the Illots de Binibeca, and overlooked by the tourist development of Binebeca Nou. Approach and entrance are straightforward – anchor near the middle in 3–7m over hard sand and weed, open from east to south. There is an excellent beach, very crowded in the season, with a pier, slipway and dinghy crane a short walk east. A *Club Náutico*, restaurants, shops and a hotel will be found in Binibeca Nou.

There has been talk of developing a small yacht harbour here but nothing has actually happened.

⚓ **Cala Fust (d'en Fust)** 39°49'·4N 4°13'·8E

Occasionally, and confusingly, referred to as Binibeca Vell, Cala Fust is small with many houses and a conspicuous church spire to the east (the village of Binibeca Vell). Open to south and southwest, it is suitable only for smaller yachts. There is an awash rock (Llosa d'en Fust) close east of the entrance. Local fishing craft are moored at the shallow head of the *cala*. There are the usual facilities ashore and some good examples of local rural architecture in Binibeca Vell.

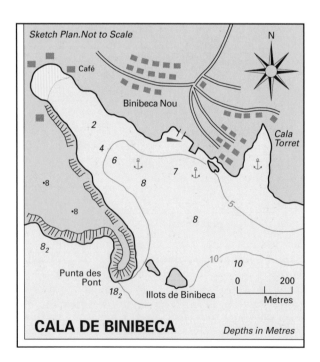

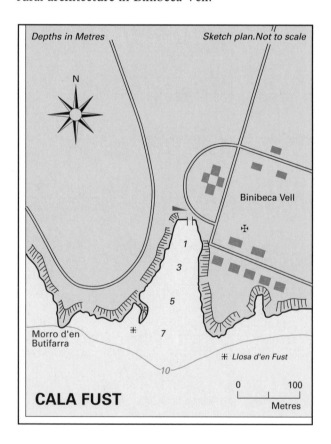

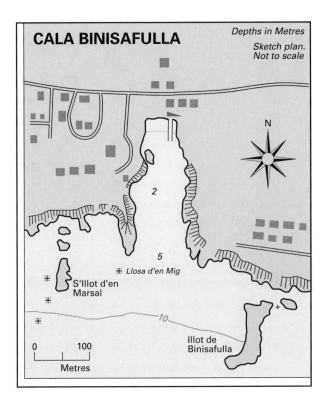

CALA BINISAFULLA

Depths in Metres
Sketch plan.
Not to scale

N

2

5

⚓ *Llosa d'en Mig*

✳ S'Illot d'en Marsal

✳

✳

10

Illot de Binisafulla

+

0   100
Metres

⚓ Cala Binisafulla (Binisafuller)
39°49'·7N 4°13'·2E

A medium-sized *cala* with some adjacent houses but not overdeveloped. Approach with care due to a number of islets and awash rocks – a course from near the southwest corner of Illot de Binisafuller clears all dangers. Anchor in 2–5m over sand and weed, open to south and southeast. Cala Binisafulla is in line with the airport runway so can be noisy.

Cabo Fonts (Es Cap d'en Font)
39°49'·6N 4°12'·6E

A low (12m) but prominent rocky-cliffed headland covered with houses. Although steep-to, several rocky islets lie to the southeast.

Calas Binidalí (left) and Biniparraitx (right) seen from the southwest. Cala Biniparraitx is longer than it appears here, a bend cutting the upper part off from view. The airport runway can be seen on the left near the skyline.

⚓ Cala Biniparraitx (Biniparratx)
39°49'·9N 4°12'·2E

An attractive small *cala* with high rocky sides, easy to approach and enter. Though inconspicuous from offshore, Cabo Fonts some 750m to the east is prominent. Anchor just short of the 'elbow' in 4–6m over sand and rock, open to south and southwest. There are rocky patches beyond the corner, and depths shoal rapidly towards the sandy beach. A few houses and a seasonal beach café stand on the east bank of the *cala*, but there are no real facilities.

⚓ Cala Binidalí 39°49'·9N 4°12'·1E

A pretty but very small *cala* just west of Cala Biniparraitx, with high rocky cliffs, a sandy beach and a few houses well set back. Strictly a fair weather anchorage, approach and entrance present no problems but as space is restricted either two anchors will be needed or a line taken ashore. Anchor in 3–5m over sand and rock, open southeast to east, but note that depths shoal rapidly towards the head. There are no facilities.

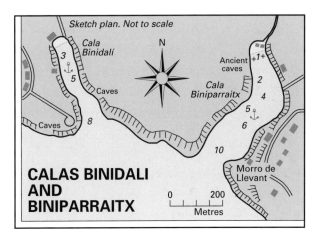

Sketch plan. Not to scale

Cala Binidalí

3

5

Caves

Caves

8

N

Ancient caves

+1+

2

Cala Biniparraitx

4

5

6

10

Morro de Llevant

CALAS BINIDALI AND BINIPARRAITX

0   200
Metres

Cabo Gros 39°50'·7N 4°10'·6E

A high (39m), rocky-cliffed headland with some houses on the top. Even so it is not very prominent and can only be seen if coasting close in. There are some prehistoric caves cut into the cliffs including a very large one on the west face.

⚓ Cala Canutells 39°50'·9N 4°10'·2E

A large and attractive S-shaped *cala* between sloping rocky cliffs, with a large tourist development to the east and many local craft on permanent moorings. Enter down the centre of the *cala* and anchor as space permits in 4–6m over sand, open to southeast and south. The upper part of the *cala* is very shallow, with a shelving sanding beach at its head which is deservedly popular with tourists. There is a café/restaurant on the beach and small shops including a mini-market in the tourist village.

The surrounding cliffs are full of caves, including two tall, arched recesses close west of the entrance and the Covas d'es Castella 800m to the east.

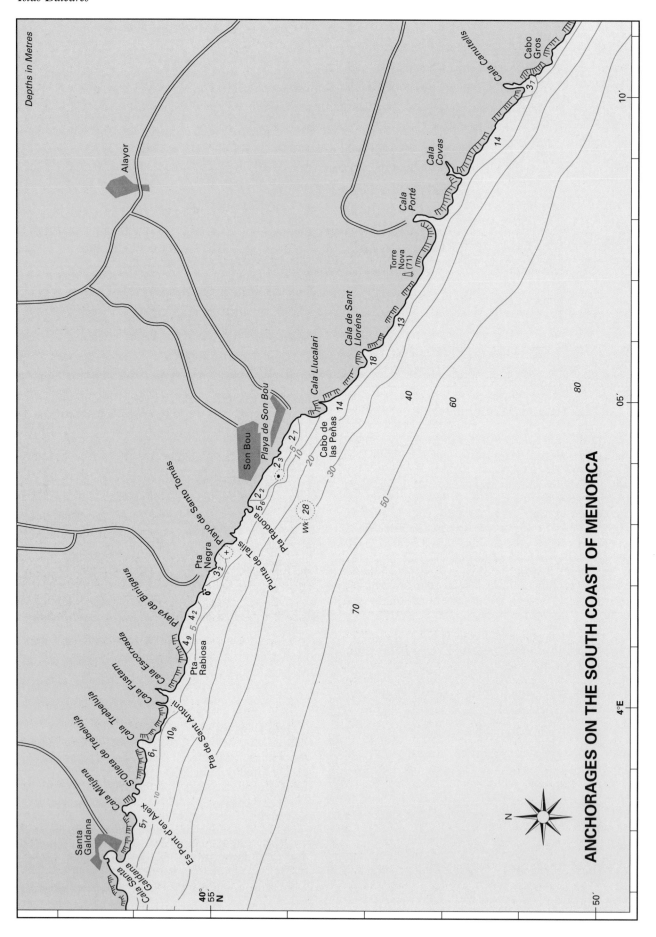

ANCHORAGES ON THE SOUTH COAST OF MENORCA

Cala Canutells seen from slightly east of south. The caves just west of the entrance show up clearly.

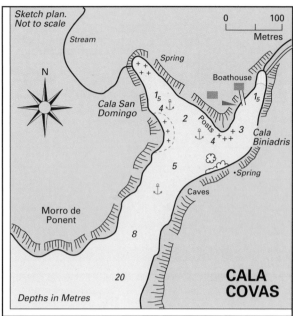

Sketch plan. Not to scale

CALA COVAS

Depths in Metres

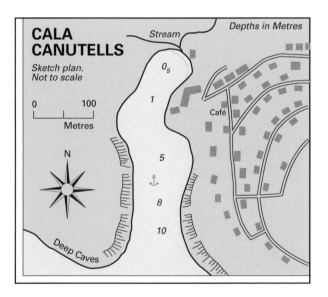

CALA CANUTELLS

Sketch plan. Not to scale

Depths in Metres

The lovely, and almost deserted, Cala Covas from south-southwest. The western arm (Cala San Domingo) can be seen clearly, the eastern arm (Cala Biniadris) less so. The sea caves around the entrance can hardly be missed.

⚓ **Cala Covas (Cales Coves)** 39°51'·7N 4°08'·7E
Arguably the most spectacular and beautiful anchorage in the Islas Baleares, Cala Covas is surrounded by nearly 150 caves, some of which are prehistoric. The entrance between two high rocky cliffs lies ¾ mile east of Cala Porté, which is easily identified by the huge housing development to its east. Anchor in 3–5m with two anchors or a line ashore to limit swinging room – there are several convenient posts on the west side of the small central promontory (see plan), but investigate first by dinghy as there are fringing rocks. Much of the bottom is rocky, making a trip-line advisable. The anchorage is open to southwest and possibly south, depending on the spot chosen.

The *cala* is deserted except for two houses, but large numbers of tourists visit the beaches every day and a litter problem has been reported. Some of the caves are inhabited in summer. There are several freshwater springs and a road inland, but no facilities.

⚓ **Cala Porté (En Porter)** 39°52'·1N 4°07'·9E
A large *cala* lying between high (48m) rocky cliffs. The valley and hillside to the north and east are covered by a mass of holiday homes, complete with hotels, shops, cafés, restaurants and discos, which make the *cala* easy to locate. The 8m Torre Nova tower stands about ¾ mile northwest.

Anchor in 3m+ over sand, open to south and southwest. A line of buoys may be laid to mark off the bathing area in front of the beach, which is good, crowded and pedalo-ridden. There are two beach cafés, while most everyday requirements are available in the tourist area.

Cala Porté from the southwest. The buildings in the photograph are only a small part of the spreading tourist development.

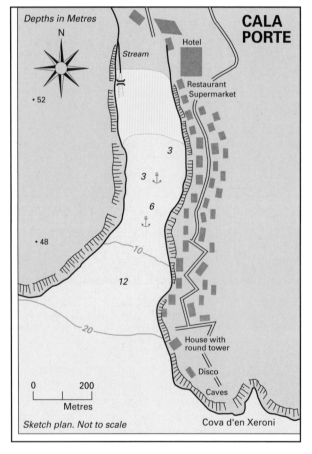

It is worth walking along the cliffs on the eastern side of the entrance to Cova d'en Xeroni, a succession of natural caves with openings through the cliffs now occupied by a bar and restaurant (and a nightly disco). There are several important *talayots* and ancient ruins on the road to Alayor.

Torre Nova 39°52'·4N 4°07'·1E
A ruined lookout tower 8m high on the edge of a 63m rocky cliff, about ¾ mile northwest of Cala Porté. It is not very conspicuous.

⚓ **Cala de Sant Lloréns (Sant Llorenç)**
39°53'N 4°05'·8E
A very small, deserted *cala* surrounded by sheer rocky cliffs with a steep-sided river valley behind. Only suitable for use by small yachts in settled conditions. Care is necessary in the approach due to several fringing rocks. Moor to two anchors over sand and rock, open to southeast and south.

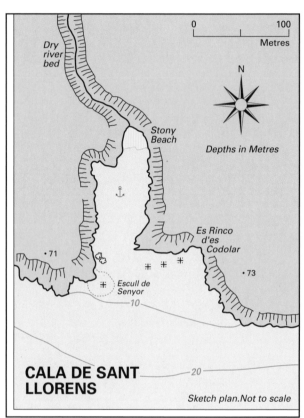

⚓ **Cala Llucalari** 39°53'·5N 4°05'E
A very small, deserted *cala* with high sloping rocky sides, tucked behind Cabo de las Peñas (Cap de ses Penyes) and backed by a dried-up river valley with a track inland. Its use is limited to small yachts in good weather. Anchor in the centre of the *cala* in 3–4m over rock and sand, open to southeast round to southwest. There is a small rocky beach but no facilities.

⚓ **Playa de Son Bou, Playa de Santo Tomás (Playa de Talis or Atalix) and Playa de Binigaus** Stretching from 39°53'·9N 4°04'·7E to 39°55'·4N 4°01'·2E
A line of sandy beaches more than 3 miles long between Cabo de las Peñas (Cap de ses Penyes) and Punta Rabiosa, broken only by the low rocky promontories of Punta Radona, Punta de Talis and Punta Negra. They are backed by several large

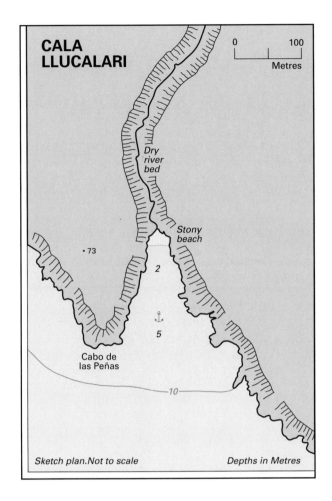

CALA LLUCALARI

0   100
Metres

Dry river bed

Stony beach

• 73

2

⚓

5

Cabo de las Peñas

—— 10 ——

Sketch plan. Not to scale   Depths in Metres

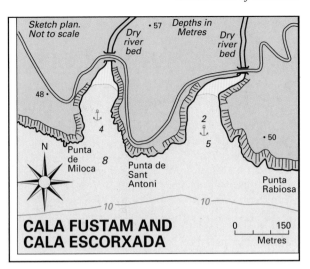

Sketch plan. Not to scale   • 57   Depths in Metres

Dry river bed   Dry river bed

48 •

⚓   4   2   5   • 50

N   Punta de Miloca   8   Punta de Sant Antoni   Punta Rabiosa

—10—   —10—

CALA FUSTAM AND CALA ESCORXADA

0   150
Metres

apartment blocks and hotels plus a number of tourist developments, including those of San Jaime Mediterráneo and Santo Tomás.

The 10m contour runs some 400m offshore, making it possible to anchor over sand almost anywhere along this stretch of coast open to southeast through south to west. There are two small islands and some rocks close inshore.

The San Jaime Mediterráneo resort at Son Bou includes a bank amongst its facilities, as well as a supermarket and the usual bars and restaurants. Santo Tomás has beach bars, restaurants, supermarkets and gift shops.

The ruins of an early Christian church dating from the 5th century overlook the eastern end of the Son Bou beach while two *talayots* lie near the road from Santo Tomás to Ferrerías, together with other ancient remains. There is a spring at the northwest end of Playa de Binigaus, which is generally less built up.

⚓ Cala Escorxada 39°55'·6N 4°00'·3E

A wide, deserted bay with low rocky cliffs and a large sandy beach, about ¾ mile northwest of the end of Playa de Binigaus. Anchor in 2–5m over sand, open southeast to southwest. Ashore there is a track to San Cristóbal but nothing else.

⚓ Cala Fustam 39°55'·6N 4°00'·1E

A smaller and narrower version of Cala Escorxada lying 300m further northwest, the other side of Punta de Sant Antoni. Moor to two anchors in 3–4m over sand, open southeast to southwest. The sandy beach is not as large as that at Cala Escorxada, but the *cala* is very pretty and totally deserted. Again there is nothing ashore other than the track to San Cristóbal.

⚓ Cala Trebeluja (Trebalúger)
39°55'·8N 3°59'·4E

A large, wide *cala* with a pinkish sandy beach. There are high (64m), sloping rocky cliffs with caves on the southeast side and lower, tree-covered cliffs on the northwest side. Anchor in 4–6m over sand, open to south and southwest.

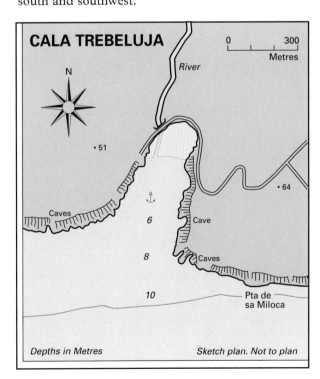

CALA TREBELUJA

0   300
Metres

N   River

• 51

⚓

Caves   6   Cave

8   Caves

10   Pta de sa Miloca

Depths in Metres   *Sketch plan. Not to plan*

A small freshwater river enters the northwest corner of the *cala*. It has a low sand bar over which a dinghy can be pulled or carried, allowing one to row up to ¾ mile upstream with the chance of seeing turtles, fish and various birds. There is a track to San Cristóbal but otherwise the *cala* is deserted.

⚓ S'Olleta de Trebeluja and Es Pont d'en Aleix 39°55'·9N 3°58'·6E

Small deserted twin *calas*, surrounded by steep rocky cliffs and only for use with great care. Either moor to two anchors or take a line ashore, as swinging room is very restricted. Open to south and southwest.

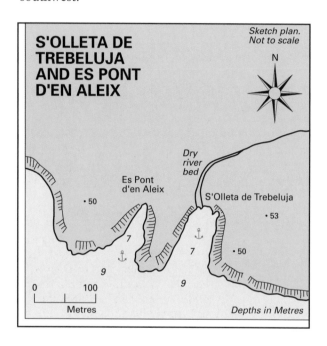

The wide, unspoilt Cala Mitjana with its backdrop of natural woodland. It is popular with tourists despite being relatively difficult to reach by land.

⚓ Cala Mitjana 39°56'N 3°58'·4E

A large *cala* more than 100m wide, surrounded by rocky cliffs but with two good sandy beaches, lying just under ¾ mile east of Cala Santa Galdana (easily recognised by its large hotels and apartment blocks). Anchor in 3–6m over sand and weed, open to southeast round to southwest. A track connects with the road to Ferrerías.

⚓ Cala Santa Galdana 39°56'·3N 3°57'·5E

Once one of the most beautiful large *calas* in Menorca, and still the largest and most sheltered anchorage on the south coast, Cala Santa Galdana has not been improved by the construction of several high-rise hotels. At least these make it easy to recognise, particularly if approaching from the east, while a latticework watertower on the cliffs east of the entrance may also be spotted. However if arriving from the west little is seen until abreast of the entrance.

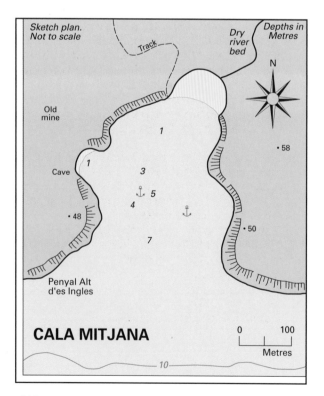

Cala Santa Galdana seen from the southwest. The high-rise hotels are almost unique in Menorca – they met with such criticism that laws were drawn up to ensure no more were built.

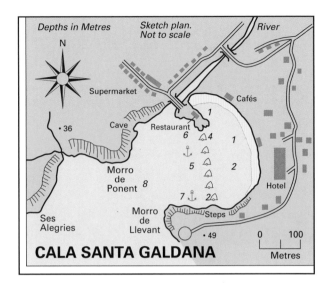

Looking directly into Cala Macarella from south-southeast. Cala Macarelleta is completely hidden from view by its high sides, but its position can be gauged by the expanse of pale rocky cliff slightly inland on the left.

A series of buoys linked by a thin line stretches from the central promontory across the *cala* to near the end of the beach, protecting the bathing area but seriously restricting the anchorage. Anchor as space permits, probably in 5m or more, over sand and weed open to south, southwest and possibly southeast. It may be necessary to lie to two anchors or take a long line ashore when the harbour is crowded. The river Barranco de Cala Santa Galdana enters the northwest corner of the *cala* and is navigable by dinghy for more than ½ mile. A bridge some 10m long and 3m in height spans its mouth, with a smallcraft pontoon beyond. A yacht harbour with around 200 berths was at the planning stage in 1997. It will presumably be situated south of the bridge.

The long sandy beach is crowded in season and the shouts of the bathers echo around the surrounding cliffs. There is also a lot of noise during the evening from bars and discos, but these usually cease around 2200. Restaurants, cafés, bars, supermarkets and tourist shops flourish in the resort.

⚓ Cala Macarella and Cala Macarelleta
39°56'·3N 3°56'·4E
A large double *cala* with two sandy beaches, surrounded by sloping rocky cliffs, scrub and trees, and easy to spot just under a mile west of Cala Santa Galdana. Anchor in 3–6m over sand and a few weed patches, open to southeast and south. The anchorage is often crowded and it may be necessary to use two anchors or to take a line ashore – Cala Macarelleta has a mooring stone complete with ring.

Three tracks bring in day tourists and there is a popular campsite nearby (caves overlooking the *calas* may also be inhabited in summer). The stream flowing into Cala Macarella is embanked with what could be Moorish masonry – the water appears clean and is recommended locally. There is a café/bar on the beach and an ancient ruined village to the west. These *calas*, together with those further east, were used as hide-outs by Barbary pirates in medieval times.

⚓ Cala Turqueta 39°55'·8N 3°55'E
A small, attractive *cala* surrounded by scrub and pine-covered rocky cliffs and with a sandy beach at its head. It lies a mile west of Cala Macarella and the same distance from Cala de Son Saura. The conspicuous Torre de Artuiz lies just west of the entrance. Anchor in 3m+ over sand with weed patches, open to southeast round to southwest, taking a line ashore if necessary (there is a mooring ring on the eastern side). Two tracks at the head of the *cala* lead inland and are used by tourists.

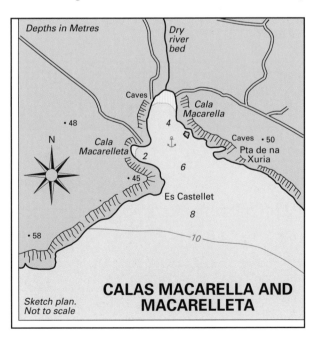

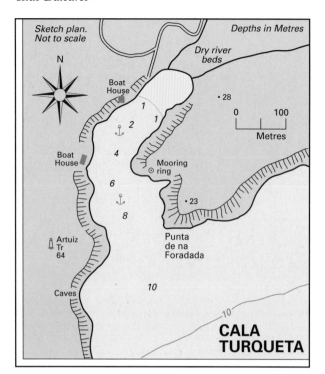

CALA TURQUETA

Sketch plan. Not to scale · Depths in Metres

N

Dry river beds

Boat House

Boat House

Mooring ring

Punta de na Foradada

Artuiz Tr 64

Caves

0 · 100 · Metres

Cala de Talé seen from south-southwest. The long narrow rock Seca d'en Barra can be seen just below the water off the narrow inlet on the right.

⚓ **Cala de Talé (d'es Talaier)** 39°55'·6N 3°54'·2E
A small and often deserted *cala* with a low rocky shore backed by scrub and pine woods, about ½ mile east of Cala de Son Saura and separated from it by Punta Gobernadó. Enter with care as there is a small islet on the west side of the entrance and a lone rock awash close inshore to the east. Anchor in 2m+ over sand, open to southeast and south. Space is very limited and it may be necessary to lie to two anchors. There is a sandy beach with a white hut at the head of the *cala* and a track inland.

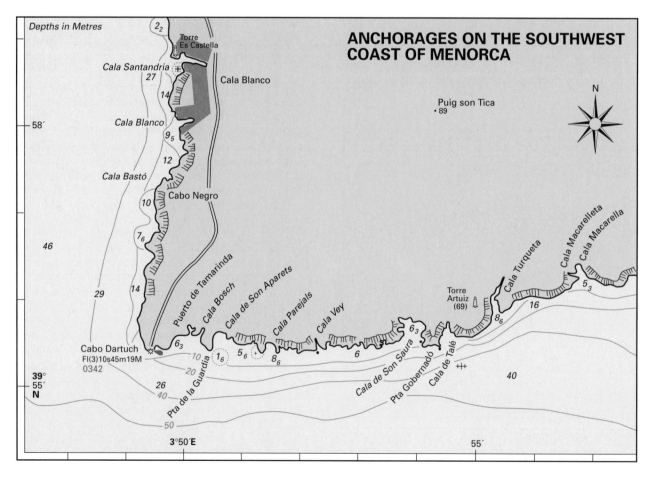

ANCHORAGES ON THE SOUTHWEST COAST OF MENORCA

Depths in Metres

Torre Es Castella

Cala Santandria

Cala Blanco

Cala Blanco

Cala Bastó

Cabo Negro

Puerto de Tamarinda

Cala Bosch

Cala de Son Aparets

Cala Parejals

Cala Vey

Cabo Dartuch
Fl(3)10s45m19M
0342

Pta de la Guardia

Cala de Son Saura

Pta Gobernadó

Cala de Talé

Torre Artuiz (69)

Cala Turqueta

Cala Macarelleta

Cala Macarella

Puig son Tica · 89

N

39° 55' N

3°50'E · 55'

190

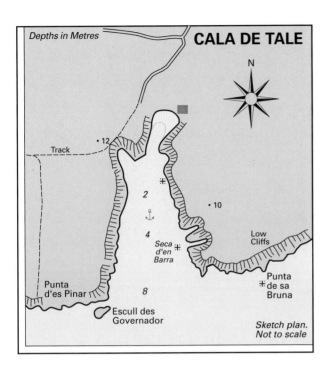

Cala de Son Saura from the southwest, dwarfing the two yachts at anchor in May 1996. As in many of the *calas* the water is extremely clear and every feature on the bottom can be picked out.

⚓ **Cala de Son Saura** 39°55'·6N 3°53'·7E

A large, semi-enclosed bay surrounded by a low, sloping rocky foreshore with dark pine trees and scrub behind. It lies close west of Punta Gobernadó and is easily recognized by its sheer size – the entrance is 500m wide and it broadens out further inside. There are two small islets on the west of the entrance and two isolated rocks near the east side, but the bay itself is clear. Anchor in 3–8m over sand and weed, open to southwest, south or southeast according to the spot chosen.

Ashore there is a long pinkish sandy beach divided into two parts by a low rocky area, with a small stream crossing the eastern beach after wet weather. There is a small fishing boat slipway, a few houses well set back and a road leading inland, but nothing else.

⚓ **Cala Vey (de Son Vell) and Cala Parejals** 39°55'·4N 3°52'·2E

Two small *calas* with rocky sides on the much indented stretch of coast between Cala de Son Saura and Cala de Son Aparets. There are numerous inshore rocks and islets, and the area should only be explored with considerable care and by experienced navigators.

⚓ **Cala de Son Aparets (Playa de Son Xoriguer)** 39°55'·5N 3°50'·6E

A large rounded bay surrounded by low rocky cliffs, behind which lie houses and some apartment blocks. The *cala* is easy to find, being a little under a mile east of Cabo Dartuch and close east of Puerto

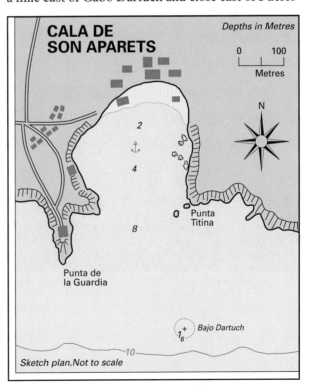

de Tamarinda and Punta de la Guardia. On the approach watch out for the isolated Bajo Dartuch which lies 400m south-southeast of the entrance and carries 1·6m – otherwise there are no hazards. Anchor in 2m+ over sand and weed, open to southeast through to southwest. The beach is good but often very crowded. There are several beach cafés and roads inland. The Puerto de Tamarinda tourist complex is a short walk away.

⚓ **Cala Bosch (En Bosc)** 39°55'·6N 3°50'·3E
A small *cala* with low rocky edges and a crowded sandy beach at its head, just east of Puerto de Tamarinda and west of Punta de la Guardia. Anchor in 2m+ over sand and weed, open to southwest and south. There are low-rise tourist apartments behind the *cala* and it is only a step across to the Puerto de Tamarinda tourist complex where there are shops and other facilities.

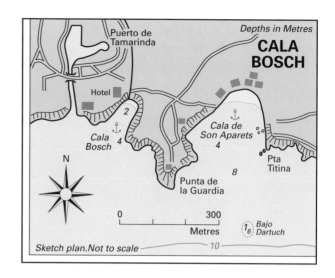

Puerto de Tamarinada and Cala Bosch, seen from the south. The 'willow-pattern plate' bridge is in clear view, together with the brownish waters of the lagoon.

Puerto de Tamarinda (Marina Cala Bosch)

39°55'·6N 3°50'·2E

Charts

	Approach
Admiralty	*2833*
Spanish	*6A, 965*
French	*7117*

Lights

No lights.

Port Communications

Puerto de Tamarinda ☎ 385238.

General

A small man-made lagoon dredged from a low-lying area and approached via a narrow channel spanned by a footbridge reminiscent of a willow-pattern plate, Puerto de Tamarinda is inaccessible to sailing vessels needing more than 10m air height. However it makes an interesting visit by dinghy and is suited to medium sized motor yachts, speedboats and smaller sailing craft. It is also used by sailboarders. The harbour is surrounded by a growing tourist development with all the related facilities such as bars, restaurants, supermarkets, chemist, a bank and tourist shops. There is a *talayot* at Son Olivaret about a mile north on the road to Ciudadela.

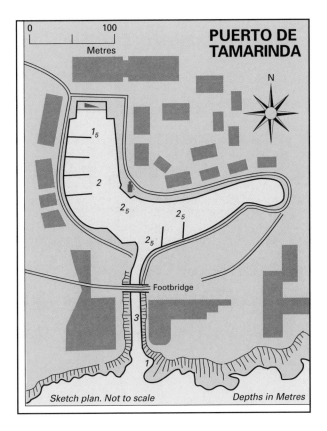

Approach

From east Follow the coast past a series of small *calas*. The large Cala de Son Aparets is easily recognised, being separated by a low rocky promontory, Punta de la Guardia, from the narrow Cala Bosch, behind which stands a group of apartment blocks. 200m west of this *cala* lies the entrance to Puerto de Tamarinda. The entrance is not obvious until close by.

From north and west Approach the prominent Cabo Dartuch with its black and white banded lighthouse. The entrance to Puerto de Tamarinda lies around 1000m east-northeast of the lighthouse and west of Cala Bosch, which will be recognised by its narrow sandy beach surrounded by apartment blocks.

Anchorages in the approach

Anchor in Cala Bosch or Cala de Son Aparets (see pages 191 and 192).

Entrance

The entrance is less than 10m wide – too narrow for anything larger than dinghies to pass each other, and much too narrow to turn. It is therefore essential to check that the way is clear before committing oneself. Approach on a northerly course to open up the channel with its conspicuous white footbridge and enter at slow speed. The water is often muddy and depths are unreliable – keep a close eye on the echo-sounder. If in any doubt about mast clearance it would be wise to anchor in Cala Bosch and walk round to measure the bridge – and possibly the mast!

In strong winds and swell from the southerly quadrant it would be dangerous to attempt to enter Puerto de Tamarinda. Equally it is not a harbour to be entered at night without prior knowledge.

Berthing

Secure in any vacant berth – the harbour is unlikely to be full. An official will allocate a berth in due course. Charges are believed to be low.

Facilities

Slipways A very wide slipway at the head of the harbour.

Water At the base of some of the pontoons, otherwise from one of the cafés.

Electricity On some (but not all) of the pontoons.

Fuel A fuel berth was under construction in May 1996.

Ice From the nearby bars and cafés.

Bank In the tourist complex.

Shops/provisioning Small supermarket and other shops in the tourist complex.

Hotels/restaurants/cafés etc. A choice of each.

Hospital/medical services In Ciudadela, about 4½ miles away.

Communications

Taxis By telephone from Ciudadela, or enquire in the tourist complex.
Buses Buses to Ciudadela.

Cabo Dartuch (Cap d'Artruix)
39°55'·4N 3°49'·6E

A prominent headland of low (10m) dark cliffs surmounted by a conspicuous lighthouse (Fl(3)10s 45m19M, white tower with three black bands on white building 34m) surrounded by a low white wall. The headland is steep-to.

Cabo Negro (Cap Negre) 39°57'·2N 3°49'·7E

A relatively inconspicuous headland of black rock, 12m high and steep-to. Easily seen if coasting close inshore.

⌇ Cala Bastó 39°57'·4N 3°49'·8E

A very small *cala* close north of Cabo Negro and about 2 miles north of Cabo Dartuch, surrounded by low (8m) black rocky cliffs and to be used with extreme caution. A small breaking rock lies on the south side of the entrance. The *cala*, which is open from west to north, has no beach and is generally deserted.

⌇ Cala Blanca 39°58'N 3°50'E

A narrow *cala* between low rocky sides, Cala Blanca is easy to identify due to an unusual building with

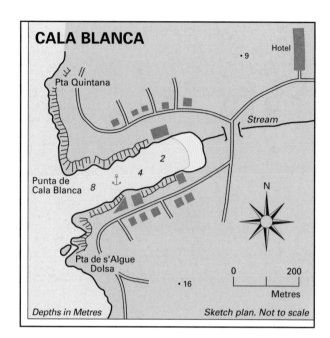

deep verandas on its northern side and a huge white apartment block/hotel in the background. Anchor in 4–8m over sand, open to southwest and west. The sandy beach at its head is often crowded, and there are hotels, restaurants, cafés and houses nearby. The Caves of Parella a few hundred metres inland are worth visiting.

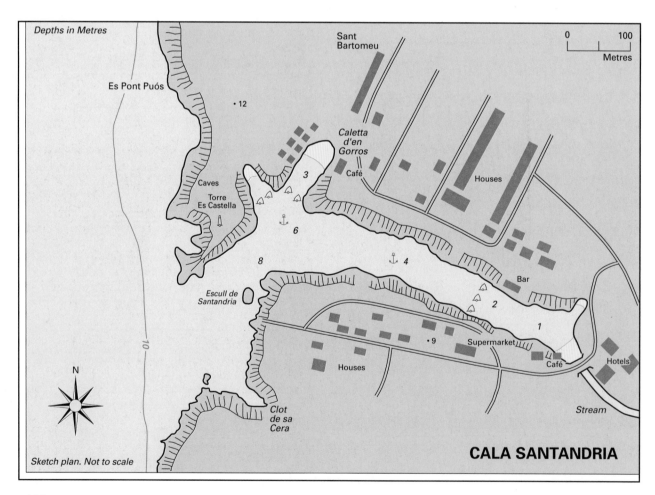

Cala Blanca seen from just north of west.

The popular Cala Santandria, only a mile south of Ciudadela, viewed from a little south of west. The restored Torre Es Castella shows clearly on the left – more prominently than it would from ground level – and the lines of buoys marking off the bathing beaches can also be seen.

⚓ **Cala Santandria** 39°58'·8N 3°49'·9E

A long *cala* with several shorter branches, Cala Santandria lies between low, pinkish, rocky cliffs just over a mile south of Puerto de Ciudadela. The entrance is not easily picked out, but the Torre Es Castella (a restored defensive tower) on the northern headland helps – though not as much as it would if the greater part were not hidden by a moat. A small islet off the east side of the entrance is the only hazard on entering. Anchor in 3m+ over sand and weed as space permits, either lying to two anchors or taking a line ashore, open to southwest and west. Two cables run down the centre of the *cala*, so care is needed when picking a spot.

Lines of buoys mark off all three bathing beaches with their bars and cafés. Slightly further back will be found supermarkets, hotels and restaurants. There are pleasant walks on either side of the *cala* and the Torre Es Castella is worth a visit. Maréchal Richelieu landed here with his troops on 18 April 1756, *en route* to capture Ciudadela.

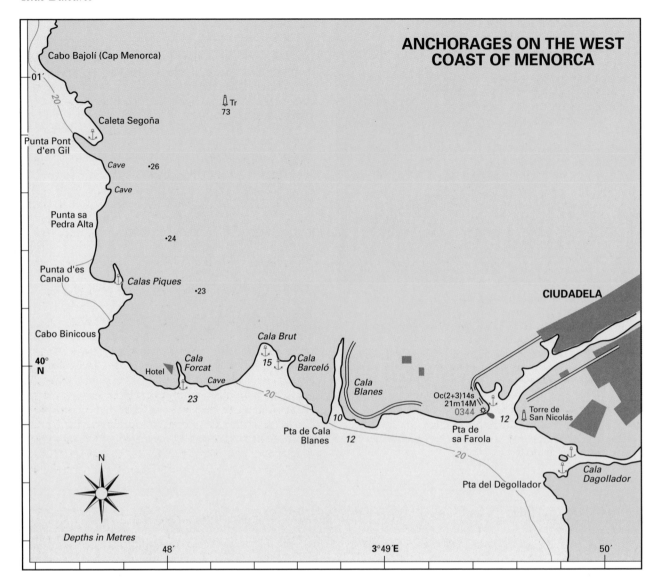

ANCHORAGES ON THE WEST COAST OF MENORCA

⚓ **Cala Degollador** 39°59'·7N 3°49'·8E

A narrow *cala* just south of the entrance to Puerto de Ciudadela, surrounded by low rocky cliffs and with two popular (and often crowded) sandy beaches at its head. Islote de la Galera, a small islet 4m high, lies in the middle of the entrance with a 4·1m shoal extending 80m northwards. Anchor in 4m+ over sand with weed patches, open to the west. It may be necessary to use two anchors to restrict swinging room as the *cala* is very narrow. See plan page 198.

Cala Degollador forms a useful alternative to Ciudadela when the latter is crowded, and has all its shoreside facilities within easy reach. Plans for turning the *cala* into a yacht harbour behind protective breakwaters were discussed at one stage, but these appear to have been overtaken by a proposal to build a marina in Cala d'en Busquets on the north side of Puerto de Ciudadela itself.

Puerto de Ciudadela (Ciutadella)

39°59'·8N 3°49'·5E

Charts	Approach	Harbour
Admiralty	2833	2833
Spanish	6A, 965	4291
French	7117	7117

Lights
Approach
0342 **Cabo Dartuch (D'Artruix)**
39°55'·4N 3°49'·5E Fl(3)10s45m19M
White tower, three black bands,
on white building 34m 267°-vis-158°
0348 **Cabo Nati** 40°03'·2N 3°49'·5E
Fl(3+1)20s42m16M White tower, aluminium
cupola, on white building with red roof 13m
039°-vis-162°
Entrance
0344 **Punta de Sa Farola** 39°59'·8N 3°49'·4E
Oc(2+3)14s21m14M White tower, black
vertical stripes, on white building 13m
004°-vis-094°

0345 **Punta El Bancal** 39°59'·9N 3°49'·5E
Fl(2)R.6s10m3M Red ■ on red metal post

0345·4 **San Nicolás** 39°59'·9N 3°49'·6E
Fl.G.3s10m3M Green square structure
on white base displaying green ▲ 4m

0345·6 **Sa Trona** 40°N 3°49'·8E Fl(3)G.6s7m2M
Green square structure on white base
displaying green ▲ 4m

0345·9 **Cala d'en Busquets, directional light**
40°N 3°49'·8E DirFl.RWG.5s9m4/6/3M
White square tower, green lantern 3m
(White sector marks centre of channel, red sector
to the north, green sector to the south)

0345·8 **Cala d'en Busquets, east light**
40°N 3°49'·8E Fl(4)R.12s11m3M
Red column on white base displaying red ■ 4m

0346·2 **Slipway** 40°00'·1N 3°49'·9E
F.R.6m2M Red tripod on white base
displaying red ■ 5m

0346 **Club Náutico** 40°N 3°50'E
F.G.7m2M Green column on white hut
displaying green ▲ 5m

0346·4 **La Muralla** 40°00'·2N 3°50'·2E
DirOc(2)RWG.9·5s8m3/5/3M
White square tower 6m. (White sector marks
centre of channel, red sector to the north,
green sector to the south)

Port Communications

VHF – Port Authority (*Puerto de Ciudadela*) Ch 9, 16.
☎/*Fax* – Port Authority ☎/*Fax* 381193; Club Náutico de
Ciudadela ☎ 383918, *Fax* 385871.

General

A most attractive natural harbour consisting of a long narrow *cala* leading to a small inner area edged with ancient quays. Only in the last decade has a new public quay for visitors been added nearer the entrance. The fascinating old town is unspoilt and can answer most needs.

Approach and entrance are straightforward but, from some angles and in some light conditions, it is virtually impossible to see the entrance itself until very close in. Entry is not advisable in strong southwesterlies because seas break across its mouth. Once inside good shelter is available, but swell finds its way up the *cala* with winds from southwest or west. During the season both harbour and town become very crowded.

Ciudadela harbour has been in use since prehistoric times, long before the Phoenicians arrived in 1600–1200 BC and gave it its first name, *Yamma*, meaning 'western' or 'west town'. The Greeks and Romans followed, and Pliny the Elder referred to it as *Iama* or *Iamnona*. The next name on record was that of the Arabs to whom it was *Medina Minurka*. With the expulsion of the Arabs by the Aragonese it received its current name of Ciudadela meaning 'little city', though very little from that time remains due to repeated attacks by pirates and Corsairs. The most notorious assault was led by the Turkish pirate Barbarrossa who, in 1558, laid siege to the town and, when it fell, destroyed its buildings and took many of the inhabitants away as slaves.

The approaches to both Puerto de Ciudadela and Cala Degollador seen from the southwest. The 17th century Torre de San Nicolás backed by an unusual S-shaped hotel makes a good landmark – the wide and tree-lined Paseo San Nicolás is less obvious from sea-level. Cala d'es Frares is also visible on the left.

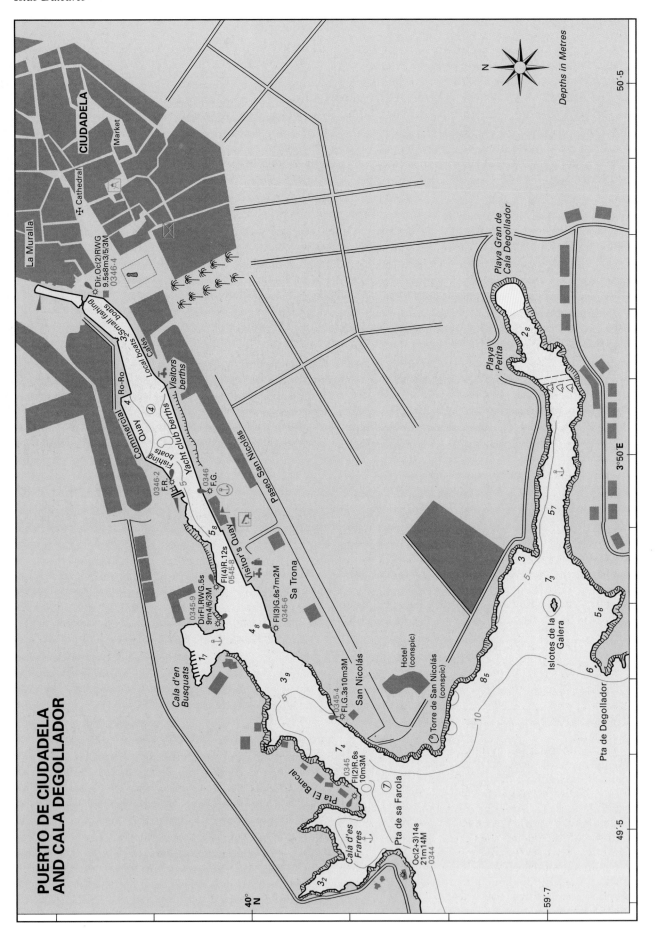

**PUERTO DE CIUDADELA
AND CALA DEGOLLADOR**

Looking northeast into Puerto de Ciudadela. On the left is Cala d'en Busquets, with the *Club Náutico* quay and clubhouse opposite on the south bank.

Even so Ciudadela remained the capital of the island (and the see of a bishop) until 1722 when the British transferred the administration to Mahón, the better natural harbour, leaving the bishop at Ciudadela together with the old nobility.

The town is a delight to explore, with pavement cafés under the arches of Ses Voltes and a contrast between the palaces of the old families fronting the open squares and the tiny houses of the artisans packed apparently at random (intended, it is said, to confuse the all too frequent intruders with a succession of blind alleys and unexpected turns). The 14th century cathedral merits a special visit, but Ciudadela is a town oozing antiquity and interest on every side.

Three miles out of Ciudadela, just off the road to Mahón, lies the Naveta d'es Tudóns, which lays claim to being the oldest building in Europe and is undoubtedly the oldest in Spain. The *naveta* (so-called because the ground plan resembles a ship) is built of large stone blocks and has two storeys. It measures 14m by 6·5m and was used over many centuries as a communal tomb.

Ciudadela's final distinction lies in its *fiesta* of San Juán on 23-24 June, famed for its daring equestrian displays to which the usual drinking and merrymaking are only a sideshow. The build-up to the *fiesta* begins the previous Sunday and it can be guaranteed that there will not be a free berth in the harbour. On 2 July the *Fiesta Patriótica* is celebrated, commemorating the town's resistance to Turkish pirates in 1558.

Future developments

Plans have been approved to dredge and enlarge Cala d'en Busquets on the north side of the harbour, in order to establish a full service marina. There is little doubt that such a facility would prove extremely popular – and equally little that it would be very costly to create. Work had not started by early 1997.

Approach

From south or southwest Cabo Dartuch, a low rocky-cliffed promontory topped by a very conspicuous lighthouse, is easily recognised. The entrance to Puerto de Ciudadela lies 4·4 miles to the north – there are no offshore hazards. The buildings of Ciudadela, and in particular the Torre de San Nicolás together with the large curved hotel behind, can be seen from afar.

From north or northwest Cabo Nati with its lighthouse, Cabo Bajolí with its 10m tower and 20m brick signal station, and Cabo Binicous further south, are all prominent headlands. Follow them round at 400m until heading east-southeast, when the buildings of Ciudadela will be seen less than 2 miles away.

Anchorages in the approach

There are several nearby *cala* anchorages, the largest of which is Cala Degollador some 400m to the south (see page 196). North and west of the entrance lie Cala d'es Frares, Cala Blanes and Cala Brut (see below and opposite).

Entrance

The entrance can be difficult to identify until close in, but the Punta de Sa Farola lighthouse on the north side and the Torre de San Nicolás to the south are good landmarks. Southwesterly gales produce breaking seas across the entrance and swell inside the harbour, and in these conditions an alternative destination should be sought. See also the note regarding sea levels below. Due to the steep cliffs on either side the wind can be very variable and fluky.

Follow the centre line of the *cala* keeping careful watch for other traffic – sizeable Ro-Ro ferries use the harbour and not surprisingly have right of way. There is a 3 knot speed limit.

Sea levels

The level of the sea rises with a southwest wind and falls with north and northeast winds by as much as 0·5m. Under certain meteorological conditions, usually when a depression and spring tide coincide, a phenomenon known as *resaca* or *seiche* occurs, causing the level to rise and fall by as much as 1·5m every ten or fifteen minutes, an oscillation which may continue for several days. Local fishermen often give warning when they expect it to occur.

Berthing

Although there are a variety of berthing possibilities, Puerto de Ciudadela is often full to capacity during the summer. On the starboard side just short of the *Club Náutico* is a stretch of quay capable of taking seven or eight yachts in line ahead, rafted four or five deep. Although owned by the Port Authority this is franchised to the *Club Náutico*, who admister the area and collect mooring fees.

Beyond the *Club Náutico* local yachts and smallcraft lie bow or stern-to, with Port Authority moorings for a few visiting yachts, also stern-to, at the far end just short of where the harbour narrows.

Much of the port side is taken up by the commercial quay – often occupied by large fishing vessels – and the Ro-Ro ferry berth. However if no ship is due yachts may be allowed to lie alongside overnight. The wash caused by ships passing can cause surge problems on the western quay, particularly if rafts have grown to more than three yachts deep, in which case the outer yachts may be told to leave in order to clear the channel.

Anchorage in the harbour

It is currently possible to anchor in the entrance to the small Cala d'en Busquets on the north side of the harbour (see plan). Bow and stern anchors are likely to be needed. The *cala* itself is full of moorings. However, as mentioned on page 199, plans are afoot to build a marina in the *cala*.

Charges *(see page 6)*

- *Club Náutico de Ciudadela quay* High season daily rate – Band B; low season daily rate – Band C. Water and electricity extra. Cash only accepted.
- *Port Authority quay* High season daily rate – Band D (15m), Band C (10m); low season daily rate – Band D. Water and electricity extra. Cash only accepted.

Facilities

Boatyards Small boatyard by the slipway west of the commercial quay.

Cranes On the commercial quay and at the *Club Náutico* (5 tonnes).

Slipway At the west end of the commercial quay. The slightly rustic cradle can handle up to 5 tonnes.

Engineers Centre Nautic Ciudadela (☎ 382616, *Fax* 385679) are agents for Ecosse, Volvo Penta and Yanmar.

Chandlery Near the cathedral.

Water At all three quays listed above.

Showers At the *Club Náutico*. A small charge is made, payable at the bar.

Electricity On the *Club Náutico* and Port Authority quays.

Fuel Diesel and petrol pumps on the *Club Náutico* quay.

Ice From nearby bars.

Yacht club The Club Náutico de Ciudadela (☎ 383918, *Fax* 385871) has a fine clubhouse fronting the harbour with bar, lounge, terrace, restaurant and showers.

Banks Several in the town, with credit card facilities.

Shops/provisioning A good selection of supermarkets and specialist food shops.

Produce/fish market Small open-air market in the town, with a fish market in its centre.

Hotels/restaurants/cafés etc. Many hotels, restaurants, cafés and bars.

Laundry In the town.

Hospital/medical services In the town.

Communications

Car hire/taxis Available in the town.

Buses Bus service to Mahón, Fornells and elsewhere.

Ferries Car ferries to Alcudiá, Mallorca.

⚓ Cala d'es Frares 39°59'·9N 3°49'·5E

A short double *cala* on the north side of the entrance to Puerto de Ciudadela, surrounded by low (6m) sloping rocky cliffs. Anchor near the entrance in 4m± over sand, open to the south and to swell from the southwest. The western of the two arms has a small sandy beach.

⚓ **Cala Blanes** 39°59'·8N 3°48'·8E

A long narrow *cala* between low (9m) undercut cliffs leading to a crowded sandy beach, about ½ mile west of Punta de Sa Farola lighthouse and the entrance to Puerto de Ciudadela. There is a large hotel with a small white tower on its roof near the the head of the *cala* which can be seen from the entrance. Anchor in 5m+ over sand and weed, open to the south – it may be necessary to use two anchors or to take a line to one of the rings ashore. In summer a line of buoys marks off the bathing area at the head of the *cala*, which is in any case shallow with some dinghy moorings.

A tourist resort is growing around Cala Blanes, complete with the usual hotels, restaurants, beach bars etc. Most day-to-day items can be purchased in the resort, though it may be simpler (and cheaper) to go into Ciudadela.

⚓ **Cala Barceló** 40°N 3°48'·6E

A very small, almost circular *cala* surrounded by 10m rocky cliffs, open to the southwest. In May 1996 there appeared to be a few mooring buoys occupying most of the space available. There is no beach or other attractions.

⚓ **Cala Brut** 40°N 3°48'·5E

A small narrow *cala* at the head of a wider inlet about ¾ mile west of the entrance to Puerto de Ciudadela. Anchor in 5–10m over sand in the entrance to the *cala*, open to southeast and south. There are rocky bathing terraces on either side and a large hotel near the head.

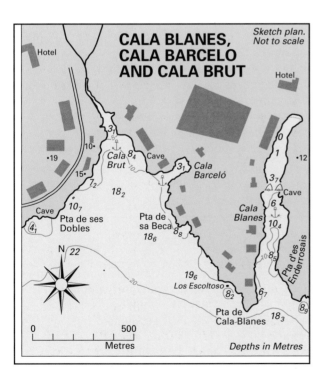

⚓ **Cala Forcat** 39°59'·9N 3°48'·1E

A very small Y-shaped *cala* dwarfed by an immense reddish-orange hotel, Cala Forcat is suitable only for smaller yachts and dinghies. It is surrounded by low (10m) rocky cliffs and is open to the south. Anchor in 4–5m over sand and rock, using two anchors. All the usual facilities of a large modern hotel are available.

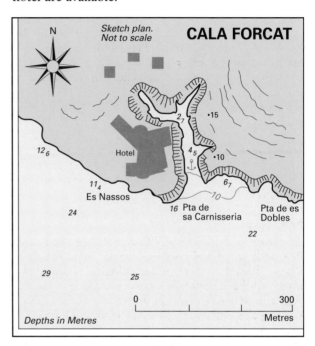

⚓ **Anchorages between Cabo Binicous (Cap de Banyos) and Cabo Nati**

The following deserted anchorages should only be attempted by experienced navigators in settled conditions with no swell – all are surrounded by high rocky cliffs (24–64m) and there are no beaches, houses or roads. The bottom is rocky and 10–15m deep.

⚓ **Calas Piques** Very small, open to southwest and west.

⚓ **Caleta Segoña (Cigonya)** Just north of Punta Pont d'en Gil (see below) where there is a natural archway through the rocks. Open from west to northwest.

⚓ **Cala de la Falconera (Es Pop Mosquer)** A small *cala* under very high cliffs on the north side of Cabo Bajolí (see below), open northwest and west.

⚓ **Cala del Amarradó (Raco de S'Almarrador)** A very small *cala* open to west and northwest.

⚓ **Cova d'es Tabac** Close south of Punta Espardina, open to southwest and west.

⚓ **Cala Be (Cova de Son Salomó)** An open *cala* with a sandy bottom and some caves, open west and northwest.

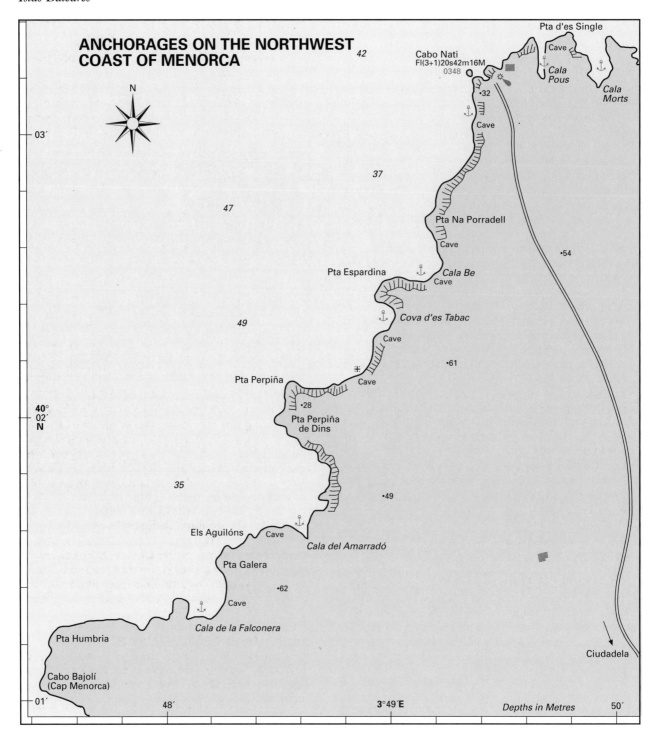

ANCHORAGES ON THE NORTHWEST
COAST OF MENORCA

42

Cabo Nati
Fl(3+1)20s42m16M
0348

Pta d'es Single

Cave

Cala Pous

Cala Morts

•32

Cave

37

47

Pta Na Porradell

Cave

•54

Pta Espardina

Cala Be

Cave

49

Cova d'es Tabac

Cave

•61

Pta Perpiña

Cave

•28

Pta Perpiña
de Dins

40°
02'
N

35

•49

Els Aguilóns

Cave

Cala del Amarradó

Pta Galera

•62

Cave

Ciudadela

Cala de la Falconera

Pta Humbria

Cabo Bajolí
(Cap Menorca)

01'

48'

3°49'E

50'

Depths in Metres

N

03'

40°
02'
N

Punta Pont d'en Gil 40°00'·8N 3°47'·7E
A long, thin, rocky-cliffed point with a large natural arch leading through into Cala Segoña (see above). The arch is about 10m high and 8m wide and can be used with care by dinghies and small motor boats.

Cabo Bajolí (Cap Menorca) 40°01'N 3°47'·5E
A large headland, high inland (72m), sloping down in a westerly direction to dark, rocky, steep-to cliffs. A disused semaphore signal station is located on the highest point.

Cabo Nati 40°03'·3N 3°49'·6E
A prominent 32m headland of dark cliffs sloping to the northwest, with a conspicuous white lighthouse (Fl(3+1)20s42m16M, aluminium cupola on white tower above a white building with a red roof 13m) set inside a white-walled enclosure a hundred metres or so inland. The cliffs are steep-to, but with several small rocky islets close inshore.

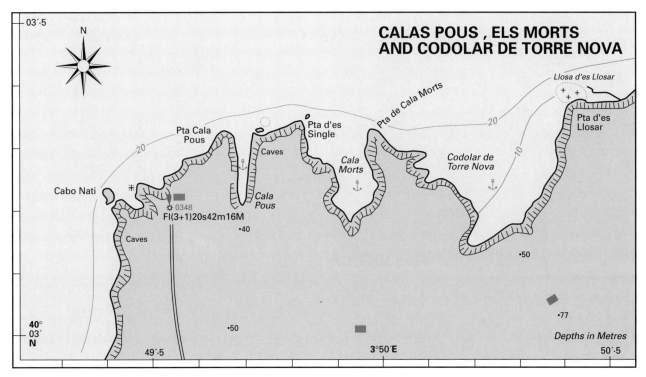

**CALAS POUS , ELS MORTS
AND CODOLAR DE TORRE NOVA**

Depths in Metres

⚓ **Cala Pous** 40°03'·3N 3°49'·7E
A small, narrow, rocky *cala* amidst rugged surroundings 300m northeast of Cabo Nati lighthouse, with a small high islet on the east side of the entrance. The inlet lies between 30m sloping cliffs and has a small stony beach at its head. Anchor over rock, weed and sand, open to wind from the north and to swell from northwest to northeast. A road runs from the lighthouse to Ciudadela.

⚓ **Cala Morts** 40°00'·3N 3°49'·9E
A larger, wider *cala*, again between 30m rocky cliffs and with a stony beach at its head, separated from Cala Pous by Punta d'es Single. Two conspicuous islets to the west of the entrance and a *talayot* on the skyline make identification easy. Anchor in sand, rock and weed open to northwest round to northeast. There is absolutely nothing ashore other than a great many *talayots*, large and small.

⚓ **Codolar de la Torre Nova** 40°03'·2N 3°50'·3E
A large, open deserted *cala* with 40m rocky cliffs, some rocky beaches and several caves, one of which can be entered by dinghy. There are several rocky islets off Punta d'es Llosar on the east side of the entrance and two *talayots* on the skyline. Anchor in 10m or less over sand, rock and weed, open to the northerly quadrant.

Punta del Escuá and Els Escullasos
40°03'·6N 3°52'·2E
Three small rocky islets lie close inshore under the high (79m) sloping cliffs of Punta del Escuá (Punta de s'Escullar). 350m further north-northeast lie two breaking rocks (Els Escullasos) with foul ground extending for 100m around them.

⚓ **Cala Morell** 40°03'·4N 3°53'·1E
This small, almost landlocked *cala* with sloping rocky cliffs was once a very beautiful place, but is now rather spoilt by the many houses on the

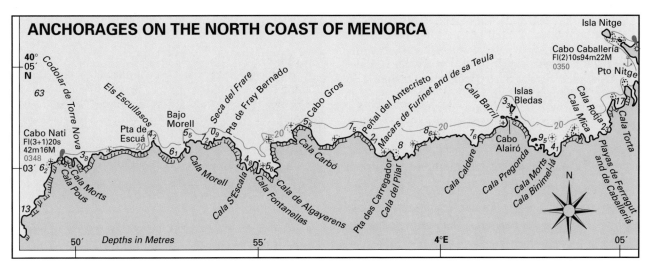

ANCHORAGES ON THE NORTH COAST OF MENORCA

Depths in Metres

Looking southeast into Cala Morell, with the unmarked rock clearly visible opposite the entrance.

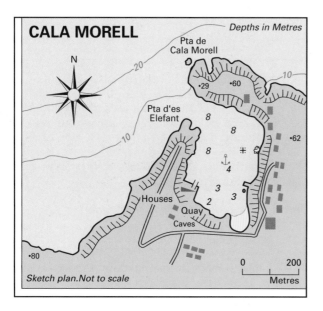

dinghies. A restaurant and basic shopping is available in the village. There are a number of caves in the area which are second only in importance to those at Cala Covas. A main road leads to Ciudadela.

Bajo (Baix) Morell 40°03'·8N 3°53'·1E
This breaking rock lies 400m northeast of Punta de Cala Morell with foul ground reaching for 100m around it. There are two other similar rocks very close inshore. There is a passage 150m wide and 16m deep between the *bajo* and the shore – use with caution.

Seca del Frare 40°03'·6N 3°53'·8E
An isolated rock carrying less than 1m, 650m west-northwest of Pta de Fray Bernardo (Punta d'es Fra Bernat). Not to be confused with an unnamed rocky islet 50m from the shore to the southwest.

⚓ Cala S'Escala (Codolar de Biniatramp)
40°03'·1N 3°54'·7E
An open bay surrounded by a sloping rocky shore with a stony beach, Cala S'Escala can be identified by the bleak Escull de s'es Ginjoles (14m) off the headland to the east. Anchor over sand and rock, open to the northern quadrant. There is a track leading inland but otherwise the bay is deserted.

⚓ Cala Fontanellas 40°03'·1N 3°55'E
A pleasant anchorage surrounded by green shrub-covered hills, with a small sand and rock beach. Escull de s'es Ginjoles (14m) lies on the northern side of the entrance. Anchor over sand, rock and weed near the head of the *cala*, which is open to the north but also feels swell from northwest to northeast. A few seasonal moorings may be laid for local boats.

There are a one or two houses in the vicinity and fishermen's huts on the northern side. Much of the beach at the head of the *cala* is taken up by a short stone quay and slipway for the use of small motorboats kept on the foreshore.

surrounding hills. The entrance is difficult to spot until well into the outer bay. If coming from the west, on rounding Els Escullasos (see page 203) a group of white houses will be seen above Punta d'es Elefant on the southwest side of the entrance. Coming from eastwards a few houses on Punta de Cala Morell may be seen (the greater part of the planned development has yet to be built), but the *cala* itself only opens after this point is astern. Allow generous clearance to Seca d'es Frare and Bajo d'en Morell (described below).

Anchor in 4–6m over sand and weed near the centre of the *cala*, avoiding the unmarked 0.8m rock on the eastern side (see plan and photograph). Holding is patchy and a few summer moorings are usually laid for local boats. If winds from between northwest and northeast are forecast it is adviseable to leave immediately, as even the latter kick up a nasty swell. There is a small sandy beach at the head of the *cala* where a seasonal stream enters, and a miniature quay, slipway, crane and boat park for

Looking almost due south into Cala de Algayerens (left) and the smaller Cala Fontanelles (right). Punta Rotja (bottom left) lives up to its name of 'red point'.

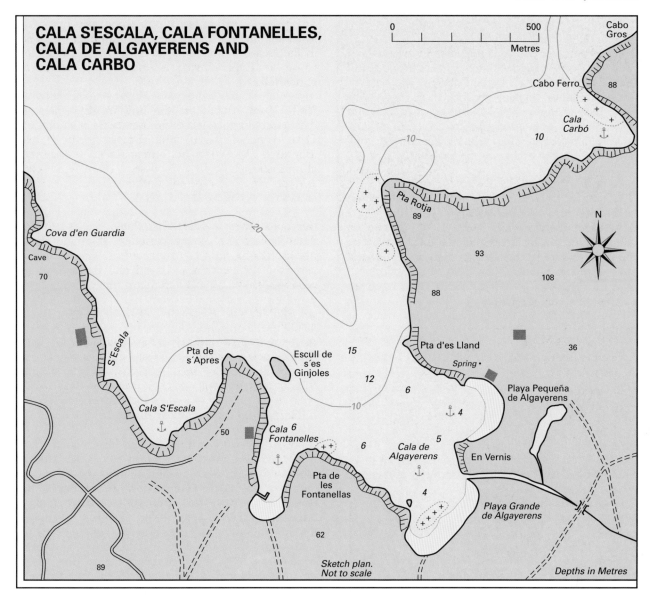

CALA S'ESCALA, CALA FONTANELLES, CALA DE ALGAYERENS AND CALA CARBO

Sketch plan. Not to scale

Depths in Metres

⚓ Cala de Algayerens (d'Algaiarens)
40°03'N 3°55'·3E

A wide bay with two good beaches, Playa Grande de Algayerens (Platja Grau d'Algaiarens) to the southwest and Playa Pequeña de Algayerens (Platja Petita d'Algaiarens) to the northeast, divided by an angular headland. If approaching from the north keep well off Punta Rotja which has foul ground extending up to 200m from its base. Anchor off either beach over sand with weed patches in 2–6m open to northwest and north, though swell from the northeast may find its way in. A rocky reef lies close to the beach of Playa de Grande Algayerens.

There is a boathouse on Playa de Pequeña Algayerens with a spring, the Font d'en Cumar, nearby, but no houses. Several roads and tracks allow visitors to reach the beaches and they are popular in summer. A large lagoon with much wildlife lies inland.

⚓ Cala Carbó (Carabó) 40°03'·6N 3°55'·9E

A small rocky *cala* tucked under the west side of Cap Gros. Enter with care as awash rocks line most of the northeast side and parts of the southwest. Anchor over sand, stones and rock, open to northwest and north. There is nothing ashore other than the ruins of a prehistoric village.

Cabo Gros 40°03'·9N 3°56'·1E

Cabo Gros (96m) has steep cliffs and several small islets and awash rocks close in, particularly to the northwest. Both it and Peñal del Anticristo 1·2 miles further east are composed of the same distinctive rust-red rock as Punta Rotja (see photograph opposite). It is sometimes erroneously referred to as Falconera, which is actually the high peak (205m) which lies a mile south-southeast. A ruined prehistoric village and wall lie south of the headland, not far from Cala Carbó.

⚓ Macars de Furinet and de sa Teula
40°03'·4N 3°58'·4E

Two ends of an open bay surrounded by sandy and rocky cliffs, to be used with care. There are rocks off the western beach (Macar de Furinet), while Punta des Carregador to the east has rocks and islets extending at least 100m northwest. Anchor off either beach over sand and rock, open to the northerly quadrant. There is a hut behind the stony eastern beach but otherwise the area is deserted.

⚓ Cala del Pilar 40°03'·3N 3°58'·8E
(Incorrectly identified as Cala la Teula on BA 2833, which also has Illa d'es Pilar wrongly placed)

A small bay between high (69m), sloping, reddish cliffs. Numerous awash rocks and small islets line the coast to the east, but an approach on a southerly course leaving Illa d'es Pilar 50m to port clears all dangers. Anchor over sand and rock open to northwest round to northeast. There is a spring 100m southeast of the beach, but no track or houses.

⚓ Cala Caldere 40°03'·6N 4°01'E
A fairly wide *cala* with sloping redddish cliffs on either side and scrub-covered hills (57m) above. There are two awash rocks close inshore, one each side of the *cala*, and at its head a sandy beach crossed by a stream bed. Anchor off the beach over sand and rock, open to northwest and north. There is a track leading inland with a few houses and two prehistoric *navetas* at Sant Jordi about ½ mile away.

⚓ Cala Barril 40°03'·9N 4°01'·8E
An anchorage off a rock and sand beach close west of Cabo Alairó (Cap de s'Alarió) and the Islas Bledas (Illa Bledes), easy to locate by a track embanked with a stone wall. Careful navigation is necessary because of a small island, an awash rock and an islet to port of the approach. Enter on an easterly course leaving Escull de Cala Barril about 50m to port. Anchor off the beach over rock and sand, open from west through northwest to north and swell from northeast. There is a track and one or two houses ashore.

Passage inside Isla Bledas (Illa Bledes)
40°04'·2N 4°02'E

A passage 100m wide and 5m deep, which requires careful navigation due to some awash and isolated rocks. A reliable bow lookout is advisable.

From the west, enter on a southeasterly course about halfway between Isla Bledes (60m) and Isla d'es Coloms, keeping careful lookout for Escull d'en Biel, which must be left to starboard, and an unnamed awash rock some 60m south of Isla Bledas, which must be left to port. When this latter rock has been passed, change course to northeast and leave Escull d'es Caló Fred to starboard. If coming from the east a reciprocal course may be used.

If passing outside Isla Bledas, allow an offing of at least 600m in order to clear the isolated Llosa de s'illa Bledes.

⚓ Caló Fred 40°04'N 4°02'·1E
A very small *cala* hidden away behind the Escull d'es Caló Fred, only for use only by experienced navigators in good weather. More a place to explore than to anchor, the *cala* is open to the northeast, has no beach and a rocky bottom, and a few houses and a road ashore.

⚓ Cala Pregonda 40°03'·5N 4°02'·6E
A pleasant anchorage in a large bay partially protected by rocky islets, Cala Pregonda has become popular and is no longer deserted. If coming from the northeast, having rounded Isla Nitge a direct course for the entrance clears Escull de sa Nau, an awash rock off Cala Binimel-lá. Enter the *cala* on a southwesterly course between Isla Pregonda and the smaller Illot de Pregondó. There is a 2·5m rocky shoal in the entrance. Anchor off the beach in 4m± over sand, open to north and northeast and to swell from northwest. The wide sandy beach has a few houses and a road behind, and there is a second smaller beach to the east.

⚓ Cala Morts and Cala Binimel-lá
40°03'·3N 4°03'·2E

A wide bay with two sandy beaches divided by a rocky promontory. The western bay (Cala Morts) has two islets and an awash rock in its mouth and is not recommended. The eastern beach has some small rocks close inshore near its centre but is otherwise clear. Approach on a southerly course leaving the awash rock Escull de sa Nau 100m to starboard (it breaks in all but the flattest weather) and two similar rocks close inshore to port, then favour the east side of the bay, taking care to avoid a shallow patch extending northeast from the promontory which divides the two beaches. Anchor over sand and weed in 4m or less, open to northwest and north with swell from the northeast.

There is a lagoon behind the beach backed by sloping, scrub-covered hills, with one or two houses and a track inland.

⚓ Cala Mica 40°03'·6N 4°04'·1E
A wide and deep *cala* with a sandy beach and a number of islets and awash rocks both in the approach (up to 200m from the shore) and fringing either side of the entrance. Anchor near the middle of the *cala* over sand, weed and rocks, open to northwest through northeast. There is one house and a track inland, and some of the surrounding hills are terraced.

⚓ Playa de Ferragut, Playa de Caballería and Cala Rotja 40°03'·7N 4°04'·6E
Three possible anchorages in a large bay broken by rocky outcrops. Approach Playa de Ferragut on a southerly course to anchor off the beach over sand and weed, open to northwest and north with swell

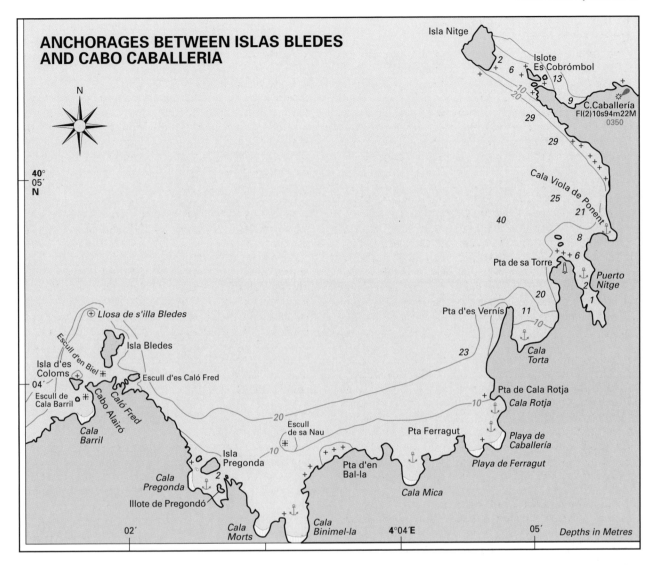

ANCHORAGES BETWEEN ISLAS BLEDES AND CABO CABALLERIA

from the northeast. At the east end of the beach there are two small rocky islets dividing it from Playa de Caballería, which is popular with visitors in summer. Take care on final approach to this latter as there is an isolated awash rock 200m off the middle of the beach – favour the eastern end, to anchor over sand and rock open to northwest and north.

Beyond the distinctive reddish point known, for obvious reasons, as Punta de Cala Rotja lies the *cala* of that name. Approach on an easterly course to anchor off the beach avoiding a patch of rocky islets, open to west and north. Various tracks run inland but there is little else.

⚓ Cala Torta 40°04'·2N 4°05'E

A large open *cala* between dark rocky cliffs with a large conspicuous tower (built by the British in the 18th century) on Punta de sa Torre to the east. On the west side Punta d'es Vernís has an islet and an awash rock off its point. Approach and entrance are straightforward – anchor off the small stony beach in the southwest corner over sand, weed and rock, open to northwest and north and to swell from the northeast. The *cala* is deserted and only has footpaths leading to it.

⚓ Puerto Nitge (Port sa Nitja)
40°04'·6N 4°05'·3E

Not a port, but rather a long, narrow inlet on the west side of the peninsula of Cabo Caballería. It was a Phoenician harbour around 1600 BC and is typical of the sites they often chose – a low, defensible promontory with the possibility of launching or anchoring boats on both sides, so that irrespective of wind direction they could escape, defend or attack as necessary. The Romans occupied the *cala* in their turn (circa 200 BC), establishing a small settlement which is mentioned by Pliny in his History.

Puerto Nitge is easy to recognise, tucked as it is close west and south of Cabo Cavalleriá and Isla Nitge (Illa d'els Porros) and with a large round tower just west of the entrance. Approach and entrance are straightforward, but without local knowledge it is advisable to pass outside the two islets lying off Punta de sa Torre even though a 50m passage carrying 5m depths exists between the islets and the point.

Favour the east side of the entrance as rocks fringe the western point and watch the echo-sounder carefully – the inner part of the inlet has silted up,

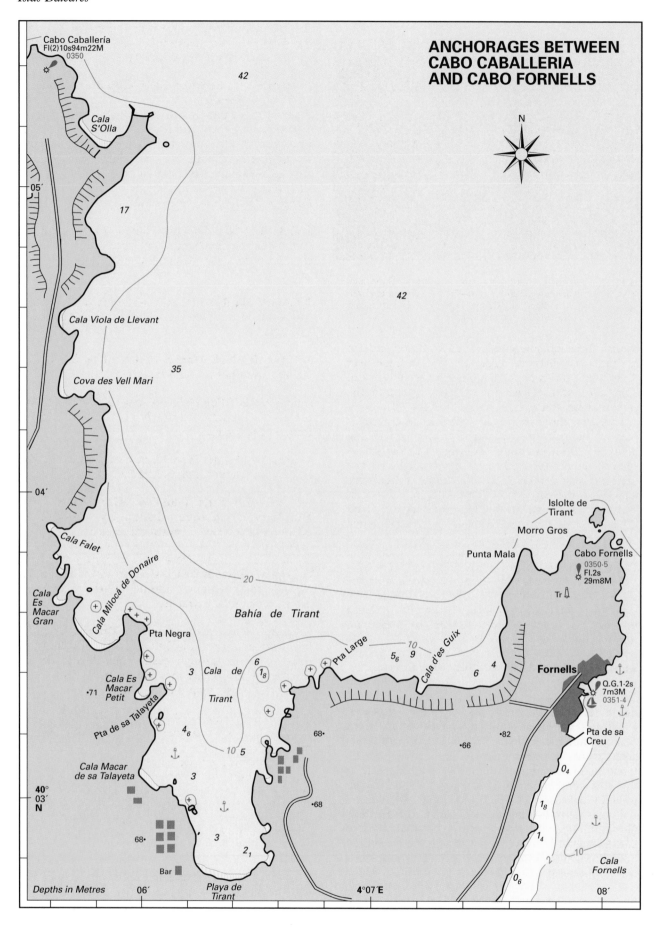

ANCHORAGES BETWEEN
CABO CABALLERIA
AND CABO FORNELLS

N

Cabo Caballería
Fl(2)10s94m22M
0350

Cala
S'Olla

05´

17

Cala Viola de Llevant

35

Cova des Vell Mari

04´

Islolte de
Tirant

Morro Gros

Punta Mala

Cabo Fornells
0350·5
Fl.2s
29m8M

Tr

Cala Falet

20

Cala Milocá de Donaire

Cala
Es
Macar
Gran

Bahía   de   Tirant

Pta Negra

Pta Large

10

Cala d'es Guix

5₆   9

6   4

Fornells

Q.G.1·2s
7m3M
0351·4

3   Cala   de

6
1₈

·71   Cala Es
Macar
Petit

Tirant

Pta de sa Talayeta

4₆

10   5

·82   Pta de sa
Creu

0₄

Cala Macar
de sa Talayeta

3

68·

1₈

40°
03´
N

3

·68

1₄

68·   ·66

2

10

Cala
Fornells

Bar

2₁

0₆

Playa de
Tirant

4°07´E

Puerto Nitge from the northeast, with Cala Torta behind and Playa de Ferragut and Cala Mica in the distance. The watchtower on the western headland stands out clearly, as do the shoals within the harbour itself.

though 2m can usually be carried for 200m and 1m for the same distance again. Anchor in 2m+ over sand, weed and rock, open to northwest and north. The sides of the *cala* are of dark rock and the surroundings somewhat low and windswept.

There are three short piers or jetties in the upper part of the *cala*, used by small motor and fishing boats, and some seasonal moorings may be laid. A stream, largely blocked by a sandbank, flows into the southwest corner. A few houses and fishermen's huts lie to the east with a large farm to the south, and there is a road out to the lighthouse on Cabo Cavalleriá. A large scale plan of Puerto Nitge appears on Spanish chart 4283.

⚓ Cala Viola de Ponent 40°04'·7N 4°05'·4E
This tiny *cala*, which lies near the east side of the entrance to Puerto Nitge, might be visited by experienced navigators in good conditions but has a number of isolated rocks. Open to west and northwest.

Passage inside Isla Nitge (Illa d'els Porros) 40°05'·6N 4°04'·6E
There is a passage 150m wide with a minimum depth of 6m between Isla Nitge and Cabo Caballería with its off-lying rocks and islets. Shape a course north-northeast (or south-southwest), equidistant between Isla Nitge and Islote Es Cobrómbol, keeping to the centre of the passage as the sides are lined with just covered and awash isolated rocks.

A very narrow fishermen's passage, the Pas d'es Cobrombol, exists between the islet of that name and Menorca. However it should not be attempted without local knowledge or first making a detailed recce by dinghy.

Cabo Caballería 40°05'·4N 4°05'·6E
A very prominent and conspicuous peninsula and headland sloping from 80m at the north end down to 5m where it joins Menorca. A lighthouse

(Fl(2)10s94m22M, white tower and building 15m) stands on the northeastern point. There is 6·5m close inshore northwest of the lighthouse.

⚓ Anchorages between Cabo Caballería and Playa de Tirant
A series of anchorages open to northeast through to southeast edge the east side of the peninsula of Cabo Caballería. All have isolated rocks close inshore and a rock and sand bottom, and should be used only with great care in settled conditions. From Cova des Vell Mari southwards they appear on the large-scale *Bahía de Tirant and Cala Fornells* insert on BA 2833.

⚓ Cala S'Olla
A wide, high cliffed (74m) *cala* close east of Cabo Caballería lighthouse which is deep close inshore. Open to northwest through north to east.

⚓ Cala Viola de Llevant
Two awash rocks on the south side of the entrance. Open northeast through southeast.

⚓ Cova des Vell Mari
Surrounded by low rocky cliffs open to north round to east.

⚓ Cala Falet (d'en Palet)
Narrow *cala* with a small beach – two other small beaches to the south. Open from east to southeast.

⚓ Cala Es Macar Gran
Narrow *cala* with a sandy beach, open to north and northeast.

⚓ Cala Milocá de Donaire (Cala Macar de Binidonaire)
A wide, shallow bay with some offshore rocks, open to north through east.

⚓ Cala Es Macar Petit
A small *cala* with an equally small sandy beach close north of Punta de Sa Talayeta, open north and northeast. There is an awash rock in the entrance.

⚓ Cala Macar de sa Talayeta (Tailera)
A wide bay with a large sandy beach backed by houses, open to north through east. (Cala Macar de sa Talayeta is incorrectly identified as Cala Es Macar Petit on the inset plan on BA 2833).

⚓ Playa de Tirant 40°02'·8N 4°06'·4E
A large deep bay surrounded by low scrub-covered hills and an increasing number of housing (presumably tourist) developments. Approach on a southerly course towards the centre of the beach and anchor in 4–5m over sand, open to the north with swell from northeast. The long sandy beach is sometimes crowded – there is a café and a good road inland. The huge lagoon behind has much wildlife.

Cabo Fornells 40°03'·9N 4°08'E
This rocky headland has a lighthouse (Fl.2s29m8M, white tower with black band on white building 6m), and a small ruined fort a little further inland. Islote de Tirant (20m) lies close off its point with foul ground between it and the headland.

Puerto de Fornells

40°03'·9N 04°08'·2E (entrance)

Charts	Approach	Harbour
Admiralty	2833	2833
Spanish	6A	4283
French	7117	7117

Lights

0350·5 **Cabo Fornells (Cap de Sa Pared)**
  40°03'·8N 4°08'E Fl.2s29m8M White tower,
  black band, on white building 6m
Leading lights on 178·5° (Isla Sargantana)
0351 *Front* 40°02'·9N 4°08'·2E
  Q.R.14m4M White pyramidal tower 6m
0351·1 *Rear*, 110m from front
  Iso.R.4s23m8M White pyramidal tower 9m
0351·4 **Harbour, northeast mole** 40°03'·3N 4°08'E
  Q.G.1·2s7m3M Octagonal green tower 6m

Port Communications

Puerto de Fornells ☎ 375104; Club Náutico de Fornells
  ☎ 376603.

General

A narrow, deep entrance channel gives access to an
inland area of water some 2 miles long by up to 0·7
mile wide, with a small and shallow harbour near the
entrance. Most of the surroundings are of unspoilt
natural beauty and development is restricted to a
few areas. The small village is picturesque but can
only offer simple facilities. Approach and entrance
are straightforward and there is a large area where
yachts can anchor in solitude, though holding is very

poor in places. A swell finds its way into the
anchorage with gales from northwest or north.

The fishing village of Fornells (pronounced
Fornays) dates back to time immemorial, but its
claim to historic fame comes from having been used
as one of the secondary invasion ports during the
first British expedition of 1708. The British
expedition of 1798 had intended to land at Fornells,
but a headwind prevented this so the first landing
took place at Addaya (see page 217). When the wind
changed the following day Commodore Duckworth
captured Fornells.

The anchorage is surrounded by some enjoyable
walks, such as out to the tower on Cabo Fornells or,
for the really energetic, up to La Mola (123m) on
the east side of the entrance. Both offer excellent
views. Isla Sargantana makes an interesting dinghy
expedition, partly to observe the unique breed of
lizard which has evolved there (though one has to be
an expert to know the difference). At the south end
of Cala Fornells are the ruins of an ancient Christian
church.

A *fiesta* is held in Fornells during the last week of
July in honour of San Antonio.

Approach

From west The very prominent Cabo Caballería with
its conspicuous lighthouse projects nearly 2 miles
out to sea and has two outlying islands to its
northwest. Immediately to the east of this

The entrance to Puerto de Fornells looking slightly west of south.
On the left are the distinctive heights of La Mola, with Punta d'es
Murté below and Monte Toro clearly visible in the distance.

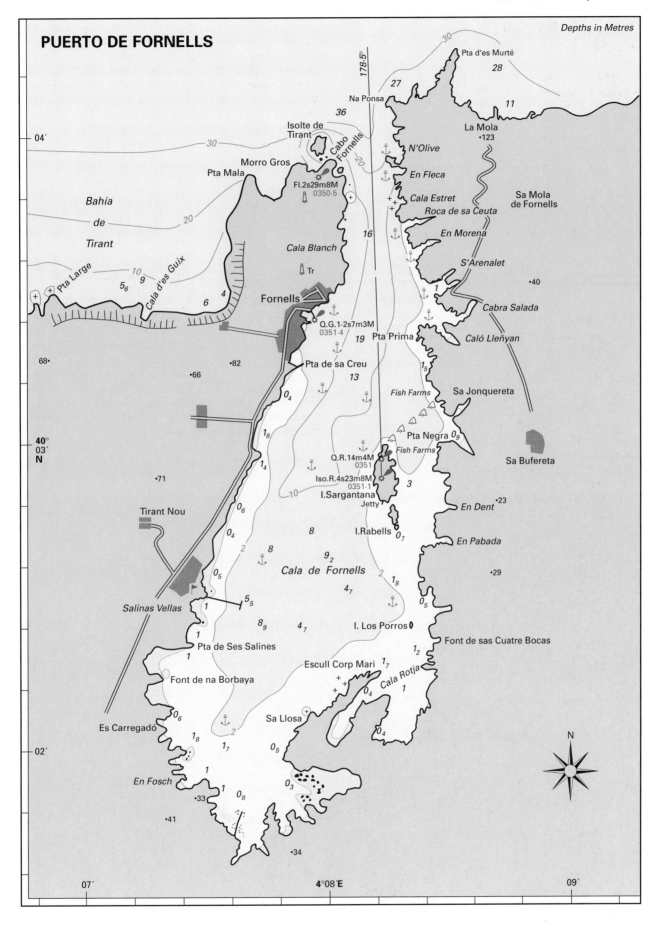

PUERTO DE FORNELLS

Depths in Metres

178·5°

Pta d'es Murté
28
27
Na Ponsa
11
36
La Mola
•123
Isolte de
Tirant
N'Olive
Cabo
Fornells
Morro Gros
En Fleca
Pta Mala
Sa Mola
de Fornells
Fl.2s29m8M
0350·5
Cala Estret
Roca de sa Ceuta
Bahía
de
En Morena
20
Tirant
S'Arenalet
Cala Blanch
Tr
Cabra Salada
Pta Large
10 9
Cala d'es Guix
5 6
4
6
Caló Lleñyan
Fornells
16
Q.G.1·2s7m3M
0351·4
19 Pta Prima
Sa Jonquereta
1 5
Pta de sa Creu
13
68•
•66 •82
0 4
Fish Farms
Pta Negra 0 9
Sa Bufereta
40°
03′
N
1 8
Q.R.14m4M
0351
Fish Farms
•71
1 4
Iso.R.4s23m8M
0351·1
3
10
I.Sargantana
Jetty
En Dent •23
Tirant Nou
0 6
8
I.Rabells 0 7
En Pabada
0 4
2
8
9 2
Cala de Fornells
2 1 8
•29
0 5
4 7
Salinas Vellas
1
5 5
0 5
8 9
4 7
I. Los Porros
1 2
Pta de Ses Salines
Font de sas Cuatre Bocas
1
Escull Corp Mari 1 7
Font de na Borbaya
Cala Rotja
0 4
1
0 6
Es Carregadó
1 8
2
Sa Llosa
1 7
0 5
0 4
1
En Fosch
1
0 8
0 3
•33
•41
•34

N

211

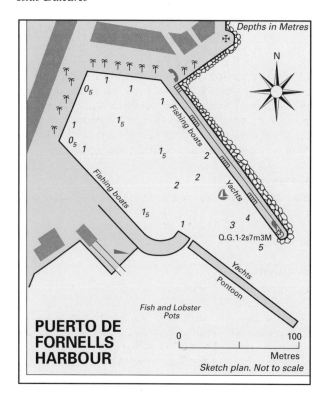

PUERTO DE FORNELLS HARBOUR

Depths in Metres

N

Fishing boats

Yachts

Q.G.1·2s7m3M

Fishing boats

Yachts
Pontoon

Fish and Lobster
Pots

0   100

Metres
Sketch plan. Not to scale

Puerto de Fornells harbour looking north-northeast, with several yachts anchored off. As can be seen, the whole area is surrounded by shallows.

promontory lies the deeply indented Bahía de Tirant which is separated from Puerto de Fornells by another promontory, Cabo Fornells (41m). This is much smaller than Cabo Caballería and has a very conspicuous isolated tower on its top. To the east of the entrance lies La Mola (123m) and Punta d'es Murté, composed of steep, angular cliffs falling to a gentler slope below (see photograph page 210). Approach when the entrance bears due south.

From east After rounding Cabo Pantinat (25m) follow the coast past Punta de na Guiemassa (50m) to Punta d'es Murté with the lofty La Mola (123m) behind. On rounding Punta d'es Murté the entrance lies to the south.

Entrance

When positive identification of the entrance has been made, approach on a southerly course. Isla Sargantana with its two white beacon towers will be visible in the middle of the bay just over a mile away. Line up the towers on 178·5° to enter (or alternatively keep the island bearing 180°). The sides of the entrance channel are steep-to.

Entrance at night should present no particular problems, so long as the leading lights are identified before entering the channel and followed until opposite or beyond the small harbour. See also the notes regarding anchorages.

Anchorages

There are many possible anchorages in this large bay (see plan page 211), though holding is poor in the more popular areas due to over-use and elsewhere because of beds of long, dense, grassy weed. For close access to the town, anchor about 100m east or southeast of the harbour in 5m over soft mud and weed. An area just south of the harbour is used to moor lobster keep boxes, which float just level with the water and are difficult to see. Southwest of the harbour is shallow with many moorings.

The area between Punta Prima and Punta Negra (northeast of Isla Sargantana) is occupied by two large fish farms, and a line of buoys runs from the northern tip of the island to the shore. Although it is possible to anchor further north on the east side of the *cala*, these anchorages are suitable for daytime exploration only and should be used with caution.

Holding is reported to be reasonably good equidistant between the harbour and Isla Sargantana in about 8m over mud and weed. The Club Náutico de Fornells has its clubhouse and dinghy jetty at Ses Salines in the southwestern part of the bay, near which there are several further anchorages particularly favoured by those who carry sailing dinghies or windsurfers.

If entering and anchoring after dark, follow the leading lights until the single harbour light (Q.G.1·2s7m3M) bears 230°, alter course onto 215°, and drop anchor in 8m or so when the light bears due west.

Berthing

The harbour is small with room for fewer than twenty yachts not exceeding 10m or so – check by dinghy first as it becomes very crowded in summer and there is little chance of a vacant berth. If space permits, berth stern-to the northeast mole or on the pontoon extending from the southwest quay. Confirm depths before bringing the yacht in, as the harbour mouth is reported to be silting up.

Charges

The northeast mole is a public quay and charges are reported to be low. The southern pontoon is slightly more expensive. As of 1996 there was no charge for anchoring.

Facilities

Boatyard Work is carried out on local craft at the head of the slipway.
Slipway A wide slipway lies southwest of the harbour, but depths off it are limited. In 1996 the state of the (14 tonne) cradle appeared dubious.
Chandlery Small chandlery near the harbour.
Water On the southern pontoon, also by container from the *Club Náutico* and other sources including the village fountain.
Showers At the *Club Náutico*.
Electricity On the southern pontoon.
Fuel No fuel berth as of 1996.
Ice From the fishermen's co-op southwest of the harbour (likely to be icebox quality only) or from a bar opposite the north corner of the harbour.

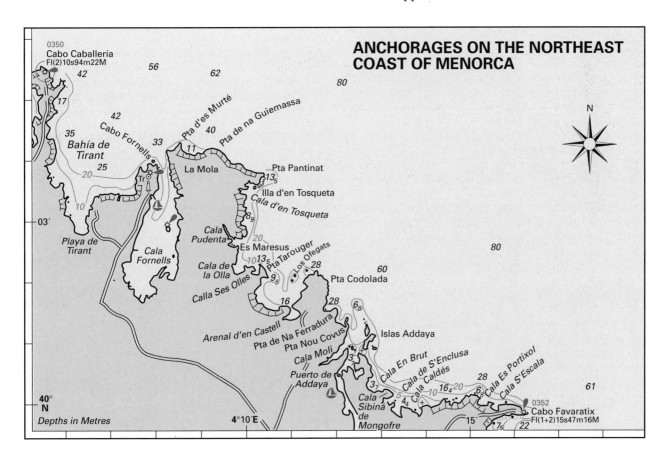

Yacht club The Club Náutico de Fornells (☎ 375103), located at Ses Salinas about 1¼ miles south of the harbour and main anchorage, has a bar, restaurant, lounge, terrace and showers.

Bank In the village – open mornings only.

Shops/provisioning Supermarket and other shops in the village.

Fish market It may be possible to buy fish at the co-operative southwest of the harbour.

Hotels/restaurants/cafés etc. A hotel or two and many restaurants and cafés. Fornells has long been famous for its lobsters, served either with *mahonésa* or as *Caldera de Langosta* (lobster stew).

Communications

Post office In the village.

Car hire/taxis One car rental company in the village.

Buses Buses to Mahón and Ciudadela.

Punta d'es Murté (des Murter), Punta Na Guiamassa and Cabo Pantinat

40°04'·2N 4°08'·6E to 40°03'·7N 4°10'·5E

A 1·7 mile wide promontory with three distinct headlands, the westernmost backed by the heights of La Mola (123m). As a whole the headland slopes downwards from west to east. Steep-to other than two rocks awash close inshore off Punta Na Guiamassa.

⚓ Cala d'en Tosqueta 40°03'·5N 4°10'E

A well protected *cala* tucked away under Cabo Pantinat, with a sand and shingle beach and rocky cliffs. Approach leaving Illa d'en Tosqueta to starboard (rocks also extend off the headland to the northeast) to anchor off the beach over sand and rock, open to southeast with swell from the east. A second beach lies 100m southwest and there are two more further south. There is a fine view from the headland and two caves to explore. Cala d'en Tosqueta is a popular anchorage which often becomes crowded in summer.

⚓ Cala Pudenta and Es Maresus

40°02'·6N 4°09'·8E

A smallish double *cala* with low rocky sides and small sandy beaches. The approach is straightforward, but look out for two awash rocks either side of Es Maresus. Anchor in sand over 3m or less, open to northeast through southeast. There is a spring behind the northwest beach, a track inland and a parking area, but little else.

⚓ Cala de la Olla (Arenal de Son Saura)

40°02'·2N 4°09'·8E

A nearly circular *cala* with a large sandy beach and sloping rocky sides. A small islet lies off the northwest corner, and there are awash rocks close inshore on the northwest and southeast sides. Anchor in 3–5m over sand, open north and northeast and to swell from the east. There is an extensive tourist development on the eastern headland, and a large lagoon with much wildlife about ¼ mile to the southwest.

⚓ Cala Ses Olles 40°02'·2N 4°10'·3E

A small, rounded *cala* close east of Cala de la Olla, surrounded by low cliffs and with no beach. Enter with care sounding carefully – an awash rock, Escull d'en Tarouger, and several islets lie up to 50m off the point on the east side of the entrance and there are some small rocks close to the shore to the southwest. Anchor in 3–6m over rock, open north and northeast and to swell from the east. There is a large tourist development between the two *calas*.

⚓ Arenal d'en Castell 40°01'·5N 4°11'·1E

A large, almost circular, bay with a long sandy beach surrounded by large apartment blocks, hotels and houses. If approaching from the west, round Punta Codolada with a least offing of 350m and continue due west until the entrance bears 160° before

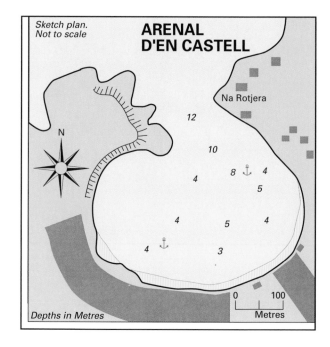

Looking into the almost circular Arenal d'en Castell from the north. As so often in the Islas Baleares the water is almost crystal clear.

turning south – this avoids three small islets off the headland, plus the low rocks to the west known as Los Ofegats (Esculls d'es Augegats). In most conditions the latter's breaking crests will be clearly visible.

Anchor off the beach in 4–8m over sand and weed open only to the north. There are smallcraft moorings on the western side of the bay and the northern part has a rocky bottom. There is a considerable amount of development behind the beach, with all the usual tourist shops, restaurants and cafés.

Punta Codolada 40°02'·2N 4°11'·6E
A low rocky headland with outlying rocks and islets. Allow at least 350m clearance.

Puerto de Cala de Addaya
(Puerto Deportivo de Addaya)
40°01'N 04°12'·4E (entrance)
40°00'·5N 4°12'E (yacht harbour)

Charts

	Approach
Admiralty	*2833*
Spanish	*6A*
French	*7117*

Lights
No lights.

Port Communications
VHF – Yacht harbour (*Puerto Deportivo de Addaya*) VHF Ch 9.
☎/*Fax* – Port Authority ☎ 366883, *Fax* 366459;
Puerto Deportivo de Addaya ☎ 188871, *Fax* 150030.

General
A long, narrow estuary, its entrance guarded by a line of islands, Cala de Addaya is a very pleasant, secluded and sheltered anchorage with a small and helpful yacht harbour in one corner. Considerable tourist development is taking place around the *cala* and forty or more houses are planned for the slopes overlooking the yacht harbour, together with a yacht club building and sports club. Fortunately this development appears to be of the distinctly upmarket – and therefore less intensive – variety.

The entrance to the *cala* requires care and in some conditions of light it is difficult to see. Entrance would be impossible in strong winds from northwest right round to east, though vessels already in the lagoon would be both safe and comfortable. Facilities are limited, but adequate for everyday needs. Mahón is less than 10 miles away by bus.

The harbour has been in use since Roman times and many amphoras and other remains have been found. The last British expedition to Menorca landed near Na Macaret on 7 November 1798 under the command of General Sir Charles Stuart, mainly because the three frigates and troop transports were unable to enter Fornells in adverse winds. The Highland Scots troops were amazed to find the hills covered with heather similar to that at home. In five days the 3000 British troops captured Menorca from 3600 Spanish without the loss of a single British soldier. In 1861 three Dutch ships carrying bullion – the warship *Wasaner* and two escorts, the *Sint Laurens* and *Sint Joris* – were wrecked off Cala de Addaya.

Approach
From northwest Round the wide promotory comprising Punta d'es Murté, Punta Na Guiamassa and Cabo Pantinat, without off-lying hazards, then head south-southeast for Punta Codolada 1·8 miles away. There are a number of *calas* in the intervening bay. On rounding Punta Codolada the Islas Addaya will open up ahead, with Punta de Na Ferradura and Punta d'en Falet on the starboard hand. In

215

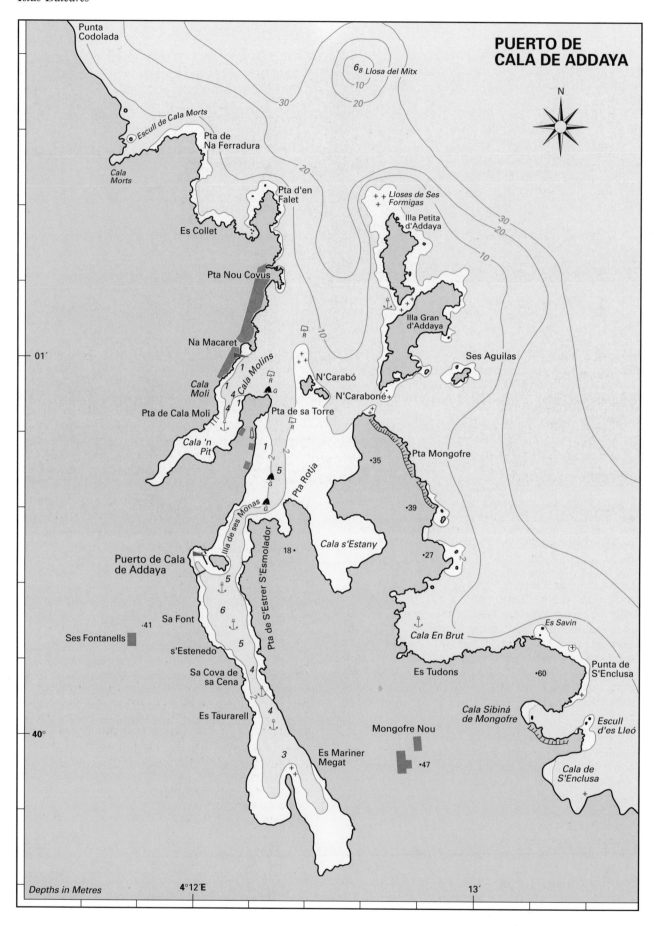

PUERTO DE CALA DE ADDAYA

N

Punta Codolada

6 8 Llosa del Mitx

10

30

20

Escull de Cala Morts

Pta de Na Ferradura

Cala Morts

20

Pta d'en Falet

Lloses de Ses Formigas

Illa Petita d'Addaya

Es Collet

30

20

10

Pta Nou Covus

Illa Gran d'Addaya

Na Macaret

01′

Cala Moli

Cala Molins

R

N'Carabó

Ses Aguilas

1

1

4

4

G

1

N'Caraboné

Pta de Cala Moli

Pta de sa Torre

R

Cala 'n Pit

1

Pta Mongofre

2

·35

5

G

Pta Rotja

·39

Illa de ses Monas

G

Puerto de Cala de Addaya

18 ·

Cala s'Estany

·27

5

Pta de S'Estrer S'Esmolador

Sa Font

6

Ses Fontanells

·41

Cala En Brut

Es Savin

s'Estenedo

5

Es Tudons

·60

Punta de S'Enclusa

Sa Cova de sa Cena

4

Cala Sibiná de Mongofre

Escull d'es Lleó

Es Taurarell

4

40°

Mongofre Nou

Cala de S'Enclusa

3

Es Mariner Megat

·47

The approach to Puerto de Cala de Addaya looking southwest. In the foreground are the Lloses de Ses Formigas (breaking), with Illa Petita d'Addaya and Illa Gran d'Adday on their left. Isolated just left of centre are N'Carabó and N'Caraboné, opposite Punta de sa Torre. On the far right is Punta d'en Falet.

heavy weather Llosa del Mitx (Llosa d'Emmig), a rock with 6·8m depth, may break about 550m offshore but at other times it poses no threat. Aim to pass Punta d'en Falet about 200m to 300m off, rounding the headland at this distance to take a southerly and then south-southwesterly course into the channel between Punta Nou Covus (mis-spelt Punta Na Cous on BA 2833, as well as being somewhat misplaced) and Illa Petita d'Addaya (see plan).

From southeast After rounding Cabo Favaritx, a low headland with a conspicuous lighthouse of black and white diagonal stripes, steer 300° towards a position off Punta Codolada. Stand on well past the Islas Addaya and the off-lying Lloses de Ses Formigas rocks, only heading in towards the coast when Punta d'en Falet bears 235° or less. Close the headland to a distance of 300m before taking a southerly and then south-southwesterly course into the channel between Punta Nou Covus and Illa Petita d'Addaya (see plan).

Note Night approach, without good local knowledge, is not advisable – for preference a first visit should be made in light winds and good visibility. Although fishermen use the passage between Punta Mongofre and the Islas Addaya as a short cut if heading eastwards, it is far from straightforward and requires local knowledge.

Anchorage in the approach

There is a good daytime anchorage just west of the gap between Illa Gran d'Addaya and Illa Petita d'Addaya in 5m+ over rock and weed, open to north and northwest.

Entrance

Once past Punta Nou Covus the channel is buoyed approximately as on the plan, though the buoys may be positioned slightly differently each season. Head for Punta de sa Torre (low, with houses and a car park – the tower itself is well back from the point), passing at least one small red port-hand buoy. If in doubt favour the west side of the channel – the chief danger is posed by rocks north of the islets of N'Carabó and N'Caraboné.

A much larger red buoy lies close off Punta de sa Torre and MUST be left to port. A large green starboard-hand buoy sits within a stone's throw of the headland. Turning to port through this 'gate' a smaller red buoy may be seen ahead marking the southwest side of N'Carabó, and two or more green buoys may show the extent of the shoals fringing the east side of Punta de sa Torre (some indication is also given by the extent of smallcraft moorings).

Looking down the channel into Puerto de Cala de Addaya from a point almost directly above the Lloses de Ses Formigas. The rocky islets of N'Carabó and N'Caraboné are on the left, with Punta de sa Torre in the centre. The shoals fringing both sides of the channel towards the yacht harbour can be seen clearly, as can the red and green buoys off the Punta.

Proceed slowly parallel to the western shore as there are further, unmarked, shoals to port.

A little short of Punta de S'Estrer S'Esmolador a mudbank, normally marked by two small green buoys, extends out from the western shore putting an S-bend in the channel. If these two buoys are NOT in place, once past the tower (see plan) steer for the centre of Punta de S'Estrer S'Esmolador ahead, turning west only when depths off the headland begin to shoal. In calm conditions the mudbank will be clearly visible as a brownish patch, but should a mistake be made the bottom is soft and the position sheltered.

Keep to the centre of the gap between Illa de ses Monas and the eastern bank before turning into the yacht harbour or coming to anchor in the pool beyond.

Warning The above channel buoys may not be laid until well into the season (May or June). If cruising the area for the first time earlier in the year do not attempt the entrance unless conditions are favourable. If the buoys are not in position proceed very slowly as above with a lookout on the bow and a careful watch on the echo-sounder.

Berthing

Round Illa de ses Monas about 50m off and Puerto Deportivo de Addaya will open to the northwest. Visitors normally berth bow or stern-to outside the southern pontoon, though space is at a premium during the high season – if in doubt about space or depth anchor off and investigate by dinghy. Alternatively consult the yacht harbour staff on VHF Ch 9.

Puerto Deportivo de Addaya is one of the Balearics' smallest – and many would say nicest – marinas, with less than a hundred berths covering all sizes. However there are plans to expand, with additional floating pontoons to take a further 80 yachts up to 15m LOA.

Port and starboard buoys are sometimes laid to indicate the channel into the yacht harbour, but these were not in place in 1996.

Anchorages

Anchor in 6m or less in the pool south of Illa de ses Monas, with good holding and all-round shelter. It is also possible to anchor further up the *cala* (see plan), and though it shoals towards its head it should be possible to carry 2–3m to where the water divides. Much of the bottom in the upper stretches is weed covered. The land around the *cala* is privately owned.

There is a small pontoon directly in front of the harbour office where crews of anchored yachts may

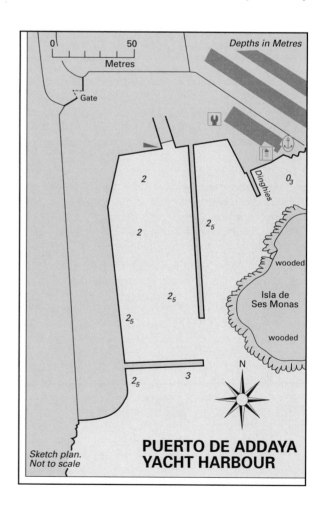

Puerto Deportivo de Addaya from the northeast. Visiting yachts moor to the pontoon on the left – the yacht harbour office is in the building topped by the distinctive white tower. Although relatively empty when this photograph was taken in late May 1996, during the season visitors are unlikely to find a free berth.

land by dinghy. As of 1996 there was no charge for anchoring – and the birdwatching was excellent.

Owners of shallow-draft yachts may wish to investigate Cala Moli (Molins) on the west side of Punta de sa Torre. Proceed with care – the bottom is uneven and there are many moorings. There is a small sandy beach off the holiday village of Na Macaret, where there are restaurants and basic shops.

Moorings

There are a number of mooring buoys in the pool but all are private.

Charges *(see page 6)*

High season daily rate – Band C (15m), Band B (10m); low season daily rate – Band D. Water and electricity included. As of 1996 there was no charge for anchoring.

Facilities

Boatyards Mardaya SC (☎ (908) 636666, *Fax* (71) 372290), based at the yacht harbour, can handle repairs, maintenance, painting etc.

Travel-hoist (a cross between a travel-lift and a trailer, since it uses the slipway) of approximately 10 tonne capacity.

Slipway On the north side of the harbour, reportedly shallow.

Engineers Addaya Motor Servicios (☎/*Fax* (908) 630784), based at the yacht harbour.

Sailmaker Mardaya SC handle canvaswork.

Water On the pontoons – yachts anchored off are charged 1110 ptas to come in and fill tanks (1996). If asked politely the harbour staff usually allow portable carriers to be filled *gratis*.

Showers By the harbour office. Free if berthed in the yacht harbour, otherwise 380 ptas per head (1996).

Electricity 220v AC points on the pontoons.

Fuel Not available, though it may be possible to arrange small quantities via the harbour office.

Ice From the harbour office.

Yacht club A yacht club is planned.

Banks In Mahón, though there is an exchange bureau up the hill from the harbour.

Shops/provisioning The supermarket up the hill to the west of the harbour plus shops at Na Macaret (west of Cala Moli) can provide everyday requirements.

Hotels/restaurants/cafés etc. A small hotel at Na Macaret, restaurants and cafés up the hill from the harbour, bar in the harbour itself.

Laundrette Up the hill from the harbour.

Hospital/medical services In Mahón.

Communications

Car hire/taxis Car hire agency nearby, or can be arranged from Mahón.

Buses Bus service to Mahón and elsewhere along the nearby main road (ask for directions in the harbour office).

⚓ Cala En Brut 40°00'·4N 4°12'·9E

An open bay surrounded by high sloping rocks, recognisable by a conspicuous white building with a tower on the hill behind. There are a few islets close inshore on north side. Anchor over sand, open to north and northeast.

⚓ Cala Sibiná (Sivinar, Savinar) de Mongofre and Cala de S'Enclusa 40°00'N 4°13'·2E

Twin *calas* surrounded by high (40m to 63m) rough hills and separated by a rocky point. Cala Sibiná is the smaller of the two and has rocks awash close inshore on both sides of the entrance. Cala de S'Enclusa has an islet with an outlying rock, Llosa de s'Enclusa, east of the entrance and a single breaking rock in the southeastern part of the *cala* itself. Both *calas* are mainly sand and are open to north and northeast with swell from the east. A conspicuous white building with a tower and red roofs stands on the hill to the east. There are several sandy beaches and some tracks inland, but otherwise nothing.

Cala de S'Enclusa (centre) and Cala Sibiná de Mongofre (right) looking southwest. The 'conspicuous white building' mentioned in the text can be seen above Cala Sibiná de Mongofre with the headwaters of Cala de Addaya behind.

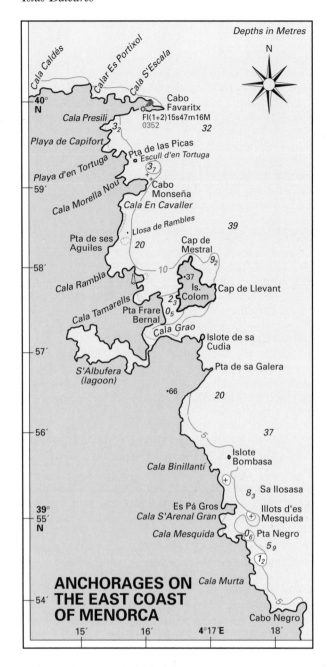

ANCHORAGES ON THE EAST COAST OF MENORCA

⚓ **Cala Caldés** 39°59'·9N 4°13'·8E

A small *cala* at the mouth of a narrow valley with high (30 to 70m) hills each side and a small stony beach. A group of five rocky islets lies to the west of the entrance and two awash rocks plus an islet to the east. Enter on a southerly course midway between the two groups to anchor off the beach over sand and rock, open to the north. There is one small house in the valley with a track inland.

⚓ **Cala Es Portixol** 40°00'·1N 4°15'·3E

A large open *cala* amongst rocky cliffs and hills, with a smaller *cala* in the southwest corner in which there is a sand and stone beach. Several islets lie close inshore on either side of the entrance. Anchor off the beach over rock with sand patches, open to northwest round to northeast. The road from Cabo Favaritx to Mahón lies only 200m inland.

⚓ **Cala S'Escala** 40°00'N 4°15'·6E

A small round *cala* with an islet in the middle of the entrance, surrounded by low rocky cliffs and sloping hills (15 to 21m). Inshore islets line either side of the entrance – enter with care favouring the eastern side and anchor off the beach, open to the north. There is a small sandy beach backed by sand dunes in the southeast corner and the road to Mahón 100m inland.

Cabo Favaritx 39°59'·8N 4°16'·3E

A very prominent low (12m), broken rocky headland with a conspicuous lighthouse (Fl(1+2) 15s47m16M, white tower with black diagonal stripes on white building 28m) set slightly back from the point itself. It is steep-to but with two islets on its south side.

⚓ **Cala Presili** 39°59'·6N 4°15'·4E

(Incorrectly identified as Cala Algaret on BA 2833) A very open *cala* with sandy beach, dunes and small sloping hills behind. Anchor off the beach over sand and stone, open to northeast through southeast. Three rocks with some 2m over them are reported to lie about 100m off the beach. If approaching from the south see the note regarding Punta de las Picas and Cabo Monseña, below.

⚓ **Playa de Capifort and Playa d'en Tortuga** 39°59'·4N 4°15'·4E

(Incorrectly identified as Cala Presili on BA 2833) A larger sandy beach just south of the above *cala* with a smaller beach still further south. Anchor off the beach open to northeast and east. If approaching from the south see the note regarding Punta de las Picas and Cabo Monseña, below.

Punta de las Picas and Cabo Monseña 39°59'·2N 4°16'·1E

Keep well off Cabo Monseña (Cap Monsenyar Vivas) and Punta de las Picas (Cap de Ses Piques) both of which have reefs and islands extending up to 600m offshore.

⚓ **Cala Morella Nou** 39°59'N 4°15'·7E

A *cala* with two sandy beaches separated by a rocky point. Enter on a southwesterly course between the islets and reefs off Cabo Monseña (Cap Monsenyar Vives) to port and Punta de las Picas (Cap de Ses Piques) to starboard. The latter has a small island, Escull d'en Tortuga, some 400m offshore which must also be left to starboard. Anchor off either beach in sand, open to north through east. There is a track inland and a few houses.

⚓ **Cala En Cavaller** 39°58'·8N 4°15'·8E

A small *cala* just south of Cabo Monseña, with a sand and shingle beach and a small islet on the south side of entrance. Anchor off the beach open to east and southeast. A tree-lined valley with sloping rocky sides runs inland. If approaching from the north see the note regarding Cabo Monseña and Punta de las Picas, above.

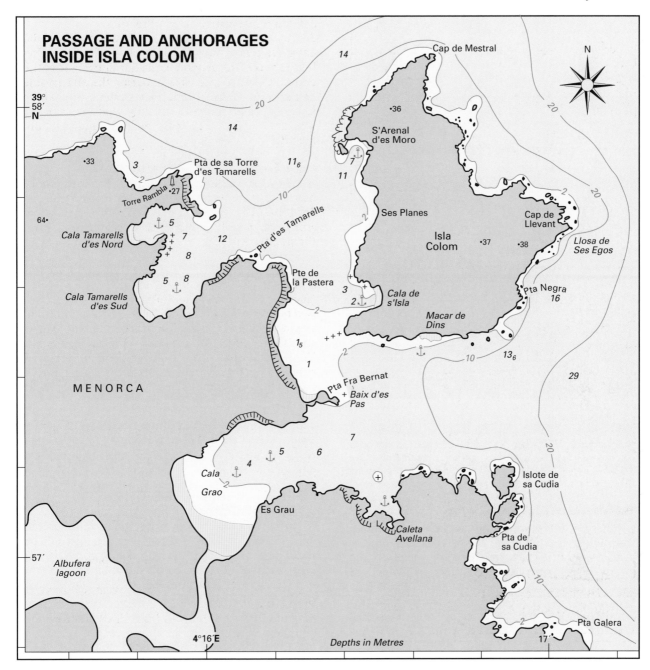

PASSAGE AND ANCHORAGES INSIDE ISLA COLOM

⚓ Cala Rambla (Cala sa Torreta)

39°58'N 4°15'·5E

A large double *cala* with low rocky cliffs on either side and the Llosa de Rambles reef some 400m north of the entrance. Enter on a southwesterly course to anchor over sand off the western beach, open to north and northeast plus swell from the east. The eastern *cala* has some awash rocks scattered across its entrance though there is a good sandy beach behind. There is a single house between the beaches and a track inland. A standing *taula* and a *talayot* will be found just over ½ mile inland, together with a ruined village at Sa Torre Blanca.

Isla Colom Bisected by 39°57'·7N 4°16'·8E

An almost deserted island with rocky cliffs, Isla Colom is 0·6 mile long by 0·5 mile at its widest point and up to 42m high. There are two attractive small beaches to which daily boat trips are run from Es Grao, and one large house, Lloc de s'Illa, plus a hut. Inevitably, the island has its own unique species of lizard.

Passage inside Isla Colom

A doglegged north–south passage inside Isla Colom, little more than 1m deep and usually about 100m wide, normally exists close to the coast of Menorca, avoiding the end of a sand bar with rocks inshore which stretches 150m west from the southwest tip of Isla Colom. Caution must be exercised since winds and currents can alter the extent of this bar and change the soundings in the channel. Note also two awash rocks extending 100m east from Punta Fra Bernat on the Menorcan shore.

Looking southwest over Isla Colom and the shallow passage which separates it from Menorca. In the right foreground, with a yacht at anchor, is S'Arenal d'es Moro, with Cala Tamarells d'es Sud on the far side of the channel. In the left foreground is Cala de s'Isla, with the broad bay of Cala Grao behind. In the distance can be seen the lagoon of S'Albufera.

Anchorages behind Isla Colom

Apart from Mahón and Addaya, the anchorages behind Isla Colom offer the best shelter on the northeast coast. They are, however, open to the northwest and to swell from the north, and are therefore not suitable in heavy weather or in winds with a northerly component, since the two anchorages that might be thought to give all-round shelter (Cala Tamarells d'es Nord and S'Arenal d'es Moro) are too small to provide adequate swinging room in a blow.

⚓ Cala Tamarells d'es Nord 39°57'·7N 4°16'E

The northern, and smaller, of a pair of *calas* divided by a rocky promontory. The conspicuous Torre Rambla (Es Colomar) stands on the north side of the entrance. Rocky islets and awash rocks lie close inshore around this point and off the central promontory – favour the south side of the entrance to anchor in 5m± over sand and rock. Shelter is good from all directions, but there is restricted swinging room even for a single yacht and it may be necessary to moor using two anchors at the bow.

⚓ Cala Tamarells d'es Sud 39°57'·6N 4°16'E

A much larger anchorage than its northern twin, with better protection than might be expected. There are off-lying rocks around both headlands as well as the central promontory – keep to the south and west sides where there are a couple of sandy beaches. Anchor in 5–8m over sand and rock, open to the northeast. There is a track inland but nothing else.

⚓ S'Arenal d'es Moro, Isla Colom
39°57'·8N 4°16'·5E

A small *cala* surrounded by sloping, scrub-covered hills. A small islet, Illot d'es Moro, lies just off the north side of the sandy beach, which itself has an off-lying ridge of rock carrying less than 1m. Anchor in 5–7m over sand and weed in good shelter, though swell from the northern quadrant would probably work its way in. Swinging room is in short supply and in all but the lightest winds it may be necessary to moor using two anchors at the bow. S'Arenal d'es Moro is a popular spot with daytime visitors but is deserted at night.

⚓ Cala de s'Isla, Isla Colom 39°57'·5N 4°16'·5E

A small, shallow, but very pretty *cala* just north of the passage between Isla Colom and Menorca, surrounded by low sloping hills and with a house set back from the northeast corner. Two rocks just below waterlevel lie in the northern part of the anchorage, while the southern side is fringed with rocks merging into those of the southwestern headland. Approach the centre of the *cala* on an easterly course to anchor in 2–3m over sand open to north and northwest. Like the beach further north, Cala de s'Isla is a popular destination for tourist boats from Cala Grao but is very quiet at night.

⌕ **Macar de Dins** 39°57'·4N 4°16'·6E
Strictly a lunch stop on the south side of Isla Colom, off a small beach with rocks awash near its centre. In settled northerly weather it is possible to anchor almost anywhere between Macar de Dins and the southwestern promontory, open to east and southeast.

⌕ **Cala Grao (Cala de la Albufera)**
39°57'·2N 4°16'·1E
A popular anchorage in a large, rounded *cala* scattered with moorings and overlooked by the holiday village of Es Grao. Approach and enter on a westerly course keeping near the centre of the *cala*, which shoals rapidly towards the beach – keep an eye on the echo-sounder after crossing the 10m line. Anchor in 3m+ off the beach, open to the east. Es Grao has a supermarket, restaurants and cafés (which also sell ice). There are also slipways and quays for dinghies and small boats.

A broad stream leading from the vast Albufera lagoon drains into the southwestern corner of the *cala* and would make an interesting dinghy excursion. The lagoon and marshes, which extend more than a mile inland, are a wildlife and nature reserve.

⌕ **Caleta Avellana (Cala Vellana)**
39°57'·1N 4°16'·5E
A small *cala* between sloping rocky sides close east of Cala Grao, with an isolated rock in the middle of the entrance. Approach from slightly west of north sounding carefully to anchor over sand, weed and rock open to north and east.

⌕ **Cala Binillantí** 39°55'·6N 4°17'·1E
A very small, deserted *cala* inshore of Islote Bombasa (En Bombarda) and north of Punta Sansá. Approach on a southwesterly course and anchor off the beach, open to north through east. Do not confuse Cala Binillantí with one of a series of five even smaller *calas* to the north.

⌕ **Cala S'Arenal Gran (Grau)** 39°55'N 4°17'·4E
This large *cala* lies immediately north of Cala Mesquida and Punta de sa Torre (topped by a large pale stone tower), and south of Punta Pá Gros. This latter has groups of off-lying rocky islets of which the outermost, the Illots d'es Mesquida, are 400m offshore. Leave all these islets to starboard on the approach and anchor over sand off the northern end of the beach, open to east and southeast. The southern part of the beach has rocky outcrops running out into the *cala*. There are a few houses and a road, but no facilities.

Looking east towards Menorca, with Isla Colom on the right and the twin *calas* of Tamarells d'es Nord and d'es Sud behind it. On the left is Cala Grao, backed by the S'Albufera lagoon. The rocky islet in the left foreground is Islote de Cudia.

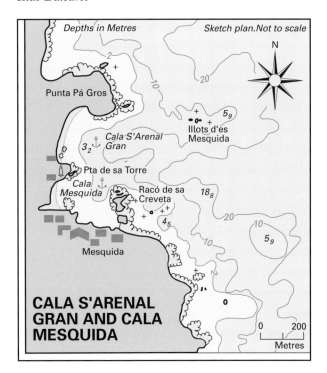

CALA S'ARENAL GRAN AND CALA MESQUIDA

⚓ **Cala Mesquida** 39°54'·8N 4°17'·4E

An angular *cala* with a small beach, close south of Cala S'Arenal Gran and Punta de sa Torre and its prominent tower (which has the proportions of a medieval castle keep). Leave the Illots d'es Mesquida to starboard and steer southwestwards towards the small beach, leaving Racó de sa Creveta and its associated rocks to port. If approaching from the south keep at least 500m offshore until due east of Punta de sa Torre before heading in. Anchor between Racó de sa Creveta and the tower in 5–6m over sand and rock, open to north and northeast.

Do not approach the beach without a previous recce by dinghy, as a reef runs most of the way across it in a northwesterly direction from the rocks near the further buildings. A shallow river flows into the head of the *cala*. There is a dinghy harbour and slipway in the southeast corner, in front of a café/restaurant backed by several streets of houses.

It was here that the heavy siege train of the Duc de Richelieu was finally landed in April 1756. It had originally been landed at Ciudadela, but was held up by the destruction of the road to Mahón and was re-embarked.

Spanish chart 4282 comprises a large scale plan of Cala Mesquida.

Punta Negra 39°54'·4N 4°17'·8E

A low (12m) headland with houses on its summit, not to be confused with the much more prominent Cabo Negro (37m) 0·7 mile to the southeast. Rocks lie off the point.

⚓ **Cala Murta (Es Murtar)** 39°54'·3N 4°17'·8E

A wide *cala* just south of Punta Negra, with a series of rocky beaches and many houses to the north. Approach the middle of the *cala* on a westerly course to anchor in the northwest corner over rock and sand, open to east and southeast. Care is necessary because the coast is foul in parts.

Cabo Negro (Cap Negre) 39°54'N 4°18'·6E

A high (37m), prominent point of black rock with steep sides sloping seawards. A small islet and awash rock lie close to the promontory, which has some sea caves.

⚓ **Cala Els Freus** 39°52'·9N 4°18'·7E

A narrow *cala* on the north side of the isthmus of La Mola, which is foul on its southern side. Bajo de las Aguilas, a low islet with awash rocks, guards the approach 500m to the east-northeast. The *cala* is open to north through east.

Punta del Esperó 39°52'·7N 4°19'·7E

A high (78m), conspicuous, flat-topped promontory with sheer cliffs, sloping gently downwards towards Puerto de Mahón. A large fort and other conspicuous buildings occupy the plateau, with a lighthouse (Fl(1+2)15s51m8M, white round tower with two black bands on white building 11m) at the eastern tip. There are two awash rocks close to this point but it is otherwise steep-to.

Appendices

I. CHARTS

Charts and other publications may be corrected annually by reference to the Admiralty *List of Lights and Fog Signals Volume D (NP 77)* or weekly via the Admiralty *Notices to Mariners*.

Note A few charts appear twice in the following list under different island headings. The index diagrams only shows large-scale charts where the diagram's scale permits.

British Admiralty charts

Chart	Title	Scale
Approaches from the Spanish coast		
1701	Cabo de San Antonio to Villaneuva y Geltrú including Islas de Ibiza and Formentara	300,000
Ibiza		
1702	Ibiza, Formentera and southern Mallorca	300,000
2834	Islas Baleares, Ibiza and Formentera	120,000
	Chs between Ibiza and Formentera	50,000
	San Antonio Abad	20,000
	Ibiza	10,000
Mallorca		
1703	Mallorca and Menorca	300,000
2831	Mallorca: Punta Salinas to Cabo de Formentor including Canal de Menorca	120,000
	Puerto de Alcudia	20,000
2832	Mallorca – Punta Salinas to Punta Beca including Isla de Cabrera	120,000
3036	Approaches to Palma	30,000
	Palma	10,000
Menorca		
1703	Mallorca and Menorca	300,000
2833	Islas Baleares, Menorca	120,000
	Bahia de Tirant and Cala Fornells	15,000
	Mahón	12,500
	Ciudadela	10,000

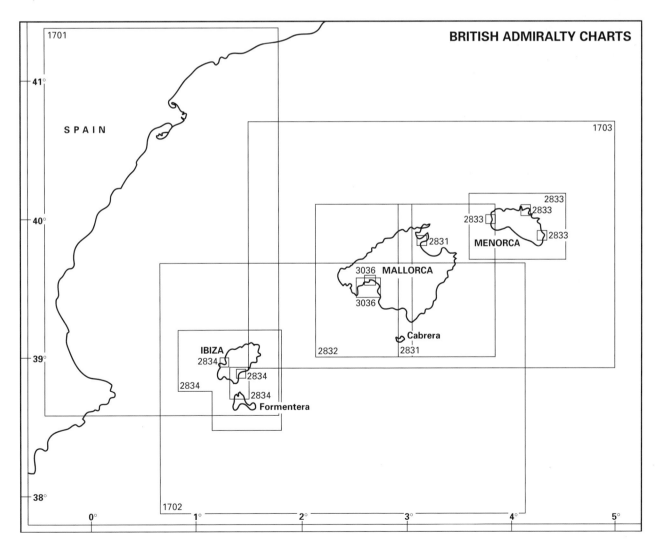

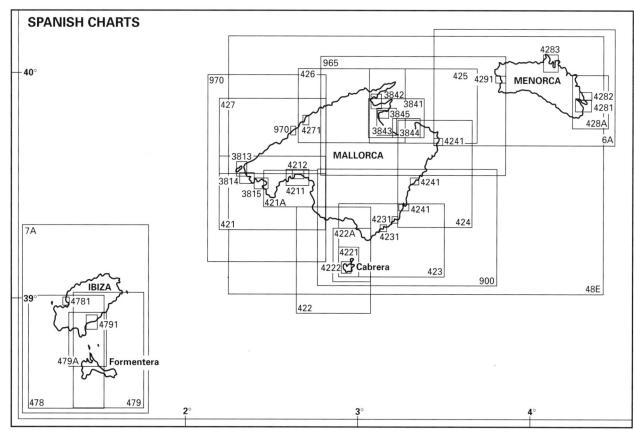

SPANISH CHARTS

Spanish charts

Ibiza

7A	Isla de Ibiza y Formentera	97,500
478	De cabo Negret a cabo Berberia	50,000
479	De cabo Berberia a Punta Arabi	50,000
479A	Freus entre Ibiza y Formentera	25,000
4791	Puerto de Ibiza	10,000
4781	Puerto de San Antonio Abad	5,000

Mallorca

48E	Islas de Mallorca y Menorca	175,000
900	De cabo Blanco a punta de Amer	100,000
965	De punta de Amer al Morro de la Vaca	100,000
970	De Morro de la Vaca a cabo Blanco	100,000
	Plano inserto: Surgidero de la Foradada de Miramar	12,000
421	De isla Dragonera a cabo Blanco	50,000
422	De cabo Regana a punta Salinas	50,000
423	De punta Plana a Porto Colom con la Isla de Cabrera y adyacentes	50,000
424	De cala Llonga a cabo Farrutx	50,000
425	De cabo Pera a cabo Formentor	50,000
426	De la bahía de Alcudia al puerto de Sóller	50,000
427	De Cala de la Calobra a Isla Dragonera	50,000
421A	Bahía de Palma. De islote El Toro a cabo Regana	25,000
422A	Freu de Cabrera	25,000
3841	Bahía de Alcudia	25,000
3843	Bahía de Alcudia. De playa de Sas Escortjas a Isla de Aucunada	12,500
3844	Bahía de Alcudia. De cabo Farrutx a playa de Sas Escortjas	12,500
4221	Isla de Cabrera y adyacentes	12,500
3813	Freu de Dragonera	10,000
3814	Puerto de Andraitx	10,000
3815	Ensenada de Santa Ponsa	10,000
4211	Bahía de Palma. De las Illetas a islote Galera	10,000
3842	Puerto de Pollensa	7,500
4231	Porto Petro y Cala Llonga	7,500
	Cala Figuera	2,500
3845	Puerto de Alcudia	5,000
4212	Puerto de Palma	5,000
4222	Puerto de Cabrera	5,000
4241	Porto Colom	5,000
	Porto Cristo o Cala Manacor	5,000
	Cala Ratjada	5,000
4271	Puerto de Sóller	5,000

Menorca

48E	Islas de Mallorca y Menorca	175,000
6A	Isla de Menorca	96,103
428A	De punta Binibeca a cabo Favaritx	25,000
4283	Ensenada de Tirant y Cala Fornells	7,500
	Planos insertos: Puerto Nitge	10,000
	Dársena puerto	1,000
4281	Puerto de Mahón	7,500
4282	Cala Mesquida	5,000
4291	Puerto de Ciudadela	5,000

French charts

Ibiza

5505	Iles Baléares	319,000
7114	Ibiza et Formentera	
	Cartouche: A – Ibiza et Formentera	100,000
	Cartouche: B – San Antonio Abad	20,000
	Cartouche: C – Puerto de Ibiza	10,000
	Cartouche: D – Passages entre Ibiza et Espalmador Abords de puerto de Ibiza	30,000

Mallorca

5505	Iles Baléares	319,000
7115	Mallorca – Partie Ouest – De Punta Beca à Punta Salinas	100,000

7116	Mallorca – Partie Est –De Punta Salinas à Cabo de Formentor	100,000
7118	Abords de Palma – De Isla Dragonera à Cabo Blanco	40,000
	Cartouche: A – Puerto de Andraitx	10,000
	Cartouche: B – Cala de Santa Ponsa	10,000
7119	Ports et mouillages de Mallorca et Cabrera	
	Cartouche: A – Puerto de Pollensa	12,500
	Cartouche: B – Puerto de Alcudia	10,000
	Cartouche: C – Puerto de Soller	10,000
	Cartouche: D – Puerto Colom	15,000
	Cartouche: E – Cala Ratjada	10,000
	Cartouche: F – Surgidero de la Foradada	12,500
	Cartouche: G – Cala Figuera	5,000
	Cartouche: H – Puerto Cristó ou Calá Manacor	5,000
	Cartouche: I – Puerto de Cabrera	12,500
	Cartouche: J – Porto Petro et Cala Llonga	12,000
6775	Baie de Palma – De Las Illetas à l'îlot Galera	10,000

Menorca

5505	Iles Baléares	319,000
7117	Menorca – Ports et Mouillages de Menorca	
	Cartouche: Menorca	100,000
	Cartouche: A – Puerto de Ciudadela	10,000
	Cartouche: B – Bahia de Tirant et Cala Fornells	15,000
	Cartouche C: – Puerto de Máhon	15,000

Navicarte charts (published by Editions Grafocarte)

E01	Majorque Est – Minorque
E02	Majorque Ouest – Ibiza – Formentera

Imray

M3	Islas Baleares	356,000

II. FURTHER READING

Many navigational publications are reprinted annually, in which case the latest edition should be carried. Others, including most cruising guides, are updated by means of supplements available from the publishers (see *Correctional Supplements*, page 2). Further corrections or amendments are always welcome (see *Corrections*, page 2).

Admiralty publications

Mediterranean Pilot Vol I (NP 45) and *Supplement* covers the south and east coasts of Spain, the Islas Baleares, Sardinia, Sicily and the north coast of Africa

List of Lights and Fog Signals, Vol E (NP 78) (Mediterranean, Black and Red Seas)

List of Radio Signals

Vol 1, Part 1 (NP281/1) Coast Radio Stations (Europe, Africa and Asia)

Vol 2 (NP 282) Radio Navigational Aids, Electronic Position Fixing Systems and Radio Time Signals

Vol 3, Part 1 (NP 283/1) Radio Weather Services and Navigational Warnings (Europe, Africa and Asia)

Vol 4 (NP 284) Meteorological Observation Stations

Vol 5 (NP 285) Global Maritime Distress and Safety Systems (GMDSS)

Vol 6, Part 2 (NP 286/2) Vessel Traffic Services, Port Operations and Pilot Services (The Mediterranean, Africa and Asia)

Yachtsmen's guides, almanacs etc

English language

Imray Mediterranean Almanac, Rod Heikell (Imray Laurie Norie & Wilson Ltd). A biennial almanac with second year supplement, packed with information. Particularly good value for yachts on passage when not every cruising guide is likely to be carried.

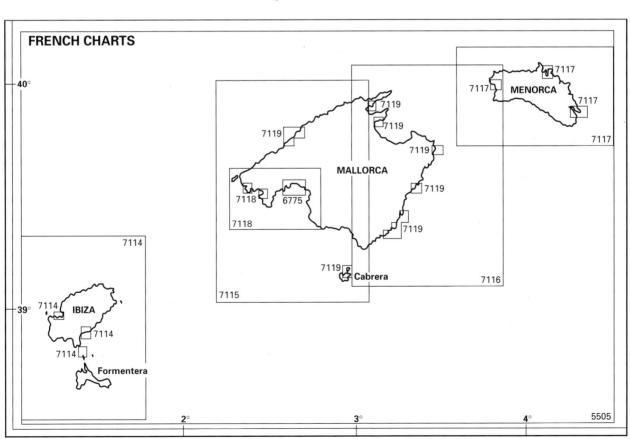

Mediterranean Sailing, Rod Heikell (Adlard Coles Nautical 1988). Useful information on techniques such as berthing bow or stern-to, clothing, storing up etc.

Mediterranean Cruising Handbook, Rod Heikell (Imray Laurie Norie & Wilson Ltd, 1990). General information on cruising areas, passages etc., some of which is now slightly out of date.

East Spain Pilot – Costas del Azahar, Dorada and Brava, and *Costas del Sol and Blanca*, Robin Brandon (Imray Laurie Norie & Wilson Ltd, 1995). Companion volumes to *Islas Baleares*, both currently undergoing major revision. Each book is accompanied by an Imray chart of the area.

South France Pilot – Golfe du Lion, Côte d'Azur and *La Corse*, Robin Brandon (Imray Laurie Norie & Wilson Ltd, 1993, 1990 & 1991 respectively). Two volumes cover the French coast with one on Corsica.

Mediterranean France and Corsica – A sea guide, Rod Heikell (Imray Laurie Norie & Wilson Ltd, 1990). Covering the same ground as the above guides, but in a single volume.

North Africa, Hans van Rijn (Imray Laurie Norie & Wilson Ltd, 1991). The only yachtsman's guide to the coast between the Strait of Gibraltar and Tunisia.

Italian Waters Pilot, Rod Heikell (Imray Laurie Norie & Wilson Ltd, 1995). Covering the west coast of Italy, Sardinia, Sicily and Malta.

Spanish

Guia del Navegante – La Costa de España y el Algarve (PubliNáutic Rilnvest SL, revised annually) in colloquial English with a Spanish translation. Not a full scale pilot book, but an excellent source of up-to-date information on local services and facilites (partly via the advertisements) with phone numbers etc.

Guia Náutica Turistica y Deportiva de España by the *Asamblea de Capitánes de Yate*. An expensive and colourful guide book covering all the Spanish coasts and including some useful data on harbours but no pilotage information. The plans are in outline only. Written in Spanish with a partial English translation. Because symbols are lavishly used, much of it can be understood with only a limited knowledge of Spanish.

Guia Náutica de España. Tomo II, Costa del Azahar, Blanca and Baleares. One of a series of books featuring attractive colour pictures, some of which are out of date, and some text. Written in Spanish but an English version is sometimes available.

El Mercado Nautico (The Boat Market). A free newspaper published every two or three months and available from yacht clubs, marina offices etc. Written in Spanish, English and German it includes, amongst other things, a useful (though by no means comprehensive) listing of current marina prices.

French

Votre Livre de Bord – Méditerranée (Bloc Marine). French almanac covering the Mediterranean, including details of weather forecasts transmitted from France and Monaco. An English/French version is also published which translates some, though by no means all, the text. Published annually.

Ports & Mouillages – Baléares (SHOM). A recent (1994) French guide in a series which also covers western Italy, Sardinia and the Lesser Antilles. Colour photos and plans.

Les Guides Nautiques – Baléares, J C Alvarez (Edition Eskis). Written in French in colloquial style, lacking in detail and with basic plans.

German

Spanische Gewässer, Lissabon bis Golfe du Lion, K Neumann (Delius Klasing). A seamanlike guide and semi-pilot book, which includes sketch plans of most harbours. Harbour data is limited but it contains much good general advice on sailing in this area.

Die Baleares, Bernhard Bartholmes (Edition Maritim). Well laid-out with good detail and some excellent, though out of date, aerial photographs.

Häfen und Anker Plätze, Gerd Radspieler. A useful book but with very basic plans and lacking in detail.

Background

The Birth of Europe, Michael Andrew (BBC Books). An excellent and comprehensive work which explains in simple terms how the Mediterranean and surrounding countries developed over the ages from 3000 BC.

The First Eden, David Attenborough (William Collins). A fascinating study of 'The Mediterranean World and Man'.

The Inner Sea, Robert Fox (Sinclair-Stevenson, 1991). An account of the countries surrounding the Mediterranean and the forces which shaped them, written by a well known BBC journalist.

Sea of Seas, H Scott (van Nostrand). A half-guidebook half-storybook on the western Mediterranean. Very out of date and now out of print, but a delight to read.

Travellers' guides

Essential Mallorca, Ibiza and Menorca, Tom Burns (Automobile Association, 1995). A handy, pocket-sized tourist guide with a little bit of everything – what to see, where to shop, restaurant recommendations, countryside and wildlife etc. Excellent colour photos.

Baedeker's Majorca (which also covers Menorca) and *Baedeker's Ibiza*, Peter M Nahm (Automobile Association, 1994). Serious, informed guides, well illustrated and particularly strong on culture – history, architecture etc. – though with some notable omissions and many errors in the index. A pocket in the plastic cover carries an island map.

Landscapes of Ibiza, Han Losse; *Landscapes of Mallorca*, Valerie Crespí-Green; *Landscapes of Menorca*, Rodney Ansell (Sunflower Books, 1995, 1994 & 1996). Three pocket-sized volumes of car tours, walks and picnic suggestions, plus some public transport schedules.

The Rough Guide: Mallorca & Menorca, Phil Lee (Rough Guides, distributed by the Penguin Group, 1996). A new addition to the worldwide series for land-based budget travellers, but useful to anyone wanting practical information. Town plans, no photographs. Also 46 pages on the Islas Baleares in the *Spain* volume (1994).

The Balearic Islands, Helen Thurston (Batsford, 1977). No so much a travel guide as a detailed history of the influences which have shaped the islands over the centuries. Slightly out of date but highly readable.

The Balearic Islands (Nagel Publishers, 1969). Thumbnail descriptions of places in the Islas Baleares, with historic details and suggestions for visits. Companion volume on *Spain*. Getting distinctly out of date.

Mallorca and Menorca, Berlitz Travel Guide. By 1995 this book had reached its 24th edition – what more can one say!

Period accounts

Jogging Round Majorca, Gordon West (Black Swan Books, 1994). First published in 1929 when 'jogging' meant a leisurely stroll, this is a charming glimpse of the island before tourism arrived. Also available on cassette.

Highly recommended.

A Cottage in Majorca, Lady Margaret Kinloch (Skeffinton, 1936). Another mirror into the past written with great affection. Long out of print, so not an easy book to track down.

Majorca Observed, Robert Graves and Paul Hogarth (Cassells, 1965). Probably the most famous author to live and write in Mallorca before mass tourism.

Road maps

Euro-Map – Mallorca, Minorca, Ibiza (GeoCenter International). Detailed but comprehensible road map giving contours, place names (sometimes both Castilian and local versions) historic sites, street plan of Palma etc. Scale 1:150,000. Useful for any form of travel.

The Firestone road map of the Islas Baleares is also reported to be excellent, but may be difficult to obtain in the UK.

III. SPANISH GLOSSARY

The following limited glossary relates to the weather, the abbreviations to be found on Spanish charts and some words likely to be useful on entering port. For a list containing many words commonly used in connection with sailing, see Webb & Manton, *Yachtsman's Ten Language Dictionary* (Adlard Coles Nautical).

Weather

On the radio, if there is a storm warning the forecast starts *aviso temporal*. If, as usual, there is no storm warning, the forecast starts *no hay temporal*. Many words are similar to the English and their meanings can be guessed. The following may be less familiar:

Viento **Wind**
calma calm
ventolina light air
flojito light breeze
flojo gentle breeze
bonancible moderate breeze
fresquito fresh breeze
fresco strong breeze
frescachón near gale
temporal fuerte gale
temporal duro strong gale
temporal muy duro storm
borrasca violent storm
huracán, temporal huracanado hurricane
tempestad, borrasca thunderstorm

regular moderate
mala poor
calima haze
neblina mist
bruma sea mist
niebla fog

Precipitación
Precipitation
aguacero shower
llovizna drizzle
lluvia rain
aguanieve sleet
nieve snow
granizada hail

El Cielo **The sky**
nube cloud
nubes altas, bajas high, low clouds
nubloso cloudy
cubierto covered, overcast
claro, despejado clear

Names of cloud types in Spanish are based on the same Latin words as the names used in English.

Visibilidad **Visibility**
buena good

Sistemas del Tiempo
Weather Systems
anticiclón anticyclone
depresión, borrasca depression
vaguada trough
cresta, dorsal ridge
cuna wedge
frente front
frío cold
cálido warm
ocluido occluded
bajando falling
subiendo rising

Lights and Charts – major terms and abbreviations:

A	*amarilla*	yellow
Alt	*alternativa*	alternative
Ag Nv	*aguas navegables*	navegable waters
Ang	*angulo*	angle
Ant	*anterior*	anterior, earlier, forward
Apag	*apagado*	extinguished
Arrc	*arrecife*	reef
At	*atenuada*	attenuated
B	*blanca*	white
Ba	*bahia*	bay
	bajamar escorada	chart datum
Bal	*baliza*	buoy, beacon
Bal. E	*baliza elástica*	plastic (elastic) buoy
Bco	*banco*	bank
Bo	*bajo*	shoal, under, below, low
Boc	*bocina*	horn, trumpet
Br	*babor*	port (ie. left)
C	*campana*	bell
Card	*cardinal*	cardinal
Cañ	*cañon*	canyon
	boya de castillete	pillar buoy
cil	*cilíndrico*	cylindrical
C	*cabo*	cape
Cha	*chimenea*	chimney
Cno	*castillo*	castle
cón	*cónico*	conical
Ct	*centellante*	quick flashing (50-80/minute)
CtI	*centellante interrumpida*	interrupted quick flashing
cuad	*cuadrangular*	quadrangular
D	*destello*	flash
Desap	*desaparecida*	disappeared
Dest	*destruida*	destroyed
	dique	breakwater, jetty
Dir	*direccional*	directional
DL	*destello largo*	long flash
E	*este*	east
edif	*edificio*	building
	ensenada	cove, inlet
Er	*estribor*	starboard
Est	*esférico*	spherical
Esp	*especial*	special
Est sñ	*estación de señales*	signal station
ext	*exterior*	exterior
Extr	*extremo*	end, head (of pier etc.)
F	*fija*	fixed
Fca	*fabrica*	factory
FD	*fija y destello*	fixed and flashing
FGpD	*fija y grupo de destellos*	fixed and group flashing
Flot	*flotador*	float
Fondn	*fondeadero*	anchorage
GpCt	*grupo de centellos*	group quick flashing
GpD	*grupo de destellos*	group flashing
GpOc	*grupo de ocultaciones*	group occulting
GpRp	*grupo de centellos rápidos*	group very quick flashing
hel	*helicoidales*	helicoidal
hor	*horizontal*	horizontal
Hund	*hundida*	submerged, sunk
I	*interrumpido*	interrupted
Igla	*iglesia*	church
Inf	*inferior*	inferior, lower
Intens	*intensificado*	intensified
Irreg	*irregular*	irregular
Iso	*isofase*	isophase

L	*luz*	light
La	*lateral*	lateral
	levante	eastern
M	*millas*	miles
Mte	*monte*	mountain
Mto	*monumento*	monument
N	*norte*	north
Naut	*nautófono*	foghorn
NE	*nordeste*	northeast
No	*número*	number
NW	*noroeste*	northwest
Obst	*obstrucción*	obstruction
ocas	*ocasional*	occasional
oct	*octagonal*	octagonal
oc	*oculta*	obscured
Oc	*ocultatión sectores*	obscured sectors
Pe A	*peligro aislado*	isolated danger
	poniente	western
Post	*posterior*	posterior, later
Ppal	*principal*	principal
	prohibido	prohibited
Obston	*obstrucción*	obstruction
Prov	*provisional*	provisional
prom	*prominente*	prominent, conspicuous
Pta	*punta*	point
Pto,	*puerto*	port *(1)*
PTO	*puerto deportivo*	yacht harbour
	puerto pesquero	fishing harbour
	puerto de Marina de Guerra	naval harbour
R	*roja*	red
Ra	*estación radar*	radar station
Ra+	*radar + suffix*	radar + suffix (Ra Ref etc.)
RC	*radiofaro circular*	non-directional radiobeacon
RD	*radiofaro dirigido*	directional radiobeacon
rect	*rectangular*	rectangular
Ra	*rocas*	rocks
Rp	*centeneallante rápida*	very quick flashing (80-160/min)
RpI	*cent. rápida interrumpida*	interrupted very quick flashing
RW	*radiofaro giratorio*	rotating radiobeacon
s	*sugundos*	seconds
S	*sur*	south
SE	*sudeste*	southeast
sil	*silencio*	silence
Silb	*silbato*	whistle
Sincro	*sincronizda con*	syncronized with
Sir	*sirena*	siren
son	*sonido*	sound, noise, report
Sto/a	*Santo, Santa*	Saint
SW	*sudoeste*	southwest
T	*temporal*	temporary
Te	*torre*	tower
trans	*transversal*	transversal
triang	*triangular*	triangular
troncoc	*troncocónico*	truncated cone
troncop	*troncopiramidal*	truncated pyramid
TSH	*antena de radio*	radio mast
TV	*antena de TV*	TV mast
U	*centellante ultra-rápida*	ultra quick flashing (+160/min)
UI	*cent. ultra-rápida interrumpido*	interrupted ultra quick flashing
V	*verde*	green
Vis	*visible*	visible
	vivero	shellfish raft or bed
W	*oeste*	west

Note (1): 'puerto' is applied to any landing place from a beach to a container port.

Ports and Harbours

a popa stern-to
a proa bows-to
abrigo shelter
al costado alongside
amarrar to moor
amarradero mooring
ancho breadth (see also manga)
anclar to anchor
botar to launch (a yacht)
boya de amarre mooring buoy
cabo warp, line (also cape)
calado draught
compuerta lock, basin
dársena dock, harbour
dique breakwater, jetty
escala ladder
escalera steps
esclusa lock
escollera jetty
eslora total length overall
espigón spur, spike, mole
fábrica factory
ferrocarril railway
fondear to anchor or moor
fondeadero anchorage
fondeo mooring buoy
fondo depth (bottom)
grua crane

guia mooring lazy-line (lit. guide)
nudo knot (ie. speed)
longitud length (see also eslora), longitude
lonja fish market (wholesale)
manga beam (ie. width)
muelle mole, jetty, quay
noray bollard
pantalán jetty, pontoon
parar to stop
pila estaca pile
pontón pontoon
práctico pilot (ie. pilot boat)
profundidad depth
rampa slipway
rompeolas breakwater
varadero slipway, hardstanding
varar to lift (a yacht)
vertedero (verto) spoil ground

Direction

babor port (ie. left)
estribor starboard
norte north
este east
sur south
oeste west

Phrases useful on arrival

Donde puedo amarrar?	Where can I moor?
A donde debo ir?	Where should I go?
Que es la profundidad?	What is the depth?
Que es su eslora	
Cuantos metros?	What is your length?
Para cuantas noches?	For how many nights?

Administration and stores

aceite oil (including engine oil)
aduana customs
agua potable drinking water
aseos toilet block
astillero shipyard
capitán de puerto harbour master
derechos dues, rights
duchas showers
dueño, propietario owner
efectos navales chandlery
electricidad electricity
gasoleo, diesel diesel
guardia civil police

hielo (cubitos) ice (cubes)
lavandería laundry
lavandería automática launderette
luz electricity (lit. light)
manguera hosepipe
parafina, petróleo, keroseno paraffin, kerosene
patrón skipper (not owner)
gasolina petrol
título certificate
velero sailmaker (also sailing ship)

IV. CERTIFICATE OF COMPETENCE

1. Given below is a transcription of a statement made by the Counsellor for Transport at the Spanish Embassy, London in March 1996. It is directed towards citizens of the UK but doubtless the principles apply to other EU citizens. One implication is that in a particular circumstance (paragraph 2a below) a UK citizen does not need a Certificate of Competence during the first 90 days of his visit.

2. a. British citizens visiting Spain in charge of a UK registered pleasure boat flying the UK flag need only fulfil UK law.

   b. British citizens visiting Spain in charge of a Spanish registered pleasure boat flying the Spanish flag has one of two options:

   i. To obtain a Certificate of Competence issued by the Spanish authorities. See *Normas reguladore para la obtención de titulos para el gobierno de embarcaciones de recreo* issued by the Ministerio de Obras Publicas, Transportes y Medio Ambiente.

   ii. To have the Spanish equivalent of a UK certificate issued. The following equivalencies are used by the Spanish Maritime Administration:
   Yachtmaster Ocean *Capitan de Yate*
   Yachtmaster Offshore *Patron de Yate de altura*
   Coastal Skipper *Patron de Yate*
   Day Skipper *Patron de Yate embarcaciones de recreo*
   Helmsman Overseas★ *Patron de embarcaciones de recreo restringido a motor*
   ★The Spanish authorities have been informed that this certificate has been replaced by the International Certificate of Competence.

3. The catch to para 2(a) above is that, in common with other EU citizens, after 90 days a UK citizen is technically no longer a visitor, must apply for a *permiso de residencia* and must equip his boat to Spanish rules and licensing requirements.
   In practice the requirement to apply for a *permiso de residencia* does not appear to be enforced in the case of cruising yachtsmen who live aboard rather than ashore and are frequently on the move. By the same token, the requirement for a British skipper in charge of a UK registered pleasure boat flying the UK flag to carry a Certificate of Competence after their first 90 days in Spanish waters also appears to be waived. Many yachtsmen have reported cruising Spanish waters for extended periods with no documentation beyond that normally carried in the UK.

4. The RYA suggests the following technique to obtain an equivalent Spanish certificate:
   a. Obtain two photocopies of your passport
   b. Have them notarised by a Spanish notary
   c. Obtain a copy of the UK Certificate of Competence and send it to the Consular Department, The Foreign and Commonwealth Office, Clive House, Petty France, London SW1H 9DH, with a request that it be stamped with the Hague Stamp (this apparently validates the document). The FCO will probably charge a fee so it would be best to call the office first (☎ 0171 270 3000).
   d. Have the stamped copy notarized by a UK notary.
   e. Send the lot to the Spanish Merchant Marine for the issue of the Spanish equivalent.

It may be both quicker and easier to take the Spanish examination.

V. VALUE ADDED TAX

The Spanish phrase for Value Added Tax (VAT) is *Impuesto sobre el valor añadido* (IVA), levied at 16% in 1996. Note that for VAT purposes the Canaries, Gibraltar, the Channel Islands and the Isle of Man are outside the EU fiscal area.

Subject to certain exceptions, vessels in EU waters are liable for VAT. One exception is a boat registered outside the EU fiscal area and owned by a non EU citizen which remains in EU waters for less than six months.

For a boat built within the EU fiscal area after 1985 the following documents taken together will show VAT status:
a. An invoice listing VAT or receipt if available
b. Registration Certificate
c. Bill of Sale

For a boat built prior to 1985 the following documentation is required:
e. Evidence of age and of ownership. The full Registration Certificate will serve but the Small Ship Registry Certificate will not.
f. Evidence that it was moored in EU fiscal waters at midnight on 31 December 1992 or, in the case of Austrian, Finnish and Swedish waters, 31 December 1994.

Any boat purchased outside the EU by an EU resident is liable for VAT on import to the EU.

EU owners of boats built within the EU, exported by them and which were outside EU fiscal waters at the cut-off date may be entitled to Returned Goods Relief. In the latter case, HM Customs and Excise may be able to issue a 'tax opinion letter'. The office has no public counter but may be approached by letter or fax. The address is: HM Customs and Excise, Dover Yacht Unit, Parcel Post Depot, Charlton Green, Dover, Kent CT16 1EH (☎ (01304) 224421, *Fax* (01304) 215786).

All the rules change when a yacht is used commercially – most commonly for chartering.

VI. CHARTER REGULATIONS

Any EU-flag yacht applying to charter in Spanish waters must be either VAT paid or exempt (the latter most commonly due to age). Non-EU flag vessels must have a valid Temporary Import Licence and may also have to conform to other regulations.

Applying for a charter licence can be a tortuous business. Firstly the *Director General de Transportes* at the *Conselleria d'Obres Publiques i Ordenacio del Territori* must be approached with a pre-authorisation application. This obtained, the application itself is sent to the *Capitanias Maritimas* together with ships' papers and proof of passenger insurance and registration as a commercial activity. A safety and seaworthiness inspection will be carried out. Finally a fiscal representative must be appointed and tax paid on revenue generated.

It will probably be found simpler to make the application through one of the companies specialising in this type of work. Try NETWORK, Edificio Torremar, Passeo Maritimo, 44 – 07015 Palma de Mallorca (☎ 403903/403703, *Fax* 400216), who will also deal with VAT and legal matters.

Index